KU-592-136

The Twenties

Books by Edmund Wilson

AXEL'S CASTLE

THE TRIPLE THINKERS

TO THE FINLAND STATION

THE WOUND AND THE BOW

THE SHOCK OF RECOGNITION

MEMOIRS OF HECATE COUNTY

CLASSICS AND COMMERCIALS

THE SHORES OF LIGHT

FIVE PLAYS

RED, BLACK, BLOND AND OLIVE

A PIECE OF MY MIND

THE AMERICAN EARTHQUAKE

APOLOGIES TO THE IROQUOIS

WILSON'S NIGHT THOUGHTS

PATRIOTIC GORE

THE COLD WAR AND THE INCOME TAX

O CANADA

THE BIT BETWEEN MY TEETH

EUROPE WITHOUT BAEDEKER

GALAHAD and I THOUGHT OF DAISY

A PRELUDE

THE DUKE OF PALERMO AND OTHER PLAYS

THE DEAD SEA SCROLLS: 1947–1969

UPSTATE

A WINDOW ON RUSSIA

THE DEVILS AND CANON BARHAM

THE TWENTIES

EDMUND WILSON

The Twenties

From Notebooks and Diaries
of the Period

Edited with an Introduction by

LEON EDEL

HERTFORDSHIRE
COUNTY LIBRARY
818/W14
719102
£7.50

© Elena Wilson, Executrix of the Estate of Edmund
Wilson, 1975

Introductory material © Leon Edel 1975

All rights reserved. No part of this publication may be
reproduced or transmitted, in any form or by any
means, without permission.

SBN: 333 18830 6

A portion of this book appeared originally in *The New
Yorker*.

First published in Great Britain 1975 by
MACMILLAN LONDON LTD
London and Basingstoke
Associated companies in New York Dublin
Melbourne Johannesburg & Delhi

Photoset, printed and bound
in Great Britain by
REDWOOD BURN LIMITED
Trowbridge & Esher

Contents

The letters and records of writers of genius are one of the ways we have of finding out how life was really lived in any given time and place.

Edmund Wilson

What a gulf between the self which experiences and the self which describes experience.

I Thought of Daisy

Editor's Foreword

Edmund Wilson was working on *The Twenties* at the time of his death in 1972. He had assembled the greater part out of old notebooks of the time and inserted certain passages of memory which gave the book an autobiographical cast, like his *Prelude* of 1967 and his *Upstate* of 1971. These volumes, also derived from old notebooks and diaries, had covered early and late experiences. He now wished to fill in the intervening decades.

Since he did not live to complete the book, it lacks the full personal gloss of his earlier volumes. His instructions were that he should be edited with a light hand. I have filled in such historical information as might be useful, and Edmund's correspondence has thrown light on specific passages. The notes speak for themselves, in their fragmented yet often piercing glimpses of the decade in which they were written; they provide perhaps the largest authentic document of the time, the observations of one of the principal actors in the American twenties. Edmund gives a good deal of the grim side, the rawness of America with its increasing industrialization and its laying waste of national treasures, the mad side of Hollywood, the literary infighting in New York, the gossip and anecdotes of his peers; we meet Scott Fitzgerald, Edna Millay and John Peale Bishop; there are vignettes of Mencken and Dorothy Parker; we hear the voices of E. E. Cummings and Dos Passos and encounter Eugene O'Neill and the earlier artist life of Cape Cod. Nowhere have we had a picture less varnished and so rich in focused detail. Some of the material was used by Edmund in various books—for these were Edmund's working notebooks. Readers may recognize passages which served in *I Thought of Daisy* and *Memoirs of Hecate County*. Where possible I give brief indication of this, but Edmund used and reused his materials in so many cunning ways, always revising, that the full study may be left to future textual scholars.

In a letter to his publisher, Roger Straus, Edmund wrote long ago that he wanted his editor to correct and "clean up" his text. "If I don't live to edit the whole thing myself, it will have to be done by my literary executor, and here I want to put it on record that if he is dealing with the handwritten volumes that I shouldn't have got around to having typed, I don't want him to have them published in the strictly scholarly way that is getting to be the academic fashion. That is, I don't want him to reproduce my contractions and ampersands, misspellings and faulty punctuations. If words have been dropped out, they should be supplied in brackets. They ought, from this point of view, to be made as readable as possible." In reviewing Hemingway's *Islands in the Sun*, he also spoke of this problem. "The author is not to be charged with the defects of manuscripts which he did not choose to publish and for which he can now take no responsibility, nor his editors with making those works more coherent, if the editing has been done with good judgment."

I take as my principal guide the injunction to make the notebooks "as readable as possible." I have been aided by the memory of certain conversations with Edmund even before I knew he intended me to be the editor of his posthumous papers.

Wilson's notebooks, deposited in the Beinecke Library at Yale, comprise 2,125 manuscript pages, in forty-one stout ledger-type copybooks. There are also miscellaneous pages. Edmund wrote indiscriminately in pencil and ink. He is at times almost illegible; but he also often writes the neat careful hand which most of his correspondents know. When he is *very* legible, we may assume that he is transcribing from rough notes taken *sur le vif*. His note-taking habit may explain the minutiae of his descriptions; he was remarkably visual, he saw much more than most persons, and he did not like to rely only on memory.

In the notebooks we meet for the first time the distinctively *personal* Edmund Wilson. There is the sentience behind the curious critical eye, the passion behind "cool" statement—a passion packed into hard intelligence. We discover how much Edmund used his eyes, his nose, his ears, his sense of smell, and he reveals always the *tone* of his mind. Wilson's interest in notebook-keeping was an artist's interest in himself and his world; the notebooks are often the equivalent of a painter's sketchbook and as such are the intermittent record of a constant onlooker and an adventurous mind. He grasps at evanescent bits of life; he wants to hold on to them before they disappear. He picks up anecdotes and jokes; he deals both with profundities and inanities; there are uncanny phonetic renderings of the slidings and elisions of American speech. He has a faultless ear. He is attentive to the dress of women, their jewels, their undergarments—there is quite a bit of bedding—and the self is portrayed in undress with the same care as when the slight young man in Greenwich Village sallied forth to parties in matching ties and socks.

Edmund had drafted a prefatory note to *The Twenties*. I give it in its entirety, for it suggests his awareness of the personal way in which he looked at people and events, his sense of his fallibility, and his doubts about publishing obsolete or redundant passages because they had meaning for him, if not for his potential readers. "I don't want to cut any corners," he once explained to me, and when I replied, "They're your own corners," he still demurred. Drastic reviser of his earlier published work, he came at times, in old age, to feel some diffidence about letting go of the past embodied in his old notes. Here is the prefatory note:

This volume has been compiled from my notebooks and diaries of the period. I have had, in connection with it, a special kind of problem. On the one hand, I have wanted to supply documentation on myself by including material relevant to my emotions and ideas in my youth; and, on the other, not to let myself down by publishing inferior material. My poetry comes under the latter head. My only advice to the reader is to skip any verse that he sees coming. Another warning that I ought to give the reader is that my reports are probably to some extent unfair, because it is always easier to tell about the ineptitudes and absurdities of other people than it is about similar occurrences on the part of oneself. The reader should make allowances for this and not allow me to give the impression that everyone else was *gauche* or ridiculous. It is difficult—even in a novel that is told in the first person—to put oneself in the wrong. The proper names are sometimes substitutions. The book will be more easily understood if one has read *A Prelude* first.

I have omitted such passages as I have already used in my books, such as the description, in *I Thought of Daisy*, of my seeing the shores of America from the ship on which I returned.

Edmund's omissions were not consistent; and in the editorial process further prunings—mainly of redundancies—have been made.

The reader can readily distinguish between Edmund Wilson's interpolations, which are in the first person, and mine, which are in the third. I have followed Wilson's own form of referring to himself by his initials. In the editing of this volume I have had the consistent help and counsel of Elena Mumm Wilson, her husband's literary executor, who gathered in with great promptness Edmund's far-flung literary correspondence. She and Professor Daniel Aaron, of Harvard, named by Wilson as alternate editor of the papers, will bring out a comprehensive selection of his letters. Roger Straus and Robert Giroux, EW's publishers, have been very helpful in supplying me with books and materials, and constant encouragement, and I am grateful as always for the assistance of Donald Gallup at the Beinecke Library at Yale. I am indebted too for a certain amount of library research carried out for me by Louise Hazlett, one of my graduate students at the University of Hawaii, and to my secretary Arlene Ishikawa for her patience in transcribing the often difficult handwritings of the subject and his editor.

My work has benefited by a generous grant from the National Endowment for the Humanities, which has enabled me to organize the editing of the Wilson papers with greater rapidity than anticipated, and thus make available an important part of his legacy to American letters.

The University of Hawaii   L.E.

A Portrait of Edmund Wilson

I. The Wound

They might have peopled a play by Chekhov or a Russian novel—young Edmund Wilson, Jr., an only child, reaching out to a brilliant, moody, melancholy father, often "in eclipse in some sanatorium for what were then called 'neurasthenics,'" and to a deaf and strong-willed mother. They lived in a self-contained world, like the Bolkonskys or the Karenins, in relative affluence, but without the aristocratic trappings, an assortment of aunts and uncles and cousins who came and went in their particular exclusive corner of New Jersey, soon overrun by suburbs. The ancestry had been Presbyterian; the Calvinism lingered. There were distinctions of caste and a sense, however powerless, of being "gentry" in a private universe. Edmund Wilson painted them with candor and vividness in *A Prelude* (1967): the gentility of the upper middle class, marriages within closed circles ("because there was no one else"), tensions, terrors, explosions. Edmund would write, "I had known almost no one but the members of my own family." This was before he went off to prep school. And when he emerged from college, he was "unable to get on with ordinary people." Riding a bicycle at thirteen or fourteen, he said to himself suddenly, "I'll eventually have friends with whom I'll have something in common."

He had many friends and the admiration of the world when he died in 1972 at seventy-seven, but there was to the end something aloof and shut in, as if he were still reaching out from behind obsolete invisible barriers, using the full force of his intellect to establish a truce with mankind. Between the lines of his remembrances one can see the walled-in childhood, a life of solitary discoveries, of self-help and early resource, in a situation that, in a less robust and tenacious child, might have led to collapse. It led instead to a kind of forcing of observation and expression. Perhaps Edmund Wilson's tenacity and his drive to strength came from the assertion of a young spirit unwilling to capitulate as his father recurrently did.

He learned early how to be independent in his confining environment. His father, Edmund Wilson, Sr., was a lawyer, and in middle life attorney general of the state of New Jersey, first under a Republican and then under the Democrat, Woodrow Wilson (no relation). The younger Edmund always had mixed memories of Red Bank, N.J., where he was born May 8,

1895. The atmosphere of his home, when he reached the age of recognition, was "oppressive." His father's relapses into apathy, his mother's deafness, which had come early, were the central facts; but Edmund Wilson told himself later that even if his mother had been able to hear, he doubted whether they would have had much to say to one another. He remembered in his teens making methodical notes on the train home from school—"notes of topics about which I could communicate to her." On the day she took him to the Hill School, at Pottstown, Pennsylvania (*aetat* thirteen), she called him "Bunny" in front of the boys. The vigorous, slim, good-looking youth found himself reduced then and there to "Bunny" and for a lifetime. He fought the jeering boys; then he accepted the reality, and ultimately signed himself Bunny to his intimates. His being Edmund Jr. bothered him less, perhaps because his father was so often absent from the family scene.

He was not so much an "alienated" child as one in whom there had been certain rechannelings of emotion, a development of strong defenses; such was the effect upon the male child, mentally alert and possessing acute senses, trained in coping with strange obstacles. Edmund's own way of expressing this (in his major essay on Dickens) was that "lasting depressions and terrors may be caused by such cuttings-short of the natural development of childhood." Whole areas of being could be clamped off, large energies had to find new outlets. In some such way extraordinary lives compose themselves, out of extraordinary circumstances. Edmund Wilson's chapters on "family" in *A Prelude*, his earlier sketch of his father, his tributes to his old masters Rolfe and Gauss, provide hints of his quest for solutions. Books, language, the world of imaginative reconstruction, established some kind of communion with the remote "outside." He seems to have developed a particular meticulosity of mind, cultivated doubtless against chaos, and yet somehow escaping the inevitable rigidities that might have frozen Edmund and made him a functionary, or a specialist, or a lawyer like his father. Instead, he pursued his obsessions and compulsions in literature, a wide quest for many languages, esoteric meanings, dictionaries—an almost Balzacian catholicity, but with much greater exactitude than Balzac. Later he would pursue sex in the same way. He had so little knowledge of women, and how a man should relate to them (as readers of *A Prelude* will remember), that he went to consult a doctor at Princeton when he had a spontaneous emission while reading a book. The dammed-up sexual drive was but one of many dammed-up drives and Edmund learned the secret of "conversion"—into a fascination with the macabre, for example, or sleight of hand. Edmund was always interested in monsters and became a very good magician and puppeteer. He tells us occasional dreams. They suggest some of the benign and morbid traits acquired in dealing with frustration. A dream of sleeping with his mother may have been "Oedipal," as Edmund mused, but we might interpose that it was one way for a little boy to attempt, at least in sleep, to cross the barrier that stood between him and his sphinx-like female parent. He dreamed also (an early nightmare) that his father was sharpening a knife in the kitchen to kill the entire family. This he also thought was "Oedipal." Yet we might equally see Edmund, in dream displacement, putting his father into the role he himself would have liked to have. There must have been times when a little boy so circumstanced would have nourished, in his deeper fantasies, a great desire to wipe out his difficult parents—and with flourish of a carving knife or cutlass.

The evidence of the early years clearly leads to the conclusion that Edmund Wilson reached in his old age: that his boyish self had been starved of human intercourse, except through avenues of the world's wonder, the comfort of storybooks and the "reality" of people in those books. Perhaps his insatiable curiosity, which remained to the end and had in it a buoyant youthfulness, stemmed from this childhood filled with unanswered riddles, the *Why?* the *What does it mean?* of a juvenile facing an impassive sphinx. In the family annals we discover certain friendly aunts who helped more than they perhaps knew: Aunt Laura Kimball, "I learned a good deal about books from her"; Cousin Helen Stillwell, who drew pictures of dragons and imaginary monsters, nourishing the macabre and a latent interest in sadism. His later war experience would give him horrors sufficing for a lifetime. She also sang English music-hall songs, read him Mrs. Gamp and Uncle Remus, played by ear the entire score of a musical comedy she had just seen. This amazed and delighted him. Another cousin, fifteen months older, provided companionship. "Sandy" gave Edmund Havelock Ellis, and thus at least printed knowledge of sex. Exuberant, lively (they were much together during an early trip abroad), "Sandy" turned out to have *dementia praecox*, as schizophrenia was then described: and when Edmund returned from the war he found his favourite cousin locked away—for life. His regular visits to Sandy reported in the notebooks show both compassion and malaise. There is a living recall of the way his father was so often locked away from him; and Edmund perhaps had a latent fear that he too might have in him the strain of mental illness that haunted the family.

To understand Edmund Wilson's particular talents as writer and critic we must look closely at his father. *A Piece of My Mind* (1956) ends with an essay called "The Author at Sixty." Yet the essay is not about the author; it is about his father, who died at sixty-one. This suggests an ambivalent identification. The account of his father shows that the senior Wilson was a highly gifted freewheeling lawyer, always able to keep his family in comparative affluence. He practiced law with resource and skill, and had great successes; he lost only one case, and was careful thereafter to take cases he was sure of winning. His method of handling a jury, as described by his son, could be applied to the way in which Edmund composed one of his own literary essays. The father attacked the jury "with a mixture of learning, logic, dramatic imagination and eloquence which he knew would prove irresistible. He would cause them to live through the events of the crime or the supposed crime, he would take them through the steps of the transaction, whatever this was, and he would lodge in their heads a picture that it was difficult for the opposing attorney to expel." Edmund, later describing the effect that reading Taine had on him, paid the same kind of tribute. Taine "created the creators [in his history of English literature] as characters in a larger drama of cultural and social history, and writing about literature for me, has always meant narrative and drama." Behind Taine and Michelet, there was the figure of his father and his courtroom dramas. And the son was impressed "by the intense concentration" that the feats of persuasion cost his father. "They could not be allowed to fail"—on the occasions when he prepared a brief at home.

A legal personality so erratic and so uncompromising could find no permanent berth. He was invited to join large New York legal firms but declined. He took cases for corporations and won them; he also fought the corporations; he hated the railroads and sought litigation with them at the drop of a hat: a package of books and sweets shipped to Edmund at school was damaged in transit; the father sued the railroad and won the price of the damaged goods. The father was deeply versed in the law—and Edmund's cultivation of "literary arcana" may have stemmed from Edmund Sr.'s way of digging into legal obscurities. Challenged by Governor Woodrow Wilson to get rid of the Atlantic City bosses, Edmund Wilson, Sr. (then attorney general), told himself he could never get a convicting jury in that politics-ridden city. So he found an old law that permitted importation of jurors when a change of venue was impossible—and sent the Atlantic City politicos and many of their henchmen to jail. It was a great success. But the father shook his head. He knew that there would be new political bosses and a new system of patronage as soon as the storm blew over. He had demonstrated, however, what research and resourcefulness could do. When Woodrow Wilson became President he offered the senior Wilson a seat on the Supreme Court as soon as one should fall vacant. The father said it might be "interesting." No vacancy occurred, however, and he never achieved this highest office. In spite of success, he had great periods of apathy. He cared nothing for atmosphere. He seems to have modeled himself a little on the ruggedness of Abraham Lincoln, another moody man of law. Edmund remembered his father's dreary office, always the same one, an uncomfortable room over a liquor dealer's store, "rather pleasantly permeated by a casky vinous smell." Even this was lost on the father. He never drank.

In his professionalism and commitment, the father set an example the son would always follow. He was without snobbery or racial bias: but he showed always the innate pride and aristocratic stance of a member of the gentry. Edmund said "he dealt with people strictly on their merits" yet always "to some extent *de haut en bas.*" Edmund too looked at life and art—and his fellow writers—from a higher plane. It was a part of his individualism. He never joined writers' organizations; he refused honors—save those that carried money awards. He worked most of his life like his father, distinctly alone and with great concentration and thoroughness when he became genuinely involved in a subject. The senior Edmund's private methods of inquiry were also Edmund's. The lawyer liked to travel and "from the moment he arrived in a city he began asking people questions, beginning with the driver of his cab." Those who knew Edmund Wilson remember how relentlessly he could cross-examine in private talk; how on entering a room he instantly came to the point, either delivering himself of recondite material he had discovered, or seeking the total satisfaction—it could never be satisfied—of his curiosity. The son's intellectual process, his ability to sort, organize and use literary evidence, his sense of drama, had its origins in the example of this gifted and unhappy parent; and perhaps the senior Edmund's greatest gift to his son was the gift of intellectual sympathy. "I was always surprised," Edmund wrote in his portrait of his father, "by the sympathy, or rather perhaps by the judicial detachment, with which, in important decisions, he treated my point of view." No better description could be given of Edmund's finest writings.

This then was perhaps the deepest emotional experience in Edmund's early life, and one that it must have been difficult for him to recognize and face: to have so attractive and magnetic a father, and yet to be shut away from him, was a painful mixture of possession and loss of which Edmund's later card tricks and sleight of hand may have been a caricatured expression. "Now you see it and now you don't." Edmund loved his father and yet there could be no expression of that love. The photographs in *A Prelude* of the senior Wilson show a handsome man, with fine mustaches, distinctly a "personality," and yet something veiled and mysterious, with depths of depression, in his eyes. His father and his cousin Sandy represented an element of "loss" in Edmund's experience, of ache and yearning, a feeling for masculine strength and tenacity that contrasted with the motherly presence that was not in the least "motherly." Mrs. Wilson, the former Helen Mather Kimball, was a woman of limited intelligence, prosaic, self-confident and self-assured. One who knew her in her later years said "her criterion of success was making money and the status that money gave—which both her husband and son despised." She would much sooner have had her son be an athlete; even when a very old lady she continued to attend the Princeton football games. She never read Edmund's writings. Her feelings were directed into the simplicities of her gardens, and she enjoyed the brightness and variety of the flowers, and no doubt the smell of the tractable earth. Her soundless world could touch the soundlessness of bulbs and flower patterns and she could show love and sympathy and a kind of spontaneous creativity in her feeling for the plants. In all his adult years Edmund kept only one picture of his mother, taken in a group of relatives when she was young. But he always kept around him pictures of his mother's gardens at Talcottville and Red Bank.

She provided, in her fixedness, a kind of stability that Edmund's early-learned rage for order could not find in the paternal self-abandonment. The sphinx was frustrating; she didn't even ask riddles. She was obdurate, pleasure-loving, often openly hostile to her ailing husband. Her deafness may have been partly psychological. She had taken Edmund Sr. to see a great specialist in England; the specialist pronounced him "mad" and the wife during the voyage home suddenly became totally deaf. As it turned out, her husband was far from mad; he simply dropped into despondency for long periods. But the mother had walled herself in, and she was impregnable. She seemed masculine in areas in which the father tended to be feminine. Edmund Sr. vowed, when his son was naughty, that he would whip him within an inch of his life—but he never did. Mrs. Wilson spanked effectively, using a metal hairbrush, and complained that the proceeding dented the metal. The image of a woman, of women, modified for Edmund by less punitive and impregnable aunts and cousins, nevertheless remained; they could inspire fear. It is perhaps no accident that in *I Thought of Daisy* and "The Princess with the Golden Hair" the contrasting women define Edmund's problems in wooing and courtship. Women could be elusive— as Edna St. Vincent Millay was, brilliant, intellectual, independent in love—and therefore unattainable; or they could be down-to-earth creatures, with whom one went to Coney Island and played games. The "democratic earthly woman" pitted against the woman of mystery, the socially attractive aloof princess with the golden hair, an idealized version of Edmund's mother. She is a dream, not flesh, when he finally is able to bed with her. But the little dance-hall girl who becomes the narrator's mistress and tells her stories of low life is a lively human partner. (The record of this story fills many of the notebook pages.) Perhaps Edmund was most at his ease in earlier years with waitresses, dance-hall girls and prostitutes: he could relate to them in a more human way, they were below his social level and therefore outside his early experience. Men of course were easier and more accessible and Edmund's school world was then wholly a man's world.

The words Edmund uses about his mother can often be applied to the less attractive side of himself. She was "brusque and gruff." She was also, and these became benign traits in Edmund, "positive, self-confident, determined." By the time the boy was thirteen he had achieved discipline and self-assurance; he had conformed, and been imaginative enough to find his own solutions and escapes within that conformity. Edmund Wilson, Jr., realized, when he grew older, that there had been little "in the way of human relations" that could afford his mother happiness. Yet his mother's harsh stability was more acceptable to an outgoing and life-seeking boy than his father's self-defeat. This must have fortified Edmund's will to persevere and to conquer.

Enlargement of his world and escape came at thirteen—his prep school and later Princeton flowed together as a continuous experience. The "Bunny" Wilson who was escorted to the Hill School in 1908 by his mother was singularly prepared—as few boys are—for the rougher discipline of school away from home. He brought to this Presbyterian institution his orderly mind, and the carapace derived from his mother. The school itself was run (as Edmund later said) with all the efficiency of an industry or a corporation. It was well organized, well staffed, well equipped. It made the boys aware of duties and responsibilities. It stimulated individuality (strange as this may seem to modern American eyes) by its refusal to be permissive. "Our whole life was regulated by bells"—but it *was* regulated. The students were drilled, and they were well drilled. Every moment was put to use for work or play. As a result, Hill students were rarely turned down by the Ivy League colleges. In the remorseless paternalism of the school, Edmund at first found "the suffocating repressive effect of the Pennsylvania mill town." But a later essay and later memories show an awareness that Hill had given him solid foundations on which to build his life, and diminished the wear-and-tear of life in his family. He disliked intensely the first weeks. He was not accustomed to being with crowds of boys and to rushing about on the double. How little "suffocating" the school ultimately was may be found in Edmund's implication that "home" was even more suffocating. He hated going home for holidays. His precocious tales and verses were published when he was a freshman in the Hill School *Record*. He was a serious yet fun-loving boy, in a Puritanical straitjacket. There was, moreover, a master of Greek named Alfred Rolfe who gave him a standard, a focus, a sense of personality; Edmund has described him in a finely written essay (in *The Triple Thinkers*) with the same affection he later bestowed on Christian Gauss at Princeton. Rolfe had the maternal assurance and firmness; Gauss was a highly literary but healthy version of the paternal brilliance. At Hill, Rolfe, tall, well dressed, with blond mustaches that hid his lips and masked expression, was merciless in his demands;

his gentlemanly sarcasm was without ambiguities. He taught Homer and made the students "translate every word into an English not unworthy of the original." Edmund was forced to scan every line, to understand every form. Of Rolfe he said "the first time that you heard him read aloud a passage of Homer in class you knew what Homer was as poetry." Later the master would take a personal interest in his gifted student, give him access to his library, share Edmund's admiration for Bernard Shaw. And if he imparted a soaring feeling about ancient Athens he spoke for an American Athens as well—Rolfe came from New England and was Edmund's "only personal contact with the Concord of the great period, and I feel that if I had not known him, I should never really have known what it was, and what a high civilization it represented." Hill School and Rolfe—and Homer; but he studied also routine subjects and—at last—had friends of his own age to make up for the lonely years. In *A Prelude* he describes these friends in some detail; they made him aware of other families, other worlds, showed him that life was not necessarily composed of Wilsons, Kimballs, Knoxes. They offered also a further resource; he paid visits during his summers, another way of prolonging his absences from Red Bank.

Edmund entered Princeton in 1912. The story of his four years at college has often been told in the lives of other members of the brilliant group of young men who graduated just before America's entry into the 1914–1918 war. F. Scott Fitzgerald was "the first educated Catholic I had ever known" and John Peale Bishop, who became Edmund's close friend, was a handsome West Virginian, a Southern aristocrat who quoted Shelley and Swinburne, when he appeared on the college scene. In Edmund's day it was the old Princeton "between the pressures of narrow Presbyterianism and a rich man's suburbanism." The young adult could dedicate himself to his vocation—poetry, fiction, style, form, verbal elegance, a reaching out to grasp the universality of the human imagination. Behind this passion there was a profound interest in ideas, in essences. In art, and in life, Edmund was a product of an aristocratic ideal. The eighteenth century had lingered in his family and Wilson seemed to be a distillation of it as he moved out into larger experience. His point of attachment, besides his devotion to the *Nassau Lit.*, was Christian Gauss, who illustrated "man's divine pride of reason and imagination." Gauss had "shuttered" eyes, but when he looked they were "clear green" and "as hard and as fine as gems." Gauss's preceptorials—his informal seminars for half a dozen students—seemed in the end like a conversation begun in youth which was continued into maturity and old age, for in later years Wilson never lost touch with him. He was "the most accessible of talkers." Edmund would himself be quite as accessible—when he was interested. He also knew how to listen. He admired Gauss's precision of thought, his unhurried pace, the way in which he

opened for students the two great literatures of the Latin world. At the pin-
nacle was Dante and in more immediate times he was a votary of Flaubert,
exemplar of style achieved through tremendous will. One can discern how
many Old World values were implanted by Gauss in Edmund; he gave him
a feeling, never lost, for the interrelation of literatures; this led him to an
extraordinary mastery of French and Russian, and to studies in Hebrew and
Hungarian. If Rolfe was a link to Concord, Gauss was a link to the 1890's, in
his anecdote of his coming upon Oscar Wilde (after the *débâcle*) sitting in
melancholy exile before piles of unpaid saucers. Gauss had bought him
drinks and talked with him. Rolfe opened the ancient world to Edmund;
Gauss opened the modern—opened we might say the way to Axel's Castle
and the highway to the Finland Station. Edmund would travel the first at
the end of the 1920's, the second at the end of the 1930's.

The young Princeton student was still virginal, still afraid of women, still
rigidly Puritanical. He did not drink—he would never smoke—and he was
shy and distant in the presence of young females. Today he might be dubbed
a "square," yet this would be mitigated by the effect of his lively hedonism;
he wrote a Princeton Triangle Show; he made friends with the frivolous
playboy students, he was always ready for fun, and even those who thought
him priggish and arrogant admitted his force, his clarity and his integrity;
he refused very early to accept the commonplaces of college life and
expressed forthright opposition to the war. When he graduated, he asked
himself what he could do to be closer to the society of his time, to descend
from the clouds of intellect and literary expression. His life had been spent
in books, fancies, writing, learning. His immediate solution might seem
strange, given his hostility to the war. He went to a military training camp
at Plattsburgh, which had been set up in preparedness for possible American
entry. He was looking, he said, for "something more active, something
closer to contemporary reality." He may have simply followed certain
friends into this camp, as a way of spending another summer away from
home. If he sought information about the army, he found out soon enough.
He was bored; he was completely convinced "that I could never be an
officer." And at this juncture he made his rueful remark about not being
able to get on with "ordinary people." Plattsburgh did not help, for he
found college and Hill friends, and life went on as before, only it was under
canvas. He read a great many books and was a miserable failure at the rifle
range.

His second attempt to move out into the world was made that autumn of
1916. He got a job as a reporter on the New York *Evening Sun*. He did not,
however, have the "push" required of fledglings and his shyness prevented
him from invading privacies to get a "story." He preferred to write about
the arts, and did some descriptive reporting. He lived comfortably on his

$15 a week, with an occasional supplement from his father, in a shared apartment in West Eighth Street; by pooling resources, he and his two friends could afford a Chinese servant and they gave pleasant dinner parties. Scott Fitzgerald had a memory of Edmund of this time—glimpsing him from a taxi. He was wearing a tan raincoat over his brown getup. "I noted with a shock that he was carrying a light cane." He seemed to Fitzgerald "no longer the shy little scholar of Holder Court; he walked with confidence, wrapped in his thoughts and looking straight ahead, and it was obvious that his new background was entirely sufficient to him." Fitzgerald added: "That night in Bunny's apartment life was mellow and safe, a finer distillation of all that I had come to love at Princeton. The gentle playing of the oboe [by Edmund's friend Morris Belknap] mingled with the city noises from the street outside, which penetrated into the room with difficulty through a great barricade of books."

Such pleasures, still collegiate, did not endure. America entered the war in 1917 and Edmund Wilson experienced the first crisis of his ordered, organized and outwardly placid life. His dedication was to civilization and to the imagination. His country invited him to "glory"—"Uncle Sam Wants *You*," the famous poster said with a pointing finger. "I did not know what to do," Edmund wrote. He reminded himself of Plattsburgh. How deep his anxiety was, we may judge by his saying (and he would repeat this more than a decade later when he had a nervous breakdown): "I usually know exactly what I want to do, and it has been only when I could not make up my mind that I have really gone to pieces." He did not go to pieces. In August 1917 he found a solution. In this he followed the dictates of his humanitarianism. He did not want to be drafted; he accordingly enlisted—and asked for duty in Base Hospital 36, which went into camp in September. He was on his way to France in November. Shortly after landing, he wrote to F. Scott Fitzgerald, "I feel that the door of the house of mirth, and in fact any normal human occupation, is shut till the war is over." And he added, "Remember me to Gauss; I think of him often in France. In spite of the fact that I had been here before, years ago, it was chiefly because of what he taught me that I felt so little a stranger when I arrived here a couple of weeks ago."

Edmund Wilson's fragmentary army notes and the two vivid Maupassant-like tales he reprints in *A Prelude* ("Death of a Soldier" and "Lieutenant Franklin") reflect the depths of his experience abroad. Hill and Princeton had been Arcadia—out of which Wilson stepped into regimentation and then horror. If he was not a stranger to France, he was a stranger to death. At first the student of Homer and Dante went through the usual indignities. "I feel a fool, a cipher," he wrote to a friend. By its very nature, the army forced on Edmund a lower valuation of himself—lower, Edmund mused, than any he had had in prep school. He surrendered the direction of his life: a painful thing for someone as independent as he was. He received orders blindly, when all his faculties had been trained to examine and to question. The only element he welcomed in his new life was the fellowship of a host of Americans from all parts of his land. It opened democratic vistas. The army broke some of his shyness, helped him to feel a bit closer (though inwardly still aloof) to persons outside his narrow world. Death soon became routine, and he learned to live with it. This was an abrupt end of his youth, a sudden sealing off of an earlier existence during his twenty-third and twenty-fourth years. Stationed at Vittel, the French watering place, where the luxury hotels had been turned into hospitals, he was first a stretcher bearer. There were few ambulances then; the great age of the motor was yet to come and the stretchers met the wounded as they arrived by train in the thin gray dawn or in the midst of snow-storms. Edmund remembered the screams of mustard-gas victims, their swollen membranes and genitals; his passage on chemical warfare in *The Cold War and the Income Tax* derives its vigor in part from that terrible memory. He also would remember piling the bodies of dead American soldiers as if they were logs during the flu epidemic of 1918. He saw victims of shell shock and also of syphilis, and after a season in the charnel house appealed to his father to get him moved to another part of the army. His endurance of horror apparently had given out. The elder Wilson did manage to pull strings in Washington, and just before the Armistice Edmund was made a sergeant and assigned to military intelligence. In Chaumont briefly he translated documents from French into English; he then got a glimpse of Trier and the occupation (the scene of the story "Lieutenant Franklin") and finally shipped back to be demobilized. A passage in this short story suggests the essence of his feelings after his exposure to war—and its byways—during the previous twenty-four months:

> All about them outside this room, the desolation of Europe opened: the starved fatigue of the living, the abyss—one could not look into it!—of the dead; that world had been cursed for four years with the indictment of every natural instinct, the abortion of every kindly impulse. And tonight in this bright-lit room, where still the wine from Moselle grapes was yellow, where still Schubert music swam in sun, the fellowship of men was reviving . . .

His war notes list some two hundred books read between August 1917 and the time of the Armistice, little more than a year later. It is a formidable list. It includes the then unknown Joyce (*Dubliners*), the posthumous novels of Henry James, just published, Edith Wharton, Edna Millay, whom he had not yet met, Kipling, Rebecca West, Lytton Strachey, Renan, Rémy de

Gourmont, Compton Mackenzie, Walt Whitman (*Leaves of Grass* and *Democratic Vistas*), Zola, Chesterton. He returned to New York with the letdown that comes after a routinized life devoid of everything but simple army responsibilities. He said he could "never go back to the falseness and dullness of my prewar life again. I swore to myself that when the war was over I should stand outside society altogether."

We know that Edmund Wilson did not stand outside society "altogether." The words were spoken in disillusion: yet they reflect also that part of Edmund which had always stood outside (and always would). To be sure, he had fled an enclosing family, an inhibiting clan; and his conscious energies were clearly directed toward as much "involvement" as possible. He was less aware, however, of the stratagems, defenses, subterfuges he had developed during many years to placate the family sphinx. They were by now his second nature, even when he was in the heart of the Village, drinking bad gin. His novel, written at the end of the twenties, is highly documentary. His protagonist thinks of "the terror, the terror mastered by the mind, and clutched and wrenched into beauty," and again "what a gulf between the self which experiences and the self which describes experience." By the time Edmund Wilson wrote *I Thought of Daisy* he was aware that he carried within a subversive *persona*, a kind of chronic presence, or call it a wound which at times negated his highest impulses, his naturally expansive and generous feelings. Familial attitudes and residual Puritanism imposed constraints, hesitations, guilts, and caused him to use guile and indirection. These in turn created subterranean distress. To reach for warm human companionship and love—a part of the natural order of things—required unremitting effort; in Edmund it was self-conscious, sometimes "bunny" shy, sometimes the activity of the satyr. The conflict is expressed in the title of his novel; he *thinks* of Daisy, the good down-to-earth girl with whom he can go to Coney Island, an idealized version of his down-to-earth mother. But he loves Rita, the poet, and "her terrific images of the commonplace." And he sees in her "the fierceness with which only a woman, when woman's narrow concentration has been displaced from its ordinary objects, can concern itself with art."

His character Hugo embodies this dichotomy of the spirit. Edmund describes himself when he writes, "Hugo was on close terms with no one. As soon as he had sampled a conversation and caught the social flavor of a household or a group, he would simply go straight away and bottle a specimen for his books." Hugo regards women "as the most dangerous representatives of those forces of conservatism and inertia against which his whole life was a protest." These thoughts, applied to various characters in the novel, show moods, doubts, conflicts, a tug-of-war *within*, which progressively led to depression and a brief period of panic break-down. He came to see that he was wounded—a wounded artist—who struggled to practice his craft *against* attitudes formed in his early experi-ence. There is a reference to Philoctetes in *Daisy*, the Greek archer, whose suppurating wound prevented him from using his unique skill. In the pages devoted in these notebooks and in his novel to literature as "fraud" and "imposture," Edmund seems to be mulling over Freud's early theories of art and neurosis, the classic disabling which both intensifies creation and can undermine it. We find thus the seeds of the influential essay Edmund would write ten years later entitled "The Wound and the Bow." Edmund's trouble was that his interests were scattered. He owned too many bows. This meant that he did not have the single-mindedness of his successful peers, F. Scott Fitzgerald, or John Dos Passos. Wilson's struggle was be-tween beauty and outrage, between life as he wanted to live it and the life his primary self imposed on him, guided his creations, dictated his aloof social behavior, and at the same time—for it had its benignity within the morbidity—gave him extraordinary acuity.

If we read between the lines of *The Twenties*, and see the despair in his novel, we gain some measure of the strain under which Edmund carried on his fertile work on the literary magazines. When the strain proved too much for him, he lapsed into depression; and then he sought relief in drink. At one period during treatment he became briefly addicted to a drug—paraldehyde; but he had the strength promptly to cease using it. He worked his way out of his 1920's depression by studying the subjective worlds of the moderns; they too were wounded, and their wounds gave them insight into the symbolic order of life. *Axel's Castle* was the fruit of Edmund's struggle, a struggle which took him ultimately to the Greek myth of Philoctetes, whose universality he would demonstrate. It pointed at the same time to the central problems of his own life—his quest for the right bow among the many that his childhood and youth had brought into being.

II. The Bow

The myth of Philoctetes, and his terrible wound, which prevents him from using his god-given skill, is rooted in the mental and moral history of man. Aeschylus and Euripides had treated it; but only incomplete accounts remain of their plays on this theme. The extant play of Sophocles served Edmund Wilson as the basis for his essay "Philoctetes: The Wound and the Bow" which he first published in *The New Republic* and then made the title essay of a volume containing "Seven Studies in Literature" published in 1941. As epigraph he used lines from a poem by James Joyce, one of the most wounded artists of our time: "I bleed by the black stream, For my torn bough." Philoctetes, with his enchanted bow, his poisoned arrows, his supreme archery, not only bleeds, but his wound (originally a snake bite) is an offense to the nostrils of society. He has been set aside like a leper; exile has forced upon him the life of an *isolato*, on an island, itself a symbol of disconnectedness from mainlands. Alone, he staunches the painful and foul-smelling hurt which will not heal. However, the Greeks—the world—need his great bow. Troy cannot be conquered without it. The crafty Odysseus seeks ways to use—to exploit—the weapon. He plots to steal it from this unapproachable pariah.

Edmund Wilson tells the story with characteristic sobriety and leisure, in his most matter-of-fact way, so that he makes the myth speak for itself, with the simplicity and directness of a parable. It is not difficult to see why Wilson was drawn to this myth out of all the myths of the Greeks, although few modern writers were attracted by it. André Gide had written it into a characteristic intellectual version, linking mystical experience with the homoerotic overtones of feeling between Philoctetes and the youth Neoptolemus. In America, early in the century, John Jay Chapman, the Boston literary amateur, had adapted the Sophoclean version into English; but then Chapman carried an actual wound. He had plunged his hand up to the wrist into hot coals in a youthful moment of Puritanical self-immolation. One tended to avert one's eyes—and nose—from Philoctetes' oozing wound; it seemed morbid to dwell on it. Edmund's war experiences, however, had inured him to all kinds of wounds. And he was drawn to both principal characters: to Philoctetes as the supreme craftsman who is prevented by his wound from exercising his craft; and to the youth Neoptolemus, for particular reasons which we must examine. Aware of his own chronic hurt, he grasped the deepest symbolic significance of the Sophoclean play.

The second part of the play allows us to trace the fuller drama of Edmund Wilson's mind as he rewove the drama of Sophocles. In the ancient play, Odysseus sends Neoptolemus, the son of Achilles, a mere youth, to steal the magic bow of Philoctetes. The youth approaches the wounded man with understandable caution and diffidence; the stench is overpowering. And yet he is eager to accomplish his mission. What he discovers, with the quick empathy of his years, is a suffering human being—whom he has been asked to rob. Something holds him back. He endures the horror of the wound; he nurses Philoctetes through delirium; he sees the blister break and drain and experiences the agony of his prey. Out of his deep sympathy comes recognition: the guile of Odysseus has overlooked a fundamental fact. The unique bow needs its unique bowman. Neoptolemus cannot bring himself to cheat or to steal. He faces the wrath of the suffering man by confessing his proposed treachery. The better solution he feels is to help the archer, instead of stealing the instrument of his craft. Edmund writes: "It is in the nature of the things of this world where the divine and the human fuse, that they cannot have the irresistible weapon without its loathsome owner, who upsets the processes of normal life by his curses and his cries, and who in any case refuses to work for men who have exiled him from their fellowship."

We must recognize the delicate question of "identification." It is not easy to identify with Philoctetes; he is a creature of pitiable suffering; he is ill, ostracized, turned in on himself. A spectator's identification tends to be with health, not sickness. The wound is physical, and symbolic. Edmund's wound was psychological. We may hazard a guess that the former stretcher bearer and stauncher of soldiers' wounds, the caretaker of the dead and the dying, felt a profound link with Neoptolemus, even while his intellect focused on the craft and dilemma of Philoctetes. The passage that ends the essay is devoted entirely to the role of the young man in the Sophoclean drama:

> Only by the intervention of one who is guileless enough and human enough to treat [Philoctetes] not as a monster, nor yet as a mere magical property which is wanted for accomplishing some end, but simply as another man whose sufferings elicit his sympathy and whose courage and pride he admires. When this human relation has been realized, it seems at first that it is to have the consequence of frustrating the purpose of the expedition and ruining the Greek campaign. Instead of winning over the outlaw, Neoptolemus has outlawed himself as well, at a time when both the boy and the cripple are desperately needed by the Greeks.

Neoptolemus, in this re-creation, becomes a kind of archetypal critic, as Philoctetes represents the archetypal artist; he reflects, even more than the archer, the image and vocation of Edmund Wilson. We can discern in this essay's biographical depths the double identification of the triple thinker: the Edmund Wilson whose wound prevented him from being poet, playwright, novelist on the scale of his contemporaries, and the Wilson whose gift of intellectual penetration and of sympathy made him one with the "common humanity" of art and society, one with Neoptolemus. In his last sentence Edmund tells us that "in taking the risk to his cause which is involved in the recognition of common humanity with the sick man, in refusing to break his word, he dissolves Philoctetes' stubbornness, and thus cures him and sets him free, and saves the campaign as well." In defining Neoptolemus, Edmund Wilson defined himself.

The vision came to Edmund by degrees. He had made himself a mediator between art and the world, between the cunning of men like Odysseus, who "used" art, and those who were dedicated to true creation. He had tested the arts and tried his hand at poem, story and play. He had moved from the high-flying life of the 1920's to the "proletarian" era of the economic depression. And now, at the beginning of the new world war, with heightened vision he was able to merge his diverse weapons into the single, powerful bow of humane criticism; he accepted himself at last for the supreme critic he was, and entered into the role with a renewed vigor and all his acquired authority. No other of our critics had served quite so long in preparing himself; beside Edmund, the much respected Desmond MacCarthy in England, with his fineness of mind and delicacy of spirit, seemed a gentleman amateur; the brilliant V. S. Pritchett came closer, but he was more specialized. Van Wyck Brooks was more historian than critic; and then he disliked the moderns. Brooks's wound—vividly described in his memoirs—had taken him backward to Concord instead of forward; he seemed to move with Emerson and Thoreau; he studied the "wound" of Mark Twain. The far-ranging criticism of Edmund was Edmund's particular bow, the one right instrument created by the necessities of his particular life experience. He could lend himself in a true humanistic spirit to the literary arts in America; and, with his extraordinary skills of reportage, to politics and society as well. He could practice the "sympathy and judicial detachment" he described in his father. He could offer himself—even if it made him an outlaw—as a "general touchstone" and be neither judge, schoolmaster, nor dilettante, but a helper, a brother of the artist. More than intermediary, such a critic partakes of the law of the healer as well as the philosopher. He becomes the enemy of the deceivers and the entrepreneurs. To be such a truth-bearer it was necessary to be open to language, psychology, history: he must understand the strivings even of the little men of art, a Harold Frederic or a Henry Blake Fuller, or the travail of a John Jay Chapman—quite as much as the protean artists who transcend place and time and speak to the entire world. Art, an obstinate record of man's imagination, far from being a magician's sleight of hand, becomes in this light the fullest expression of the artist's being, his despair, and his serenity; it was the duty of criticism to see the grand lines, the sweep of a great work, its impact upon society and its time, and on posterity.

Edmund was multiple-minded; he had more in common with the universal minds of the eighteenth century than with the hurt lyricists of the nineteenth. He could never prevent himself from ranging far afield. He was based in literature but he wrote of the Zuñi and the Iroquois; he journeyed to Israel to learn about the Dead Sea scrolls. He was an adventurous traveller. He had to master languages. "I always find a pleasure almost sensual," he wrote, "in attacking a new language." He annexed Russia as a large province of his intelligence and sensibility. And he was never satisfied with his conquests. One day at Harvard he suddenly said to me, "You have never taken me to the grave of Henry James." I had thought he had long ago visited that quiet spot in Cambridge. So there was an afternoon's pil-grimage, a long ramble in the Cambridge Cemetery, with pauses and dis-course before the resting places of the Howellses and the Jameses, and of many Cambridge worthies who lie on that hill within view of Soldiers' Field. Edmund seemed always to have more ideas than he could use, more arrows than he could shoot. It would take him years to synchronize and unify his hyperactive talents. With time he created the series of books by which we know him, extraordinary gatherings-in of the fruit of his thrust-ing mind and his unappeased curiosity. He came to recognize in the end that he had a great mastery of "the short." His training as literary journalist, the necessity of publishing in the magazines, made the briefer forms con-venient, mandatory. And then he brought the whole of himself to such powerful focus and concentration on any problem—a given career, a movement of ideas, a social phenomenon, the character of Casanova, the perversities of Sade—that tension could not be long sustained. He was in-capable—perhaps he was too impatient—of writing a long and meditated work. His best writings are consummately organized scenes and pictures, miniatures and portraits. His masters were Taine and Michelet: and he as-sociated to them the insights gained from the Greeks and classical psycho-logy. A series of essays on modern writers became *Axel's Castle*, his seminal work on symbolism; a further series "in the writing and acting of history" ended as *To the Finland Station*. By the same method he brought into being his "literary chronicles."

What characterized Wilson's criticism was his probity, his search for the truths of a given problem, his interest in curious byways which illuminated the whole, and his refusal to compromise with the commonplace. He refused also to use criticism as an instrument of power—or as an expression of his personality, a common failing among dictators of public taste. He remained aloof, detached, objective, sometimes stern, and even when he dealt with certain types of mediocrity it was in a spirit of enlightened inquiry. Yet he remained always attached to his works of the imagination. I remember him saying to me with some vehemence (one day in Prince-ton): "Why do you speak to me always of my criticism? I have written plays, poems, stories, light verse, novels. I am a writer—a writer of many things." Nevertheless, the world knew him best as critic and explorer of faraway regions of the mind. In the pages of *The New Yorker* he was the analytical traveler, the student of Russian literature, the vigorous ques-tioner of races and cultures, the incorruptible reviewer. Fulfillment came and belated fame. His whole life is a study in creation and re-creation, writing and revision, the continuing self-discovery and self-renewal within which he was able to retain an overview of the world; and with this his compassion for the sufferings out of which art is born.

I remember an evening in Princeton in Edmund Wilson's house, in 1953. He was spending the winter there. Elizabeth Bowen, the novelist, was visiting, and John Berryman and I called after dinner. Berryman was writing his "Homage to Mistress Bradstreet." The poem had filled him to repletion, so that he seemed constantly to overflow, and he had brought some pages he had just written. We sat in the big room in its pools of light, within the outer chiaroscuro, Miss Bowen with her controlled stutter and natural charm, Elena Wilson, the essence of warmth and sympathy, and Edmund, large, expansive, magisterial. Edmund asked Berryman to read from his work in progress. The poet had then—before he cultivated his Whitman-esque beard—a hard-seamed face and his voice was tightly drawn. He mumbled his lines, he dropped his voice, he often lost words, he drowned in his personal anguish, pushing on blindly and only half coherently in the reading. Edmund, sitting beside him, listened with all the intentness of which he was capable. After a bit, he began quietly to feed some of the lines back to Berryman—and by the same token to us. He fell into this quietly, tenderly, with a voice that was almost a caress. The suffering poet hardly heard him. He plunged ahead and I felt as if I were listening to a discordant Gregorian chant, in which Berryman's splutter of words was followed by a modulated and repetitive response. It was the poetry of reiteration, a vocal embrace, an administration of aid: Neoptolemus and Philoctetes. I felt myself in the presence of the highest form of sympathetic criticism—the critic as help-mate, as explicator, as friend, not only of the common reader, but of the artist himself.

LEON EDEL

Chronology

1895   Edmund Wilson, Jr., born May 8, in Red Bank, New Jersey, to Edmund and Helen Mather (Kimball) Wilson, their only child.

1908   First trip to Europe. In autumn, enters the Hill School, Pottstown, Pennsylvania.

1912   Graduates from Hill. Enters Princeton. Meets Christian Gauss; fellow students include John Peale Bishop and F. Scott Fitzgerald.

1916   Graduates from Princeton. Summer in military camp at Plattsburgh. In autumn, becomes reporter on New York *Evening Sun*.

1917   Enlists and asks for service with hospital unit. In France attending the wounded and the dying in hospitals in the Vosges.

1918   Becomes sergeant in Intelligence Corps. Goes to Germany at war's end.

1919   Returns to U.S. in July. Demobilized.

The Twenties

1919   Settles in New York and begins writing as a freelance.

1920   Becomes managing editor of *Vanity Fair*. Meets Edna St. Vincent Millay.

1921   Trip to Europe, "Edna having gone abroad." Becomes managing editor of *The New Republic*. Visits England, France, and Italy.

1922   *The Undertaker's Garland*, in collaboration with John Peale Bishop, published by Alfred A. Knopf. Rejoins *Vanity Fair*.

1923   Marries actress Mary Blair. Continues at *Vanity Fair* but also becomes drama critic for *Dial*. Death of father. Birth of daughter, Rosalind.

1924   Goes to California for Swedish ballet to induce Charlie Chaplin to take role in ballet written by himself. Chaplin declines. Provincetown Players produce *The Crime in the Whistler Room* starring Mary Blair. Rejoins *The New Republic*.

1925   Separation from Mary Blair.

1926   *Discordant Encounters*, a series of imaginary conversations. Visits New Orleans.

1927   Spends summer in Peaked Hill, Eugene O'Neill's house in Provincetown. Begins work on essays for *Axel's Castle*. Visits Boston during Sacco and Vanzetti demonstrations.

1928   Works on *I Thought of Daisy*. Visits California and rewrites novel.

1929   *Daisy* completed. Enters Clifton Springs Sanatorium for treatment of "a kind of" nervous breakdown, but continues work on *Axel's Castle*. Leaves sanatorium after three weeks. Summer at Cape Cod. *Poets, Farewell!* and *I Thought of Daisy* published by Scribner's. Divorced from Mary Blair. Marries Margaret Canby, 1930.

The Twenties

Edmund Wilson was discharged from the army on July 9, 1919, and on August 10 moved into an apartment at 114 West Sixteenth Street, sharing it as before with school friends. Four days after his return to Manhattan he wrote to F. Scott Fitzgerald: "I'm not writing a novel, but I'm writing almost everything else—and getting some of it accepted." His wide-ranging interests and his mental agility and playfulness made him popular in the magazines and showed him to be a master of the brief article, the short essay.

He found work almost at once on *Vanity Fair*; there had been a staff shake-up, and that handsomely printed popular journal needed a managing editor. He worked there with his Princeton friend John Peale Bishop, who had served in the trenches during the war; and it was here that the two of them met and fell in love with Edna St. Vincent Millay. Between the lines of his notebooks, in his late memoir of Miss Millay, and in his novel *I Thought of Daisy*, we can see how the poet made these years poignant for Edmund, and provided perhaps the only truly "romantic" passion of his life. He would love other women, and seek endlessly to be gallant, in the starved way of a Puritan-reared man. He was sensual, and also grasping. Miss Millay was not to be grasped. She remained from the first an elusive flame, but Edmund found the flame gave off too much heat. Miss Millay was indeed burning the candle at both ends as she would say in celebrated lines. Edmund also resorted to fire imagery:

> I who have broken my passionate heart
> For the lips of Edna Millay
> And her face that burns like a flame
> And her terrible chagrin.

When later he came on her line "Here is a wound that never will heal, I know," he said: "This poem plucked the strings of chagrin." He realized the wound was caused by one of her many lovers—not himself. Edna Millay said: "I get my whole life messed up with people falling in love with me." Perhaps it was symbolic that Edmund mentions taking her to see *Heartbreak House*. Between the lines of his memoir one reads a great deal of heartbreak, and it is written into his novel in the vibrant figure of Rita

Cavanagh. In Edmund's erotic experiences, as we have remarked, women can be divided into the two types he projected in *I Thought of Daisy*—the Daisys and the Ritas. His Daisy (also identifiable) is nevertheless an extension of Henry James's Daisy Miller; so was Fitzgerald's in *The Great Gatsby*. But Rita came to him whole, out of Greenwich Village. The play of life and literature was important for both Edmund and John Peale Bishop, although Bishop seems to have burned with a more somber passion. Readers may be amused to read in the notebooks the description of Miss Millay in the arms of both her lovers on a farewell evening—she was about to go away. In one letter we find Edmund saying: "I had one magnificent evening with her in the spring during which all old quarrels were repaired." Early in their meetings we get a touch of the Princetonian Edmund in a sentence describing his going with Edna to a party at the home of the actor Richard Bennett: "I sat on the floor with Edna which seemed to me very Bohemian."

He would become very Bohemian indeed. The bad liquor of Prohibition, the speakeasies, the parties, the passionate and sometimes tortured sex—we glimpse the 1920's in phrases, bits of speech, miniature scenes. Edmund never forgot, when he was with Edna, "the things she noticed, for she charged them with her own intense feeling. This power of enhancing and ennobling life was felt by all who knew her." The trip to Europe, which he made in 1921, seems to have been motivated by a desire to see Miss Millay, then abroad. In his memoir Edmund brings her to life as she first looked to him in 1920 in the Greenwich Village spring—dressed in bright batik, with her not-yet-bobbed reddish hair, her animations and intensities, her purity of speech, her long throat and full figure and her "intoxicating effect on people." It was an intoxication Edmund had to live through. As he wrote in 1921 to his old friend Stanley Dell: "My affairs of the heart (confidential) are badly entangled. I suppose it is old mother nature's revenge for my long period of freedom from these troubles that I should have spent this last year occupied with women at the expense of everything else."

By that time he had acquired, in spite of various *chagrins d'amour*, a considerable, if limited, reputation. He was not a celebrity like Millay, or Fitzgerald, or Dos Passos during these years; but his voice on literature, on the arts and on the social scene gave to his name an unquestioned authority. He moved in and out of *Vanity Fair*, and he became a staff writer for the then comparatively new *New Republic*. That journal, over whose literary department Edmund would intermittently preside, published some of his best work during the 1920's. One has to read his review of *Ulysses* in the pages of *The New Republic* or his notice of *The Waste Land* in *The Dial* to see how these works of literary modernity were promptly grasped and explicated by Edmund, while other critics read with bewilderment. By the time he reviewed such works, he understood the "modern movement" in its historic depths, recognized the preeminence of the subjective modes and the victories of symbolism over the naturalists.

His review of *Ulysses* sees at once the brilliance and shoddiness of Joyce, at a time when readers were only dazzled by the brilliance; he questions whether parody and mockery are effective ways for dealing with reality in the novel, yet he values the strength and virtuosity of the Irishman's gift. And then he saw through—as his notebooks show—the tinsel of Fitzgerald, whom he criticized mercilessly, yet praised with candor. Fitzgerald listened; he respected Edmund too much to want to be seriously hurt. As for Edmund's explication of *The Waste Land*, it remains the first large critical statement in America on T. S. Eliot.

This by way of margin to the notebooks, which are fragmentary during these years. After his passion for Miss Millay had burned itself out, Edmund married the actress Mary Blair, who was playing successfully in the Provincetown Players' productions of Eugene O'Neill. She took the lead in Edmund's play *The Crime in the Whistler Room*, produced in MacDougal Street October 9, 1924. Edmund did not succeed as a playwright, and he spread himself into so many cultural activities that he published none of the books he was planning during this period, save a collaboration with John Bishop. In 1923 he became the father of a daughter, Rosalind Baker Wilson, born September 19. He had by then left *Vanity Fair* and was enjoying his work on *The New Republic*. The journal's offices were located in two old houses that seemed almost to be in the river on the West Side. When the weekly became interested in him, he was entertained by each of the editors in turn, much to his amusement, as if he were being admitted into a fraternal organization. Lunch was served daily in these houses in a particular dining room and the editors conferred and came and went as they pleased. At these lunches, more private and more searching than the performances of the round table at the Algonquin, Edmund found Walter Lippmann the "liveliest" of the lot. He described *The New Republic* as "a chilly and unfriendly home for anybody but a respectable liberal of at least middle age." It remained his literary home, however, long enough to harbor some of his finest early essays, set pieces and imaginary conversations. Edmund Wilson had acquired (by the middle 1920's) a certain Johnsonian celebrity from this editorial perch, which he would carry over into the columns of *The New Yorker*.

His collaboration with John Peale Bishop was a book called *The Undertaker's Garland* which Alfred Knopf published in 1922. It reflected Wilson's and Bishop's war experiences: and it mocked death. It is a bitter book and a witty one, and the preface, which Edmund wrote, speaks largely in his ironic voice, of the death force in America as against the life force of the centuries. He would play with this theme in another form in *The Crime in the Whistler Room.* "New York is no more fitted for love than it was designed for art," Edmund wrote. "Money was the thing to get, not music, not wine . . . we have decided that we shall best interpret our country in a book devoted to death . . . at the darkest point in the Middle Ages people made a farce of death. To the people of the XVth century death itself had more life in it than life has today." The all but final section treats of the "death of God"—who asks man to forgive him for his bad job.

The book was a miscellany of Wilson's and Bishop's tales and poems. But by the time it came out, the 1920's were on their binge of prosperity and liquor; the war had receded; and while a few, like Mencken, praised the book, it had little sale and attracted only passing attention. Death is never a popular subject. However, its appearance in the year of *The Waste Land* and *Ulysses* suggests how much it was in the spirit of its time.

1919–1925

After the War

[My intelligence unit was not mustered out, on account of our being non-combatants and hence low on the list of privilege, till after the Fourth of July, 1919. My father and my mother came to see me separately at the rest camp at Southampton, Long Island. My father had gratified me at the camp when he first complained of the army's inefficiency in not letting him in to see me sooner, then when the officer in charge warned him that that way of talking was treasonable, telling him that there was nothing in what he had said that violated any law. I had written my mother to bring me Witter Bynner's poems, Ezra Pound's *Lustra* and H. L. Mencken's *American Language*, the first edition of which had just appeared. I read them all on the camp's board benches.

My mother had an upsetting revelation to make. My favorite cousin Sandy (Reuel Baker) Kimball was a schizophrenic case (schizophrenia was then called *dementia praecox*). He was only fifteen months older than I was and had in our early years been my closest friend: we wrote stories, made phonograph records, played checkers and got up charades together. We had been sent to different prep schools, had belonged to different clubs at college and had become rather alienated from one another. He was a year ahead of me at school and college, and during those years we saw little of one another. But that he should have gone insane was a shock that I had difficulty absorbing. It was an amputation of a whole relation. His mother had brought pressure on him to become a successful doctor like his father, but his instructors at Physicians and Surgeons had advised against trying to finish, and he flunked his examinations. He had proposed to and been rejected by the spirited redheaded daughter of one of his neighbors in the country. (He had rather disturbed me by telling me with a certain amount of enthusiasm of his homosexual experiences with another boy at his prep school.) And he had worried about not taking part in the war. When I was in France, he had written me letters about this, and I had answered that once you had enlisted in something, you were preoccupied with your work and its hardships and never gave your patriotic duty a thought. His father, after a taxing and assiduous life of work, had now collapsed and become quite helpless, relapsing into a second childhood; and his mother, who had never understood him—it was a mistake for him to continue to live in her house—could not bring herself to relinquish her ambitious plans

41

for his future. His unfortunate sister Esther had to act as a buffer between
him and his mother, whose tendencies were irreconcilable. Sandy had first,
after giving up medicine, had a job in a chemical department in Washington and afterwards worked as a clerk in Scribner's bookstore; then, his condition making this impossible, was sent to private sanatoriums, where he at
first partly retained his intelligence. He wrote a parody, *The Great Hater*, of
Rupert Brooke's *The Great Lover* and a story in which he figured as the in-
adequate son of a great old king (my now disqualified Uncle Reuel). He
made friends at the sanatorium with a young member of the Proctor family
of Keith and Proctor, the vaudeville producers, and they used to kid one
another, joking about their illnesses. He spoke once of going to Europe, and
I pretended to take this seriously, but "How can I go when I'm insane?" he
said. My very boyish-minded Uncle Win attributed Sandy's deterioration
to his having been sent to St. Paul's instead of, like the rest of the family, to
Andover or Exeter. His Knox uncles, products of St. Paul's, were considered decidedly weak-minded by my more energetic and competent
Kimball uncles. Sandy soon passed into eclipse in the state hospital at Middletown, New York. His disappearance from the world made upon me a
deeper impression than I might have expected, and it was for long felt as
something of a trauma.

It was only after coming back from the war that I found that it had come
to be possible to talk naturally to my father on something like a plane of
equality. He did not express outrage at my then rather radical opinions; but
though himself still a mainly loyal Republican, he was horrified by the il-
legality of the arrest and deportation of radical aliens without either war-
rant or trial. Our conversations had become more comfortable. He talked
frankly about politics—told me that Warren Harding, though a Republican, represented the lowest grade of the machine politician and regaled me
with funny stories about local New Jersey figures.]

Upper New York. One saw the first beginnings of the city in the open
boulevard: the façades of apartment houses, laced with fire escapes, the
many garages and automobile stores.

A local doctor named Sam Patterson once sat in the New Jersey Senate. It was
the custom at that time, when a bill had been proposed which was likely to
restrict any large corporation, for the senators to await offers from the corporation before declaring which way they would vote. Votes were usually
bought for a reasonable enough sum—a few hundreds—but on a certain
occasion this man Patterson demanded $5,000. The corporation's lobbyist
expostulated with him, but Patterson claimed that his conviction was so
strong that he should vote the other way that nothing short of $5,000 could

persuade him to change it. The lobbyist finally consented and made an appointment with Patterson to meet him the day that the bill was to be voted on in a certain water closet in the Capitol lavatory. When the roll was being called for the vote on the bill, Patterson went to the W.C., as agreed, but the lobbyist did not appear. Just as they were nearing Patterson's name in the roll, however, the fellow turned up with a wad of bills "big enough to choke a horse." "My God! hurry up!" he said, "or you won't get a chance to vote at all!" "Hold on now! Wait a minute! I want to count these bills!" "Why, man alive! they'll be past your name, if you stay here another minute!" Patterson went up and voted. When he finally counted the bills, there turned out to be a good $100 bill on the outside and nothing but counterfeit money inside. So great was his rage at first that he threatened to have the lobbyist arrested for passing bogus money.

Charley Walker [a Yale friend of EW's, later internationally known for his expertise in labor relations and his translations of Greek plays] came down to Red Bank. I had not seen him since before we went into the war. He had been doing the long shift with the blast furnace in a steel town and looked as if he had been baked in the fires of hell. He had decided to devote himself to Labor, because that was the great coming force. I regarded myself as pretty far to the Left, which Charley was still far from being—he saw everything in terms of employment conditions, had nothing of the radical vocabulary. I had been much excited by the big steel strike of 1919. But Charley was a serious person, he had not gone in for selling bonds like so many other college graduates. I did not then become so acutely aware as I afterwards came to be of the difference between the college graduates who were carrying out the tradition of the time when the men who went to college were all, with few exceptions, destined for what were called the "learned professions," but I found the visit of Charley had a fortifying effect on my own morale.

[I decided that I had now been innocent long enough and decided to buy a condom. I went to a drugstore on Greenwich Avenue and watched nervously from outside to be sure that there were no ladies there. I then went in and inquired. The clerk withdrew to the back counter and produced a condom of rubber, which he highly recommended, blowing it up like a balloon in order to show me how reliable it was. But the condom, thus distended, burst, and this turned out to be something of an omen. I soon got over my shyness with women, but I was a victim of many of the hazards of sex—from which I might have been saved by previous experience: abortions, gonorrhea, entanglements, a broken heart.

I went back after the war to sharing an apartment—this time on West

Sixteenth Street—with my old friends David Hamilton, Larry Noyes and Morris Belknap. We had, to cook for us, a mulatto West Indian woman, who would become exasperated with me for bringing unexpected guests home to dinner. We entertained many Yale and Princeton friends as well as other friends: Gilbert Troxall, Phelps Putnam, Charley Walker, Fred Manning, Douglas Moore, John Bishop, Scott Fitzgerald, Kenneth Hayes Miller, Adele Brandeis, Morris Belknap's stepmother, and others whom I have forgotten. The arrangement, pleasant while it lasted, eventually, however, had to fall apart.

David Hamilton soon got married to Margaret Bentley, a girl from Chicago to whom he had been engaged from before the war. She was the daughter of a Chicago lawyer who looked after the interests of the McCormicks. I had been to school with her brother Dick, a tough-spoken but likable boy who went to Yale and afterwards himself became a lawyer. But Margaret had or thought she had artistic tastes and on that account, I think, married David, who wanted to be both a writer and a painter. There was a big very affluent wedding in Chicago, to which we all went out and at which we all were ushers. Margaret was a strong-minded dynamic girl, with more character, I think, than David, who was languid and had always been rather coddled by an indulgent mother and sisters. He was to publish two or three novels of an unemphatic ironic humor and do a certain amount of drawing and painting of which I never saw much except enough to be sure that it was very far from first-rate. He and Margaret had two daughters, then Margaret at an early age died.

Morris Belknap came from Louisville, Kentucky, where his family were evidently quite well-to-do. He had lost both mother and father early, and his father had married again a handsome and very able woman, who was extremely kind to Morris. His only brother was "not all there," a case of arrested development. Morris's invariable companion was a cultivated Jewish girl, from a well-known and well-to-do family, who had pretty and distinguished sisters but was herself rather dumpy and unattractive. She came to New York to be near Morris, and I imagined always hoped he would marry her. They had their love of the arts in common. Morris was both a painter and a musician, but a kind of spiritual impotence, quietly resigned and morose, nullified his artistic aspirations. He went to the Art Students League, where he sat under Kenneth Hayes Miller and was very much influenced by him in the direction of psychoanalysis. He painted nudes of both sexes; they seemed always to turn a turbid green, as if they were already dead.

Morris Belknap contributed in a small way to my musical education: he played on the piano Gluck's *Euridice* and Mussorgsky's songs of death, read the memoirs of Berlioz and talked about them, and he led me to explore

Berlioz's *A Travers Chants*, with its literary descriptions of Beethoven's symphonies—I read it with the same kind of avidity that I was beginning to read Paul Rosenfeld's musical articles, and Morris played so many times the oboe's part in the *Meistersinger* overture that I was finally able to whistle it. He was an extremely friendly good-tempered fellow, but in the long run rather dampening. He exemplified the sour side which I noticed as characteristic of one of the two classes of graduates of Yale. There were those who had proudly belonged to the best senior societies and fraternities, for whom Yale was a kind of religion, and those—of whom Sinclair Lewis was one of the most embittered examples—who had never belonged to anything and could never forgive Yale. (I remember that Paul Rosenfeld told me that it was only his summers in Europe that made it possible for him to stand four years of New Haven.)

Larry Noyes was a homosexual, but though I had roomed with him two years at school and in spite of his occasional pederastic jokes and a rather ambivalent pal that he brought back from his period in the navy, I never suspected this and knew nothing about it till after we had parted. He was evidently somewhat embarrassed about this side of his life. I was told later that it was his great regret that his being homosexual had prevented him from belonging to the Racquet Club. He came from St. Paul and had known Scott Fitzgerald but, due to the Fitzgeralds' straitened means, there was a social barrier between them. Scott did not like Larry and, referring to him in *My Lost City* says of him, in his description of what he regarded as my enviable New York household, that "only the crisp tearing open of invitations by one man was a discordant note." Larry, when Scott became famous and had died, said of him, like a patronizing elderly lady, that it was a pity he had not lived to do more because he was "*such* a clever boy." I thus learned that although in Louisville it was a social disadvantage to have too much money, it was, on the contrary, in a Middle Western city a handicap not to have a good deal. Yet Larry was the kind of Middle Westerner who, regardless of Middle Western fortunes, depends much on the prestige of his Eastern connections. His sister was married to a De Forest; his mother was related to the Gilmans; Katherine Ludington, a kind of liberal patroness, was also a relation of his. He was the most complete case I have ever known of Eastern-oriented Western snobbery.

Larry had a job in New York with a very smart firm of architects, but having been given the commission for a millionaire's house in the West Indies or some other exotic place, he got into trouble for attacking a native and was apparently in his office relegated to a minor role. I got him, at some time in the forties, to remodel an old Cape Cod house I had bought, and found that since his driver was a boyfriend who occasionally presumed to treat him with a rather undue familiarity, he did not like either to leave him alone or to ask us to have him to dinner. It was equally impossible for me to tell him that I really didn't care. We finally invited them both.]

One of the young Rockefellers and his wife rode up on horseback to the Duryeas' house. Mrs. Duryea went out and began to talk to them. Mr. Rockefeller's horse caught her little finger in his mouth and began to grind and munch it as if it were an apple, while poor Mrs. Duryea jumped up and down with pain. When she had finally got her finger out of the teeth of the horse, Mrs. Rockefeller remarked: "Oh, I hope he hasn't bitten your finger off." Mrs. Duryea excused herself, saying that she felt faint and sick, and withdrew to the house. The colored servant came to her in great agitation. "I tell you, he was no gentleman, Mrs. Duryea, or he would have gotten off his horse! . . . You leave him to me! I'll go out and fix him!" The Rockefellers simply left word that they had come to invite her to dinner and would she telephone whether she could come? Mrs. Duryea called in the doctor and had her finger bandaged up. She waited purposely for some time to see if the Rockefellers would call up and inquire after her, but nothing happened, and she was finally obliged to call up herself and tell them she could not come; they never mentioned her finger. The only kind of situations they knew how to deal with were dinner invitations and, confronted with anything else, they were helpless, did not know what to say.

Gordon Bodenwein used to treat Trixie [Gilbert] Troxall abominably when they roomed together at Yale. He would prod him with a fork or chase him around the room with a knife. "You little hussy!" he would say. "You horrible little monster! You're the kind of thing that the kings used to pick up, when they were riding through the country, to be their court fools!" He would, in fact, do everything possible to hurt and insult Trixie. He seemed to be possessed by a perverse demon. After he got out of college, Gordon quarreled with his father and went into a monastery; he broke out later, became a Catholic and is now teaching and flogging little boys in a Catholic school at Hackensack. He had excellent taste and loved the arts, which went strangely with his fanaticism. [Gilbert was a friend of ours whom, in spite of some peculiarities, we liked.]

Trixie and Gordon, after a year together, separated for a year, then resumed the combination.

Larry (Noyes) on the Gardenia. When Larry was on the tugboat *Gardenia*, whose business was to meet incoming ships, he used to get shore leave every five days. When he came back, he would sleep for three or four days on end, sustaining himself with chocolate till he gave himself indigestion and became incapable of getting up, but lay there in a stupor. One day, the captain came down into the hold where they slept and asked: "Are there any rats down here?" "Hell, no!" answered somebody, who didn't see who it was. "No rats could live down here!"

The Palisades in October. In the autumn haze, they looked very remote, and the green and gold of the trees, which clothed the cliffs like metal scales of armor, was infinitely faded till it blent with the brownish gray of the many-fissured side of the naked rock. And against that ancient background, so somber and wild, the white gulls rose and fell on languid wings. And downstream the river and sky were melted to silver together.

New York to Newark on the way to Red Bank or Princeton. Coming out of the Hudson tunnel, one finds oneself emerging from a hill on whose barren sides are seen the straggling frame houses of suburbs, the last city streets of some New Jersey town which is itself a suburb of New York; one stark church stands up in the sordid landscape, where one is surprised to see even the outer semblance of a religion; if it is actually the house of a religion and not merely a building designed mechanically, in an obsolete form and by architects who had more taste for designing factories, as an inexpensive recognition of a respectable convention; it is a religion hardened and begrimed and divested of beauty, which has assumed protective coloring in order to live at all. It is a country forever tarnished by a dingy haze of dampness and smoke. At the foot of the hill lies a vast marsh of swamp grass, bleached by the fall, with patches still persisting in a feeble verdancy and with stagnant pools corrupted by a vivider green; the whole of this dead meadow is laced with telephone wires and occasionally traversed by muddy roads that seemed to be foundering. The one touch of color and life was the series of large board signs that advertised New York hotels and theaters, underclothes, candy and shaving soaps. Then one saw the factories with tapering smokestacks; one of them had four chimneys and lay like a ship in the marsh. The landscape bristled with chimneys and with cranes along the railroad tracks. And there were human habitations: feeble-looking houses, unpainted and gray, which, but for an occasional line of clothes drying in the tainted air, would have seemed bleached to as complete a death as the sea they were islanded in. At last, after ten minutes' ride in a world of factories, one reaches a body of water, perfectly black and still, where the hulk of an old steamboat, as black as the river, has been rotting and sinking slowly for several years and shows only its warped upper deck and its blackened wheel. This is Newark Bay, and the city is Newark: more factories here, but jammed together; small factories and machine shops, pattern-makers and electroplaters, press close beside the train—manufacturers of castings, blowpipes, paints, chemicals, mattresses, fountain pens, ketchup, refrigerators, phonographs, bacon, chewing gum, safety razors, cigarettes, carpet sweepers, licorice drops, flours,

letter openers, typewriters, umbrellas. The city and the bay produce a
curious impression of mingled life and death: there is business, one can see
that; there is lots of work being done; there is prosperity in the cheap stores
and solid buildings; but in the dirtiness of the streets, the dull colors of the
city, the lack of any sign of a love for cleanness or brightness, the impression
of life grown heavy and sordid in those thousands of brick-walled rooms
behind those dirty windows, one felt that death was rotting and blackening
the city, as it had that old steamboat hulk which no one had thought to destroy or save.

At Perth Amboy, one saw something like a great common, full of mangy
bare spots in the thin dirty grass; it seemed partly to be used as a dumping
ground for refuse, for it was strewn with tin cans and papers; beyond these
were frame houses, which, but for the smoke from their chimneys, might
have seemed, like the papers and cans, old rubbish worn out and thrown
away and defaced by the weather out of all recognition as things which had
once served human life.

The skyscrapers in November. From the Jersey City ferry, on a gray morning of November, the skyscrapers stood out distinctly in a hard light and
seemed no more dignified, but only larger, than the hideous utilitarian
buildings of the small towns—like them, of the drabbest and most grimy
colors and of a square machine-made architecture which excluded imagination.

November, Red Bank. The fine bleak gray and gold of a November sunset
in the west, and in the east the dry and faded corn stacks in the dry and faded
light; a wood fire on the hearth; the little mice come in from the fields when
the corn stacks are taken down and seek shelter from the cold in the walls of
houses, where they are heard running and gnawing and chirping like birds;
there is nothing but white and rusty-red asters in the withering green of the
garden.

Beside the road stood the dry skeletons of Queen Anne's vanished lace;
the bleached crests of the thistles had commenced to scatter and the milk-
weed pods were splitting and strewing the air with spun silver. The air,
which was not yet harsh with winter, filled the throat like cold wine. And
though the golden vesture of the trees had begun to wear thin and dull, they
gave the landscape everywhere a toned and faded richness. At night, the
frosty moon filled up the world, as if by some liquid, with a bluish-gray
light which just seemed to bring out the green of the grass with a faint silver
luminosity, and, in the morning, one saw on the fields the whitish bloom of
the frost.

November in New York. The sky was full of wild dramatic clouds above the bleak gray streets. Outside my window, the rusty leaves rustled dryly on the vines, which were quite bare in places and looked like tangled string; the roofs and chimneys were cut out sharply against the bleak yellow of the sunset, and the red brick house backs were blackened and made mysterious by the sooty winter twilight.

One saw the livid violet lamps strung sparsely in the dark.

Lincoln Park, Chicago. From the Parkway Hotel in Chicago, Lincoln Park, for all its black winter trees, seemed shadowy and soft under the snow and in the light of the lamps that hung everywhere like great round pearls. Occasionally, a taxi would thread its deserted ways.

The Hamilton-Bentley wedding. Dick Bentley, handing out the ushers' gloves: "Have you got your mitts?"; handing out the gardenias: "Isn't that pretty nasty, though?"

Just as the bridal procession was about to start down the aisle, a very old lady appeared and demanded a seat. She was clad in an enormous ermine cloak over what looked like a corselet of mail. She must have been blind or had a glass eye, for her glance was lifeless and strange. She was accompanied by a meek-looking old gentleman without presence or magnificence, but it was she who did most of the talking, in a very loud voice and apparently with only an imperfect realization of what was going on around her, but with a very vigorous conviction of her own importance to it. Morris Belknap said that she looked as if she had ruined four or five people in her life.

Mrs. Belknap is like the goddess Athena, γλαυκῶπις, a New England Puritan type of magnificent distinction. One feels that she should be ruling an empire, that she can hardly realize all her capabilities in the Louisville house of the Belknaps. She should have been drawn by Holbein.

Johnstown, Pennsylvania, etc. In a valley, which brims with smoke, as if it were a vessel, a huge-chimneyed blast furnace dominates everything else: the muddy and turbulent little stream and the bare smoke-colored houses perched along the barren hillside. On a bank lie great husks of scrap iron like the fragments of carcasses. Between those iron hills one can see nothing which is not desolate. The forests have been burned away and left only a few blackened spikes, as if it were a battlefield in the late war. The towns of the Middle West, like Gary, and of western Pennsylvania, like Altoona, are even more completely sordid and crass than Eastern towns like Elizabeth, which at least catch a faint metropolitan atmosphere from the proximity of New York, whereas those other places, in their flatness and coarseness, seem the natural products of a peasantry richer, to be sure, than that older one which lived on the land, but one which is incapable of imagining or desiring anything better than this dingy, crude and colorless material life without even the customs and costumes and the strong-flavored sensuality that we find in the pictures of Hals and the folk songs of Europe.

Uncle Win. Uncle Win [Winfield Kimball, a brother of EW's mother], after living in the Royalton for twenty-some years, is now obliged to move out, because the building is to be torn down, and this seems to worry him more than any family catastrophe has ever done. He says that there are no other bachelor apartments in New York and that rather than go to the trouble of getting established alone somewhere else, he is almost willing to get married. "Have you got your eye on anybody in particular?" we asked. "No," he replied, "but they better not fool around with me now!" [Mrs. Knox had tried to get him to marry one of her Todd connections; but he had balked at this.] He said further that he was much worried for fear the family name should become extinct. "I asked one girl, and she said: 'When they get to be as old as you are and nobody's got them, there must be something wrong with 'em.'" His mind seems to run constantly on this subject. When Aunt Laura gave him his choice of neckties for a Christmas present and remarked that, when men got to be as old as he was, they probably preferred darker ties, he said: "That's just when they want the bright ones! When a man gets to be that age, he's gotta wear sump'm to make 'em lamp him!"

—A Jap butler had given him cream cheese for butter to put on his pancakes.

"Aw, they used to have the wildest dinner parties you ever heard of—every Thursday night. About six or eight men, all Princetonians; you used to hear the inside dope on everything—all the gossip, all the scandal! I used to go along as the archaic old thing to lend some air of respectability to the party; I was the only one there who didn't drink. —But I've cut out those drinking parties. It's an awful bore for the man who doesn't drink, you know. It's amusing for about the first twenty minutes, but, after that, they either begin to put their arms around you or they begin to curse you—one or the other!" [The drinking of his two brothers had made him a teetotaler for life.]

Hecker [a friend of my army days. His grandfather had played a role in the '48 revolution]. I have sometimes thought that there is a great man locked up in Hecker. If so, the locks have tightened and hardened with age, and, having always kept so firm a hand on himself and never let himself go, he will probably never do so. The army and the war convinced him, he said, that humanity was not worth dying for, and yet he comes near to being the type of man who does die for humanity. It is really priggishness which stands in his way in this as in little things. Still, he might be a great Puritan . . .

The white winter sun over the gleaming snowy road. On the way to Chicago, the whitenesses of the frozen lakes under the moon.

New Year's Eve. The dinner party belowstairs began with the popping of corks and the braying of a phonograph: about one in the morning; the company were apparently on the crest of the wave. When the phonograph was played, I could hear what sounded like a large heavy man joining loudly in the refrain of the melody. After every burst, he would stop and laugh boorishly at his own clumsy efforts, surprised that his exhilaration should have tricked him into enjoying so unfamiliar and ludicrous a thing as music.

The volume of Anatole France lay lightly on the table, its lemon-colored cover curling a little at the edges. Its proportions were as slender and graceful as those of a French window.

[The incident that really put an end to my ménage with these woman-avoiding companions was a visit from Edna Millay. She was living then in the Village in a wretched cold little one room, where she had to share a bathroom with the other tenants. She asked to take a hot bath at my apartment. I told her the bathroom was at her disposal, but when she took advantage of it, this had, I believe, on Morris and Larry a profoundly shocking effect. It was then that Ted Paramore and I took an apartment at 777 Lexington Avenue. This place, though it was over a furrier's loft and smelled, as Ted said, like wet cats, had from our point of view an ideal arrangement. A long "railroad apartment," it could be divided into two parts with a convenient bathroom between, and this could be shut off on either side. We were thus able to entertain our girls without interference with one another. We had only gas heating, so the atmosphere was suffocatingly fetid, but I would sit reading *Ulysses* or *The Wings of the Dove* with my feet on the gas heater. I had rather fought shy of Ted at school—I think he was a year behind me and he went around with the air of an alert bull terrier who might become scrappy. But I now found him agreeable and great fun. He had a fine fund of improvised humor, embellished by occasional tags from Shakespeare—especially "a fair hot wench in flame-colored taffeta." When Ted was alone, I would find him on his bed, always with a hangover but always cheerful, the daily newspapers, which he read attentively, strewn on the floor around him. I had the bad taste, when I was asked by Larry to send him some things of his I had carried off, to include a box of old condoms. He answered, "I wonder you can spare them."

Paul Rosenfeld once told me that my typical friend was someone clever

but dissipated who looked rather the worse for wear. He was evidently
thinking of Phelps Putnam, Scott Fitzgerald and Ted Paramore, the last of
whom was a perfect example of this. For all his cleverness, he never got anywhere with the projects—usually theatrical or connected with the
movies—which always kept him sanguine and allowed him to assume an
air of having important business to see somebody or other about. His actual
productions were very few. He did a Menckenesque article for the *Smart Set*
which predicted that the United States would be immensely improved if
conquered by the Japanese. The only thing he ever wrote that had any kind
of general success was *The Ballad of Yukon Jake*, a parody of Robert W. Service, of which, in response to the many demands, we had to have offprints
made. It was eventually published as a small book and had almost as much
popularity as a piece for recital on convivial occasions as Service's own ballads. It was accepted by Crowninshield, the editor of *Vanity Fair*, on which I
then had a job, but due to what he shrank from as its crudity, he could not
for a long time bring himself to print it. As a result of this, it lay around the
office and was from time to time retouched by John Bishop and me and
made to read somewhat more smoothly. It was indeed very funny. Ted in
those early days did succeed in getting one play produced—a detective
affair which was dominated by a very sharp but dignified old lady, obviously inspired by Ted's ideal of his mother. He and I at one time began a
comedy based on the commercial exploitation of a prehistoric monster reported in a South American lake; but we did not get very far. Scott Fitzgerald, when he went to Hollywood, asked for Ted to work with him on a
script; but he said that he was soon discouraged by the extreme banality of
Ted's ideas. Ted had a great gift for inventing comic songs that were parodies of popular numbers:

> Take me back to South Dakota—
> That's the place I love the best.
> And I don't mean Minnesota—
> It's just one state further west.

One of Ted's principal pastimes was seducing his more inexperienced
girlfriends. His principal instrument for this was a pioneer guidebook to
sex, the predecessor of the present avalanche, by a certain Dr. Robey, which
aimed to remove inhibitions by giving you permission to do anything you
liked. He would put "old Dr. Robey" into the hands of the girls and count
upon their yielding reactions. Another provoker of temptation was the
desire of the ladies to save him from his drinking and disorderly living. He
was in some ways so sensitive, so infectiously amusing and so apparently
well-intentioned that it seemed a pity and quite unnecessary to allow him to
go to waste. I had myself at first this illusion. But though he played on other

people's faith in him, he must have known in his heart, or at least his sub-conscious, that he could never be reformed. He used to remind me of a well-liked dog who looks docile when forbidden to do something which he has every intention of doing. His theatrical ambitions were chimeras, and his real fundamental aim was to go on, under the inspiration of liquor, playing bridge in Santa Barbara, where his family lived and where he always spent part of the year, while he sustained himself with hard liquor. His formula with women seemed always to work. One of his girls did much better than Ted by marrying a rich man, who very soon after died. Another married Ted and had a son by him but was soon deserted. He married a second time, and then a third. His latest wife was much younger than Ted, the pretty daughter of the Russian actress Anna Sten, who had been brought to this country by Blumberg but who had never found a place in our films.

Ted's death was sudden, shocking and senseless. He was sitting in a car which had been raised in a garage on one of those elevators which they use when making repairs. The contrivance fell and killed him. This happened on the West Coast, and I heard nothing further about him till I was told about the accident by Norah Sayre.

The somewhat raffish tone of what later follows is partly determined by my association with Ted. I maintained more respectable connections, but this world seemed rather exotic, and I chronicled it very minutely.

Vanity Fair. When I was first living in New York and trying to get some-thing published, I adopted a system—which I have always recommended to young men who wanted to write. I made a list of all possible magazines and another of all my pieces which I could imagine being accepted. I did not allow myself to be unnerved or discouraged by rejection slips, but tried with each of my products every one of the magazines on the list, and when I had sent each of them out and got it back, I began sending them out again. This proved to be a good idea. At that time, the man who was supposed to read the manuscripts submitted to *Vanity Fair* was an old magazine editor, Albert Lee, who supplemented his general nullity by a pince-nez attached to a black ribbon and who simply, without reading them, sent the manu-scripts back with rejection slips. I gathered that he and Frank Crownin-shield had once worked in the same office and that Crowninshield had arranged for him this sinecure. I had revised one of my undergraduate pieces that had first appeared in the *Nassau Lit.*, a memoir of an imaginary *fin de siècle* writer called Edward Moore Gresham, and I sent it a second time to *Vanity Fair*. Dorothy Parker was now reading the manuscripts, and she brought it to Crowninshield's attention. Crowninshield called me up. There was a crisis at *Vanity Fair*. Dorothy Parker had offended Billie Burke, a popular comedy actress, who was married to Florenz Ziegfeld,

and Ziegfeld had made a fuss to Condé Nast, the publisher of *Vanity Fair*,
and had evidently insisted that Dorothy be taken off writing about theaters:
she was constantly offending actresses; and Crowninshield had to submit.
As a result, not only did she resign but Robert Benchley, the managing editor, and Bob Sherwood also resigned, out of sympathy. This left the *Vanity
Fair* office empty except for Crowninshield's woman secretaries; and I was
called on to fill in, and was at first tried out on reading manuscripts.
Benchley and Dorothy joked about my being a "scab," but were kind
about showing me the ropes and took me for the first time to the Algonquin. When I had first met Dorothy in the office, she had been, I thought,
overperfumed, and the hand with which I had shaken hers kept the scent of
her perfume all day. Although she was fairly pretty and although I needed a
girl, what I considered the vulgarity of her too much perfume prevented me
from paying her court.

Very soon I became aware that, except for the woman secretaries, whom
Crowninshield knew how to charm, the people who worked for
"Crownie" were not very much attached to him. Benchley came from
Worcester, Mass., and there was something "la-dee-da" about Crowninshield that offended his New England taste. He told me how Crowninshield had watched from a window some parade of American troops, and
commented on their sloppiness and lack of good form in comparison with
the soldiers of other nations. I was somewhat shocked by what I thought his
lack of manners when, having taken me to lunch at the Coffee House, a
little lunch club which he had founded, as I was told, in order to recruit
contributors to *Vanity Fair*, he explained to the men on his right, telling me
to turn away and not listen, that Benchley had absurdly "got excited"
about their treatment of Dorothy Parker. Frank Crowninshield was not a
sympathetic character. It used to annoy me that he would always be solicitous as to whether I needed money and, with the utmost cordiality, offer to
lend me some—I never borrowed more, I think, than fifty dollars; but immediately after this start badgering me to pay it back. I was interested to
find that, in a memoir of his uncle, a nephew of Frank's says that he was bad-
gered in a similar way. Crowninshield, in his well-pressed gray suits that
harmonized with his silvering hair, would travel around the office with a
gait at once strutting and mincing, with the upper part of his body bent forward.

He was a type of which I have known a few—the born courtier who
lacks an appropriate court. He had first worked for Frank Munsey, the
owner of *Munsey's Magazine*, had shepherded him to Europe and arranged
to have him meet some titles; and he was now playing the courtier for Nast,
the glossiest bounder I have ever known, who was incapable of saying good
morning without a formally restrained but somehow obnoxious vulgarity.

The legend was that Crowninshield had once attempted to get up a bridge club in order to arrange for Nast an entry into Society, but that people had refused to join when they found out about this purpose. Frank Crowninshield's own stifled resentment against his position on the "Nast publications" occasionally came out in the flare-up of a word of impatient contempt. I once sat in on some kind of conference at which business affairs were discussed and was struck by what seemed to me the brutal tone of Nast in dealing with his social sponsor. *Vanity Fair* was always "in the doghouse" as the money-losing member of the Nast group, of which *Vogue* was the great success. It was true that Condé Nast had transformed fashion publishing in America by importing a French format and typography—he was in origin St. Louis French; but his capacity for innovation ended abruptly there. The family of Crowninshield had been identified with New England. The first Crowninshield in this country, he told me, had been a Swedish doctor in Boston, and the family had been mostly distinguished in connection with the navy and the sea; but I never observed in Frank any suggestion of this nautical tradition, and he had traveled very far from Boston. His father, Frederic Crowninshield, a mural painter and an instructor at the Boston Museum of Fine Arts, had been director of the American Academy in Rome. Frank had grown up partly in Italy and spoke Italian well. When he was interviewing me for a job, he tried me out in Italian and must have found my Italian very academic. He would refer to Boston with a kind of disdain. Hiram Powers's "Greek Slave," once so much admired, was only too recognizable as really "Mrs. Wigglesworth of Boston"; Longfellow was a middle-class mediocrity whom the elite had never taken seriously. On one occasion when Crowninshield had to go to Boston and had lunched at the Somerset or some other superior club, and had asked, after using the urinal, where he could wash his hands, he had evoked the exclamation, "You New York dudes!" But he spent all his weekends with his mother at Stockbridge, and remnants of a decorous training would be revealed under his Manhattan adaptation. His only book, *Manners for the Metropolis*, published in 1908, is a mixture of easy satisfaction at frequenting the then rich and ostentatious world of Newport, Long Island, and New York, and of satire on that weekending, champagne-drinking and bridge-playing world. I had reason to dislike and resent him, but, in spite of his unscrupulousness and occasional meanness, I enjoyed his frivolously amusing side. He liked to get up games in the office such as the "Rape of the Sabine Women," when we carried out the girls into the hallway, and he did have moments of delightful humor. I remember a disquisition on the change in one's psychological attitude when one put on a silk hat and on the peculiar impression produced on him whenever he called on the pompous wife of a then famous newspaper magnate. He had a friend with whom he played an amusing game: when they ran into one another at luncheon and Crowninshield was lunching with somebody else who did not know the friend, the latter would assume a role—sometimes that of an Italian noble, and Crowninshield would play up to him. He was much in demand as a toastmaster, a function for which he was peculiarly suited. John Drew, once a "matinee idol" who ravished so many of the ladies by his ability to "be such a gentleman," was by that time a rather stiff old man, a member of the best clubs, who wore spectacles with very thick lenses and who surprised me on one occasion by expressing extreme indignation at opinions he had read in *The Nation*—he seemed never to have seen it before or to have any idea of what had been appearing in the then current "liberal" weeklies. When some sort of anniversary occasion was to be celebrated for John Drew at the Coffee House, Frank Crowninshield rightly foresaw that, Drew being by that time a kind of wooden image, this occasion would be likely to be boring, and he decided to handle it in a new way. He conspired with other members to counteract the stuffy dignity of Drew by a series of outrageous memoirs. His introduction ran something like this: "I remember when I first visited Marseilles that, desiring to see the sights of the city, I was taken to a luxurious establishment of almost overpowering elegance, which I learned was a deluxe cathouse. When I entered, I saw a man coming hurriedly down the staircase with a French woman shrieking after him. He was evidently an American, who knew no French. It seemed to be a question of money. I spoke to the woman and appeased her and paid her the sum she demanded. That was my first meeting with John Drew." This I found rather endearing, as was also Crowninshield's attitude toward an "efficiency engineer" recently installed by Nast. We would find on our desk slips that showed exactly how many minutes we had been late in arriving at the office. Crowninshield, when he saw them, would crumple these up and throw them into the wastebasket.

I have been asked whether Frank was a homosexual; but, in spite of his not very attractive habit of seizing you by the arm in a way that seemed calculated to establish some kind of affectionate ascendancy, I do not believe that he was. He once told me that he had a girl who came to see him once a week; and this seems more in line with his cautious habits, for he was careful in his personal relations and, in spite of his show of friendliness, always managed to keep people at a discreet distance.

The *Vanity Fair* office was, however, not lacking in a homosexual element, which Crowninshield accepted and ignored. This flourished in the men's wear department, the main representative of which asserted that our London correspondent was no good because he himself was not "queer," a prerequisite for a writer on men's fashions. At first, for a long time, we did not have a men's wear department—Crowninshield thought this quite unnecessary: "A gentleman knows how to dress"—but it was evidently imposed on him by Nast. In the early days, we had periodical visits from a singular character called Hogan, who plastered on heavy eyebrows and daubed his scant hair down with eyebrow paste that gave him a peculiar smell. He wore a derby and pretentious clothes which, however, were meant to seem preeminently correct. I never could figure out who he was or why he had this entree to the office. When one day I asked Crowninshield about him, his only answer was, "He's not a mucker." Hogan was full of salacious rumors: "They're saying that Jack Barrymore is having an affair with Tappé [a well-known homosexual couturier]. Nothing in it! It's completely ridiculous!" But the fellow who wrote on men's fashions was an almost childlike little man who must, I thought, have been sent to Crowninshield with a request to do something for him. Revising his copy was one of my duties. His writing was pellucid in its innocent way, and he was perfectly easy to work with. But he and Hogan were always at cross purposes—Hogan assumed some authority in this department—and complaining about one another. Each accused the other of being queer: Hogan was "just an old queen," and the boy was all too plainly "just a little fairy."

The constant presence of pretty actresses and amiable secretaries more than neutralized, however, these two. The more important actresses were photographed by a man who called himself Baron de Meyer—his invariable method was, as Crowninshield said, to highlight their faces from below by putting electric bulbs in their corsages. The secretaries were very jolly, because Crowninshield, by exercising his charm for women, always kept them in good humor. Jeanne Ballot, of French origin though from Brooklyn, became indispensable to Crowninshield and still, since his death, works at *Vogue*. She was delightful and got along well with everybody. I brought in the poet John Peale Bishop and Seward Collins, both of Princeton. Elinor Wylie, by that time divorced, was given a sort of part-time job. She and I used to write one another whimsical poems of devotion. We printed in *Vanity Fair* the poems of Edna Millay, whose first trip to Europe was arranged by Crowninshield and paid for by her contributions of the sketches signed Nancy Boyd. Crowninshield complained to someone that he found it rather a nuisance to have his two editors, John and myself, in love with the same girl.

When I married Mary Blair, the actress, who had attracted considerable attention by appearing at the Provincetown Players in O'Neill's *Diff'rent*, but of whom my mother disapproved, my father came up to New York to talk over the matter with Crowninshield. The latter handled this interview with the usual lack of tact and exercise of false judgment that went with and often spoiled his determinedly smooth address. He told my father that my being married might have the desirable effect of stimulating me to more serious effort. He explained that the failure of his brother Edward had had the effect on him, Frank, of stiffening his moral backbone and spurring him to work and make money. Edward, he said, was a confirmed drug addict, who had always been a problem to the family. He had none of Frank's elegant mannerisms and couldn't have been less foppish. He talked, also, like a canny old New Englander, whom one would not suspect of taking drugs. The only example of the Boston accent that I ever remarked in Frank was his pronouncing his brother's name "Ed-ward," with a marked gap between the syllables. I believe it was the bad example of Edward that had made Frank a teetotaler for life as well as extremely intent at hanging on to a job; but I thought it rather indelicate for him to expose this personal matter to my father, whom he had never met before and who heard him out with the polite silence of one to whom this kind of man was alien. I never knew anyone who talked as much as Crowninshield about being and behaving like "a gentleman" and one who exemplified this less in his own relations. This has made me suspicious ever since of people who talk much about "gentlemen." I think it ought to be a warning to be careful and hold on to one's wallet. The career of Frank Crowninshield, I suppose, did have its pathetic side: there was the "gentleman," the personality to which he aspired and which he rather too ostentatiously acted, and the treacherous opportunist who so often destroyed these pretensions.

My relations with Crowninshield came to a crisis when I asked for a raise in my salary—which was well below a hundred dollars a week. I pointed out that I was getting a good deal less than the little man who wrote about men's fashions and was only just trying his hand at journalism—to which Crowninshield replied that he could get any number of people who would be competent to do my job but that it was hard to find anyone who could do men's fashions. This enraged me so that I quit. Walter Lippmann, who had written for us occasional articles, now offered me a job on *The New Republic*, which I very gladly accepted.

This does not mean that Frank Crowninshield was quite devoid of journalistic decency. When George Putnam, with whom he was on friendly terms, was publishing a flimsy novel by Heywood Broun, he came into the office to ask me what I was going to do about it. I told him that it was not worth notice, and he immediately made a scene to Crowninshield, who I was rather surprised to find stood by me. And an article which I had written on Hawthorne's European notebooks was evidently, for some reason which I did not understand, not at all what Crowninshield had expected. He was rather cross about it, but then later came back and apologized. He said that he now saw what I was aiming at. The most shocking thing I ever knew him to do—an incident that I never quite got over—was the result of our needing for some reason to print the text of a letter of Voltaire's. He sent down to Putnam's bookstore below us and borrowed a volume of an expensive and splendidly printed edition of Voltaire, then simply cut out the pages with the letter and sent the volume back, knowing that this would not be detected.

Years later, when I was writing for *The New Yorker*, he invited me to lunch at the Coffee House, from which I had resigned when I left New York. It was evident that he did not know anything about what I had been doing in the meantime and that the only thing that impressed him was that I had finally made good by being given the *New Yorker* job of writing weekly about books. For Crowninshield, this was a peak of success, whereas for me it was a means of paying off back debts incurred during the writing of *Hecate County*, and a possible provision, if necessary, for publishing this book at my own expense. (The textbook editor at Scribner's, an influential person in the firm, had characterized it, I was told, as "the most unpublishable book" he had ever seen.) Frank said that he was proud of my recent success, that I showed my brilliant proficiency in being able to write appropriately about such a variety of kinds of books: "You can do a Renoir, and then the next week you can turn around and do a Van Gogh." He was much more responsive to painting, on account of his father's career, than to any of the other arts. I do not think he was interested in it in any very serious way, but he did have an accurate instinct, in judging modern art, for what was going to be important, or at least for what was going to come into fashion. He bought the pictures of a number of painters who were likely to command higher prices, and he reproduced in *Vanity Fair* the works of such native artists as Charles Burchfield, who had at that time been hardly heard of. In concocting captions for works of art, he was expert in a half-humorous way: they were to some extent parodies of the eloquent copy of such writers as Walter Pach, whom he sometimes got to do articles for *Vanity Fair*. Late in life, when he needed money, after *Vanity Fair* had been discontinued, he sold his art collection and, before the sale took place, bought up as many as possible of the special editions of French books illustrated by well-known artists, on which he was able to realize a profit.

The Algonquin. It was, as I have mentioned, the people from *Vanity Fair* who introduced me to the Algonquin. The proprietor was then Frank Case, a witty and sharp-eyed Irishman who attentively supervised the customers and made of his little hotel frequented by actors and writers something almost in the nature of a club. A large round table in the room opposite the lobby was reserved for a circle which consisted of Alec Woollcott, Heywood Broun, Robert Benchley, Dorothy Parker, Marc Connelly, George Kaufman and, I think, occasionally Franklin P. Adams. I was sometimes invited to join them, but I did not find them particularly interesting. They all came from the suburbs and "provinces," and a sort of tone was set—mainly by Benchley, I think—deriving from a provincial upbringing of people who had been taught a certain kind of gentility, who had played the same games and who had read the same children's books—all of which they were now able to mock from a level of New York sophistication. I found this rather tiresome, since they never seemed to be able to get above it. At one time, their favorite game consisted of near-punning uses of words. "Have you heard Dotty's *Hiawatha?*"—"Hiawatha a nice girl till I met you." Marc Connelly's *Honduras*: something about "the big Hondurance [endurance] contest." Somebody else's Benchley: "Benchley [eventually], why not now?" (This was an advertising slogan.) Visitors to Woollcott in the country were made to play croquet.

I found Woollcott disagreeable at first. I did not then know that an early attack of mumps had rendered him sexually impotent, and that this did a good deal to explain his uncomfortable personality. Dorothy Parker told me that he had gone to Jung for psychoanalysis and that what this revealed was that Woollcott had been in love with Harpo Marx. He was the off-spring of a Fourierist "phalanx," an exploit in communist living not far from Red Bank, New Jersey. My grandfather had delivered his mother; and when he came to realize this, his attitude toward me changed. He recognized me as the son of "Lawyer Wilson," who had rescued his uncle, a painter, from bankruptcy, taking no compensation save a painting of the Phalanx screened by trees, which I still have in my Talcottville house. My grandfather and my father now took their places in his personal mythology. Heywood Broun was a big soft lazy man who figured as very advanced since he called himself a socialist and had allowed his wife to retain her maiden name. Connelly and Kaufman, who at one time wrote plays together, both came originally from Pittsburgh and were distinguished by the crackling Pittsburgh wit. Connelly had no pose or pretension and, with his drollery, was one of the most agreeable of this group. Kaufman, unlike Connelly, whose reputation rested mainly on *Green Pastures*, an adaptation of someone else's book, had concentrated on self-advancement. I remembered how he heralded his advent to New York by a series of contributions to Franklin P. Adams's column, invariably signed G.S.K. This had made him a somewhat mysterious character whose coming one awaited with suspense. In New York, he was always being sued for plagiarism. He always won these suits, though I believe that, in certain cases, the charges were well founded. I happened to see a play by Walter Lowenfeld, which came in as a book at *The New Republic*, and it was evident that, as Lowenfeld claimed, one of the songs in Kaufman's musical *Of Thee I Sing* had been plagiarized from it almost verbatim. But Lowenfeld's suit did not succeed.

Scott Fitzgerald was convinced that Kaufman had plagiarized his play *The Vegetable* but announced that he was not going to sue him.

The relationship between Benchley and Dorothy Parker was special and rather peculiar. After leaving *Vanity Fair*, they took an office in the building of the Metropolitan Opera House and decorated the door with the sign: "Eureka Nut and Bolt Company." They always referred to one another as "Mrs. Parker" and "Mr. Benchley." Benchley, as I first knew him, had the manner of a quiet and modest young Harvard graduate, with whom it was pleasant and easy to deal. Later, when he went to Hollywood, where he had some success doing comic shorts, he seemed to have become transformed. He was florid and self-assertive. He at one time became obsessed by an unimportant girl on the stage, whom Dorothy thought to be very inferior. I remember this girl's saying once that she had to leave us to try out for "a leg and fanny show"; but he used to insist to Dorothy that she entered a room with the presence "of a queen." He got to drinking heavily and died of cirrhosis of the liver. I used, in the days I first knew him, to urge him to do serious satire; but he proved to be incapable of this. His usual character for himself was that of an unsure suburban duffer who was always being frightened and defeated, and this, even in his Hollywood shorts, seemed to be the only role in which he was able to appear. He lived out of town with his family in a perfectly conventional way, and I believe that his rather obnoxious phase was an attempt to counteract this. Dorothy regarded him as a kind of saint, and he did have some admirable qualities. He testified in court at the Sacco–Vanzetti case that Judge Thayer had shown his prejudice at the golf club by threatening "to get those anarchist bastards" or something of the kind.

Dorothy Parker was the only personality who interested me in this group and whom to some extent I cultivated. She was naturally spontaneously witty, and the conflicts in her nature made her interesting. She could associate on an equal basis with such people as Elinor Wylie and the Gerald Murphys, with whom the other Algonquinites would have been uncomfortable and out of their depth. One had to become reconciled to knowing that she was unreliable and even capable of a certain treachery. She would always get out of an engagement if something more tempting turned up, and she would alternate effusive affection with remarks, once the object was no longer present, of a well-aimed and deadly malice. Lillian Hellman, in *An Unfinished Woman*, has given an analysis of Dorothy, based on an intimate acquaintanceship, which is unlikely to be bettered by anyone else. It seems that her youth had been wretched: she had lost her mother at an early age and was ill-treated by her father's second wife, and Miss Hellman believes that her waspish barbs and her habit of unhappy love affairs were a protection against caring too much about others, against expecting others to care. When I told her once—what she didn't know—that a former lover of hers had died, a young, good-looking and well-to-do fellow who had suffered from tuberculosis, she said crisply, "I don't see what else he could have done." On one occasion, after the *Vanity Fair* crisis, we ran into Condé Nast in the lobby of the Algonquin. He said that he was going on a cruise: "And, Dorothy, I wish you would come with me." "Oh, I wish I could!"— immediately followed, as soon as Nast had gone on, by "Oh, God, make that ship sink!" She was beglamoured by the idea of Scott Fitzgerald, and I arranged to have her meet him and Zelda. We sat at one of those Algonquin tables, too narrow to have anyone across from you, so that one sat on a bench with one's back to the wall: "This looks like a road company of the Last Supper." When Scott died in Hollywood and she went in to see his body, I am told that she echoed Gatsby's former guest looking in on Gatsby's body: "The poor son-of-a-bitch!"

I was struck by the enormous reverence that the Algonquinites felt for Ring Lardner. He never mingled with them. He lived at Great Neck, Long Island, and came into town only for business; I never saw him at the Algonquin. He was somehow aloof and inscrutable, by nature rather saturnine, but a master whom all admired, though he was never present in person. It may be that all any such circle demands is such a presiding but invisible deity, who is assumed to regard them with a certain scorn.

The Coffee House. This little lunch club of artists and writers, which included a few actors, had been founded by Frank Crowninshield as a sort of feeder for *Vanity Fair.* One sat at a long table with everyone else and ate an inexpensive lunch. As almost the only younger men, John Bishop and I were somewhat out of our element. I used to say that the other members were men of the eighties who had never caught up with the nineties. Charley [Charles Hanson] Towne, with his incessant insipid jokes, was the quintessence of that second-rate generation. John said truly that he resembled a chestnut worm. John also said that John Jay Chapman gave the impression of an old owl, who looked wise but never said anything; but I decided, when later I read his books, that this impression was produced by the fact that, always existing on a much higher plane than most of the other members, he could not really communicate with them and could only smile or chuckle at their jokes and shop gossip. They treated John and me with a certain alienated apprehension. Ezra Pound was then a kind of bugaboo for those mediocre novelists, dramatists and journalists who were comfortably at home in their limbo and did not want to be disturbed: such people sometimes baited us with some such challenge as, "I suppose you admire Ezra Pound." Chapman, however, would ask our opinion as if he were interested to know what we thought. In other words, he had better manners than most of the other members. Crowninshield more or less presided and tended to call everyone "old boy."

A great convenience was that at the Coffee House you could order dinner ahead and dine alone with your guest in the other room at a separate table. When I was press agent for the Swedish ballet, I entertained one of the ballerinas there. She turned out to be a very correct Swedish lady, who was not exciting in the least and who only corroborated the judgment of Cocteau, when I discussed the ballet with him in Paris, that the Swedish ballet were simply "des suédois qui dansent."

John Bishop's friend Townsend Martin was the nephew of Frederick Townsend Martin, a "philanthropist" who had achieved a certain reputation as well as provoked some ridicule as the author of such books as *The Passing of the Idle Rich,* in which, himself a rich man and a figure in New York "society," he took to task the other members for their frivolity and wasteful luxury. His nephew Townsend had also an adequate income but nothing of the philanthropist or prophet. He liked to keep up an illusion that he was going to write witty plays but actually most of the time amused himself at smart resorts in Europe. He invited John Bishop, who was always hard up, to make use of his New York apartment, which, though small, was quite luxurious: an Oriental screen, an antique fourposter bed and I forget what other furnishings. It perfectly suited John, who liked to live in a lordly fashion and did its honors so well that many people thought the place was his own. He presided with the same distinguished taste and style as he had as president of his Princeton club, and the apartment became something of a gathering place for the Fitzgeralds, Alec McKaig, myself and other friends of John's. John had his job at *Vanity Fair*, to which I introduced him, but was mainly preoccupied with his poetry. Alec McKaig used to imitate him as he tried it out in the mornings, declaiming it to himself, at the same time as he was brushing his teeth.

But Townsend would return from the Riviera and find John, in an ornamental dressing gown, playing host to his merry company with a wit and a wealth of discourse which Townsend, for all his suavity, could never hope to match, and he came to resent this. John on his side was irritated by Townsend's continual gossip about the royalties and bearers of noble names with whom he had been intimate abroad and to whom he always referred as Toutou and Nicky and Bobo—I am improvising these nicknames—as if anybody who was anybody would be sure to know whom he meant. John could not accept his position. He was a Southerner and was never at home in New York; his work at the office tired him terribly. He had survived a lingering illness and had been cared for with affection by his mother and sister. He had not enjoyed earning money as a tutor to some rich people's children. When his residence at Townsend's became uncomfortable, he married Margaret Hutchins, who was equipped with plenty of money and who had over him a hold, I think, based on strong physical passion. She carried him away to live in France, of which he had had only a glimpse in the army. It was inevitable that he should have been taken over by a woman who would stand behind him and guard him; but it was perhaps unfortunate that he should find himself dominated by a woman who was otherwise rather out of harmony with his temperament. He had at this time already established a fairly intimate relation with Elinor Wylie, and it was sometimes thought he would marry her. But she was much older than he and, although immensely amusing and clever about poetry, so self-centered that she could hardly have supplied for him the solicitous attention he needed.]

January. The dull brown landscape seemed to be melting dirtily away in slush and mist.

Uncle Win: "When Rusty Moore was so sick then and the doctor came to see him, he said: 'Say, Doc, don't you think it's time I began practicing on the harp?' That's the kind of a fellow he was! Funny as a goat!"

January, on the way to Red Bank. I rubbed a peep-hole in the frost-glazed window and saw through it a vignette of the snow that looked gray in the rain, and the fences strung with wires of ice and the bushes and trees with the frozen rain decking them like crystals.

During the snowstorm in early February. From the windows of the *Vanity Fair* office I saw the masses and square pinnacles of the city melting into the thick blue dark, where the electric signs seemed hung in the sky like fiery writing on the air.

Fitzgerald: "I'll tell you what the situation is now: I wouldn't care if she [Zelda] died, but I couldn't stand to have anybody else marry her."
[He did marry Zelda not long after. John and I were invited to meet her at the Fitzgeralds' hotel. We drank Orange Blossoms, a kind of cocktail then in vogue. Zelda was lying on her back on a couch, looking very pretty and languid. When I reminded her of this years later, I found that she was rather embarrassed to remember the too fancy clothes with which her mother had outfitted her—they were appropriate for a Southern belle but not the right thing for New York. She was still apologetic about her mother.]
"When I'm with John [Bishop], I say: 'Well, John, you and I are the only real artists,' and when I'm with Alec [McKaig], I say: 'You and I are the only ones who understand the common man,' and when I'm with Townsend [Martin], I say: 'Well, Townsend, you and I are the only ones who are

really interested in ourselves,' but when I'm alone, I say: 'Well, Fitz, you're the only one!'"

The Vanity Fair staff lunch at Delmonico's. Presided over by the Business Manager. Mr. Melville, an efficiency expert, speaks; a florid Western-looking man with yellow hair, pink cheeks, blue eyes and round bone-rimmed spectacles; very indignant about the cavalier way in which Crowninshield and others had been treating the tardiness slips: "I send the slips in and the department heads throw them in the wastebasket. Then we have a meeting and I bring the matter up and they say they'll attend to them. Then I send the slips in again and they destroy them . . . Why, I was amazed when I saw the records of some of the people in this organization! I could hardly believe my eyes! How a man or woman can pretend to belong to the Nast publications and then be habitually late—half an hour, a whole hour—I can't understand it!" —Mr. Wright, editor of *House and Garden*, protested that there was a certain human element in the question: "The weather is very bad and the traffic is frequently held up; a stenographer coming to the office in the morning may get in a crowded car and be carried all the way down to Fourteenth Street without being able to get out." —Question of getting a nurse: Mrs. Chase [editor of *Vogue*] suggested that they should get a really good one—"'a lady,' as Mr. Crowninshield would say, someone who could look after not only the health of the girls, but also spread a little moral propaganda—I'm sure they need it!" —The editor of Spanish *Vogue* (I think it was) remarked that he thought it would be a good idea to get a nurse who would actually nurse. He had once worked in an office where a stenographer had been sick and stayed away. The nurse was sent to check up and, having ascertained that the girl was actually sick, came immediately away. The girl, who was rather poor, nearly died, and the editor had been obliged to attend to her medical treatment himself and to have her sent to Atlantic City. —Throughout, Mr. Albert Lee sat with a strange fierce look, full of indignation and a high contempt and pride but not intelligent enough to be proud of anything worth having or contemptuous of anything worth despising.

Early April. I heard the rain beating softly with brisk and muffled drums.

April. At the Red Bank station I saw the blue robes of the night sewn with its bright specks of silver trailing in the filth and rubbish which was the town.

Imagination and the Unusual. The reason that more unusual and startling things are not done is not that they are particularly impracticable but that most people have not the imaginations to conceive them.

Shaw is the greatest master of literary sleight of hand the world has ever known: give him a platitude and in the twinkling of an eye he will transform it into a paradox.

Zelda [*Fitzgerald*]: "John [Bishop], I like you better than anybody in the world: I never feel safe with you!—I only like men who kiss as means to an end. I never know how to treat the other kind." —Bill Mackie: "I've been twirling the thyrsus tonight in Greenwich Village—[gazing passionately at Zelda]—I can feel my ears getting pointed!" —He finally became so much aroused that he was obliged to withdraw to the bathroom. He was found in a state of collapse and murmured: "She made provoking gestures to me!" One night he was found by Townsend Martin weeping piteously under a tree outside Townsend's house. —When Zelda first began kissing John and Townsend, Fitz tried to carry it off by saying: "Oh, yes, they really have kisses coming to them, because they weren't at the wedding, and everybody at a wedding always gets a kiss." But when Zelda rushed into John's room just as he was going to bed and insisted that she was going to spend the night there, and when she cornered Townsend in the bathroom and demanded that he should give her a bath, he began to become a little worried and even huffy.

Crowninshield: "It seems that Nat Wills married a famous circus rider. The morning after the wedding, as they sat at breakfast, he began reading the comic supplement—'Yellow Kid,' etc. She picked up a mess of pancakes that had just been brought in and heaved them into the midst of the paper: 'Say, have I married one of these here bookworms?'"
"—And some like the little prancing girls."

Philadelphian Society [the religious organization at Princeton]. Buchman [of Moral Rearmament] gave a talk on the confession of sins, urged the students to confess in public. One of them arose and said that he had played craps one evening last year from seven to eleven and hadn't felt right about it since; after that, another got up and said that, when he had been company clerk at Camp Lee, a cake had come into the office for a man in the company, and that he and another Princeton man (whom he named) had eaten that cake. —Walter Hall [a young history teacher] had the curiosity to go for an interview with Buchman. Buchman began as follows: "I'm a dirty low-down scut and you're another!" Walter answered: "Well, I don't know about you, Mr. Buchman; but I can tell you I'm nothing of the kind."

Crowninshield: "Munkittrick used to come into an editor's office with a poem about six feet long, don't you know—and the editor would say: 'Why, that's too long! We can't use that!' and Munkittrick would say: 'Well, I can cut it into six-inch lengths . . . it's arranged so that it can begin and end anywhere—if you shuffle the verses up, any verse can follow any other verse.' And if the editor said he didn't want a serious poem, he wanted a humorous poem, Munk would put his hand in his pocket and pull out a couple of comic snappers, don't you know—to put on the end and make it a humorous poem. Or if it was a poem about spring and he wanted to make it into a Christmas poem, he'd look through it and find a cow—there was a cow in the manger, don't you know—and make that part of it into a Christmas poem. Oh, he was the greatest fellow!—he had all these poems on file, don't you know—Easter poems, Christmas poems, spring poems— he knew just exactly when you had to begin sending around Easter poems for the Easter magazines. He'd begin sending around Easter poems on the 27th of February, don't you know."

George Wood [a newspaperman from my *Evening Sun* days whom I had afterwards found in the army]: "John Reed's a mushhead . . . You don't realize how bad the newspapers are now till you've seen them from inside . . . Government by headlines is what we're having now! People think in headlines . . . Do you know why [Leonard] Wood and Cox were featured so in the papers? Because they're short words of one syllable!—they're easier to get in a line; consequently, they were popular with the make-up men and the head writers . . . There was nothing doing with Lowden and Harding at all . . . The Wood boom was two-thirds the work of the head writers! . . . I've seen those cuts, and I know they're not made of rubber: they're made of metal."

Mr. Rolfe [*my teacher of Greek at the Hill*] *and the Others.* When I went to dinner with George Wood and Hecker at Columbia, I saw Mr. Robins (of Hill, who taught Ancient History) coming out of the University Commons just as we were going in. My first impulse was to go over and greet him, but I was checked by a second thought: I reflected that this man had made intolerably dreary and dull all the beauty and nobility and interest of Greek history, and I remembered how, in agony of mind and a desperate attempt to concentrate, I had once stretched myself out on the hard top of his desk and tried to memorize the dates of the Peloponnesian Wars, which I would then get up and write on the blackboard in a column of figures like an addition sum. So I passed into the building without making myself known to him. But, just as we were entering the dining room, I saw Mr. Rolfe coming out. He didn't notice me either, but I went over and spoke to him. He was surprised and apparently pleased. It was five or six years since I had seen him, and I had come to think of him, rather, as a crabbed old Concordian drying up in a narrow and puerile environment; but, as I talked to him, I was much impressed by the attractiveness of his face: it was one of the saddest faces I have ever seen—he is really getting old now—

but it was also full of an unusual sort of kindliness and humor pleasantly tempered with irony. I invited him to dinner and he couldn't come—he asked me what I was doing, etc. Then I joined Hecker and Wood —But, in the dining room, I felt as if I were in some sort of delirium, in which all of my early life was confusedly passing before me. It seemed as if I were surrounded by the complete combined faculties, not only of the Hill School but also of Princeton, and none of them recognized me: I seemed to walk among them invisible, like Aeneas among the Carthaginians. I decided not to speak to them. What was the use? They didn't interest me. There were men there—Mr. Lester and Mr. Beament—to whom I undoubtedly owed something—but I was a little contemptuous of them all. So I let them pass by. —And when I analyzed the situation, afterwards, it seemed to me significant and interesting that of all those men under whose instruction I had spent two years of my youth the only one whom I still respected and whom I cared to see again was the one with whom I had first read Homer. [This emotion led EW to write, twenty years later, his essay on Rolfe included in *The Triple Thinkers* (1938).]

[I remember seeing the Fitzgeralds only once when they were living at Westport. It was announced to me more or less solemnly that Zelda had decided to change her style and behave like a conventional lady, paying and receiving calls and making polite acknowledgments. This was touching but could not have lasted. I heard not long afterwards that Charley Towne and George Nathan had been on a visit to them which had become so disgracefully debauched that Towne on the way home, to the great amusement of Nathan, was full of horrified compunction. Zelda at some point had broken down and sounded the fire alarm just for fun in order to see what would happen—calling out the fire department and getting them into trouble.]

I had just met Edna Millay and was full of her. I sent her a copy of the following poem, and when I saw her again, she said, "That was a strange poem you sent me." Rereading it now, I see how strange it *was*, as well as how extremely bad. These early poems are quite embarrassing. John Bishop used to say that it always made him nervous when I resorted to a high romantic vein.

At the time of the first piece that follows, Zelda had been left with Marion Cleveland, who was married then to Stanley Dell.

When I motored down to Princeton on May Day
With John Bishop and Scott Fitzgerald
And we saw the mist of green that hung in the trees and fields
And when we rode into the town with gilt wreaths on our heads,
Singing a rag of Swinburne,

There was something running in my mind
Deeper than the spring and the laughter;
For I could not forget your poems
And the things I had heard about you
And your face that was sometimes a flower
But more often a flame.

Poor Fitz went prancing into the Cottage Club
With his gilt wreath and lyre,
Looking like a tarnished Apollo with the two black eyes
That he had got, when far gone in liquor, in some unintelligible fight,
But looking like Apollo just the same, with the sun in his pale yellow hair;
And his classmates who had been roaring around the campus all day
And had had whiskey, but no Swinburne,
Arose as one man and denounced him
And told him that he and his wife had disgraced the club and that he was no longer
    worthy to belong to it
(Though really they were angry with him
Because he had achieved great success
Without starting in at the bottom in the nut and bolt business).
At any rate, he was dreadfully hurt
And felt he could interpret himself no longer
In the face of such a Philistine and hostile audience,
And he went straight back to New York
By the seven o'clock train.
And when they told me about it, the humanism
We had come down to celebrate
Seemed scarcely real to me:
I could think of nothing but the cruelty
At the roots of life;
And the thought drove all the dreams from my head
With its sharp sword—
And Princeton fell away
And there seemed to be nothing real
Among intangible shadows,
Except a light here and there, a light I had known of old,
And your flame in New York
That that cruelty did but feed.
I sat in a bare room
Talking to Christian Gauss
And watching his clear green eyes, as hard and as fine as gems;
I heard him speak of books and politics and people,
With his incredible learning and his cloudless mind,
But he was really talking of life
As something that made him suffer
But about which he could not tell lies

Nor tell other people lies—
(For he could not make moral judgments nor praise inferior things);
And I thought of him, as I have always done, as a short stocky naked man
Holding an impossible post
At the edge of an abyss,
With bleak and uncontrollable storms
Crashing about him,—
While he stood without panic or complaint,
Looking out with straight hard eyes,
A last champion of man's divine pride of reason and imagination
Against all that tumult and stone . . .
And Princeton that I had loved was nothing to me:
I was swearing again an oath I had many times sworn already:
That, so long as I should live, I should honor nothing but Gauss
With his back against the rock,—
But, while I swore, your bitter beauty
Filled the room,
And I saw it was you who were standing
Against the rock,
Who were taking the hurricane
On your "fierce and trivial" brow.

The mist of green, as we motored back, meant almost as little to me
As the gray and barren streets of Weehawken and Newark;
And Hardwicke Nevin was telling me things about you
That he didn't understand.

August 27, 1920

A Perverse Thought

Sometimes I wish I had been born
Among that calm race of "ladies and gentlemen,"
Who thought Bayard Taylor a great poet
And took a chaste joy in visiting Rome
And never asked a real question or were racked by a real passion—
That happy race whose image I have caught
In Frank Crowninshield's unclouded countenance;
I wish that I had lived among them
And been "refined" like them:
I should have been a bit of a Bohemian,
But with a heart as good as gold
(And no dangerous notions—)
I whose life has been one long anger
Against the meanness and ugliness of my time;
Who have spent two years as an enlisted man
In the American army
And known Europe, not as she appeared

To the bland eye of Henry James,
But agonized and mad with war,
With her barbarity lying bare;
Who have seen the anatomy of society
Performed under my very nose
Without the assistance of ether;
I who have broken my passionate heart
For the lips of Edna Millay
And her face that burns like a flame
And her terrible chagrin.

August 29, 1920

The Ideal

Oh, poor hard heart that pain has made so cruel!
   Oh, cruel mind that understands so much!
What curse is this that turns all life to fuel
   For desperate scorn, that blights ears, sight and touch?—
That I should find all men enrage or bore me,
   Loving passionately only her, from love set free,
Who has trod the terrible path too long before me
   To slake her dry bitter heart from me.

Be still, you wailing fool, there is no place
For gods among your blind and limping race.
Best laugh and do your work and take your pay:
Your heart will kill you any other way,—
And you would much regret—you know you would—
To lose your books and friends and fame and food.

Edna on the machine-carved mantelpiece in our apartment: "Ah, that mantelpiece! It's like life: there's been so much work and care put in on it, and then look at it!"

March, 1921

Ah, my hard councilor, you have come at last!
Lacking your word, I trembled in the street.
I have seen the flesh of soldiers writhing gassed
No rawer than my heart in its defeat.

But now you have swept the floor clean of love's bones
And now the hot and lonely days are dead,—
My tenderness spilt like water among stones,
Her tenderness like a little wind long fled.

"Ah, you who would have had the love of a proud queen
And noble partings and long-honored vows,
Who told you love and pain had that high scene?
The action passes in a bawdy house.

"And all the grief that made you harsh and blind
And all the weight that stayed your steps like stone
Have bought you but the splendor of your mind—
That never can live but baffled and alone."

September 1920–July 1921

[I indicated this lapse of time in my notebook. I was so much demoralized by my love affairs that I made no entries in it, and it was not till I got away on a trip to Europe that I began making notes again.

1953. I have written at length elsewhere about my relations with Edna Millay (*The Shores of Light*, "Epilogue, 1952, Edna St. Vincent Millay"). The passages below were originally written with the idea of including them in this memoir; but I decided to leave them out.]

. . . In any case, a romantic idealism combined with a certain shyness had hitherto kept me from falling in love in any serious way; and Edna ignited for me both my intellectual passion and my unsatisfied desire, which went up together in a blaze of ecstasy that remains for me one of the high points of my life. I do not believe that such experiences can be common, for such women are not common. My subsequent chagrin and perplexity, when I discovered that, due to her extreme promiscuity, this could not be expected to continue, were rather amazingly soothed by an equanimity on her part which was also very uncommon.

[Our farewell evening with Edna]

. . . After dinner, sitting on her day bed, John and I held Edna in our arms—according to an arrangement insisted upon by herself—I her lower half and John her upper—with a polite exchange of pleasantries as to which had the better share.

She referred to us, I was told, as "the choir boys of Hell," and complained that our both being in love with her had not even broken up our friendship. John Bishop thereafter always referred to her as "the Great Queen."

Opportunity in America. In America, everyone has an equal chance: the mill hand, the shopkeeper, the factory worker, the Italian bootblack: he has an equal chance with everyone else to become a rich bourgeois, to employ two thousand laborers, to own a whole chain of shops, to belong to country clubs and to possess automobiles.

Prostitution: A point of view [I invented this]. "I always give the whores as little as possible: I don't think that prostitution ought to be encouraged."

Gauss. EW: "I come down here for comfort and assurance when I am particularly overcome by life—to recuperate. —Because you are familiar with all the same phenomena as I am and you yet remain calm."

CG: "Oh, I see! But you don't want to mistake that calm for the serenity of philosophy. It's really only senility."

Laurence Vail reported by Edna. He was worried as to what he should do: "I'm almost as old as Christ was when he died. And yet Christ really did a very remarkable thing. —But I don't think I have much talent for that sort of thing."

Mencken. The first time I met him—at the Coffee House—he suggested to Owen Johnson and W. L. George that perhaps women didn't really have an enormous influence on men's lives, that anything a man really had to do would probably get itself done anyway without being much affected by the women who came into his life. "Yet no novelist would ever think of telling about his hero without telling about his women. —There's *Barry Lyndon*, of course, and *Huckleberry Finn* and some of Conrad." . . . The second time I met him was in the street: I steered him on and off the El and down Sixteenth Street. He talked much about *The New Republic*, which, he thought, had been "sick," but was now recovering. They had made a mistake in falling for the war . . . [Upton] Sinclair's *The Brass Check* was "flattery . . . No, really!" . . . The third time was when he summoned me to the *Smart Set* about *The Undertaker's Garland* [by John Bishop and me, which we had sent to him]. Nathan was lighting his cigar, and he explained: "This is Mr. Nathan, my secretary: he lights my cigars for me." They made me sit down between them in a chair narrowly fitted in between the two desks and with its back against the wall. Mencken, in his shirtsleeves, had his feet on the desk. We had a very good idea there, he thought. Here were two young men who had undertaken to spit in the eye of Death, treat it as a joke . . . But we needed something very sardonic, he thought, —something about the physical side of death. For instance, he saw a good deal of the doctors at Johns Hopkins, and they told him that, out of the whole number of autopsies performed, it was evident in about 80 percent of the cases that the diagnosis of the disease had been wrong. (This was rather horrible, of course!) . . . Another idea: the death of an archbishop. The archbishop is about to die, and he begins to think about his life. He thinks: "Well, now I'm going to die, I wonder if it was really worthwhile; there was that beautiful girl I passed up back in the eighties . . . And then, all the weddings I've been to, where I was kind of a killjoy. I'd have to perform the service and leave afterwards before the guests could have any fun . . . And now I've read a book by Huxley that proves there's nothing in the whole business, and I'm going to hell, anyhow . . . It's been proved that the Old Testament was written by Rabelais, the whole thing is a joke." . . . I said that he ought to write that himself. "Well," he replied, "no man can give another man an idea." . . . His own *Death: A Discussion* would have gone well in the *Garland*, he thought . . . He confessed that he hadn't read the poems: he found as he got older that he became less and less able to read long poems. The first time he strikes an inversion, he thinks it would have been better in prose . . . Nathan interjected sharp bits of badinage: one felt he was much less spontaneous than Mencken. When I told them that the Fitzgeralds were going to have a baby, Mencken said, "Good!", and Nathan remarked that it would probably be a cross between the Ziegfeld Follies and Moore's restaurant. Nathan had suggested that we might have a living dead man in the *Garland*—"Oh, he likes the Follies, he's perfectly happy." . . . There was a bottle of gin between them on the left side of Mencken's desk. On the wall were patent-medicine and old burlesque-show posters. —Fourth meeting: "I want to get there on time: it's a mania with me." He wanted to see Ernest Boyd: Boyd's family had been great friends of Mencken's family, and he always made a point of seeing him. At Boyd's door, a friend came up and inquired about his hand, which was bandaged up. He explained that it was a great nuisance, "and then, right on top of all my other troubles, Cardinal Gibbons died, so I'm all up in the air spiritually!"

The New Republic (conversations at our lunches)

Alvin Johnson, when Olgin explained that a Menshevik was someone who wished that the Bolshevik coup d'état hadn't happened, remarked: "He's in the same situation as a liberal in America." —He spoke of the harvest in the West, when the men and women worked all day and in the evening lay in the hay sleeping or courting the whole night through . . . He told Harold Stearns, who wanted him to do the economic article for his book on civilization in America, that "in the first place, Harold, you're taking as a subject something that doesn't exist."

[*Herbert*] *Croly*: "I don't see why generals shouldn't be allowed to make fools of themselves as well as anybody else."

[*Walter*] *Lippmann*: ". . . It was a gross breach of international something or other."

[*Francis*] *Hackett*: "I went all the way up to Milwaukee to see his play [Percy MacKaye's] *Anti-Matrimony*, you know . . . Oh, it was terrible! He was the only person in the theater who laughed. He laughed all through it. I noticed 'm shaking beside me and I didn't know what was the matter! I thought he had the ague! . . . He was laughing!" . . . "Oh, my God, is Walter well? I'd hoped he was good for a month! I'd got all ready to pick up the *Times* every morning and see a bulletin on the front page signed by four Jewish doctors—all specialists!" . . . He said, when I described Paul Elmer More as looking like an engraving of a Roman: "Like a bank building in the classic style . . . Really very good, you know—but a bank building." . . .

When Croly said at lunch to Hallowell, to whom something was being passed: "I've got a letter to read you," or something of the kind, Johnson said: "Take a piece [of cake] quick, Bob." —He quoted Horace's account of the Roman theater apropos of something, and, on another occasion, indulged in a long serene fantasia on the subject of using goats in America for meat and milk and to clear the land; the prejudice against goats was due entirely to the fact that they had been made comic . . . A letter from a correspondent on the subject of jazz led him into a discussion of its possible appearance in the ancient world: What about those soft Lydian measures that Horace said nobody could resist? What about the measures to which Catullus' *Attis* was written? Jazz had invaded the ancient world from Asia Minor . . . On one occasion, he asserted, without explanation apropos of what, that Ovid was a better poet than Virgil. He liked particularly the *Epistolae*. I protested that Virgil was greater, but he insisted that Virgil was greater only as Ezra Pound was greater than Edna St. Vincent Millay: "Ezra Pound is more pretentious, but it's evident that Edna has it all over him." I said that I had thought Ovid artificial, that Virgil was really trying to produce something beautiful, etc. He answered in his calm way of flat contradiction with a gentleness almost disdainful (his low voice, equanimity, mildness, casualness, commonplaceness): "Now, you say he's artificial, for example. Ovid's style is nearer to the natural order of speech than that of any other Latin poet . . . Of course, you have to have read an awful lot of Latin to know that." . . . He told of having read the notes which someone had kept on a series of conversations between John Burroughs and John Muir: "It was the most doddering stuff you can imagine. John Burroughs would say: 'Well, John, if you could live three thousand years now, what would you do?', and John Muir would say: 'Well, I'd spend the first thousand studying the great mountains of the world and the second thousand studying the great forests of the world and the third thousand studying the great bodies of water of the world.' And John Burroughs would say: 'Well, John, I guess maybe you'd never get to the great bodies of water!' — Then John Muir somehow got it into his infantile brain that he wanted to get under a waterfall at night and see the moon through the waterfall. So, after immense trouble, he succeeded in getting under the waterfall; but the wind came up and blew the waterfall in on him and nearly drowned him, and he had to be rescued and brought back to life." . . . One day, when some dispute was being agitated, Alvin Johnson remarked to me: "I don't suppose you had any idea when you came here that there was any discord in this magazine." [The dissension was a bitter feud between Francis Hackett and Walter Lippmann.] I replied that it always looked very smooth when you read it. "It's like a sausage," he said, "that comes all smooth out of the sausage machine, but it is really made of the meat of two bulls who died fighting." He also remarked that he supposed that, while he was away for the summer, somebody would be fired: it always happened. His preceding remark had been that he supposed the staff would all have eaten each other up . . . His yellow mane hanging over his collar; his socks wrinkled around his ankles and his great blunt shapeless black shoes; his thick square carpenter's fingers and his heavy red hands like beefsteaks; his terrible low voice in which he says the most crushing things so mildly; his habitual continual irony; his love of paradox, to which he gives the appearance of seriousness, carefulness, moderation and weight—of complete reliability; his complacency; his thorough saturation with the academic manner and habit of mind (in spite of the fact that he apparently detests the academic life as unnatural and narrow), and his custom of never admitting anyone else to the conversation on equal terms, because he has formed the professor's habit of always talking to mental inferiors; his probable satisfaction in his perfect Olympian manners and his ability to preserve them in any company, in spite of the fact that his father was an immigrant carpenter and he himself originally of the shop and farm; his hard and ceaseless maintenance of his own judgment and his eyes, without genuine warmth of benevolence or friendliness, always saying: "My judgment is well balanced and independent: you can't buy *it*! You can't make me swerve a hairsbreadth from my independent judgment, for geniality, politeness or philanthropy!"; his fundamental love of justice and humanity, much vitiated, overlaid and kept in second place by many of the qualities mentioned; his almost naïve pride in his knowledge of the classics (he is said to have taught himself Latin by reading Caesar's *Commentaries* through, first without either dictionary or grammar and then with a dictionary, as who should say to the leisure classes: "You claim this as your privilege and field, the mark of your superiority. Well, I know more about it than any of you, and I am a democrat and man of the people who not only has been through the classics but has used his great intellectual competence to study your society and analyze its economic structure and who knows that you have no importance in the perspective of human history and in the mass of human beings, of which you are always the perishing remnant"); his shyness and self-consciousness; his childlike inability to keep from grinning when he has said something clever, with his customary calm and his invariable transformation of the grin into a frank smile, with his great thick lips curled back and his head lifted—the nearest approach to a real frankness of expression that he ever makes—and this is something which he has assumed to protect himself (though there is some genuine good humor in it, too, and some spontaneity breaking through the restraint of his habitually repressed manner); his curious childlike appearance; his extra-large coffee cup; his pipe; his fine clear handwriting which errs just a little in the direction of commercial soundness and neatness; his old-fashionedness dating somehow from the gentle genteel *American* nineteenth-century period; his hatred of cruelty, which has become perhaps very largely only one of the ways in which he feels his mental superiority—remarking on one occasion of the 100 percent Americans: "Soon they'll be reviving the rack and crucifixion," and explaining, when I said that Kipling would have made Johnson's other-man story a piece of *The Day's Work*, that, if Kipling was interested in the painful things people had to do, *he* was interested in the painful things they didn't have to do.

[This is another case of mounting resentment against somebody I couldn't talk back to (like the colonel I have mentioned in a previous volume). I had first known Alvin Johnson at Columbia, when I had taken a course under him on some aspect of labor in the summer school there. In describing the vicissitudes of the labor struggle, he had displayed the same smugness and calm that afterwards annoyed me at *The New Republic*. He would walk up and down the room, smiling to himself, as he would say, "The early years of the factory system in England are among the blackest pages of human history." Stanley Dell and I called him "the laughing economist." I was surprised to find him at *The New Republic* and soon developed a silent antagonism toward him. This was intensified later on when I took to see him my old army friend John Andersen, thinking that a Danish boy from the farm who had made good might be sympathetic and helpful with a Danish boy who had aspirations. John could not have been received more coldly. When I had first broached the subject with Johnson and told him of John's desire to write, he said only: "I hope he doesn't suffer from the Danish sentimentality." John was angry, after the interview, at the behavior of his compatriot, and so was I. This hadn't happened, I think, at the time when I wrote the above portrait; but I obviously felt strongly, because I took the time, in Florence, to sit down and write at length about him. He was a complacent old fraud, no doubt—Ben Stolberg once said about him that he was "a stuffed shirt with his fly unbuttoned"—but he was not in the least formidable. After cherishing him for years as a pet abomination, I was suddenly and completely deprived of this comfort when I met him one day, years later, at a party in New York that Sherwood and Eleanor Anderson gave. Johnson was there and came over to me and talked with what for him was friendliness, saying that it was a long time since he had seen me and speaking appreciatively of my literary articles in *The New Republic*, with which he had long since ceased to be connected. This puzzled me rather at the time, but I understood it later when I discovered that he had just published a novel, and, realizing then that he was seeking for my good opinion, I never felt resentment toward him again.]

[Myself imagined as a character]
He comes to New York, reads the papers, sees the theater advertisements and begins calling up friends. —Even before calling up the friends, he says to himself, "I love this!"

Failure of perverse erotic fantasies when he is confronted with his old love: no longer biologically possible—propagating and perfecting the race hits him in the face, sends him away.

Growing up in the early nineteen-hundreds, at the end of the Big Money period, he has felt himself somewhat at a disadvantage in respect to the richer people; later, after the slump and in the period that follows, he feels he has special advantages, of which he was scarcely aware before: he is closer than other people to the nonmechanized America, where political, intellectual and moral ideals had to be realized in relatively primitive conditions. He still had something left to live for besides a high standard of living.

That she had understood and enjoyed making love when they were both partly drunk.

He should sometimes have plain drastic thoughts, which he puts to himself bluntly, about society, sex, war, etc.—but usually doesn't dare to speak.
He must cast up his gains and losses—moral defeats and successes. This is the Protestant tradition.

Great reaction against New England when he goes back: Greek looks like machinery and women look dead; the men are getting to be like the legendary New Englanders. Very faraway point of view on everybody. —Left alone in the cold room with its low ceiling.

Up to a certain time, American professional and landowning society more or less homogeneous; then divergence appears, during second half of century, between those who, for local (perhaps Southern), individual, perhaps eccentric reasons, stick to the old idea, and those who, consciously, against their wills, or, unconsciously and gradually, wanting what they can get of power, went along with what was on the upgrade. The difference, the split, takes effect, after college, before we know it. — Then, later, there is an impulse to get back to the original relationship (meetings, after an interval, with Bill Osborn, Stan Dell, Charley Walker) . . . does it really amount to anything? In any case, you appreciate the original thing, from which the U.S.A. had departed before you knew it and even before you were born—this doesn't much help most of the breaches that have occurred, though. —First divided from, then united with, an idea; but can you ever really be in solidarity of action?

When he goes among some group of people that he has so much enjoyed in their jolly kiddish phase—at a moment when he is neurotic and is sinking out of life and can see in them only either (what he takes for granted) that they are still jolly and normal (can support him in his collapse)—or that they are like him: unhappy, neurotic and all but lost.

[I used to see a good deal of Elinor Wylie and became quite addicted to her—although there were elements in her personal life that affected me rather unpleasantly. She had lived as a young woman in Washington, where her father was solicitor general. Her family had been rather erratic. A sister, who had married a German landowner, shot herself with her husband's hunting pistol; a brother had also killed himself; another brother, who married Tallulah Bankhead's sister, jumped overboard from an ocean liner but was rescued before he drowned. Elinor, who was married and had a son, ran away, when she was thirty-five, with a Washington lawyer, Horace Wylie, who was also married. A friend of mine told me that not long before this he had dined somewhere with Elinor and there had been much conversation about H. G. Wells's *New Machiavelli*, a novel in which the married hero runs away with another woman. This was followed by Elinor's elopement. This kind of thing was in the air. Not long afterwards the friend who told me, also a married man, ran away with a young girl. When Elinor and Wylie got to Paris, Wylie's attention one day was attracted by a man who recognized him on the other side of the street. He told Elinor to stay where she was but went over to speak to the friend. When he came back, he warned Elinor to note and remember the other man and never to have anything to do with him: "He has syphilis. His name is Walter Berry." Walter Berry, who is supposed to have been the object of Edith Wharton's affections, had a great reputation as a ladies' man.

Elinor's husband, she said, was a schizophrenic and eventually became quite insane. Her son committed suicide. She saw this son, she told me, only once after her elopement with Wylie. Wylie's wife for several years would not give him a divorce, and he and Elinor lived in England under an assumed name. When it would come to light that they were not married, their English friends would drop them and they would go somewhere else to live. Horace Wylie, who had given up everything else for Elinor, had nothing now to do except to play bridge for money, at which he became expert. He had an enormous fund of information, by which he at first kept Elinor fascinated. She told me that he could hold her attention for an hour any evening telling her about volcanoes. But he was fifteen years older than she, and when they came back to America, she divorced him—by this time they had been married—and for a time lived alone in New York.

She had been considered a beauty, but by the time that I knew her was almost skeletally thin, and she had the harsh voice of a peacock. She was vain but not in a disagreeable way. Her humor and her literary culture made her a delightful companion. She had at this time come to live in Greenwich Village, and one had felt she was always available. She brought with her her pictures and furniture, which, although rather grand, were a little bleak, but they gave her a civilized setting which in the Village was rather rare. She eventually married William Rose Benét, who had been a friend of her brother's at Yale. I was somewhat shocked by this and remonstrated with her about it. It seemed to me that from a literary point of view he was so inferior to her that it made her marrying him inappropriate. I did not know then what bad results can follow from the competition of two writers or artists on anything like a plane of equality. Bill wrote a hideously bad long blank-verse poem called *The God That Was Dust* about his relations with Elinor. When I had expressed my doubts about their union, she had said with her harsh and rather callous laugh: "Yes, it would be a pity that a first-rate poet should be turned into a second-rate poet by marrying a third-rate poet." I once brought Scott Fitzgerald around to see them and was surprised when she told me that her poem "Twelfth Night" in *Black Armour* had been inspired by her protective attitude toward Bill, aroused by the incursion of Scott, of whom I had not thought as intimidating. I missed her extremely when she died of a stroke—she had refused to take any precautions and continued to drink against the doctor's orders—and Dos Passos, who used also to go to see her, said he missed her as acutely as I did.

Her last poems were addressed to a man whom she had met on a visit to England, where she had gone without Bill. I thought they were somewhat inferior and believe that they had been prompted—she had never before gone in for sonnets—by a desire to compete with Edna Millay. Bill seemed to take his rival quite calmly. In general, I felt that the influence of the poetry written by the Benéts had a little cheapened Elinor's. She became infatuated with Shelley, with whom, I think, she identified herself. This bored me, and I could not read her novel, *Orphan Angel*, about him.]

Djuna Barnes's story about Carl Van Vechten. She said that he was very "prissy." He had gone into a bookstore in some provincial city and put on a name-spending act: "I read this book of Cabell's in manuscript"; "Conrad told me that he was not really satisfied with this novel," etc. At last, the bedazzled bookseller said: "May I ask who you are, sir?" "Oh, I," said Van Vechten in a camping manner, "am Edna St. Vincent Millay!"

Gauss, while working very hard over the Endowment Fund for Princeton, told me that, as he had mailed some letters on matters of business, he had reflected: "Well, there are four letters to people who don't interest me in the least!"

France, England, Italy

[EW's note here reads: "Though I had not been long at *The New Republic*, I wanted to see more of Europe than I had been able to do in·the army. I imagined that I could make enough money by writing articles for *Vanity Fair* and *The New Republic* but my father had to help me out." EW's correspondence gives us more information. To earn money for the trip, Edmund gave himself a strict schedule in which he would devote evenings to his work, "Edna having gone abroad." This suggests that his evenings had been very much occupied with her—and also that he apparently was eager to follow her to Europe. Elsewhere in his letters he expresses a need to "escape" from "this so-called country." He published a number of articles during late 1920 and early 1921, including one of the earliest popular essays on psychoanalysis, in *Vanity Fair* ("The Progress of Psychoanalysis"), and two essays of what he called "destructive criticism" on "Things I Consider Over-rated." He followed these with an essay on things he considered "under-rated." He spent a great deal of time reading Hawthorne and discussed in an essay his attitude toward the nude statues he had seen in Rome—"The New Englander Abroad, with an Account of Nathaniel Hawthorne's Infidelity to the Venus di Medici." Just before sailing for Europe he published an article on H. L. Mencken in *The New Republic*. He arrived in Paris June 20, 1921, and two days later was writing to Scott Fitzgerald of the "humiliating" effect on him of French artistic and intellectual "standards." This led him to make a capital statement on what the absence of standards meant in America: "In America I feel so superior and culturally sophisticated in comparison to most of the rest of the intellectual and artistic life of the country that I am in danger of regarding my present attainments as an absolute standard . . . I don't mean to say, of course, that I can actually do better work than anybody else in America; I simply mean that I feel as if I had higher critical standards and that, since in America, all standards are let down, I am afraid mine will drop, too; it is too easy to be a highbrow or an artist in America these days; every American savant and artist should beware of falling a victim to the ease with which a traditionless and half-educated public (I mean the growing public for really good stuff) can be impressed, delighted and satisfied; the Messrs. Mencken, Nathan, Cabell, Dreiser, Anderson, Lewis, Dell, Lippmann, Rosenfeld, Fitzgerald, etc., etc., should all beware of this; let them remember that, like John Stuart

Mill, they all owe a good deal of their eminence 'to the flatness of the surrounding country'!—I do think seriously that there is a great hope for New York as a cultural center; it seems to me that there is a lot doing intellectually in America just now—America seems to be actually beginning to express herself in something like an idiom of her own. But, believe me, she has a long way to go. The commercialism and industrialism, with no older and more civilized civilization behind except one layer of eighteenth-century civilization on the East Coast, imposes a terrific handicap upon any other sort of endeavor: the intellectual and aesthetic manifestations have to crowd their way up and out from between the crevices left by the factories, the office buildings, the apartment houses and the banks; the country was simply not built for them and, if they escape with their lives, they can thank God, but would better not think they are 100 per cent elect, attired in authentic and untarnished vestments of light, because they have obviously been stunted and deformed at birth and afterwards greatly battered and contaminated in their struggle to get out."

Europe afforded EW an opportunity to do some leisurely traveling and thinking. He had led in New York so strenuous a life in the year and a half since he had left the army that he enjoyed looking at European art and architecture, reading the new writers, and meeting some of them. Later he spoke of having in these travels "convalesced very pleasantly from my two years in New York." In Paris he visited various Americans ensconced in Montparnasse and elsewhere on the Left Bank. And he had his sought-after meeting with Edna Millay, as his interpolated passage reveals.]

On the boat, the Belgian automobile man entertained Aunt Evie and her niece with the story of how he had rigged up an infernal machine (which he had brought with him and displayed) for the purpose of catching one of his partners, whom he had suspected of robbing the cash drawer. The machine was a success and blew up the man's hand (by means of a revolver) and filled his face with shot. He was found in a pool of blood. The Belgian remarked that, if the man had died, they might have made trouble for him; he might have been charged with manslaughter. "Why, how unjust!" cried Aunt Evie. "If the man was a thief, he deserved to be blown up." "Yes," said the Belgian. "If his hand wasn't where it belonged, why—" "It's just like the pheasant parks in England," continued Aunt Evie. "I remember when I was a girl that there used to be signs up saying: 'Whoever enters, enters at his peril.'" . . .

I had to share a stateroom with this salesman. He was a very unpleasant character. He corrected my French.

On the Rue du Four, the crash of the market trucks going to the Halles in the very early morning made the whole room vibrate, and I, who, even in

bed, felt the jolt and the rattle of the vehicles, came to feel as if I were a part
of the real life of the city.

Littlefield McCoy, an old Hill friend, whom I met in Paris, told me that Dr.
Frank Crane, who wrote a kind of "uplift" column, was a lecherous old
creature, with a sardonic smile and a terrible line of filth, who felt up
moving-picture actresses in public (at some studio, I think). His wife, he
claimed, was the daughter of some Middle Western farmhand, who was
tremendously impressed by her husband's success and prestige and was
always talking about "when I first knew Frank." He said that what he
wrote did no harm, was intended to have a good influence—told people to
brush their teeth and be good to their wives.

McCoy had also a story about when they had danced among the cabbages
at the Halles and drunk Calvados at the Boule de Cidre. A medical student
had taken Laurence Vail's sister, who had just entertained them with a
stomach dance, into the back room, where he could be seen talking earn-
estly to her. She finally came out and announced: "I've just had really a very
good proposal. He wants a mistress for his father."

Djuna Barnes's friend, a bony, tarnished spinster-like Villager, seeing the
picture of Jane Heep on the mantel, had asked: "Who's Hamlet?" [Jane
Heep was well known as a Lesbian, who dressed in near-masculine clothes.]
—"Marsden's very upstage with drunks." He [Marsden Hartley] was then
in Paris.

In the *Luxembourg Gardens*, the trees in the long alleys had begun to rust,
but the grass and the red and white and pink geraniums were still bright in
the sun.

Djuna Barnes said that she was getting used to the dirt of Paris, it was a
relief after *The Little Review*, anyway. "You know they always used to
wash the soap before they used it." . . . "My husband was a scholar, he
really had a fine mind . . . He works on the *American* to earn a living—and
uses his money to buy books . . . He's writing a book on the philosophy of
criticism—but it'll never be finished. He's been working on it seven years
. . . He had me absolutely stunned so that I didn't know whether I was
coming or going . . . Oh, you couldn't pry me away from him . . . The
amount that man knew was appalling: he knew about all sorts of different
editions and things . . . But he thought earrings were very foolish; he
couldn't understand why I should want to wear earrings . . . But I couldn't
stand it any longer."

Robert McAlmon—Djuna Barnes—Ezra Pound. When McAlmon said that
perhaps I worked harder than they did, Djuna said: "Oh, no, he lives like a

pet pony!" . . . "I come high!" [to some admirer] . . . "Be simple, Ezra, be simple!"

Rue de Vaugirard, on the way to the Luxembourg: the glimpse, through a doorway, of a little court at the end of a short dark corridor: square paving stones in the wet, a low window and vines and ferns vivid green in the rain.

[I made the acquaintance of a very likable prostitute, who lived on Montmartre and called herself Loulou Fanguet. I was impressed by her good sense. She thought that President Wilson was "très chic," but when I tried to convince her that the prostitutes of Paris ought to organize in a union, she said that this was impractical, and it evidently shocked her sense of propriety. She took me one evening to call on a friend of hers, who was living with an automobile salesman. Though this was certainly for the girl an advantageous situation, which Loulou, I think, rather envied, one was aware that her temporary protector was committed to nothing by this relation and could drop her at any time.

I flew to England to see Kemp Smith, my old friend and philosophy teacher from Princeton. I took a Goliath plane from Paris. One of the engines broke down and we flapped around lopsided in the air. A young woman married to a pilot was obviously very worried. I watched the haystacks below to see whether they were getting bigger. We landed on the edge of the Channel at a little town called La Crottoye. I spent the night at Calais and crossed on the boat the next morning.]

At Boulogne, one saw the gray strip of water bristling with shipping, behind it the hotels and shops, gray buildings with narrow windows and thin-lathed blinds, and, above them, ancient houses clustered unevenly on the hill, with yellow-brown walls and dull red roofs subdued and mellowed by time.

At Calais, the vast dreariness of the hotel—the most complete desolation of its kind that one could ever imagine; its dull damp dark cold quality, without any pictures or any sort of ornamentation; its small lounge with a clock under a glass and its trade magazines—*Exporteur Français*, etc.; the enormous dark hall upstairs, lined with doors on either side, at the other end of which a chambermaid would be dimly seen, a dark form, a creature of the shadow; the bedroom with the large mirror, the huge bed covered with its red insulation, dark red walls and red plush furniture, enormous bulk of everything, triple windows with heavy, close-sealing croisées, its stillness and profundity as of death; its woman-at-the-desk in a great glass-paned cage, from the depths of which she transacted business entirely without excitement or eagerness to please or represent the hotel as attractive (being

necessarily without the possibility of making the guest stay) of the ordinary
hotelkeeper; the perfunctoriness of the hors d'oeuvres.

Kemp Smith. He had spent a vacation with Gauss in Pike County (Pa.)
and visited a saloon where they cried "Help! Help!" when they wanted
their glasses refilled . . . At St. Andrew's, one of the professors had been got
rid of when it was discovered that he had given the same lecture twice in
succession. But at Edinburgh, he told me with pride (he occupied the chair
of Moral Philosophy which had been held by Sir William Hamilton and
others), you couldn't be removed: you could "lead a bad life or anything."
In the case of one man who drank, they had simply appointed an "assistant," who acted as substitute . . . "There's probably no such thing as a
totally disinterested motive . . . Yes: it's easy enough to improve the character. You can always correct the fault. But it's like an India-rubber ball with
a dent in it, ye know: you can always straighten out the dent, but another
dent appears somewhere else. If you try to improve your intellectual life,
you find that you're neglecting your personal life. You try to be sincere and
you find you're becoming rude." The sexual instinct, he said, was certainly
very badly regulated—no wonder Schopenhauer based his pessimistic
philosophy on it . . . The other day they shot a collie dog . . . "Now, why
did they do that?" . . . He surprised me by telling me that he had been worried at having lost his temper with a waiter on the Continent. The waiter
had looked as if he might have syphilis.

[I had letters from Crowninshield to Mme Picabia and Jean Cocteau.
Mme Picabia had organized that summer an outdoor place of entertainment
called le Théâtre de l'Oasis, with Yvette Guilbert and other vedettes of the
nineties, which included even Aristide Bruant. I adored Yvette Guilbert,
whom I regarded and still regard as one of the great French artists of her
time.] I spent many evenings at the Oasis, and when it closed I followed her
to the Trocadéro, where the theater was much too large for her and the
house was never filled. The French public had not kept pace with her. She
had been away for years in New York. She had married an American
doctor and conducted an original kind of school for actresses, singers and
diseuses. But during these years she had studied French songs and had much
developed and extended her range. The French did not know this, and I
somewhat resented their tone when they referred to her as "une chanteuse
de café chantant."

She gave them their old favorites, too, in the costume, with long black
gloves, celebrated by Toulouse-Lautrec: *Le Fiacre* and *Madame Arthur*. But
she had also a whole new repertoire of songs from earlier periods, of which
she caught the style and accent in a most extraordinary way. Her powers of
impersonation were equal to any I have ever seen and were displayed with

hardly any change—or none at all—of make-up or coiffure or costume. Her old songs of the nineties were sung with very few staccato words, every syllable of which was made to tell. But, as a beauty of the Renaissance, she conducted an aggressive but ceremonious flirtation:

> Dites, dites, dites, dites-moi,
> Suis-je, suis-je, suis-je, suis-je belle?

With a childlike simplicity she rendered a medieval *Légende de Saint Nicolas*. As a *grue* of the Bal Bullier, she inveigled a green young man from the country, telling him, while she waltzed, of the very distinguished admirers who had thrown themselves at her feet. But

> Plaignez, plaignez
> La pauvre innocente
> Qui n'a jamais, jamais
> Connu l'amour.

As the former mistress of Béranger, in a ballad by his successor Bérat, she sat "under the old chestnut tree" and told the young people about her hero. As she recalled her girlhood, she made the old woman appear to grow actually youthful and, as she smiled, even pretty:

> Si vous saviez, enfants,
> Quand j'étais jeune fille,
> Comme j'étais gentille!
> Je parle de longtemps:
> Teint frais, regard qui brille,
> Sourire aux blanches dents,
> Alors, ô mes enfants!
> Alors, ô mes enfants!
> Grisette de quinze ans.
> Ah! que j'étais gentille!

And she caused Béranger's militant spirit to revive in a swelling echo:

> Vous parlerai-je de sa gloire?
> Son nom des rois causait l'effroi.

In *Verligodin*, she became a tough old peasant woman who seemed almost about to murder her drunken husband, also impersonated by her, who muttered his sulky defensive retorts; in a modern monologue, she talked to a former lover whom she had not seen for many years: she recalled their old good times together and the miseries that they had endured; then:

> Je vous ai dit, "Je ne vous aime plus—
> Désormais je veux rrrompre!—

(Then, after this declaration, breaking down into a friendly laugh)

Ah, mon ami, t'en souvient-t-il?

One of her most startling pieces was the woman drunk, *La Soularde*, which at one point became almost embarrassing. She seemed genuinely drunk from the beginning of the song; but then when there was laughter in the audience, she broke off to *engueuler* those who were laughing at her. One was almost ready to believe that Yvette Guilbert was really drunk. Her outburst produced a silence.

Jean Cocteau took me to lunch and of course was gratified by my admiration. I had enormously enjoyed his *Mariés de la Tour Eiffel*, performed by the Swedish ballet, which, with its ostrich and hunter in the Eiffel Tower and its general, a guest at the wedding, who is eaten by a lion—"He would have been the first to laugh about it"—seemed to me a new departure in French humor, an equivalent to English nonsense. He did not like my confusing him with the Dadaists—on account of his having made a contribution to one of Picabia's publications—and scoffed at the idea that their nonsense was perpetrated in a genuine spirit of fun: "Ils sont tous des petits Nietzsches!" Like most of the young French writers of the time, he was not enthusiastic about Anatole France, who he said was "fou de la politique." France, he said, liked to gossip about Mme de Noailles, who had an unusually large head, and to speculate as to how she disposed of it when she was lying with her lover. I wanted to talk to him about Octave Mirbeau, whom I had read during the war and whose *Sébastien Roch* I admired. Cocteau said that at the end of his life Mirbeau had been "très malade." "C'est toute une génération que la nôtre a sautée."

He talked presently with a marked brilliance. I was struck—though I did not agree with him—by his saying that Flaubert was always getting ready to shoot but did not hit the target, whereas Stendhal did not aim but hit the mark. I later found that he had simply been giving me a passage from his *Le Secret Professionnel*. I do not disapprove of this practice. I have known Santayana to do it and have sometimes done it myself.

I found Edna very much allied with the Bohemians of the Left Bank, with whom I was not much at home.

We walked in the Bois de Boulogne and joked about the signs that said "Pelouse défendu." Edna said that we could always protest, "Mais nous ne pelousons pas." She was very broke at the moment and she asked me to take her to the South of France; but I knew that she was not to be relied on and would leave me for anyone who seemed more attractive. I did not want to have to worry and suffer again. I, besides, felt committed to Mary Blair, who had promised to try to join me in France. I declined to go away with Edna, and lent her money instead.

[On July 3, 1921, EW wrote a detailed account to John Peale Bishop of his visit to Miss Millay. He described her as living comfortably on the Left Bank. He had a feeling, he said, that the stage was set for his call—she had put on "a serious black dress and was discovered sitting before her type-writer with a pile of manuscript." In this *mise en scène*, EW remarked, she was better dressed "than she has ever been before in her life." He found her looking older and more mature; she assured him "that perhaps the next day she would be like a little girl again." EW also said "she was very serious, earnest and sincere about herself." Later in his memoir, he believed that "Europe frightened her less than New York." He wondered, however, whether this wasn't "inspired by my presence." She told EW "she was tired of breaking hearts and spreading havoc, and wanted to start a new life." After noting that she was having a love affair with a British journalist, then well known in Paris, EW went on: "She can no longer intoxicate me with her beauty or throw bombs into my soul; when I looked at her, it was like staring into the crater of an extinct volcano. She made me sad; it made me sad, curiously enough, that I had loved her so much once and now did not love her any longer. Actually, of course, I would not love her again for anything; I can think of few more terrible calamities; but I felt that, im-possible and imperfect as she is, some glamour of high passion had gone out of life when my love for her died."]

[The Fitzgeralds were in Europe but I never saw them. Scott wrote me a letter in which he wondered how I could enjoy it. He had never learned French. They had just had a misadventure in Paris due to Zelda's having tried to make sure of the hotel elevator by tying it fast to their floor. I re-plied with a rather high-flown eulogy on French literature and culture.

It was only on a later visit that they got to know Hemingway and the Gerald Murphys, who apparently, with no admixture of other elements, came to constitute Europe for Scott. The Fitzgeralds seem to have lived in France without any real contact with the country, as they had not had for that matter any very close relations with New York. Hemingway, whom Scott began by adoring and by whom he remained more or less obsessed, did not represent any social level; and the Murphys were also anomalous. Gerald, as an Irish Catholic and hence not "out of the top drawer" in New York, was also a somewhat eccentric and an independent figure who could hardly be assigned to any "life style" or group. He and Scott had it in com-mon that they were both Irish Catholics, and Scott's discovery of Gerald as a man from the same semi-excluded background, but very rich as he was not and would have liked to be, with glamorous and fastidious tastes, amus-ing, sensitive and capable of fantasy, was like the realization of a dream. But I wonder that the Murphys stood Scott for so long. They remonstrated with him for asking his impudent embarrassing questions, and they would put him into Coventry for specified periods when he had thrown things into their drawing room at times when they were entertaining aristocratic French guests and had not invited the Fitzgeralds. But the lively imaginations and entertainment value of Scott and Zelda preserved them through a certain amount of troublemaking.

I believe that Dos Passos was right when he suggested to me once that Scott was by no means always so drunk as he pretended to be, but merely put on disorderly drunken acts, which gave him an excuse for clowning and outrageous behavior, because he had never learned to practice the first principles of civilized behavior. This must have been the case on the occasion of his disastrous call on Edith Wharton, who had admired *The Great Gatsby* and who was evidently disposed to like him but by whose reputation—at the moment he was unaccompanied by Zelda—he had been made excessively self-conscious. He had also an act as Prince Charming, and I have been assured by a lady who had met him only once that in this role he was quite irresistible. I saw him assuming this personality when I took him for a drink with Léonie Adams, the poet, whom he had never seen before and whose half Latin-American prettiness and obvious purity of spirit called forth all his instincts of chivalry. But this lasted for only about three minutes before the sloppy boor took over. I think he may have been too much aware that I would have been surprised by his access of conscious charm.]

Men are seen at their worst with women; women at their best with men.

Walking the picture galleries of other men's minds.

Paris. The Tuileries and the Louvre were a blank gray embankment; the river lost itself in gray on either side, where the dotted lines of lights of the bridges reverberated one another; to the west, above the river, the smoky twilight was faintly tinted with rose. —From the Left Bank one saw the yellow stars, which seemed to make the night a milky green, beneath the trees of the Place de la Concorde, from which the Obelisk lifted its pale blade.

The Rue de Richelieu. The long crowded windows of the gray façades strung with twisted-iron balconies, where one saw the tarnished gold letters that announced firms and products; the narrowness, the oldness of the street; the very impression one got of the stuffiness and moldiness and darkness and dirt of the interiors somehow having a richness and dignity as of a life which, in spite of its inferior neatness and spick-and-spanness, was essentially more serious and finer than our own—as if the less well educated people than oneself were yet more sophisticated: they had seen the Revolution. A small gray square with a large iron fountain and some trees, closed in by gray. —Along the Chaussée de la Muette, the little leaves were yellowing and powdering the walk, and the light of the withdrawing sun itself was yellow and faded and rusty; there was a faint haze in the park, where the children were playing about the simple little skeletons of the folding iron chairs.

Rue de Varenne. Through an archway in a gray stone façade, with stone balconies and white persiennes, one saw a smooth-cobbled little street, closed in with fine-looking hotels—a glass semicircle above a door, trees turning yellow in a garden, the fine-leaved foliage overflowing the black iron grills—which turned and closed off its perspective. —Everywhere, the Corinthian columns inlaid between the long windows, above which are arcs of stone or masque-like faces (of Cupids?)—the gray many-windowed façades—the lacelike effect of the streets, with their stiff fringe of lightning rods and chimney pots—the subdued changes of the autumn, without tragic splendor or bravado—the smooth brightly lighted fields of the Champs-Elysées at night. The leaves behind the Hôtel de Biron looked tiny as if they had been engraved and were yellowing in a dull pale fashion and the engraving had faded.

Versailles. There was a golden core to the Bosquet de la Reine, where the yellow leaves, strung up the high trees, were almost translucent to the light of the sun and fell among four Roman busts . . . A wide alley, now disused, where the tender green of grass showed through the brown estampement of leaves and the slender green treetops met above like fine fingers brought tip to tip . . . The little leaves made a light tan carpet and dappled the dark bronze green of the round basins, where black iron sea gods and cupids disported among black iron rocks . . . At the end of an alley, as the twilight began to fall, I saw the limbs of a young god, as slender and as gray as the stems of the screen of young trees . . . Dark box hedges and above them the elms clipped flat like a wall but higher, bellying out and overflowing; they were rusting with a rich metallic brown . . . The sun a great star of silver fire behind the high green screen . . . The great elms like some monstrous pompous eighteenth-century headgear of plumes . . . The round leaves drifted down very slowly, languidly, almost drowsily, turning in the air, detaching themselves noiselessly and ceaselessly . . . The long thin flower borders, walled in with little lines of box and packed with geraniums, daisies and rose geranium.

The artists working with all their might to make life look interesting and attractive; the philosophers and historians to give it some sort of meaning.

Côte d'Azur. Some gleaming town of rose and white, there where the Alps like elephants come down to kneel beside the calm and azure sea. On the sky and the water lies a hard glaring glaze of gold. The Mediterranean, level and smooth, lips the shore with a slow rise and fall of sound like the breath of a sleeper—a gentle insistent rhythm—brushing the beach with sound. The cactus clumps (aloes) like spiky octopi. The palms that stud the Croisette at Cannes with *tignasse* tufts and thick pineapple stems. At night, the pale dark peppered with stars like the finest of silver tinsel. The last soft red streamers of the sunset faded behind the gray silhouette of the Esterel, and from the jetty I saw the green trees and the red roofs of the houses that mount the little hill to the square Saracen town grown somber and black above the silver blue-gray water of the harbor, where the little boats were neatly moored in a fringe about the shore: above the boats was the low avenue of lindens and along between their trunks were the lights of the shops.

Ninette Fabre, whom I had known at Vittel during the war. Her father had a café there in summer and a café in Cannes, which he opened in winter. I had greatly admired Ninette and by good luck found her at Cannes, where she happened to be visiting an aunt. I told her that her nose was cold—"Comme les petits chiens qui se portent bien. Il me faut deux années pour digérer les baisers. Après, je vais recommencer. Vous devez me prendre pour une fille légère! vrai? A coups de cravache" (this was the way her father had bossed the natives in Indochina). She had an admirer who was a croupier at the Monte Carlo casino, and we went on a holiday there.

Human beings are tiny centers of consciousness in the void, with only their frail bodies to keep out the overpowering nothing of infinity which presses in on them—little creatures growing and building against the annihilation of space and the inorganic world.

The melancholy thing about happiness is not that it doesn't exist but that it doesn't last (in reply to Leopardi's Torquato Tasso dialogue.)

Venice's cloying flamboyance.

Eleventh-century text of Homer. Brown ink against yellow, traced over darker where someone had tried to restore the effacements; greasy, worm-eaten and soiled; its λ's, κ's and ξ's like wormholes and conveying no more than wormholes to the monks in whose hands it was found—a formidable forest tangled and bristling with loops and dots and barbs; written in three different hands, with great holes and stains on the pages (of vellum, *membranaceus*); a caricature, as of a human heavy-jowled dog with huge paw; scrawled with schoolboy drawings and scribbled letters; glossed here and there in the margins; thick heavy brown cover.

The fifteenth-century text, on the other hand, was copied on clean cream-colored pages in a clear beautiful hand. The first page of the *Iliad* and the first page of the *Odyssey* and the initials to all the books were done in wonderful red and blue and green and pink and thick bright gold.

[Echoes from the *New Republic* days]. Hackett, who had evidently been snubbed, or fancied he had been snubbed, by Lytton Strachey, thought that, since it was a question of "the most fatuous of human institutions: monarchy," Strachey should have attacked it openly in his *Victoria*, instead of only leaving it as one of the inferences to be drawn. "Culturine." He said that the canned salmon was made from the sweepings of an automobile-tire factory.

Lippmann (when I saw him in Paris) said that Hackett was charming with illiterate people.

At Florence, the deep blue sky, dark yet of pure color, not blackened or tarnished—indigo, perhaps—set with stars, above the brown soiled old-looking buildings, in the clear autumn night. The square lay open, a wide dry brown-gray expanse lit by two or three street lamps. One night it seemed to me that the stars were thicker than in other countries: one seemed to see smaller ones—a dust of stars behind the planets, etc.

[*Florence* gave me much the impression of an old university town. The palaces which are now galleries are grim-faced and rather drab: no signs of Renaissance splendor. I did not know anybody there and spent a good deal of time simply reading in my hotel: *The Oxford Book of Italian Verse*, Vasari, and Dante's *Canzoniere*. The city seemed quite Dantesque, with its sharp outlines against a clear sky and its black spikes of cypresses above the town. I, however, picked up a copy of George Saintsbury's two-volume book on the French novel, written in his most digressive and entertaining later vein, and with a shadow of bad conscience on account of not reading Italian classics would indulge myself in reading it late at night.]

Florence in September. From the gallery or open terrace of the Viale dei Colli, one saw the first smoky sunset of September: the west a dullish red glow above the blank gray rampart of the hills and, below it, the roofs and dun walls embrowning themselves in the dusk; which thickened gradually about them, while the great harsh mountains to the north seemed to send out a more effacing haze that blotted off the edge of the city; to the west, the Arno was bright with the sunset, but, nearer, it showed its polished metallic surface of brownish green; the lamps were lit along the sides and threaded it with a double line of tiny bright points; on the hills to the west, the villas were white shadows pricked sometimes with a spark; but behind, a dark green hill, its outline spiked with stiff cypresses, still kept the colors of the day, darkened with the sun's distance, against a sky where the blue of day still showed frankly above the rusty shadows into which the valley was sinking. Between the trees of the darkening path lay the brown leaves of autumn, and two nuns, in their floating black gowns, passed silently without haste.

The Boboli Gardens [My poem "Boboli Gardens" is taking shape in this description (the poem appears in EW's *Night Thoughts*, 1961)]. Where goldfish flecking green with red drift idle in the eternal sun; winged horse; gods and goddesses, alternating with great urns, in the brown niches above the gray lichened tiers of the amphitheater; monkeys on a fountain; atrocious eighteenth-century grotto—heavily encrusted with fake moss and stalactites and with conch shells stuck in it—which drips like mud in copious clots over the mural reliefs of, on one side, a pastoral scene with sheep, their wool matted and overlaid with plaster or whatever it is, and, on the other, the river gods being smothered with a deluge of slather—on the ceiling Bacchus, in faded colors, with his leopards, apes, etc.; at the back, in the arcanum of the grot, a fountain with a nymph being squirted with water from the mouths of four satyrs, who strain forward, chinning themselves on the edge of the bowl. The oleander spreads its rose. The vaulted alleys dark with boughs, where stone benches are low in proportion to the lowness of the tunnel; no winged sphinxes guard the gate. There are no gardens there like those; lap-dog lions and goats with dolphin tails, cupids, etc., about the great fountain with the green-planted island from which the white Hercules towers; Zeus and Ganymede—this note often struck: beautiful young man with small satyr crouching at his thigh, etc.; monstrous busts à la Rome; atrocious merry yokels; enormous knight bestriding bearded and grimacing hippogriff; girl (or androgyne) pushing Amor away. And no white statues stop the alleyway; the great dark green walls close and high above the narrow path; the unexpected vistas, the variety and the labyrinthine character intended for the amusement of visitors; the smooth sloping paths shadowed or in sun; the triple-tiered fountain with silver rain. They had no gay-lettered texts. [Comparison with New England.] And the sad autumn dark with cloud. The frozen snow, the winter stars; the thin high air.

Dark green stiff trees against the pure blue of the sky.

The rococo mural style: dolphins sprouting into scrolls; winged female creatures, round-breasted and wasp-waisted, with feet turning to tendrils; frail birds and cupids flitting among the garlands; hippogriffs; mosquito-like creatures.

The sacred form of this style involved, more simply, cherubs and birds.

Florence

[I did better with this in *Poets, Farewell!*]

This is my city!—girt with hills,—not she,
   The mirror of the East, in Eastern gown
   Of yellow, rose and red, with gaudy crown,
That rots with color by the peacock sea;

But she, the dusky-toned, the brown, the dry,
   In sober garb, but crowned with that clear light
   That roofs the streets with crystal blue and white,
And cuts the cypress black above the town,—

That clearest light that, biting the straight stone,
   The low-domed hills, clipped sharp the cliffs of Hell;
     That pure and candid radiance, bright to blind,
Which brims the valley, where a vision shone
   That fled like snow—too infinite to tell—
     Or like the Sibyl's leaves before the wind.

September, 1921

[I set out to go from Florence to Naples, but my pocket was picked in Florence before the train started. The thieves resorted to what I afterwards learned was a very familiar trick. One man with a huge belly stood in a corridor so I had to squeeze past him, while another extracted my wallet. I reported this to the stationmaster, who was not in the least surprised and made notes but held out no hopes of recovery. I gave up my projected trip and very soon went back to France.]

Le Havre. The gray-faced buildings embedded in the murky night as if in some livid mud, like great squarish stones; the lighthouse raking the horizon with its long blade.

[On his return to New York during the autumn of 1921, EW wrote a discursive piece in *The New Republic* called "Night Thoughts in Paris: A Rhapsody" (XXX, March 15, 1922, 75–77). He originally intended to reprint it here, although he characterized it as "naïve." It is an impressionistic essay, in which one gets the feeling that EW had been touched deeply by his European wanderings and by his sympathy for European culture. He had been frank in his letters to his friends about America's cultural limitations, but he is a bit defensive in his essay. "Things are always beginning in America," he wrote. "We are always on the verge of great adventures." Paying homage to Europe's maturity, he remarked: "History seems to lie before us instead of behind."]

Return to New York

New York [1921]. In the early October dawn, one saw first a white-walled red-roofed building like a factory of some sort, its colors quite fresh in the light, and then the wooded shore in dingy brown and yellows like a discolored or badly printed photograph; the shore bristling with cranes on barges drawn up in a row; the gulls in gleaming white flakes; the domino faces of the pier ends ivory in the dawn. Then, as the raw hard light becomes stronger, the faint white shapes of the houses on a hill become pasteboard-sided villages; the city appears, gray and pearl, a hill, between the hard steel-gray of the water and the hard steel-gray of the sky; as one gets nearer, the black and white planes outline themselves sharply—the "packing boxes" stiffly plumed with smoke; the docks raying out from the shore; the National Biscuit Company.

Ted Paramore. Story about the man who went to the girl's room in the Lafayette—somebody there drunk already—man pretends to be house detective and puts him out. —"Look here, buddy, this is New Year's Eve—" "Now, I'll stand here and watch you go out that door." —Suggested complication: he comes back and gets into the wrong room by mistake, thereby becoming embroiled with the real house detective. —He was a small Brooks-suited fellow with a boyish and innocent face.

The girl at the fraternity (or some sort of club) dance who made the fellow take her up to get a comb and then when he offered her one said, "Aw, what the hell?" and turned the light off. In the morning, the floor was seen to be strewn with condoms, the remains of several parties of this kind.

The policeman at the Montmartre (or the Rendezvous) who, soused himself, went the rounds of the tables telling the people it was time to close and that they would have to get out. He accepted liquor from every flask and when he finally came to Ted's table and was told, in response to his demand, that they didn't have any, said, with his hat on the back of his head: "Well, I've a good mind to run yez in!"

The story about the weekend trip and the home-breaking. The former Yale professor whose wife walked out on him when he brought his mistress—"just a little smelt"—to the house—his Irish songs and the smelt's "Oh, Walterr, don't sing any more!" and "Wayrr's that dearr little dog?"

Herman Oelrichs and *Sixtus the Sixth* and the whiskey that he poured out

96

with a great gesture when he couldn't come to an understanding with Dorothy Heydell [a Santa Barbara friend of Ted's, whom Oelrichs afterwards married]. His ice machine, sliding panel, etc.

Ted's great-grandmother was a very severe old lady and was greatly outraged by the heretical opinions of one of his uncles, who had been to Yale: "So you don't believe Christ was divine?"—when the boy had come back from Yale. "No! I don't believe he was *divine*; I think he was a very good man—" "Good, eh? Good man, eh? You just wait till you die and then you'll find out how *good* he is!"

The lady who kept the bootlegger's den and who had been divorced from the socially superior husband. His family tried to high-hat her. "That codfish aristocracy!—They'd sit and knit, see? Knit!—all evening they'd sit and knit. One evening, Harry came in and said: 'Let's take a walk down the road.' 'Jesus Christ!' I says. 'You said something!'" They tried to correct her grammar. "What I said to them finally, I said: 'Say, you tried to climb the social ladder, but you didn't get any further than the window,' I says."—The bootlegger was finally arrested and put in jail: he made a business of destroying automobiles for owners who wanted to get the insurance—burning them up, driving them over cliffs, etc.

Ted Paramore: "None of Cupe Black's family were *soft*. [Cupe Black was one of his Santa Barbara friends.] —They drank seven bottles of whiskey—the bunch there—sitting on the floor—a chair was like the Eiffel Tower at that time of night. They just sat around on the floor, braced up against the wall—and Cupe would just throw down a mug of whiskey from time to time. —When the patrol wagon came, he said: 'Gee, I'm glad! I never coulda sent for a taxi!'"

Princeton in February. The delicate Japanesy limbs of the trees drawn upon the gray day, into which their lines seemed just to melt. —The day, as it got on toward six, seemed closing down with infinite hot relentless gradualness—as if some heavy and unyielding, almost mechanical, pressure were bringing darkness down to crush the light—and life. The Graduate School tower was gray against gray. The locomotive headlight looked like a jewel—a star—coming easily, beautifully, reassuringly through the grayness. —Later on, the full moon came up, at first like a disc of straw-colored paper—rather a cheap, washed-out, diluted tint; later the pale yellow vanished and left it paler still.

Djuna Barnes. When Mary [Blair] admired a nightgown she had bought in Paris: "Yes: I spent all summer looking for a night to go with that nightgown."

New Haven to New York in December. The dry meadows and forests mottled with snow; the New England towns of big box-like houses and great skeletons of trees; the streams glazed with black ice; the long flat factories.

"Don't you think our feet are congenial together? They're fraternizing across the lines."

I sometimes feel as if all the tires of my mind were deflated and my intellectual wheels were running rackingly and joltingly on their rims.

I should think that Edna Millay and Frank Crowninshield would be the two most cynical people in the world: both of them have discovered that everyone, no matter how intelligent or superior, may be made a fool of by flattery, if it is cleverly enough applied. They flatter the intellectual according to his intellect and the artist according to his art.

Newark again. The buildings strewn on the hill like the scum of a receding tide, the horizon of chimneys and gas tanks, the foundering marshes, the dilapidated shell of an old factory above a straight black iron river, a vast low brick plant enclosed in brick walls, exact piles of rusted pipes and congeries of truncated nondescript metal shapes (great arcs, like slices of boilers).—Newark: the flimsy, kindling-wood houses, the great black coalyards. The factories, buildings, etc., turning molten as the sun sets behind them.

[Eugene O'Neill was still married to and living with his second wife, Agnes—to whom he referred as Aggie. I saw quite a lot of Agnes O'Neill because she was a friend of Mary Blair's. Her father was English, a painter, and she was an English type, sensible, practical, rather lacking in elegance but likable and with qualities that commanded respect. She had also some literary ability and wrote a book about her marriage. O'Neill, on the other hand, in spite of an appealing boyish charm, was difficult to make contact with. I was grateful to him for persuading the Provincetown Players to produce my first play, *The Crime in the Whistler Room,* but I found conversation with him impossible. He was then completely on the wagon, and you were cautioned not to offer him anything to drink. But I got so bored with his nonresponsive silence that one night, having dinner with him in a Greenwich Village restaurant, I decided to prime him with some wine, which with no hesitation he accepted. For this I paid a heavy price. We talked about Greek tragedy, and I told him that in *Oedipus at Colonus* the crimes of Oedipus seemed to have been expiated when he was somehow miraculously removed by a supernatural agency. O'Neill said that he couldn't believe this: Sophocles would have had too much respect for human beings. O'Neill had a peculiar point of view on the homosexual activities of the sailors he had known on shipboard. He thought that in degrading themselves by submitting to the demands of other sailors, they were always trying to atone for some wrong which was on their conscience. He was amusing about the old female performers—Trixie Friganza and others like her—whom he had known in his early days. One of them had sat at his bedside and told him that if she hadn't been faithful to his brother, she would have come right into bed with him. Another had been warned by her friends that she would have to be very careful with the family of the groom of a pal who was having a proper wedding party at the Bellevue Stratford in Philadelphia. The friend restrained herself till the very last moment when the bride and groom were driving away in a taxi. She had collected several towels from the bathroom of the hotel and she threw them in at the window, with "I guess you'll need these!"

After dinner, we went on to my apartment at 3 Washington Square North, and, once started talking, it seemed O'Neill could never stop. What was striking was that he quite lost connection with anything that was said by me or Mary. He did not answer questions or seem to recognize that we were there at all. He disregarded all our hints. We got up and crossed the room; we made remarks which with anyone else would have brought the session to a close. But his talk was an unbroken monologue. And he drank up everything we had in the house: when a bottle was set before him, he simply poured out drinks for himself, not suggesting that we might care for any. If we said we ought to go to bed, he paid no attention to this. He told us at length about a rich man who lived near him in Connecticut. He had some tragic theory about him: he was frustrated, his conscience bothered him. O'Neill, there now being nothing more to drink, did not leave until four in the morning.

Mary Blair, having acted in *Diff'rent* and another O'Neill play, agreed to do *All God's Chillun*, in which she was to take the role of a white girl married to a Negro. The Negro was Paul Robeson, who had not long before graduated from Rutgers and had not yet a reputation as a singer. Mary got insulting letters, and somebody wrote to O'Neill he was so low that he'd have to take a stepladder to get up to a cockroach. As a result of all this, Mary came down with pleurisy, and the opening had to be postponed; but she went through with it, and O'Neill thereafter expressed a certain appreciation and exhibited a certain loyalty, telling one of his associates to remember *God's Chillun* and give her a part in one of his plays.

I do not much like O'Neill as a dramatist: he depends too much upon hatred; but I believe that *All God's Chillun* does have a certain advantage over some of the too smooth and easy films that deal with similar situations in that they show that racial antagonisms may rankle and break out after marriage. When O'Neill married again and went out to California, he ceased to answer letters from any of his old friends. He had always been quite frank in his scorn for actors and seemed to feel that he had been unfair to his father, who had had a great success as Monte Cristo and no doubt was something of a ham. O'Neill himself had once acted with the elder O'Neill. He told me that *Ah, Wilderness!*, one of his very few amiable plays, had been a kind of attempt to make it up to his father; and I suppose that *Long Day's Journey* was something of an effort in the same direction. I did not share his admiration of Strindberg, in whose poison-spitting quarrels between man and woman he evidently took satisfaction and which to some extent in his own work he imitated.]

The nymphs were said to have had hair the color of the sea.

> I sometimes reflect as I am riding in the subway
> That I have never read the tales of the Comte de Caylus,
> Nor the memoirs of his mother.
> What a polished and delightful fancy one must find in the former,
> With overtones of sophisticated naïveté,
> What a charming style and tone in the latter.
> But I am carried on, crashing, away from them
> By the subway, by the city, by the century.
> Who knows if, in the course of our journey,
> We shall ever meet them again?

Cook's Linoleum Rugs
Mill and Factory Supplies
National Pneumatic Co.
Gatto and Cogno
Cut herringbone gears
Hobbed Worm Wheels
International Automobile Body Corporation
American Metal Moulding Co.
American Platinum Works
Federal Steel Tubing—Light steel gauge tubing
Rhoad's Tannate Belt
H. W. Schrimpf: structural and ornamental ironwork
The Crucible Steel Company of America
Derricks and Pile-Drivers
Bab and Bidelow
Smelting and refining
Calendar-embossing machinery
The Aeroplane Ultimate Typewriter Ribbon
The Goerke-Kirche Co.
The American Steel Barrel Corporation

Automotive Parts
Hyatt Roller Bearing Company
Oschwald Brick Works
Simmons Pipe-Bending Works
Encaustic Tiling Co.
Mucilage and Asbestos
Manufacturers of doll voices (and condoms)

Theater, etc.

The dinner guests enter single-file and in dress suits to the sound of the stiff beats of a dirge.

The curtain goes down on one who has announced his intention of drowning his cares in drink getting sadder and sadder as he drinks and finally bursting into tears.

A simple girl—servant, perhaps—reading aloud a letter from her lover in order to inform somebody of something, reads in all the tender passages as a matter of course.

Gross and persistent flattery of a man with a balloon head; the head swells up and finally bursts (with hat) and the figure collapses on the floor. The Literary Situation: several men praising each other.

Elinor Wylie's story of dinner at Mrs. Simeon Ford's. Mercedes da Costa, Gibran the Persian, etc. Great enthusiasm for Whitman; Whitman and Christ perhaps the two greatest people who ever lived. "What poets do you like?" "Why, Milton, for example—" "Milton!!!" They cried with horror, turning to one another and saying: "She says she likes Milton!" It had to be shouted at Mrs. Ford, who was deaf; when she understood, she made a frightful grimace: "Milton!" "Why," said someone to Elinor, "I thought you were a *good* poet. You haven't been influenced by *Milton*!" "Well, why should I be? You admire Jesus Christ, but you don't behave like him, do you?"

[Of Elinor Wylie, EW wrote to John Peale Bishop at this time: "Elinor is married, as I suppose you know, and lives in an agreeable American-Victorian interior on East Eighteenth Street with Bill's little Victorian children." (She had married William Rose Benét.) "She has profited by it immensely, on the whole, I should say—looks better, behaves more calmly and puts on flesh."]

The Man in the Troll Hill

Why do you look at us so closely with anger and chagrin? we have shown you a thousand times that we are only trolls—hollow behind like masks—we live in the Troll Hill, where the days are dark, why do you

keep getting us to come out? we are not men; we do not want the light. —
Why do you keep trying to make us stop fighting? We would rather fight
than have peace: it is too much trouble to have peace. When the gray trolls
fought the gray trolls for a slice of cheese, it was much easier to fight than to
measure out the cheese, which would have involved rules and weights and
que sais-je encore. —Why do you insist on making our females behave according to the laws which you yourself have invented? They know nothing
about all that. Some like to have children and some like to have lovers, and
that's all that one can say. —We do a little mischief; we do a little harm. —
How do you know *you're* not a troll? Have you ever looked behind yourself?

February 1922—
ratty: "Well, that makes it very ratty for us."
crocko, squiffy,
boiled to the ears.

dumbbell	upstage	lousy
high-hat	rat-fuck	to crab someone or
		someone's act.

to snap one's lunch, one's cookies, one's crackers.

What's the dirt? spill the dirt!

"He's always doin' his stuff."		razz: the Royal
cuckoo	flop	Spanish raspberry
		bozo

In Europe the war was like a part of the history of the human race; in
America it was Plattsburgh plus a big advertising campaign to sell a new
breakfast food or a new kind of uplift.

The facts of his life filled up his mind like a scaffolding in a New York
street.

Porphyrio, or the Mad Prince. A Tragedy in Nineteen Acts, with an introduction explaining that what is here published amounts to no more than
fragments of the whole, but that if interested readers will raise a subscription
fund of $15,000, the authors will be glad to go to Europe and finish the
work. Explanations of the difficulty of doing any long and *written* work in
twentieth-century America. Statistics of the great compositions of the past:
Homer, Virgil, Dante, Flaubert, Ibsen; Shakespeare much the worse for
haste. The fashion of writing journalism instead of masterpieces; the
modern English novelists cases in point; the difference between them and
Strachey. The complete disappearance of the ideal of the *well-written* book:
Dreiser. Statistics on our financial needs; Detailed Budget of a trip abroad
to finish the drama, with full discussion of tips, rates of exchange, lending

money to stranded Greenwich Villagers who have come over as to the Ely-
sian Fields, Italian beggars, art galleries, baths, silk stockings for the girls at
home, etc., etc. Also, in order to make the book as learned as it should be,
we shall first have to acquire the learning, the morale: all things vain, but
we must first be able to sample these things. As for the general moral and
purport of the book, we cannot as yet even indicate this: frankly, we do not
know whether it will be optimistic or pessimistic: it all depends on what
happens to us in the meantime. Influence of personal fortunes on general
views of life: reason the old become conservative—not because they are actually wiser but because they are better established and adjusted than in
youth, when they were in a constant state of exasperation from the effort to
fit themselves to the world and the world to them; Voltaire might never
have been anything but an elegant versifier and unreal if he hadn't been
horsewhipped and thrown into jail. Chances considerable, however, that
the work will take a pessimistic turn of some kind, since Dr. Bishop believes
in the flesh and I believe in the reason, so what hope is there for either of us?

John Bishop and I had talked about doing *Porphyrio* together, but it was
he who actually wrote it: a story in his *Collected Prose* and two sonnets in the
Collected Poems.

My brain is like a piece of cheese that quivers with a million mites.

> One evening, walking through Tenth Street,
> I beheld that the house was torn down
> Where my old love [Miss Millay] once lived.
> It had been red brick with white doors
> And long fine-shuttered white blinds,
> And I remembered I had stood in the window
> One diamond winter night:
> The spacious winter stars
> Close above the low roofs of the Village
> Had brought Paris suddenly to me,
> Wide-strewn with the stars of spring,
> And my heart flew out with the thought
> That she was soon to walk for the first time
> Where Condorcet vindicates Man
> In the broad space before the Institute.
>
> Now I know that that spacious Paris
> Is a city I could never show her
> And that the winter stars I gave her
> She has long since spent for cigarettes,
> But that her house should be ripped like a cobweb
> To make place for steam-heated apartments
> Leaves the winds of April harsh.

The wall which shutters my window
Is a lusterless maroon;
Its dull brick grudges windows
And leaves hard-edged mechanical slots.
But the bolts which grip the ends of the girders
Have heads in the shape of stars.

They are blunt and ugly, it is true,
Plaqued clumsily against the blank,
But why could they not have made them square?

There is a tendency here that ought to be thwarted.

There is nothing like Lacrimae Christi which so meets with my spirit's flavor. Not even to Champagne or Château d'Yquem can I give myself without reservations: to effervesce with the one or to melt into vapor with the other still leaves my heart undissolved; there is still a hard core unawakened. But when I taste the harsh salt fire of Lacrimae Christi, wrung from the meager grapes of Vesuvius, all the fierceness of my soul leaps green; I relish its bitterness with zest. These were never the gentle tears of Christ— this sharp untempered vintage pressed raw from some deep corrosion, some bitter fury of years! They are the tart astringent tears of Maupassant, superb in his worldly pessimism and with his boy's heart broken at last by the worldliness of the world; they are the brutal tears of Swift that he never could bring himself to shed . . . Most of all, they are the tears of him who, walking the barren volcano, in mockery of human hopes, scorched with irony the poor ginestra that continued to grow on its side. They are tears that feed again, without assuaging, the passion that has provoked them, that fire higher the high kind of exhilaration which may be eventually distilled from bitterness.

Charley Walker, though his family were well enough off, had as a Hampshireman been treated rather parsimoniously. It used to be said of him at college, "Poor Charley, he's given such a small allowance." On his visits to New York, he always insisted on staying with us. If we told him there were no beds, he said he would sleep on the floor. One morning we found his socks in the breadbox.

Ted Paramore at Lexington Avenue: "I went to get something out of the breadbox and a hedgehog and two otters jumped out! One of them had been in there so long that he spoke Old French."

Our housekeeping was very sketchy. We had a woman come in to get us dinner, but although very good-natured, she took as little trouble as possible. Sometimes she came so late that we couldn't be sure of any dinner at all. This was embarrassing with Margaret Canby at the time when she had not yet broken off relations with Ted. Our housekeeper would dash in, open a can of tomato soup, cook a hamburger and open a can of peaches.

At the foot of Fifty-ninth Street, the gray-green of the Park beneath the dull lustrous pearl of the sky. (*Early May*.)

At the Charter Club [at Princeton], the morning light shone white through the luminous whites of the window curtains and behind that screen showed faintly the clear early green of May.

Late May [1922]. In the graying green the waves of iris showed faintly lavender and yellow.
The sky above the bulk of office buildings was high-piled with silver light, which left, as the silver dimmed, a canopy of dove-gray feathers.

Early June morning. Outdoors there was a blinding blaze of silver, in which the green tree-edges were melted, and the lawn was velvety with dew.

Uncle Win: "In the days of the races there used to be a line of victorias stretching all the way to Long Branch—all the statesmen, all the actresses, all the big gamblers! They used to come to Long Branch in the spring, and then, later on, they'd go to Saratoga. —I was one of the first people who ever fished in the surf—everybody thought I was nutty. —Why, the finest fish in the. world! kingfish! But for every kingfish I caught I used to catch five sallygrowers, sea robins or hammerheaded sharks. —It used to be quite an event, you know—all the children used to gather around me and hope I'd catch one of these creatures. Whenever I'd catch one, there'd be great rejoicing—they'd all cheer. —I used to be a member of the Perseverance Fire Company—we never put out any fires because the hose always broke—we could never get anything but old second-hand hose, and we usually had to train it up the hill from the millpond, so that the pressure always made it bust. Just about the time we got the nozzle up to the fire it would drop down to a little trickle and bust out all the way down the hill."

He is much against the Jews, who, he believes, are utterly dishonest in their dealings with Christians. He thinks that, if things keep on as they are doing now, we may see a revolt against them in America. —His explanation of Brandeis's appointment—he got Wilson out of some affair with a woman—Wilson "a bad actor"—Hoover a crook.

The Jersey coast. Swiss chalets bleached out like mussel shells, Italian villas with elephantiasis, turreted medieval castles like Maxfield Parrish worse debauched, giant mosques, English half-timbered manor houses swollen to a toneless hugeness, enormous stiff wooden pergolas standing bare and vineless on the treeless unfenced lawn, great pedestaled silver globes and crouching marble dogs and lions drowned in a flat sea of grass—infinitely dilapidated hotels with signs in Yiddish and English, exact concrete-sided lakes bordered by dusty motor roads, dreary gray board-walks, the infinitely desiccated bones of trees, flimsy cottages with bizarre ornaments and disconcerting excrescences ready to capsize like sand castles as a result of the lack of human care and the deadly breath of the sea, gigan-tic barn-like auditoriums dropped inappropriately in vacant lots, for which their bulk is much too great, extinct soda fountains boarded desolately through summer and winter alike. All this must once have been thought at-tractive, have possessed the charm and the movement of life—there must have been a spirit of holiday-making to have produced such monstrous bizarreries—but a blight has fallen upon it—the houses gape hideously at the road, ogling, winking and peering with the horror of the corpse of gaiety. They grin out at the dingy shreds of life which streak back and forth along the road. Here and there one finds an elegant house half smothered in a jungle of florid foliage and with the lawn high and weedy like a meadow, its waters scarcely furrowed by a path. The sea has no leeway here to spread its crests in ease and recede; it crouches, beetles and butts its forehead against the bulkheads that defend the land—though this is really, of course, the sea's fault for encroaching unceasingly on the land—perhaps it thinks the cot-tages, the hotels, the blinded and deserted shooting galleries only so much sterile debris that might better be chivied away and rhythmically pul-verized in the universal solvent of its waves.

The lawn was glittering with lightning bugs like liquid orange sparks flitting low above the grass to a quiet rhythm.

Swampscott [Mass.]. The surf was gemmed with little drops of bluey-green phosphorus which got caught in Louise's dark hair so that, when she came dripping out of the sea, she looked like a nereid. —Her black head on the water. —She capered in the cold surf with gawky rhythmic gestures. — She curled her toes in the sand as she talked, emphasizing what she said— her pleasant excitement at her daring and the stimulant of the cold winey water and her satisfaction in her young beauty.

Concord (early June). The tall-grown meadows glistening with a tinsel of fireflies; the plumy elms; the river of dark silver running between low green banks that merge into the waterside sedge—farther up, they are the unfenced lawns of houses; the precise square dark-blinded windows, the longer narrow windows crowned with low triangles; the rounded tops of doorways—of the doors of a barn; on Emerson's lawn, the pinky-white rhododendron flowers, like porcelain after the rain, behind the elegant

white palings; many rectangular windows very close together—liberal
Puritanism approximating a bay window; dragonflies with wings of black
velvet and peacock-blue bodies; the low dark-green verdure in flat strong
colors; Miss Alcott's house of dingy brown with mean tiny windows to
squint through at the world, but a close wooded slope rising behind it.

Boston. The doorways melt like music on the eye. Delicious silver-
knobbed doorways on Beacon Street—by Bulfinch—with wide fanlights
as clear as crystal and flanked by clear white-curtained panes; white doors
with Ionic columns; the exact and uniform swelling of prolonged red-brick
bow windows; the British-looking chimney pots; whole narrow high-
walled streets of the eighteenth century and wearing on their firm-laid
bricks the formidable dinginess of antiquity; the dowdily or drearily
dressed women—high-collared, in dismal light browns—their regular,
highly unsexual English features—one in lavender with lavender legs, following the mode of New York; the British block letters of the street signs;
crossing from Cambridge, the blue of water, the green esplanade, the red
row of house backs and the blue of sky again—all in colors that somehow
managed to be at once crude and old.

Walden Pond. A dark lake spike-fringed with dark trees.

Madison, Conn. Today the skies ran gray that drowned the green; aromatic clam broth; the wide low-shored coves lined with little boathouses;
green rushy sea-meadows invaded by smooth blue lakes; the houses somehow less compact than in Massachusetts, their colors less strong and clear,
wider surfaces with the windows and doors less emphasized—the whole
civilization looser and lighter.

Provincetown. The calm vista of the harbor eternally fluttered over by
gulls and bounded with its yellow rim of sand that seems to lock the town
in as a world of its own—the water all buff and blue and lavender and
green in the shallows when the tide is out and with yellow islands of sand
or palest blue and dullest sand on bleaker, less vivid days; the great un-
shadowable dunes like enormous snowdrifts or tinily crow's-footed by the
sprouting lips of moss, which in time puts forth little yellow flowers as if it
had sucked from the arid sand its last drop of vital pigment—whiffs of faint
balm from patches of bay—little white-bellied sandpipers gliding along as
if they were running on wheels—the great sea unfurrowed and bright blue,
frothing whitely over the bright yellow beach, which it chews and spits out
and chews again like a dog worrying a bird; [Eugene] O'Neill's house with
its wide square rooms decorated in the colors of the landscape—the light
but vivid yellows and blues of the sand and the sky and in the living room,
with its set of big plates each one pictured with a different kind of fish: droll

conventionalized flounders and butterfish—the mottled white and brown cat which had come in on the wreck of the barge that was smashed at their very door and which produced a snow-white kitten; the Portuguese of the town, dark, beady-eyed and squat-nosed; the houses close and thick along either side of the street, with their single row of windows looking out from under vast brooding roofs built sloping against the wind; enormous box-like buildings to store fish; a high square chocolate-colored house—as if the chocolate were moldy and melting—sounding a sudden and ungraceful note of ornate respectability with old dirty flowered window curtains and two dirty rusty old urns at the foot of the steps at the entrance—a white horse grazes on the unkempt weeds of the lawn: the house belonged to a miser, recently dead, who shut up the top floor and confined himself to the lower part—his sister used to be seen picking up driftwood on the shore; blue-silver sheets of water that lay like broken mirrors on the sand.

Uncle Winfield. The story about the nigger who called through the window of the jail to the other nigger to find out what time it was. "What do you care what time it is, nigger? You ain't fixin' to go no place!" —He always took soda-mint tablets after every meal in the country. —Oysters with or without pearls. —Old Dr. Wentworth at Exeter: "You come from down in New Jersey, don't you? Well, you better go back there. You better go back there. The winters up here are very cold; the snow is very deep! You better go back to New Jersey." The boys used to call him "Bull." Wentworth gruffly chewed his words. —In the winter, sitting in your room, you would hear the snow go "crunch, crunch, crunch" under the feet of the boys outside. Wentworth's son was fired from Harvard because, having inherited his father's mathematical brilliance, he invented a success-ful system for beating the roulette wheel in Boston. —"I don't know much about it, but I think *Vanity Fair*'s a kind of fly-by-night."

The artist sometimes begins by choosing characters too remote from him-self, which he is bound to view from the outside, and attempting to animate them: what he must do is find some type of protagonist into which he can effect a transfusion of his own emotions. It is a sort of sleight of hand; he must invent a ventriloquial figure which really speaks with his own voice. There is, of course, no such thing as real detachment. You cannot galvanize into life a being whom you really see objectively. The more kinds of char-acter a man has, the more kinds of characters he can create.

Pat Kearny's stories about spiritualism. The woman who failed to see through the trick even when the medium substituted for his hand his un-shaven cheek, because she thought that the electric pricking which she felt was only sure proof of his supernatural powers; the savant who reported to the French government that, as a result of his experiments, he had established that ghosts were warm, that their hearts beat, that they had a pulse in their wrist, that they breathed out carbon dioxide, that they had hair on their heads, etc. —His study of the psychoanalysis of magic and his projected article for the *Psychoanalytic Review*: he thought that the inspiration of conjuring tricks in the suppressed desires of the unconscious was glaringly apparent: for example, the trick in which the magician takes an empty box, fires a gun at it and a human being comes out—every fantasy has its source in the unconscious, so it is evident that there must be something sexual even about making coins disappear.

Boston to Truro. Past Middleboro, the suburbs of Boston change even their more rural aspects; sand takes the place of clay, and the face of nature changes with it: gray-stone fences; cows; lakes; wood yards; farms; scrub oak; pale-blue sky almost a pale gray; low forests of thin and scrawny pine; miles and miles of a low and arid verdure; here and there a sandy graveyard or a meager garden; the lakes growing smaller and more marshy; the train stopping at every town—of which there seemed an interminable line, some of them constituting veritable family groups of "Easts," "Norths" and "Wests"—till the journey seemed insuperably long, as if one were making one's way slowly and with difficulty into a foreign country; sea marshes tufted thickly with marsh grass; little low rootless houses strewn about the mapless downs that did not admit of being turned into villages or even netted in a cage of roads; the country tousled with scrub pine or broken out in a green rash of bay; desolate churches lodged like boxes on the highest eminences; the great hummocks of the dunes, scarred and bald; the pale green grass that draws its color from the pale gravelly sand; the sudden infinity of the gray level sea streaked with faint violet and green and scarcely fringed with white where it touches the shore.

Messages to Ted from his friends. "We will get into trouble somewhere"; "Hark, from the tomb there comes a mournful sound" (telegram to Yale Sheff. reunion); "You've got scamper-juice here!" (letter from his brother reporting what had been said by officer intervening in some Western riot).

Early June [New York]—5 a.m. The blue silhouettes of high buildings against the murky pink of the east, which changed to a pale smoky rose the even blue sky above; the trees in the Park growing green again, but the mysterious shadows of the night still lingering obscure and blue; the impression of the summer world not changing with the changes of day and night, but remaining warm, tranquil and familiar while a brief shadow merely falls upon it—it is so short a time from sun to sun—in summer the world is always sleeping gently, so that at night it does not need to fall into the deep dead slumber of winter or fall.

The rumorous hum of summer coming up through the open windows.

Among the familiar limited forms of history, fiction and thought and of the world about me as I have found it, I sometimes feel that the world is too small and its phenomena too petty and imperfect. "Human history is not good enough; humanity is not good enough; I am tired of the old repertoire; I know all their new plays beforehand; they will have a series of the same old settings and the same familiar cast of characters. I knock against the people, the geography, the events as if they were the bars of a cage. —Love especially is too little; it takes up too much of our time for such a simple and physical affair; it is appalling to think of the thought and energy expended on amorous adjustments. —I am impatient for the day when, controlling gravitation as he now controls electricity, mankind, harnessing the worlds, shall drive them around the heavens, master of the solar system and eventually of the whole universe. There will be no more books or works of art produced, because every man will be a sage and an artist. Such a man will understand everything and have no need of the records of science; and, as he flies, he will naturally and without agonizing his brain sing songs which will make the poetry of Dante and the music of Beethoven seem like the stammering of barbarians."

—Until man, having swallowed the present universe and expanded beyond it with his mind, shall have created another universe mighty enough to contain him.

—To stand on the perilous verge of time—smothering in the past, brought up against the blankness of the future—to confront the gray abyss which lies beyond the limits of the world—the little world, the nursery of an ignorant and mischievous childhood.

Bethlehem, Pa. The blast furnaces like giants at stool with their intestines wrapped around their bellies, voiding their bowels with a thunderous hissing and excreting a molten feces of gold burnt beyond gold to white ethereal yellow—shriveling the very autumn sunlight with its supreme incandescence. It seemed to be something which got light from the sun but something that outburned the sunlight, which showed through it as if through a confused white film. Cascades of intense thin sublimated gold pig iron, from which sparks burst like tiny rockets in the air—an explosive spray of fire. —Thick fly-wheels revolving through the floor, their rims almost reaching to the roof. Enormous engines pounding, throwing great pounding cylindrical rams back and forth, like phalluses in some gigantic copulation—or as if the machines were playing a game—each by itself—of batting this bolt back and forth, say, from hand to hand, trying to see how much momentum could be withstood before one of the guardian hands gave way. —In face of one of these machines, one feels abashed, immensely rebellious, a weakling in the presence of prodigious strength—like a small dog before a big dog.

The Follies: Feb. 28, 1923. The great loose-legged colt-like girl practicing kicking behind the backdrop—a man holding his hat for her to kick; Gilda Gray's small-town life-of-the-party tricks—her grimaces and clowning, her small-town idea of how a great actress should behave, clasping people's hands, "Bon soir," giving her hands to be kissed, her grand manner, her hardness, harshness, vivacity and push, her eagerness to go to England and dance for the king, her grimacing ecstasy over Will Rogers, "Oh, yes, he's clever!"; of Brandon Tynan imitating Belasco, her "That's a lot of crap!"; large ease and leisure with which the scenes seemed to be shifted, folded or unfolded from against the wall; men rushing electric apparatus in and out of the wings; little girls trooping in and out in different costumes—"Come in, dumbbell!"; little girl watching the show from the wings who raised her leg until it pointed straight up (like a clock at 12:30) and leaned, hugging it, against the scene, then brought it down and lifted the other, holding it meditatively as she watched; "Tomorrow? Eleven o'clock?"—"How long has this been going on?"; "Why, you ought to see Shean's dress suit! He's got it buttoned up clear to the throat. He don't need to wear a vest!—Why, sure! he thinks it's great. Don't let him hear you say that!—Why, sure, if he was invited to the Ritz Carlton, he'd go like that"; "Seven girls have asked about you—one girl said you could have her telephone number any time you wanted!"; fine-looking Negress wardrobe woman—reflecting that she can never be dazzling and admired like the white girls?; Mary Eaton, perfect type of American magazine-cover village belle, rubbing her feet in resin, strapping on her silk ballet shoes; the little gilded girl who has to take a shower every night [the gilt clogs the pores] and have the gilt painted on the next night; "She's a blockhead, a dumbbell—no personality, no beauty—can't act, can't sing, can't dance—stand 'em on their heads and they're all alike—*you* know!"; Gilda Gray: "Oh, you've come to make some more sketches, I suppose. —Well, you can't sketch 'em when they're leaping around like that!" (laughs derisively)—"I want to look before they leap."—"I don't think she got that—say, do they ever get anything?"; horrible skit of discordant family life—husband, wife and son in a continual raucous wrangle—I asked the old property man why they had taken off *Cuckoo Nell*—"It didn't go—no laughs in it"; military drill, setting-up exercises of grand climactic chorus marching downstairs and understage at the end of the first part; the Beauties, the Dancers, the Chickens; "Come along. Sing a song. Come along." —The green peacocks and gold garlands of the proscenium. —Hogan: "This is Miss Vigi—you ought to have her picture in the magazine—she's one of the coming dancers—she's got ability—she understudies Eaton, and when she went on for three nights, she knocked Eaton cold—knocked 'em cold. —Eaton won't let her wear the cap. —Who's that little girl over there? [Looking her up and down.] Nice-looking little girl. Got ability, too." —Much talk of a girl who had been played up lately; who was fucking her?

Ted Paramore. Sweetbreads smothered in aspirin tablets—veal cutlet with sauce Veronal. The crushed Técla pearls in the apartment.

Crowninshield: "In the days when we worked on the *Century*—with that prince of good fellows, that merry andrew—Robert Underwood Johnson—a perfect harlequin! Why, Bill and I worked in a morgue together—our work was laying out the corpses. There was Richard Watson Gilder, who was an invalid; William Brownell, who was suffering from indigence—and Robert Underwear Johnson—that was our little group." Nast: "I haven't got time for that, Frank." FC: "I have one silly suggestion to make." Nast (not turning around): "Silly suggestions are out of order." FC finally gets underway, with a guilty *empressement*, and explains that in his opinion the schedule ought to be moved up two or three days—illustrating his point by an elaborate metaphor about a man being invited to dinner for half an hour earlier than the dinner is actually to be—"Is the thing to do to stand over him while he is taking his bath—especially if it's a lady—or to—?", etc. Everybody laughs; he breaks up the seriousness of the meeting.

Marion Davies. Hearst's mistress, who wanted to be a movie actress. Hearst started the Cosmopolitan Film Co. to gratify her desire and was then obliged to put on a lot of good films to counterbalance the deficit for which Marion Davies was responsible. "You may be the world to Bill, dear—but you're only a bore to me." She is common, graceless and dull, with one stiff grimace to express every emotion.

Ted Paramore. A Yale Sheff. dance: the girl who passed out with her man on a couch—the dancers strewed them with the garlands and garnishments of the hall. Finally, the girl came to and, separating the boughs of her bower, looked through and said: "Anybody got any chewing gum?" Nobody had and she subsided. He went to sleep, drunk and naked, in a bed with a movie actress at a party—without amorous intercourse. In the morning, she rose up and, looking down at him where he lay sprawling naked on the bed, said: "You're a funny little person." Another girl said: "I thought he'd stopped comin' for it in the afternoon, but today I looked out the window and there he was! And that depressed me so that I went out to this party and got soused, and they had a fountain of pedigreed goldfish there and I said to Bill: 'Come on! I bet I can catch one before you do,' so we both dived in and all we got was a handful o' fins and we like to got drowned." . . .

Verna Tolley's "synthetic men."

Pittsburgh, March 11–12. The bald hilly scattered gritty city; the city proper concentrated and imprisoned at the point of its wedge, hemmed in and locked by its two muddy rivers, which unite at the top of the wedge to form a third muddy river; the sporadic suburbs—a city all of suburbs—breaking out here and there in the bald hills—flimsy shells of timber or massive mountains of stone—all dingy, all gritty, all branded from the root with ugliness—all, however, set apart, but rarely in long uncompromising strips like the Philadelphia suburbs—Scotch-Irish independence; enormous cottages of the architecture of the eighties, like warehouses, like institutions—one with dingy Ionic pillars and with a huge black gable carved with grapes and vine leaves; a boy in a sweater sitting working at schoolwork at an upper window, his legs hanging out toward a roof; deserted houses of gigantic bulk in which it seems incredible that anyone could ever have lived and which seem to lie so massively on the ground that they must have flattened out the hills with their weight; gulches and gullies, dingy cliffs lined with ignoble dwellings, like blackened barnacles left by a tide which has subsided and turned stagnant; a great many stained-glass windows, like the green and blue of oil in a muddy street or like the scum of stagnant water; the churches monuments of desolation; the Venice jazz café; the Carnegie Steel Works sending up nocturnal vapors of solid gold; the nerve-racking Westinghouse Electrical Company covering acres and bristling with machinery and lights; the Heinz factories in Allegheny; CRUICKSHANK APPLE BUTTER aloft on the bald hillside; the "inclines"; motor accidents; students fucking in the hallways of the Carnegie Tech; the unrivaled blackness of those buildings and of those of the Pitt School; the small hills razed and removed, leaving bare unsightly stumps; the subsidence and collapse of the Boulevard; the railroads at the bottoms of gulches; the idealized, semi-allegoric murals in the museum and the school; the hard round-headed black-eyed people; the jazz roadhouses where most of the parties went on; the cute Pittsburgh girl at the Venice; the turbid gray haze—a society smothered in smoke; an epic grimness and harshness—violence of life—people always breaking out when they did anything at all—throwing themselves over cliffs, going on disastrous joy rides, girls getting themselves with child with a sort of mechanical fierceness, terrific drinking, hard-hitting steely slang and voices, the Pittsburgh "wise-crack"; no pictures on the wall, no smartness, cinder piles for front lawns, trains and factories hooting to the hard hills—remote in the west, self-contained, cut off from culture and beauty, young people born in its hard gritty soil and beaten hard and gritty like it, striking out with a kind of persistence and intensity toward journalism, toward poetry, toward the stage—yet with a sort of blight on them forever.

Big parties at the William Penn Hotel where someone hires a suite of rooms and the guests wander from room to room in a drunken dream. Verna Tolley's *mésalliance* with the son of an eminent corporation lawyer; she deceives him during the war with a lieutenant, contracts gonorrhea, lives with the doctor who cures her, accuses the husband of giving it to her, airs all her grievances in the papers, is accused of having had intercourse with the whole regiment, is defeated, divorced and exiled from Pittsburgh by the husband's family, but manages to cover them with mud and retreats with apparent complacency—her father a small bank official, whom she speaks of as if he owned the bank—he regards her as a fine girl, a little too fond of a good time.

Little brick houses like jails; at the bottom of the smoke-smothered gully, factories spouting vapors of gold; dingy cliffs lined with flimsy dwellings like blackened barnacles left by the tide.

A skeleton in a taxi rides through town from Rutgers Place to Riverside Drive; finally he knocks at a door.

Verna Tolley [she was someone that Mary Blair knew, a trained nurse available for other purposes]. "We *must* get some clean towels. I'll get some at the Hotel Pennsylvania tonight." She told about May Collins, very tight, falling out of bed and then saying angrily, "Why did you push me out of bed?" She insisted upon steadying herself by keeping one foot on the floor. She used to get a good edge and then go around to see her elderly friend who so much admired her innocence. In his presence, she would drink nothing but buttermilk.

Ted Paramore's story: "At these parties they get absolutely soused, then they begin to get Ritzy and at the same time they keep falling off the chairs. You can't try to high-hat everybody and fall off chairs at the same time."

Ring Lardner, in his most alcoholic phase, insisted upon silence from the entire company and then told the following story: "Once there were two foxes in the bathtub together, Pat and Mike. They took turns sponging each other off. Finally, one said to the other. 'Here,' he said, 'here, you've been sponging off me long enough!'—so he kicked out the stopper. And, what do you think? the next morning they woke up in the same street." He told also about a woman who was a Lorna: "The thing about a Lorna is that they can't prune trees. That was how they found out that this woman was a

Lorna—they took her out by a tree and she couldn't prune it—and so they knew she was a Lorna."

Alvin Johnson. Someone said that he supposed all the outrageous perversions of the truth published in the provincial newspapers—"The *'Allies'* advance into the Ruhr"—really perhaps didn't make so much difference after all, because the provincials were completely indifferent about the whole business. Johnson said: "The only thing which has saved democracy is the indifference of the public to politics." The [William Z.] Foster trial in which he was indicted for criminal anarchy; the agent provocateur who had had to assume two pseudonyms—one to conceal his real identity from the Communists and one which the Communists made him take.

Ted Paramore. He went to the Fakirs' Ball at the Commodore as a "vulture"—that is, he went as a stag and spent the evening trying to pass out old men and steal their young mistresses. After the Playboy Ball, he said, he got into a sort of stable, with stalls—and each stall had a pass-out corpse in it—"it looked like Flanders Field." EW: "You spoiled my red tables with your cigarettes and your gin. Why, your gin ate circles into them, and once when you spilled some on a page of the *Daily News*, the pictures and print came off on the tabletop like a decalcomania."

At home in mid-April. The gentle dusk of spring softened more and more the soft colors of turned earth and young grass—to most mellowed and tender-toned buff and green, like the watercolors, delicate and worn, of some old engraving. The forsythia sprayed the dimness here and there with a yellow itself dim.

Playboy Ball, late April. John Amen brought a very pretty girl in vivid red, with black eyes and hair and vivid cheeks, whose bodice, apparently completely unsupported, revealed provocatively two small plump breasts; her feet and hands were tiny. She was a widow, having lived two weeks with a husband who had died in the war, and now had a little apartment in the Village and was a secretary at the Guaranty Trust. She was continually worrying about her sister-in-law, who was very young and having a baby. She would remember it every now and then and explain to somebody her anxiety or get John Amen to call up Long Island. Fitz [Scott Fitzgerald] blew up, as usual, early in the evening, and knocked Pat Kearny unconscious in the lavatory. Louise Bogan: "I feel ready to say 'Blaa!' to the whole world." "Another view of Webster Hall—from the outside . . . Milk wagons carrying the morning's milk for thousands of hungry little mouths . . . Remodeled dwellings—showing the new art element in the Village." The dance from *Liza*: silk-hatted coon advancing and retreating with quick-falling elegant patent-leather steps before yellow soubrette, who, standing still, received him in pantomime; surrendering, admiring, enjoying, rhythmically, in the same spot.

Washington Square, April [1923]. The April Square, after rain, freshened with tender green and swimming in milky pallors.

Ted Paramore. His story about the party at Irene's—elaborate ornaments, potted palms, a fountain, fluted Venetian cocktail glasses—somebody played Chopin—the actor from *Nice People,* who tried to read the poem about the lady at the harpsichord and was interrupted by the peevish barking of Irene's Pekinese—she would try to shut him up, but when the noise began again, he would begin to yelp again. Finally the actor twisted up the poem and threw it at him with great ferocity and shouted: "Shut up!—you—bastard!" After this, everybody relaxed and became vulgar, and the evening was a great success. Ted on Leon Walker: "You couldn't have him in the room with a girl fifteen minutes but you'd find a condom behind the clock. The girl who vowed that he'd never get away with any of that stuff with her—when Leon met her, he immediately stunned her with some remark that was almost a rape in itself and then began smelling her—smelling her neck—'Oh, it was just terrible, you know'—and she fell for him like a ripe fruit, brutally clubbed from a bough." He always stayed at the Yale Club till after the last big football game and then went back to San Francisco (or Santa Barbara) to stay till the next September. The Yale Club was always trying to throw him out; the room was always swimming in gin and garlanded with condoms. He and Ted used to lie in the two beds with the cocktail shaker and a forest of tumblers on the night table between them and explain over the telephone to Mrs. Walker (staying at the Ritz) that Leon's hoarseness was due to a cold—but Ted would take good care of him. His Walker's mixture of the bully and the well-bred. Creelman's story about Leon Walker: "I just give her a push and she swings for half an hour." "Oh, it was terrible—it was like two drunken satyrs on a straw pile."

Peggy Lewis told Mary that, when she was little, her mother used to shut her up in the back room when company came. When she was killed, they had to dispose of all the nice lingerie that her gambler had given her and which she had been saving till she should meet somebody she really liked. She became a little morbid about the gambler, from whom she received $50 a week, and always thought that everybody knew about it and were sneering—"This rose is off your mother's wedding dress, Verna."

[Verna Tolley and Peggy Lewis were both killed by a train while driving in a car on Long Island. They were slipping down in the world. One of them had surprised me by saying that many trained nurses were practically prostitutes.]

Rumson, mid-May. As I explored the weedy paths of a tumble-down, overgrown estate, two wild geese rose hoarsely from the marsh and went honking away.

Red Bank to Princeton, May. The lovely countryside washed in light watercolors of gray and green—the forests, the orchards and the fields clouded with white and pink.

Uncle Win, picking pansies: "Y'know, if y'look at those long enough, they'll talk to you."

The luster of the ice-water pitcher at Red Bank was dulled with a silver nebula.

Mother, when I told her that Mary was afraid of frogs: "Why, what could they do, poor things?"

Brookhaven, early June [I spent a summer there after I was married to Mary Blair]. The red translucent sunset showed through the black filigree of boughs like the stained glass of the Sainte-Chapelle.

Our back yard there turned out to be a place of rendezvous for turtles. The thicker tail of the male is his penis. He puts it into the female, who is standing in her normal position, and tilts back, leaning at an angle of forty-five degrees. He remains so, *les yeux pâmés*, for a very long time.

John Amen's pigeon, which fell from the roof of J. P. Morgan and Son and was gawped at, as it fluttered about, bruised, by an enormous crowd—to whom apparently any sight of the kind, however trivial, was a welcome relief from their work. JA: "I suppose I'll be like that in time."

John Amen told about party at Delmonico's—to which he took girl he didn't know very well—she disappeared almost immediately on arriving at the party. He never found out whose party it was—he kept asking people but no one seemed to know. It was a regular orgy—like a Roman banquet or something. Everybody was stewed very early in the evening, and the extraordinary thing was the way in which it kept right on going—it carried right through, it never stopped. There was a room surrounded with sort of couches on which couples were lying around limply—and about one o'clock a man came around with Bromo Seltzer and Veronal. There was sort of an unseen agency managing the whole thing, so that it would never be allowed to flag. An old man tripped near the top of a long flight of stairs and fell all the way down and got a terrible cut in the back of the head—but a couple of men rushed out and picked him up and a doctor appeared, and they took five stitches in his head and in about ten minutes he was back on the floor with this cocoon-thing on the back of his neck dancing and as good as ever. People just tottered in from the ballroom and fell on the couches. Two or three dinners were served during the evening which nobody could eat—wonderful dinners, you know: chicken-salad and anchovy sandwiches and things. And the orchestra was stewed: a trombone and a drum would go off in one corner, you know, and a horn and a saxophone in another; you'd hear this terrible braying all out of tune—and people kept on dancing to it. And when you went out to get a little air, the elevator boy would say, "Gee, some party—long time since I've seen anything like this!" Mary told about a dinner at Delmonico's to which Verna and Peggy had gone and at which Peggy had got drunk and sick and Verna had put her in the elevator, thinking it was a little rest room, so that poor Peggy spent half an hour or so going up and down in the elevator.

June. The Chinese white of daisies.

Evelyn Law throws her long loose legs about like a colt romping in a field. No high pressure can make her less amiable or less superb in her careless ease.

Alvin Johnson: "Norman Hapgood knows a lot about magazines in the same way that it was said of a certain woman that she knew a lot about children, because she'd buried six." Ford and Bryan were successful because they had exactly the same ideas as the ordinary man—Ford was widely admired because he did and said just exactly what the ordinary man would do if he were rich—you could raise just as many chickens as you pleased but you couldn't have a pheasant or a heron. He wanted to have Ford president, because it would be such an amusing spectacle.

One nurse girl boasted to the other that, where she worked, they had pink ice cream and, when they ate it, the master of the house turned on a pink light.

Bellport, mid-August [near Brookhaven, where Mary and I spent the summer]. The wide drying light of declining summer blown about the dry white sand and along the level beach, where the sea was scrolling lightly on the shore—when all had fallen into shadow, one threw one's gaze along the far smooth stretch and saw a tract of light again, where the sand lay bright and dry and the sea all silver-zinc on the dark first coat of blue. One's bare legs and arms were stung by the tiny blown grains of sand.

Patchogue, mid-August. From the water, low, eel-grass grown, and paved with oyster shells, till one reached a bottom of soft muddy sand, one saw the thin-walled summer buildings, the yellow-brown hotel with its square green-blinded windows and its plumy trees in front, painted white around the base, under which people sat on benches, flashing an occasional red or yellow; the little bathing pavilion that sold sarsaparilla and bright pink strawberry soda, with a white pennant that said "Bathing" flying briskly from the top; low white bungalows and a white hotel, all simple and rather early American, with their square windows in regular rows and their appearance of well-proportioned boxes; the slender pines, the tiny sailboats, the toy-like holiday character of the Bay.

Lynbrook. [For some reason, I had the job of getting their belongings from the coroner after Peggy and Verna were killed.] A paper in the coroner's safe at the Lynbrook Police Court, containing a handful of hairpins and a dilapidated velvet handbag, broken lipsticks and boxes of rouge, a powder puff or two, cigarettes, a bottle opener, a couple of gold chain bracelets, a pearl heart on a little string, a narrow bent gold band, a penny and a dime, a pair of cheap purple cufflinks and an envelope containing the cards of a dozen or more salesmen, contractors, cloak and suit manufacturers and newspaper reporters.

[EW had married Mary Blair, a leading actress with the Provincetown Players. She had been married before, to Charles Meredith, a fellow graduate of the drama school at the Carnegie Institute of Technology in Pittsburgh, but they were divorced. She joined the Provincetown Players in 1920, played the lead in *Diff'rent* and became known as "the O'Neill actress" for her performances in his plays during the twenties: *Diff'rent* (1920, 1924–25), *The Hairy Ape* (1922), *All God's Chillun Got Wings* (1924), *Marco Millions* (1928) and the one-act *Before Breakfast* (1929). *All God's Chillun* (1924) won her considerable attention when, playing the wife of Negro actor Paul Robeson, she would nightly kiss his hand on stage. The play was staged against strong opposition (including threats from the Ku Klux Klan) and O'Neill always remained grateful to Mary Blair for enduring the publicity. This incident (plus a feeling of guilt that she was not given the Broadway lead in *Diff'rent*) influenced his casting, and he gave her parts in later plays even when they were not especially suited to her. She is described as "a thin-faced girl with an intense quality about her." She was small and slim, with auburn hair and dark brown eyes. Of an Irish family, she had grown up in Pittsburgh and was raised as a Swedenborgian. She also took the lead in EW's *The Crime in the Whistler Room* (1924). EW and Mary were divorced in 1929. She retired from the theater in 1933 and died at fifty-two, after a long illness, in Pittsburgh, on September 18, 1947.]

Brooklyn. [Mary and I went to live in the Links' apartment—probably late in August (1923)—in order to be near the hospital. Rosalind was born September 19.] Blank maroon walls; an eternal quiet broken only by shrill-voiced children; an old dead white horse on Washington Street which nobody seemed to be paying any attention to; sodden drunks sprawling out into the street with their heads on dark stone doorsteps; the warm sickening fumes of chocolate from a dingy confectionery factory; Reduction Sale, low dirty Romanesque post office, elegant drugstore with lots of stained glass, a large heavy brick building with high windows cuirassed with iron grill.

The more pretentious buildings at one period—the large houses and the hotels—had a fad of ornamenting their brickwork with great armor plates of some riveted green metal—which, however, has corroded with time till it looks like the rusted sheeting of some old roof. The wooden houses and hotels still reminiscent of the frame buildings of small cities which were smart fifty years ago; sailors—sailors with blowzy coarse stupid girls; all the air of a small provincial city; Montague Street, Pineapple, Cranberry Streets; great cindered open fields near the freight yards where the children seem breeding like cats; Plymouth Church and the old respectable houses; the incessant electric pianos running all day and every day—movie music—and the voices singing to them as monotonous and mechanical as they.

Delmonico's, August 1923. "For Rent, Bertram L. Kraus"; the distinguished toned-yellow building, with its columned and ornamented windows and its dulled green rows of lamps growing like buds from the low restrained stone balcony and from the low stone railing at the top—rather like an old French palace. No name, no electric sign, the last stronghold of the old Fifth Avenue. Alec McKaig told me that his aunt from Pittsburgh always used to insist upon eating there; she seemed to have a blind inherited faith in its reliability: if you ate there, you were always safe.

Party at the Seltzers' for D. H. Lawrence. Terrific argument between John Macy and Lawrence about extent to which reviewers were prostitutes. Lawrence thinks critics influential and should realize their responsibility; F. P. Adams thinks so too; Macy tries to high-hat Adams any time he puts in a word; finally tells him he's *hors de combat* because—; "Oh, I am, am I? What do you mean by it? Didn't you hear what Lawrence has just been saying.—You old prostitute, you!" (all quite calmly, smoothly and effortlessly, thinking with great rapidity and speaking with perfect ease); Macy ridicules lunch at the *Nation*—"But have you ever been to lunch at the *New Republic*? Oh, my God!—"; Lovett and Bob Littell right there; I do everything possible to make matters worse; someone says FPA runs a column and oldish gay-fangled lady says she supposes he's very witty—he nods solemnly—"He's not so witty as his contributors, though, are you?" someone else says—Adams nods solemnly again.

[I found Lawrence's appearance disconcerting. He was lean, but his head was disproportionately small. One saw that he belonged to an inferior caste—some bred-down unripening race of the collieries. Against this inferiority—fundamental and physical—he must have had to fight all his life: his passionate spirit had made up for it by exaggerated self-assertion. (I have never seen this physical aspect of Lawrence mentioned.) On this occasion, he suddenly became hysterical and burst out in childish rudeness and in a high-pitched screaming voice with something like: "I'm not enjoying this! Why are we sitting here having tea? I don't want your tea! I don't want to be doing this!" The Seltzers, rather stodgy in their bourgeois apartment, sat through it and made no reply, and nobody else took any notice of it. Mrs. Lawrence—whom I have more or less described as Mrs. Grosbeake in *I Thought of Daisy*—also sat silent, her feet in rather large shoes or sandals, one beside the other and flat on the floor, as if she were the anchor that held him down, the Mother *Erde* on whom he depended. The furious fit soon passed, and he presently came over and began to talk to me in a conventional British way. I don't remember what he said except to ask me a question or two about myself. I had earlier been rather antagonized by his denunciation of Dante as a writer who had tried to intellectualize love.]

The Cooperative Masons and Stone Renovators; Black, Starr and Frost [Elinor Wylie and I thought this name quite poetic].

Old Franklin Sargent of the Sargent Dramatic School shot himself in a Plattsburgh Hotel. He made his will, leaving everything to his housekeeper, engaged a room, bought a large piece of oilcloth, stretched the oilcloth on the floor, bound two bath towels around his head and took off the telephone receiver, so that when the call was answered, nothing was heard but the shot, and when they arrived in the room they found Sargent lying dead on the oilcloth and on the table a note asking them to notify his office, of which the address was carefully given.

I always try to put the most charitable construction on all my sins. —You may find me indifferent and grudging in my work for other people, but just try me with some enterprise for my own gratification or advancement and see how eagerly and wholeheartedly I will cooperate. —I sometimes walk about the room composing favorable reviews of my books.

Their arms pressing against each other and then shunning each other, leaning together and then away—the human beings, beneath the critical polite good-humored conversation, trying each other, hugging each other, starting back, frightened.

Mary: "I had fancy dreams last night."

Vaudeville. "I know I'm in love: I feel terrible."—"A little song entitled *Over There Where Europe Used to Be.*"

Early October. Dahlias lemon and rusty red in the autumn dusk. —For an instant, as I drove through Red Bank, I couldn't remember whether it was autumn or spring.

Roy Gamble [of my Detroit army unit]. On the Eastlake period of architecture. "This jigsaw architecture—when they just discovered they could cut out fancy patterns—steamboat gothic."—Anecdote about Henry Ford getting smuggled into his factory in a basket, so that he could spy on his employees.

Baseball at Newark. One man reached up in a single gesture and stopped a ball with a sure unyielding hand—then they began pounding it around the diamond.

Washington Square, October. The shadows of the defoliated trees in the park were like clouds, in the late afternoon, drifting across the soft rose fronts of the houses on the north side.

Tom Smith at the Giffords', etc. "I bet Clem knocked Belle higher'n a kite before he married her."—"Are you Jewish, Otto?"—"No: I'm not but Horace is." [Horace was his brother.] Belle said that Anderson had come to her just at a time when Clem wanted her to have six children and had just bought a lot of new clothes and gone to New York and left her with a baby in a new apartment. Clem accused her of having learned passages from Ellen Key, which she quoted to him when he came back. He said he never wanted her to have six children—"Alice was an accident."—"Yes; it was just when I was having Alice that you passed that remark!"

The Miracle. I asked Pennington if it had many scenes—"No," he said. "It all takes place in the nave or something of a cathedral—it'll all take place in the storehouse soon. —Part of it's being built in a sheep pen over in Jersey—the sheep all stand around and go Blaa—Blaa!" Kommer said that he was rehearsing it in four different places and spent a large part of every day getting from one to the other in a taxi through inextricable obstructions of traffic.

"Well, Jo spiltuz bugs all over town, no wonder he hasn't got any left for me." She was childless.

Trip to California, February 1924

[EW's note: "Gilbert Seldes, whom I had met at John Bishop's and whose writings I had read at college in the Harvard literary magazine, got me a job, when I was very hard up, as press agent for the Swedish Ballet, which was visiting the United States. I had the idea that it might be possible to induce Charlie Chaplin to perform in one of its pantomime ballets, and I convinced the impresario, Rolf de Maré, of the feasibility of this. He paid my expenses for a trip to California to try to persuade Chaplin."

EW in this note omits the important fact that the ballet in question was his own: he had written, he told John Bishop, "a great super-ballet of New York" and the Swedes had shown an interest in it. Edmund recognized that the pantomimic virtuosity of Chaplin was just the sort of art that could blend with the Swedish Ballet—a recognition of capabilities Chaplin would not reveal until the remarkable dance sequence in his later *Modern Times*. We know what kind of ballet Wilson projected, for he told John Peale Bishop it would have "a section of movie film in the middle, for which Ornstein is composing the music and in which we hope to get Chaplin to act. It is positively the most titanic thing of the kind ever projected and will make the productions of Milhaud and Cocteau sound like folk-song recitals. It is written for Chaplin, a Negro comedian, and seventeen other characters, full orchestra, movie machine, typewriters, radio, phonograph, riveter, electromagnet, alarm clocks, telephone bells and jazz band."

Toward the end of 1923 EW had moved with his actress wife and his baby daughter to No. 1 University Place. He was at this time much interested in symbolism, and actively corresponding with Christian Gauss—*Axel's Castle* was on the horizon, though it would take two or three more years before the book would shape itself in his mind. Reading Wallace Stevens's *Harmonium* at this time, EW praised him as "a very distinguished poet in a fairly small way." In America, he added, "people like Stevens, or Dos Passos, in his book of poems, produce a mixture of the symbolist and metaphysical with the objective and hard."]

Beyond Harrisburg. One saw, from the lower-berth window, the great dim blind buildings and the houses with shuttered eyes, then billboards with gaudy ads close against the windows, then lonely street lamps in streets of scattered houses, nothing but the telegraph poles telling off their lengths of

wire, and then the enormous gray ashy night, where the stars were powdered like cinders.

Morning: the flat fields faintly brown dusted with frost like ashes—in
Ohio, the gray day on the flat and empty fields, where the fraying smoke
column of the train hung always before one's sight, obscuring the sparse
thin tufts of trees, the horses grazing the barren meadows and the muddy
cows in dead cornfields trampling the prostrate stalks—the pigs lost like rats
in the vastness.

The Missouri at Omaha with its mud shallows oyster-shell-iced and
beyond it the wilderness of railroad yards.

A small town in Nebraska, with the vacant vast fields about it: some houses,
a corner with a white wooden fence and a row of high elms—I thought,
"Someone has passed that corn too many times."

The little girl named Maxine from Milwaukee. She was eight years old.
Her mother and aunt put her on the train at Chicago and told the porter to
look after her. "I've got a life-size picture of you startin' out in this train in
three weeks' time from now," said the aunt to the mother. When they had
gone and the train had started, the little girl cried a little. After that, she read
Photoplay and went through the different things to eat they had given her,
sampling each one separately: Zu-Zu gingersnaps, olives, cheese sandwiches, apples and oranges, chocolate cherries and chocolate bars. When
the porter put her lower berth down, she was afraid it was going to fall on
her and hid her face in her hands. The next morning, she cried bitterly for
her mother; she said that her mother had made her her little kimono, which
she put on at night, and also the clothes for her big doll. At night she would
be frightened and homesick and cry again; and she would put off the getting into bed as long as possible, playing wildly about the aisles, hiding behind the curtains and making trips to the ladies' room—laughing almost
hysterically at her own jokes. —I am afraid she is going to grow up into a
mealy-faced, mole-specked, hard-r'd, pale-green-eyed Middle Western
girl, who says "This here" and explains gabblingly to the Milwaukians
about the swimming parties they have in Los Angeles. —She followed
Barney Google. She said, in the dining car, that her mother could make
corn bread like that—she was a good cook, mother—she used to cook in
Thompson's restaurant in Chicago. Her father, she said, was traveling.

Just out of Salt Lake City, the long silver bar in the sky reflecting itself in
the winter mist below, so that the dark mountains with their fine snow
thatching showed like phantoms traced delicately, exquisitely, in the reality of the silver light—as if a great silver tube had been held up and were
reflecting something from the other horizon. In the enormous barren
arena, the patch of cultivation of a farm, poplar-plated and laid out in great

rectangles—high open hay barns, cows in a muddy byre, where the water has settled in a fresh pool at the lower end, and beyond the fences, the dark rough-coated horses grazing the dead tufts and the snow. —Blinding silver over the bare rock-crest, cut like a blade on the sky—a crevice between the crest, etc., and the dull gray cloud-roof pulled like a drumhead across the heavens. —"Where rolls the Oregon and hears no sound save its own roaring." [This is misquoted: it should be: "save his own dashings"; but *roaring* seems to me actually better.] Rare black-chimneyed mills or plants, with their family of little wooden workmen's houses, in the arena. —Sheep and haymows on the snow. —A deserted farm with gray paintless buildings bleaching in the waste—only an old piece of farm machinery sprawling broken, frozen in the ground—a flock of small quick-flying birds flickering past it in the cold.

California: Pale pink hills under the cloudless pale blue sky—bisque green—scrub-studded soil and black silver-filamented mountains—a silver-filamented stream—the metallic dark green orange-orbed orange groves—the dry fragrance from the warm eternal noon soaking into the closed train—the sunny mission-style stations. One felt unexpected elation at first entering this country in March.

[On the train I read Sophocles' *Electra* in Greek. Since it went rather slowly, I felt a certain nervous suspense as the killings were being led up to. A somewhat morbid state of mind had already been induced by my following simultaneously the story of some gruesome murders which had taken place in California: a homosexual boy had been preying on other boys who, one by one, had come to work for him and his mother; when they were done with a boy, they murdered him in order to prevent him from talking. They buried them on their ranch. This case has associated itself in my mind with the satire by Anita Loos called *The Better Things of Life*, which first appeared serially in a magazine. It was supposed to be the narrative by a public-relations man in Southern California of his more or less successful efforts to disguise a series of ghastly local murders. Undeterred by the finding of dismembered bodies, he made a great demonstration on behalf of the attractions of Hollywood: the sunlight, the wholesome atmosphere, the optimistic exhilaration. It was only years later that Anita Loos brought herself to publish a version of this work. But her later *Better Things* was adapted to a later if somewhat different period and was very much less cynical than the first one, which would perhaps have made a scandal for Hollywood, of whose spirit it was, however, quite typical.

I stayed with the Paramores in Santa Barbara, and Ted arranged to have me see Chaplin. We found him on the set where he was making *The Gold Rush*. He was wearing the make-up of his character and, while he talked to us, stood quietly swinging his cane. I had met him already at *Vanity Fair*, when he came to have a photograph made, and he had shown me how to perform the trick of pulling his derby down on his head and having it pop up into the air—which I have had little chance to exploit since it requires the stiff and narrow brim of a derby. Though he liked to resort to such occasional tricks, he had none of the tiresome exhibitionism peculiar to professional clowns. He was good-mannered and perfectly natural. Retaining his independence, refusing to be put under management, he had established himself in a place where he accepted as colleagues and equals only Douglas Fairbanks and Mary Pickford—and even they, he once confided, Ted told me, "were Babbitts." Once when we were walking on the street, he was accosted by an unknown boy who was hoping that Chaplin would help him find a job. He stopped and questioned this boy in a kindly way, then passed on.

He came to see us in Ted's Hollywood bungalow, laughed appreciatively at my ballet—later published as *Cronkhite's Clocks*—but explained that he always had to do everything himself, invent and play his own character. Not long after, he made *Modern Times*, which dealt with a somewhat similar subject of a nerve-racked victim of "rationalized" industrialism. I doubt whether it was suggested by *Cronkhite's Clocks*; but if it was, he was welcome to whatever it was worth. The scene of automatic feeding provoked the accumulative unrestrainable hilarity—carried on beyond the point where one would think it could not be taken further—of which Chaplin (like Dickens: the trial scene in *Pickwick*) displayed a peculiar mastery. He never really left behind the old gags of the music hall but he animated them with new genius. The scene in *The Gold Rush* in which a bear is following him along a mountain pass but disappears whenever he looks around has been doing duty for years in English Christmas pantomimes—the last time I saw it in London, a space man had been substituted for the older menace— yet Chaplin made it funny, with an undertone of imminent danger. Even so late as *Limelight*, his story is simply the old hackneyed one of the clown with a breaking heart; but Chaplin did something with it that had never been done before: the music-hall song—he is playing and parodying a music-hall performer—which consists of the simple repetition of the word *love*; the scene with Buster Keaton in which the sheets of music are continually, as if impelled by a devil, slipping off the piano and having to be replaced. I have always felt in connection with Chaplin that the people who used to arouse ridicule by treating him as a serious artist were not very far wrong. When one talked to him, one found that his instant reactions were as fresh, as authentically personal, as those of a poet like E. E. Cummings. When I mentioned Santa Barbara to him, he did not show any enthusiasm but simply said that anywhere with mountains always had on him an oppressive effect.

The inequalities of his personality were embodied in those of his face, the
upper part of which was imaginative and full of intelligence whereas the
lower part was square-jawed and coarse. I do not think he ever recognized
the music-hall vulgarity of many of his characters and settings.]

[During his stay with the Paramores in California EW was fascinated by
the stories and mimicry of his friend Ted's father, E. E. Paramore. Four
years later he wrote a long obituary piece about him titled "Mr. Ed" in *The
New Republic* (LV, June 25, 1928, 251–54), which he incorporated in his
notebooks as relevant to this period. The article had never been reprinted
by EW, and is given here in the form in which it was prepared for inclu-
sion.]

"Mr. Ed," Mr. E. E. Paramore, who died in California on the twenty-
fifth of May [1928], was a personality of singular interest and charm. The
son of a Western millionaire, who had been commander of an Ohio regiment during the Civil War and who afterwards built and controlled the so-
called Cotton Belt railroad between Texas and St. Louis, he had been born
to a position of influence and means in the West of the post-war period.
And in the interests of business and pleasure, he had ranged widely and lived
much. At one time, he had organized and been president of the Portland
Cement Company in St. Louis; later on, he had had a canal company and
some rice mills in Louisiana; still later, he had cleared and developed the
land of the Red River region of Arkansas; and at the time of his death, he
was the owner of a large ranch in California. I have learned since Mr.
Paramore's death that he was an excellent businessman and successful in all
three undertakings; but during his lifetime, I never heard him speak of them
except as delightful and romantic adventures. The only thing which seemed
to have bored him a little was the Portland Cement Company, from which
he had finally resigned at the height of its prosperity, because it kept him in
the city during the summer. But otherwise one always had the impression
that his business enterprises had been a species of sport. Certainly he devoted
as much time and attention to yachting, his favorite sport, as to any of them:
his great passion was really for ships; he had sailed in all the waters of the
world; besides a river pilot's license, he had ocean captain's papers, and had
once taken the square-rigger *White Heather* from Southampton to New
York.

This wide travel and varied experience had given Mr. Paramore, as an
American, in respect to North America, something of that quality of citizen
of the world which we admire in Europeans who have seen a good deal of
Europe. (Santayana, in *Persons and Places*, says of a friend of his that "he had
a kind of cosmopolitan competence or normality that I seem to have noticed
in the best people of the American West. They moved swimmingly in the

midst of all the current conventions and noises, but they seemed to make
light of them, as your good Bostonian never could. They were not 'taken
in' by the tastes, opinions, and pleasures that they played with as in a carni-
val.") I mean that Mr. Ed was internationally-minded—something singularly rare in Americans—in regard to the United States. His relation to the
West in particular can only be described as masterly. He had been everywhere and knew how to live everywhere and how to deal with everybody.
Nor was it merely that he had had the advantage of seeing more of the
world than most people: he had been able, by imagination, to seize and hold
all that he had seen. Mr. Paramore presented, in some respects, the appearance of a type which one often finds in the cities of the Southwest, where
living is good: he had the red face and the Humpty-Dumpty shape which
we encounter, for example, so often in the Epicurean *table d'hôtes* of New
Orleans. But his appearance was in no way commonplace: it had, indeed,
that kind of oddity—it scarcely strikes one as being odd—which we sometimes find in remarkable people. His mouth was very small, and his face was
not mobile; it was almost as little capable of expression as a firmly blown-up
football; but his eyes, which were close together and a bright clear hazel-
green, like new marbles, were alight with a strange leaping and gleaming
lapidary intensity of life;his hands and feet were very small. One felt that
the singularity of his appearance was the sign of a deeper originality.

   One soon became aware of his special fineness of character and his personal point of view. "Mr. Ed" was a famous raconteur—by far the best I
have ever heard. He had the most extraordinary gift of mimicking the way
people talked and could, apparently, reproduce the local accents and dia-
lects of every part of the United States: his sarcastic New England sea cap-
tains were as faithful as his Arkansas yokels or his Louisiana niggers. He
relished, in fact, so lovingly the rich cadences of human speech that in
moments of gaiety or well-being, he could often be heard declaiming to
himself the peroration of a Baptist sermon or the big speech of a backwoods
actor, as other people whistle or begin reciting verse. I have two or three
times heard him echo the old melodrama *Davy Crockett*: "I've looked into
them eyes and I've seen thar what I never seed in the eyes of a living woman
before, and I'd lay my life down this minute—I would—as I'm a man—but
if you want to know what's on that little slip of paper, miss, you'll have to
ask a larnder man (with emotion) *than pore Davy Crockett*, for I'm a back-
woodsman—and I cannot read." (His family tried to get him to make
phonograph records of some of his stories, but the phonograph made him
self-conscious, and the records came out badly.) Yet this was not what was
most remarkable about his stories: they were not ordinary funny stories at
all: one almost never heard him tell an ordinary joke, and then only, as it
were, to make himself agreeable when such stories were going round. Nor

did his stories depend for their effect on fantasy or exaggeration. They seemed all simply to be accounts of incidents in which he had taken part or descriptions of people he had known. Nor did it ever seem to me that he was trying to improve, as many storytellers do, on the thing as it had actually occurred. His dramatic gift was so sure that one responded at once to these stories, and it was some time after I first met him before I began to ask myself why these incidents and people had struck him, why he had remembered them so many years and told about them so many times. And then I understood that, in every case, it had been some special trait of character which had interested him and which he had isolated and thrown into relief in such a way that it acquired a kind of beauty. Other than this, his best stories often had no point. It was merely the stoicism of the sea captain and his scorn for the ignorant "super-cargo"; it was the benighted squalor of the Arkansas household, where he and an old woman had sat up all night, alternately spitting tobacco juice into an unprotected fire which might otherwise have burnt up the house, it was the naïveté of the Negro, the childlike character of even his violence. He had one very long account of a Negro servant he had had during the days of the canal company in Louisiana: the man had killed another Negro, while Mr. Paramore was away, and had written him letters from jail—letters which began "Kind Captain"; when he came back, he found the Negro patiently and apparently resignedly waiting to be hanged, but Mr. Ed got him out and took him back into his service. He seemed profoundly to understand the Southern Negro of that time; I know of nothing to compare with his stories except Mark Twain's portrait of Jim in *Huckleberry Finn*. I remember especially a dialogue between a Negro and his master on a Louisiana plantation:

"Mista Charlie, I hear—I hear the niggers is free, is that right?"

"Yes: that's right, Gadson."

"Then I'se free, too, ain't I, Mista Charlie? I hear a nigger is free as soon as he's twenny-one. I'm twenny-one this week."

"That's right, Gadson, you're free now."

"Then, Mista Charlie, you got to pay me wages, don't you?"

"All right, Gadson: I'll pay you five dollars a month."

"Thank you, Mista Charlie, thank you."

"But remember you'll have to pay for your own clothes and buy your own tobacco and 'tootsie.'"

"Is that right, Mista Charlie, do I got to do that?"

"Certainly, if you want to be free you got to pay for it."

(Pause) "Mista Charlie—I guess I won't be twenny-one till next year."

But then, he seemed to have felt and caught the nature of everything he had heard and seen. Once I happened to come into a room and find him performing old-fashioned ballet steps for a little girl who had just come with her mother to call: Mr. Ed and the little girl had got off into the room by themselves and had been having a marvelous time—until other members of the family, arriving, were obliged to restrain Mr. Ed, who had lately been suffering from attacks resembling angina pectoris and was not supposed to exert himself. What astonished me most, however, was the fact that, in reproducing the old ballet routine, which he appeared to remember with accuracy, he had made me seem to see for a moment precisely the kind of thing that people had once admired in ballet dancing.

There was a remarkable variety in his stories—the mood was sometimes one of deliberately casual pathos; sometimes of joyous cynicism; sometimes of a sad and generous humor. There were elaborate practical jokes, as when some friends of his and himself had dressed up a tramp who spoke broken English and introduced him on board their yacht as a foreign nobleman. There was the man he had known at Yale who had picked out a spot on the Columbia River and announced that he was going to make his home there: when people objected that it was wild and lonely, he had replied, "But then think how far it is from Boston!"; and then when he had got out of college, he had actually gone there as a civil engineer and done valuable work in opening up the country. When it was suggested to him that he ought to name after himself at least one of the roads he had built, he had merely erected a stone which read: "This trail was built by Mike Murphy and George Biddle"; and the man had a house near the very spot which he had picked out when he was in college, and he was happy there all his life. But some of his stories were more complex. One of the best was about Henry Van Blarcom and Sam Bray in St. Louis. Henry was president of a bank and made money, and Sam was a waster and lived on him, but they were fond of one another and both understood the relationship without ever thinking of money, work or anything but their friendship. When Henry died, he had lost most of his money, but he left $5,000 to Sam—virtually all he had. While the $5,000 was still intact, Sam went down to the bank and asked the cashier for one of the $100 bank notes signed by Henry. He framed the note and hung it in his room and lived modestly for two years on the rest of the $5,000. He was too proud to borrow money, but as the $5,000 dwindled, he kept looking at the $100 bank note—"and" (lightly and humorously) "of course, the assumption is that finally he broke the glass." Sam went down to Molly Perry's, the fashionable brothel of St. Louis, and spent the money as Henry would have wished him to, ordering up champagne for the girls. Getting drunk, he gave the girls checks, as he had so often done in the past, with Henry generously making them good. Molly Perry understood, and told the girls not to cash the checks, but to give Sam a wonderful time: she seemed to have foreseen what was going to happen. At six o'clock in the morning, Sam Bray went away and took cyanide of potassium. Mr.

Paramore's story would be hardly surprising (if true) that, when Henry James came back to the United States in the later years of his life and stopped over to lecture in St. Louis, he should have said, when asked what he wanted to see, "I want to see the Eads Bridge and I want to meet E. Paramore"—whose fame had reached him in the South or the East.

But perhaps the most extraordinary thing about all these reminiscences was the love of life they revealed. One felt that the Negro murderer, the old woman who spat on the fire, were attractive and interesting people and that one had missed much in not having known them. And what would one not have given to have had George Biddle for a friend or Henry Van Blarcom! Or, most of all, to have known Mr. Ed during the days when he had lived on a houseboat in the Louisiana waters, with a nigger and a Cajun boy to work for him: he had explained to the Cajun boy that he mustn't put his coffee spoon in the sugar after he had had it in his cup, and the boy had taken pains to wipe it off with his tongue. Mr. Ed would go back to the boat in the evening and sit out on deck and think, and anchor up one of the bayous. About every other night, he would hail somebody from the shore and invite him on board to dinner. "New Orleans was fine in those days," he would say. "They used to have the Mardi Gras, and ladies and gentlemen went. Now the merchants give away tickets to their customers! But in those days, at the ball, there used to be a silk cord that fenced off the part where the ladies were from the place where the men were. Nowadays they'd have to have an iron rail—and then they couldn't keep 'em away!" Or in the early days in San Francisco when "there was so much to eat, y'know!—and you could get a splendid *table d'hôte* dinner for fifty cents." Or in St. Louis in the days of the Veiled Prophets' Ball, where as soon as you arrived, they gave you champagne in the coatroom. And even the lonely and arduous work of clearing land on the Red River seemed to have been quite jolly: all of their hardships had been amusing. And there had been a blind pilot in those days who had guided him through unknown waters—the old pilot remembered it all from twenty years ago; he would say, "Is there a house around that bend? Is there a stump beside the house?" He made you feel that there had been something noble about that pilot, as he found in all the world his own amazing vitality.

He was not a religious man, and spoke of piety and the pious with gentle rakish irony. Some of his most amusing stories were of sermons in rural churches: there had been one preacher in a little church somewhere in the wilds who had ended a sermon on Lot's wife with the following obser-vation: "And they do say, brethren, that if you go to Sodom, and you walk down the street, you can see that pillar thar to this day—but I can hardly be-lieve that, brethren, because I reckon that by this time, the rains and the cattle musta lepped it away!" When a Jew had been put up for membership in the Santa Barbara country club and some anti-Semitic feeling had been expressed, Mr. Paramore waved it aside: "Of course I never could quite forgive the Jews for crucifying Our Lord, but otherwise I've found them charming." Ted wrote me the following in a letter: "Once at a Christmas dinner he told a story I have only heard him tell once—[he was extraordinary that way, telling hundreds of stories over and over again and then suddenly surprising you with a new one] and this was the most moving story I have ever heard. It was supposed to be the story of Old Eighty-five, a horse so called because he paid $85 for him and they had run out of fancy names. Of course the story wasn't about that at all—but about the love and understanding he had about Mother, her cousin May Martin, and the fine days at Manchester by the Sea, when we had everything and he made every day a delight. I seemed to feel that that story was an expression of his attitude toward life and humanity, although there was apparently nothing in its plot except how Mother and May Martin got tight in the company of Old Eighty-five. I left the table as soon as dinner was over without waiting for coffee and sat in his study thinking about the story. He came in and he saw tears rolling down my cheeks and at first thought something was the matter. I just said, 'That was the greatest story I ever heard or ever read.' He fraudulently insisted on the humorous side of it and chuckled. But he didn't kid me or himself. That story is entirely lost, as I couldn't reproduce five percent of it."

At one time, he loaned money to farmers on the land he had cleared in Arkansas: he always referred to this as the "usury business." He kept in touch with the farmers and advised them; he had never, save on one occasion—for the purpose of proving a title—foreclosed a mortgage. On one of his rounds, a farmer had hailed him with, "Hey, Ed! I just got a fine new black stallion over in the barn. And you know what I've named him? I named him Ed Paramore!" It was not the compliment which he treasured, but the droll idea of naming a fine black stallion after a man who looked like himself. His manners had the heartiness of the West and the dignity and ease of the South: his favorite mood was one of roguish joviality. His politeness to women was extreme, and he would not tell a story involving the slightest profanity so long as there were ladies present. He drank in the old-fashioned American style, and expected everyone else to do the same. Of the anarchic goings-on of the younger generation of Westerners, he was usually unaware. He had grown up in a world inhabited by ladies and gentlemen, and he supposed that the sons and daughters of the people whom he knew must have the same standards as himself. When anything sordid or disgraceful on the part of the people about him was brought to his attention, it embarrassed him and made him silent. On one occasion, when a man of his own circle had swindled him out of a large sum of money, his attitude was one of astonishment and commiseration. "Think of how Ned G. must feel," he said, "to have to go and buy a judge, and to have to go to the club and see all those nice men and know they know he's a thief!" When he was a young man, the reading of *The Newcomes* had made a deep impression on him, and when he had first gone to England, the first thing he had done was to go to see Greyfriars, where Colonel Newcome had said "Ad sum." If he could be said to have any sort of prejudice, it was against the American East, though this was principally a joke (he had gone to college in the East and knew it pretty well). He used to tell with great delight how, when he had first visited Boston and some Bostonian had asked him what he thought of the city, he had heartily replied, "Well, Boston is certainly the Omaha of the East!" And he always used to say that when Mark Twain went East, "they had ruined him."

In his later years, when he had his attacks and had been forbidden to smoke or drink, it made him very unhappy: he regarded such a condition as something to be ashamed of, and was extremely sensitive about it. When guests came to stay at the house, it became impossible to restrain him. He tried to console and occupy himself by designing a new yacht (he had himself designed and built without an architect both the houses in which the Paramores had lived at Santa Barbara), a yacht which everyone knew, which he perhaps knew himself, he would never live to sail—and he used to spend a good deal of his time poring over the blueprints. He would take you into his study, which was decorated almost entirely with pictures of ships, and he would talk about them and tell you of the voyages they had made. "There's the old *Endymion*," he said to me once. "She made the voyage from England in ninety days, but that was the voyage that Jack B. met the girl he was going to marry. Before we left England, he was engaged. I had no idea that Jack was going to meet this girl and marry her!" I assumed that he regarded this incident as a romantic and fortunate one, but he went on to say with sadness, "I had no idea that that was the last voyage that we'd ever make in the old *Endymion*, but before the year was out, Jack had married the girl, and now he's clipping bonds downtown somewhere in New York, and the old *Endymion*'s being used for a fishing boat up off the Grand Banks!" He showed me the log of the voyage, which he had kept himself, and looked up the place where the storm had occurred. His last years were troubled by his worry about making money to leave to his sons, who were perfectly well able to take care of themselves—Jim was a lawyer in San Francisco—and who protested against his wearing himself out in the development of a ranch which, when he bought it, had been merely a section of virgin forest; but he believed that it was a primary obligation to see that one's sons were provided for, as he himself had been. He died of a heart attack on his way to the ranch, in his car.

When an artist or a writer dies, we are ordinarily consoled by the knowledge that his vision of life has survived, but in the case of Mr. Paramore, I have regretted that all that world which he had seen and heard, which he had absorbed and re-created, has vanished with him. While he was alive, I still had the feeling that the America of the old South and West had not ceased to be within my reach, that I could come into contact with it directly, and now, since I have heard of his death, I have felt as if it, too, had died, and I should never know it again.

[Mrs. Paramore was a spare red-haired woman of Irish origins, who had a constant taxing problem with her household of men. Her hiding the liquor from them got to be a sort of game. She had always to be looking for new places, and they would always succeed in outwitting her. While Mr. Ed told his stories, she confined herself to brief tart comments. "Someday I'll tell you," Ted wrote me, "about Mr. Ed's love affair with Mother—the only one he ever had, and how he tried for forty years to win her and never could. How much his attentions to her were chivalry I don't know, but I think his failure to win her was the major frustration of his life."

I did not approve of Mr. Paramore's insouciant attitude toward Ted's career. When I once tried to talk to him about the importance of getting Ted to take this seriously, I found that he himself was unprepared to think seriously about the problem. The point was that he liked to have his boys about him, that he depended on them for companionship and an audience. Ted invariably came home for the summer, and neither he nor his father could imagine it any other way. Mr. Paramore always saw to it that Ted had enough money for him to spend the winter in New York, and they were both quite content with this arrangement.

The Paramores were delightful to visit. Ted was apologetic about their new house, which he said was a sad reminder that, since their income had been diminished, they were now "in the sere and yellow leaf," but this reduction in scale of living was only perceptible by Santa Barbara standards, and the place was not only very comfortable but filled with the romantic and convivial atmosphere created by Mr. Ed. A long stay, however, would have made me impatient: though Mr. Ed appealed to my imagination, I could not really accept a life that had no aim except drinking and laughing.]

The open roadside oil stations—red-orange or blue-red-white—with their slender and elegant red-gold pumps; the story about the husband and wife at Santa Barbara who hated each other—but one night they went to a party and each became excited about someone else, so that when they came back home they slept together and had a child and have hated each other in an even more deadly fashion ever since; the party in the large oak-stage-setting-looking house with the portrait of the mistress inlaid over the fire-place, the strapping golden-skinned boys and girls playing roulette with highballs in every hand—the girl who played the piano with a terrific command of jazz—her Californian abundance of hair—*Who'll bite your neck, your Swahansdown neck after my teeth are gone?*—stumbling over the little terrace, the tinsel stars of Cannes—the eternal summer skies of the South. She was originally a singer and piano player in a little town called Stockton. "My brother happened to see her there with a friend of his and they tossed up to see which one would have her and the other man won—but nobody knows that in Santa Barbara—nobody except my brother and myself and the other man." "This is the town drunkard." "Why, Fred, you look terrible, you look like a death's-head." Lord Bingle-Bangle: story about how he ran his car into the bird-reservation lake, and Keith, who can imitate Mexican dialect, and his friends sent their cook around with a lot of medals on his chest to pretend he was the sheriff and Lord Bingle-Bangle thought he was actually arrested and every time Dominic came back they gave him another drink and the steweder he got, the higher the fine became.

The sea scrolling silver on the kelp-mottled beach—or the silver mirrors of the ebb, and, beyond, the deep wonderful blue and the brown-leaf of the kelp, and, beyond, the brown blue-washed mountains answering to the blue brown-streaked sea—or at late afternoon with a purple carpet of loam, and, beyond it, blues and purples of the sea.

Hope Ranch—the cleft sand-aisled rock—mussel clusters petaling black rocks—little pearly and pink sand crabs that bury themselves back-side foremost in the sand—a tramp fishing for sea perch—"Think of what a great life they really must lead simply living along the beach like that—once I found one who was reading a history of Italy in Italian—of course, he may have been an Italian but he spoke English without a trace of accent—we used to come out and have some cocktails and then have supper and stay till night—there was a great big full moon—we used to keep moving our blanket back as the water came further up till we were right up against the cliff and then the shale used to fall on us— This is the first time I've ever come to his place with an easy conscience—I've always been like the Ancient Mariner, don't you know? When he used to glance back for fear some terrible fiend was following him" —When we got dressed, our underclothes blew out with the tempered cold Pacific wind like sails about our bodies—the breakers so long and easy—the flapping white gulls close above us—"They make iodine out of the kelp." The shadow of Vera Cruz lay before us in the water.
Her husband had slammed a glass door on her and broken a vein in her foot. The winding precipitous roads—the beanfields,

purple-brown—"She was originally a waitress in an oil town, and they say, don't ever say this, that everybody had her, and then she got to be King Edward's mistress—I don't know how she did it but she was presented at Court." The mysterious burning of the clubhouse; was it done by a certain lady to get rid of some incriminating letters that the steward was threatening to blackmail her with or was it done by a certain man who wanted to smoke out his wife's rendezvous?—anyway, Mrs. Paramore knew that it did smoke out the rendezvous—*So we played a little game of ten toes up and also ten toes down*—we left our footprints pointing up and also pointing down—*I'm the man who did the pushin' made the spots upon the cushion*—Ted's cousin was the daughter of McLaughlin, who was a banker and quite a man in Deadwood, South Dakota, but she was educated in a convent in Washington and talked much of "ladies and gentlemen"—she had a sacrificial mania, etc.—she got the old people to give her money to carry out her husband's posthumous plans—and "Oh, they're the most terrible people you can imagine—these old people that she gets to put up money—they're sort of soupy—like soup with something sweet in it"—The quail chittering under a tree—the cactus on the tiled piazza against the white wall of the house. "We give Father a birthday party every year and last year his toupee fell off. He was just being very gallant and he happened to jerk his head backwards and it just fell off behind and he put it back on very hurriedly but he put it on backwards—so that there was this big bang down over his eyes—and the part was all wrong and everything. He didn't know it and just went on being so courteous and gallant." To master the continent. Sandyland: the little boy in the bathhouse who asked me what kind of a car I drove over in and what kind of a car I had and what kind of a car I thought was the best—he thought that the Packard was the best—he said he also liked music—highballs, sweet-flavoured cocktails and mulled claret.

Hollywood. The man who had been working on "title laughs"—"The man is threatening the girl with a knife—'Have you no heart?' she says—and then you see him threatening her again and then you have the caption again: 'No!'—and then you see them again and then you have the caption: 'Well, give me liver!'—Now, here's the gag."

"She started out to be sort of a hothouse lily, you see, and read a lot and everything and then she married this cowpuncher from Deadwood, South Dakota, that we used to call Rattlesnake Pete—the first time she ever saw him was in the train and he had a big hump in the back of his coat and he asked me if it showed and then it turned out that he had two six-shooters in there." "A gentleman by act of Congress." She turned Ted over to the Department of Justice for trying to get her to send Upton Sinclair's *Profits of Religion* to a soldier in France.

The Drummonds of Boston. The father apparently a rounder—the mother imprisoned the children, refused to send them to school or college, made each learn a trade and compelled them periodically to wait upon the servants—one, according to Ted, was an arche-typical old ápe; another a great big masturbating moron who spread scandal about Dorothy Heydell; a third, who had studied to be an electrician, went to the war and never came back but got a job as an electrician after he was demobilized and the other children are forbidden to correspond with him; and a fourth, Ellen, is a strapping tomboy all Western but for a Boston pronunciation of *darn*—she gave him a kiss and said "Hello, Passion!" "Well, isn't it about time to coït?" Mrs. Drummond a woman with a red face and a red nose and a baleful eye. Mary Craig, Ted's cousin, used to remonstrate with him about Margaret Canby and tell him how terribly she (Mary) felt about her little child, etc., and on one occasion she enraged him by taking him to task for wasting his life in drunkenness, when he ":had only been in swimming." She said, "Look at you now, your eyes are all bloodshot!" "I hadn't had a drink for a week." (Her mother was simple and nice and said things like "Oh, look at the mountainy—mountainy—mountains.") "Then she [Mary Craig] told me that I wouldn't listen to anybody's opinion on anything."

The spacious Pacific landscapes. The pink enormous mountains—the people grow to match the scenery—they expand out there more easily—they marry and divorce young—gigantic uncultivated beauties like the beauties of the prehistoric world—men playing and thriving in the raw magnificent landscapes of primordial processes and upheavals—the sun dropping into the Pacific and the red-gold holocaust of the sky.

"Hello, Mr. Pops—well, they took your son's coat and his shirt and his vest and his pants and his shoes [at bridge or poker]." [Jim Paramore to his mother] "Oh, gwan, you've got a piece o'change hidden away up there—I don't know where you put the key.—Why don't you give it to Ted?" "Give it to Ted?! Why, that would be like hanging the key to the chicken coop around the fox's neck!" They would hunt for the booze till they found it, when Mrs. Paramore had gone away—then they would drink up part of it and leave some in the bottle—"always leave some in the bottle for a nest egg"—and she would never say a word when she found that it was gone.

The highballs they had on the beach—and the sun dropping into the Pacific—their underclothes blowing about them and gulls flapping overhead—so far from the war—so far from business—so far from the troubles of the world—with only the enormous sea and the spacious Pacific landscape—living and rejoicing in life among the primordial magnificence of the world. What had he really cared then, what could he ever really care, for politics or society or learning—so long as he had that happy life to go back to, that life of eternal sun—the Pacific at night, not violent against the shore, but insistent and wild like the high sun.

The letter that Margaret wrote Ted at Yale when she had told him she was going to marry Canby and he had written and told her not to, that he loved her, and then he lay awake all night thinking about it and in the morning went out and got the letter back from the post office and sent her another letter telling her he hoped she would be very happy and all the regular conventional stuff—and then as soon as he got back from Russia, as soon as they were together again—he was taking her home from a party— they both "swooned away" together—"as soon as we got together, it was like an electric current—it used to come over me periodically while I was away—I used to miss her terribly."

Ted had had the audacity to propose to a woman friend that we should all go to Tijuana together: "Oh, Teddy, when we came back, we wouldn't be pure!"

Mr. Ed: Robert Louis Stevenson in California—the bartender who knew him and said he was a regular fellow—the rumor that Mrs. Stevenson had destroyed a story about a streetwalker— "Why, you know, nobody could have told the real story, the real pathos of those girls' lives, the way Stevenson could!"

They always called Mrs. Paramore "the dame." "About how Mrs. Paramore and I have nothing in common—I said to her the other day, 'There isn't a single thing we both like—oysters—the hard parts and the soft parts. You're takin' the second mate's drink.' Why, the second mate always takes as much as possible, y'know, because he's so seldom asked. Yes: that's a very pleasant wine [of the diluted port], drink a glass and see if you get any aroma from it."

A party where two girls tried to make up to Ted and his father. Mr. Ed didn't get on to it and when Ted explained it to him afterwards said, "Oh, you don't think they meant that!" Ted went back to see his girl—which turned to be rather depressing, since she met him in the hammock in a nightgown and he took her out in the car, and he was all cold and her legs were all gooseflesh and she didn't seem to come and he tried it again and she didn't seem to come that time either, so he gave her up and took her home.

Ted, pretending to pant like a dog: "Oh, I just saw one of the prettiest girls I ever saw in my life!—Just a fresh little smack!—Let's go back and get her." We did turn around but she had gone into a drugstore. Long privation.

Seward Collins's family at Pasadena. The radio twelve-year-old evangelist at the Los Angeles Temple who converted dozens of souls nightly: "I want to see Jesus, don't you? My Saviour so faithful and trew!" Uncle Jim, the most popular radio announcer on the Coast: "This little lady—I always forget her name—Fisher—oh yes, Fisher" . . . Bedtime story. A quartet in Los Angeles singing for the benefit of friends who were celebrating a wedding anniversary in Nebraska—*Fanny is my darling, my darling,* etc. Continually turning one off and the other on. Erotic dream of radio horns.

[I stopped off on the way back at San Francisco to see my cousin Alice Osborne. She was quite pretty and quite intelligent but rather pale and a little dry, and she never married. I found her very sympathetic; we used to go to the Exhibition together in 1915.

I found Margaret Canby living in an apartment and waiting for a divorce, with another woman, Paula Gates, who was also getting a divorce. Margaret had thought she would marry Ted Paramore, but had recently more or less given up this idea as the result of going to a dance with him, at which she said he had behaved very badly. She said that she felt that she couldn't trust him. She derived from her Canadian mother a strong streak of Scotch Presbyterianism, which gave her an indestructible sense of what was and what wasn't done. In spite of this, she said she was fatally attracted to "bounders." There had been a young Canadian officer who had jumped down from above through a great glass skylight in the ballroom of a big hotel. But when it came to a definite decision, she thought that Ted had gone too far. It never then entered my head that I should eventually be married to her myself. I still thought her preempted by Ted.]

Green Street. Their apartment—the piano, the enormous bronze Pegasus on a dark-green marble pedestal, the paintings, the quasi-French windows in the bedrooms. The Commander who wanted to take us to Honolulu—six days out and six days back—but he couldn't eat poi, the Worcester sauce of Honolulu—they ate pig practically raw—he thought the Annapolis men were superior to the West Point men because they had been around more—he started to tell us something about himself and got off onto some other officers whom he greatly admired. He wanted to marry Paula and would take her around everywhere with him, instead of leaving her behind in traditional sailor-wife fashion. He wanted to know at what age women ceased to be able to have children. The bond salesman who had been in the war and was angry when he found out that somebody had told about his having been decorated for saving a doughboy, whom he had carried back out of a shell hole—he had been twenty-six days under fire. When he told Paula that he was in love with her, she asked him if he loved her more than anything else in the world. "I can never forget the war!" His French-Canadian stories: "Well, throw it in [the anchor] anyway: it might do some good. I heard a splash and Jesus Christ it was me!" He didn't believe we were actually laughing at his stories when we laughed: "Now, you're not laughing at the story." He played the tramp song—*Goddam*—on the piano. When he left Lawrenceville he had gone to the Colorado School of Mines and he had spent a good deal of his time in mining camps. When they talked about books and things, she noticed that he didn't get it, that he simply wasn't there. The balcony opening on the bay—the city falling away in lights to the bay. The Commander only had three days leave. His Spanish poems— but Paula made him self-conscious, so that he got stuck and couldn't finish—he had elected Spanish instead of French. Margaret had an eminent optician (and professor) on a string—he was a married man with children and very kittenish when he had broken out—in the kitchen he did an Apache dance with the ice pick. The one [of Margaret and Paula] who got in first always played the piano to let the other know she was there. Paula talked about Edward Carpenter and Yoga (bending backwards, concentrating on nothing, etc.). She had gone into the Brevoort in dashing evening clothes, after driving all night in the Park, and had realized there was a child in the room and it was all so terrible and she had had a nervous breakdown and gone back West. Her father in Mexico used to beat her with a riding whip. Once she had ridden seventy-five miles in a day but she couldn't swim.

The white long-boarded houses, the first civilization of the Coast.

The locomotives, different from the Eastern ones, bellowing like lost cattle. The Sierra Nevadas: the huge rusty spine of the continent. The Great Salt Lake: the pale blue vitreous waters reflecting palely the pale clouds— crusted at the edge with salt and snow and on one side covered with a verdigris of green ice—the glistening salt desert—the black mountain wall lapped in white—the brownish haze at the base of the mountains. The brick-pink sandstone images like gods worn faceless by erosion—the brick- orange soil of the rolling hills with a gray winter coat of grass clumps—the shaggy wild brown cattle grazing them—all cut out against the lovely delicate bright robin's-egg blue sky. The long thumby clumps of the cactus (not in Utah, in California).

The dry sallow snow-dusted winter landscape of the Middle West. Ideal Cement Works (Nebraska).

Indiana—the broken bones of the corn stalks in the snow. As the afternoon wanes, the white of the snow becomes almost as gray as the sky—it has the dullness of chalk. The hogs wallop in the snow. The houses are raw and bare. The whole vast flat landscape is raw.

The little girl who had her mother read *Barney Google* to her and said "Hotsy-Totsy" over and over again at the top of her voice.

The sparse black bristles of the wood on the snowy hills.

Newark: Climax Crib Company.

[On the train back, I read as much as I could understand—I skipped the equations—of A. N. Whitehead's *Concept of Nature*, which had been recommended by Kemp Smith. I was never at home with metaphysics, but I adopted his metaphysics—a department in which I was not at home but accepted as plausible Whitehead's explanation of the world, from the point of view of its atomic constituents, as made up of what he calls "events," with God as the principle of "concretion."

I also read the manuscript of Jim Tully's *Beggars of Life*. He was a protégé of Chaplin's. I had met him in Hollywood with Chaplin, who had taken to him on account of his rough experience and his literary aspirations, and had given him a job. He bitterly complained that a type like him was excluded from consideration by what he regarded as an Algonquin hierarchy, a clique of phony journalists. His book had an amusing Irish rhythm and flow, and I gave the manuscript to a publisher, who brought it out. Tully then became something of a popinjay, an equal of any Algonquin celebrity. I don't think he ever thanked me, and I was told that he went around saying that I ought to have got him a better publisher.]

Back in the East

The summer hung close and dull.

[A speech for a character in a story or play.] *Down Sixth Avenue to Varick Street, up through Minetta Lane, 12:30 in the morning:* "And it all looked so dreadful—everything looked so blank and so dingy and deserted. Just rubbish blowing around and the shop windows full of rubbish and here and there a grimy little knot of Italians or a cat eating rubbish in the street. The only things still going strong were the big white breakfast-food factories or whatever they are, with the electric light on full blast and the taxis scooting around like cockroaches when you go into the kitchen at night."

Great Neck, mid-April. Fitz said he was going abroad because his reputation was diminishing in America, and he wanted to stay away till he had accomplished something important and then come back and have people give him dinners. There was great talk on Lardner's part of going to the Red Lion or some other roadhouse, but when we did leave—all the liquor now gone—we simply went on to Lardner's, where we drank Grand Marnier— he insisted on presenting us each with a little bottle—and more Scotch. Fitz's attempt to deliver himself of a great self-revelation—"egoism, *The Egotist.*" Lardner said, "No, you haven't got that right." —"Well, *Egoist,* then—don't interrupt me just for a little *t* like that." Lardner thought it was a good book, Fitz didn't agree with him. —"Where he sees the professor." —"Oh, yes: he was the mother of the girl." Loud laughter. Zelda had gone to sleep in an armchair and covered herself with a shawl—she was bored by Scott's chart of the Middle Ages and had made herself very disagreeable about it. Scott was sore because we had crabbed his revelation. "You pronounce too many words wrong," Lardner had said. Lardner read the golf rules aloud. (This was a little book put out by the local golf club. Lardner read these rules at length with a cold and somber scorn that was funny yet really conveyed his disgust with his successful suburban life.) —Then we went back to the Fitzgeralds'. Lardner and I started talking about the oil scandal, and Fitz fell asleep in his chair. Lardner and I went on talking about baseball, Heywood Broun, Lardner's writing, the Americanized *Carmen,* the Rascoes, etc. Deep blue patches appeared at the windows. I couldn't think at first what they were—then I realized it was the dawn. The birds tuned up one at a time. It grew light. It was seven o'clock. Scott asked what

we had been talking about. Lardner said we had been talking about him.
—"I suppose you analyzed me ruthlessly." Zelda was sick and had to have
the doctor and apologized profoundly for her "rudeness."

When we were talking about his own work, Lardner said that the trouble
was he couldn't write straight English. I asked him what he meant, and he
said: "I can't write a sentence like 'We were sitting in the Fitzgeralds'
house, and the fire was burning brightly.'"

The telephone bell blazed on the silence.

Alvin Johnson discourages one with the intellectual.

Let's go to the end of the subway line—the mysterious Broadway
subway. Idea of going on to the end of the line—at Coney Island or wher-
ever—and spending the night there. —Idea of walking up Fifth Avenue
from the Village and spending the night at the Plaza.

Roy Gamble [my old friend of the army, who came to see me on a visit to
New York]. Drawbacks of going second class—have to talk to all these
birds that ask you what business you're in, see—but still, I ain't no lecture-
hound, see. —Morris Belknap's nudes: I said that they looked all greenish as
if they were dead—El Greco looks like fresh meat beside them. "Yes, El
Greco could eat those birds up."

Jarvis: "You've got to have references to get in here now." "Mrs. ——
didn't used to ask for no references—she got Jim out of a menagerie." "But
you got to have 'em now."

Clem and Belle. "Oh, look: doesn't that man look like Fred Potts?" Clem
said he didn't look anything like Fred Potts and that Belle was always finding likenesses between people who didn't look anything alike. Belle, who,
as a matter of fact, was always finding likenesses between people who had
been in love with her at one time or another, resented this. She had seen
somebody the other day who looked exactly like a man she had been in love
with in Denver when she was ten years old. She objected to having Clem
kid her about it. If he kept on kidding her about it, she would tell something
on *him*. *"I'll* tell something on *you!"* He fixed her with a piercing and mas-
terful look— "You think I'm afraid of you! You think I'm afraid of you!"
She gave him back the savage glare of a panther. "I'm not afraid of you!
Why, I've got him just like that!—You think I'm afraid of you!—Here—
here! just look at that! that's where I hit him with the bronze off the mantelpiece. He [Clem] promised to take me out at eleven and he didn't come
back till six in the morning. And I'd gotten all ready and been waiting up
for him all night!" —She was always telling me about her lovers and then

apologizing for it or trying to explain it away afterwards. —"I hate people who say those things and I thought the minute after I'd hung up how awful I must have sounded."

The party at Betty Weston's. Alec McKaig had the heebie jeebies. The doctor told him that if he went on drinking, black and purple stripes would begin to come out on his face and his toes would drop off. But he was prepared to get drunk tonight. Betty Weston had given him a rough time when she pretended she had been engaged to him—had even tried to have him arrested when he was leaving the country. He thought it would be a very rough party. So we started out gaily enough in a taxi: the hot sultry stuffy sticky city in mid-June—the address was 249 West Eightieth Street— a sinister address—the red-light district of Englewood—"That's probably way over in the Jersey suburbs somewhere." Sensation on arriving at the number. Low half-timber and concrete gabled bogus Elizabethan front— unexpected door at side—up dirty flight of stairs—the party—the tiny dose of orange juice with just a suspicion of gin at the bottom of the tall glass. The refined and witty conversation—the tall girl with the hard *r*'s who talked rather amusingly: "Grand Street is a great Jewish-cart street— one night there I saw a man displaying—I don't know whether I ought to tell about it in this mixed company—I saw a man displaying a whole pile of men's union suits—he would hold them up and run them through his fingers." —Everybody had already done his stuff—one silent, almost invisible young man was said to play Debussy but did not do so—the young "neutral nationalities neutral-sexed" man talked continuously and rather well: Winifred Lenihan as Juliet—Winthrop Ames thought her the best one among those who had read the part for him—he must have had a great twelve hours—the Grand Street Follies—*Orange Blossoms*, designed by Norman Bel Geddes, who had contrived an intimate cottage scene so that it looked, as Paul Poiret said, like an annex to the Public Library, and a rhinestone curtain that it was impossible to light—the moving platform that Duncan had insisted on in the Francine Larrimore show—the first night they tried it in Atlantic City and Florenz Ziegfeld said, "Put it in the Atlantic Ocean!", so that was out—and then they wondered why the production cost so much—Alec on the new stage in Munich, half of which was dropped underneath while the other half was lowered into place—"Well, elevators may be all right, but in —— they had one for the props, because the stage was too small and the elevator stuck halfway, so they just went down with mallets and zongo-zongo-zongo, they just smashed it and threw the props into the alley first, and then, when that was full, they threw them into Denny's restaurant, which is next door, don't you know." On the way home: "Well, I contributed more than you did—you sat there like a saint with a bellyache or something." "Oh, he's a bum director." "Was the girl his wife?" "That's what she said."

I wanted to kiss her inside the thighs, but she said, "Closed for the day."

New York at Convention time (mid-June) was like a Princeton commencement—the same sultry sticky weather, the same influx of visitors, the same messy festival streets, the garlands of light along Fifth Avenue like the Japanese lanterns strung among the trees in front of Old North. The plank platform and enclosure in Washington Square seemed the preparation for a prom. The heaviness and undress of the summer. A last ceremonial burst, now that the real play was over. One went to the new revues, which had opened with high expectations of the Convention, a little as one had to the Triangle Club in the Old Casino. The motors roaring and speeding all night back and forth through Washington Square just as they used to do through the campus—plunging, whirring like dynamos, through the stuffy summer night, spluttering as they got underway or hurtling noisily through the night.

I took off her blunt-toed sandals and held her sweaty tired feet in my hands like two moist little cream cheeses in cloth cases. [EW inserted this in *I Thought of Daisy*.]

The man who has a big day ahead of him selling phonograph needles.

Betty Clark is such a cat that I don't doubt at all that when she was out driving with Gussie Knox she would tell Gussie that she had just had an epileptic fit, whether she had actually had one or not.

I heard the harsh march of the clock and thought: That destroys us all!

I heard her little breath as she slept—it seemed so tiny to keep all that engine of activity and feeling alive.

As limp as wet lettuce leaves.

Birds killed and run over and over by motors on concrete motor roads until they are flattened into black inorganic patches on the black surface of the road.

Little Paul Wallace [my cousin Dorothy Wallace's little boy]
He wanted to throw a torpedo at the cop.
"Where's your cooking girl?"
When he went to the hospital, he asked to have a baby.
Flowers in bloom!
He said, "I hate to see so many people run over!" when he was looking
   down from the top of a bus.

When he saw butterballs for the first time at Aunt Caroline's, he said, "What's this? candy?"

Mid-June. The summer wind at night under the open summer sky—the frondy shadows of trees blown about in the blue moonlight—the great leafy trees around the house rustling ceaselessly like a summer sea—the recurrent grinding and effortful chugging of motors murdering the quiet, as they climb up the hill.

The sea at Seabright, low and deep blue, playfully casting its silver nets for the orange legs of the bathers.

Alec on 4th of July at Esther Murphy's (Southampton). First they went over to the country club, whence, as they approached it, they heard the sound of loud male voices singing *Sweet Adeline*—Mr. Murphy and some other gray-haired old gentlemen were bounding about on the lawn. Esther was rather embarrassed and drove home. They had to telephone three times to the club before they could get Mr. Murphy to come home. When he did, he subsided immediately into a chair and said, "Where are the cocktails?" At dinner, Mrs. Murphy sat mumbling about the butler—they always did manage to have such sinister servants, don't you know? "I really feel there's something wrong about him—I'm really afraid of him—even though his wife *is* such a good cook, I really think I'll have to discharge him!" "Well, Mother, I really don't think you're very good if you allow yourself to be intimidated by your own servants!" "Well, but you don't have to be in the house with him continually as I do—I really don't think it's safe to be in the house alone with him—I really think I'll have to let him go!" And all the time Esther was sitting there doing this (with her hands) and saying, "The Duke of York had three sons and two daughters," etc., etc.—Talleyrand's bon mot: "C'était donc votre père qui n'était pas beau." "Now, what did Talleyrand have in mind when he did that? 'Fouché méprise les hommes. Ce mépris tient à ce que Fouché s'est beaucoup étudié.'"

T. S. Eliot said of Macaulay's style that it was "the ruins of a fine style in the hands of a journalist." Something of the kind is true of Frank Crowninshield's manner—which is the ruins of a fine manner in the hands of a New York editorial slave.

The July sea. Deep tan against deep blue; short waves that break with a crunch on the shore—climbing the watery mountains—the world all white light and water—they shake their fraying silver crests.

The auratum lilies having orgasms in the vase on the mantelpiece—straining back their great gilded red-flecked flesh-like white petals while their pistils emitted semen and the stamens smeared it with their brick-dust pollen. Inside the petals were stiffening white fringes like the entrance to a vagina. All the time they gave off a heavy sweet odor.

Title laughs

Somebody told her she had a large vocabulary—so now she's dieting.
Somebody's heart was so warm that he had to wear asbestos vests.
You win the barbed-wire garters!
His rival is so crooked that they named a pretzel after him.

Belle Gifford. Mrs. Collins gave her $200, and she and Clem used it to go abroad. —At *What Price Glory?*, she thought that Wolheim was horrible-looking but William Boyd handsome. I asked if he was any relation to someone of the same family name with whom she had been in love, and what had become of the latter. She understood that he was back and that his wife had had another baby: "They always seem to do that just afterwards—I've known that to happen three times." On the way home, she said she believed that, after she'd been in Europe, she'd be awfully glad to get back to America—"I don't like these frogs either—little bits of men!" —I suggested that the Italians were tall and handsome. —"Oh, the English—I'll fall for an Englishman—they're big and light, aren't they?" I asked her if she liked that big blond type. —"Um—um!—Blond with blue eyes!—And do you know who made me find out I did?—Clem's brother Alex!" She had thought that André Gide was like a little old woman.

[She had, I think, the most obvious sex appeal of any woman I have known. Clem had married her when she was still in her teens and was a neophyte dancer in some nightclub. He was from the first so uncertain of her that he would lock her up when he went to his office. She had melting and sensual brown eyes and looked in some ways rather exotic—her origins were actually German. She loved music and played the piano, and occasionally I took her to concerts. I took her to see Stravinsky conduct his own compositions at the time he had first come to this country. Her reaction was a combination of her points of view as a music lover and as a connoisseur of men, delivered in her harsh and nasal Middle Western voice that somehow had her sexuality in it.

I was not insensible to Belle's attractions, but she never, in the current phrase, gave me a tumble. When she called me up one day, I told her, full of hope, to come right around. But in spite of the fact that I performed the at that time for me heroic feat of carrying her into the bedroom, it turned out that she only wanted to tell me how worried she was about Clem's drinking. She had usually talked about her latest passion, about which she was frank to a degree that seemed even then quite extraordinary. When she felt an interest in someone, she would apparently simply go to bed with him till her appetite had worn off. It was no wonder her husband drank. She treated him, though, with affection; there was nothing very bitchy about her.]

America. The flat landscape and the frame houses and the street lamps lighted while it is still day.

John Amen's mistress. The head mannequin at Tappé's—was kept by a rich and elderly protector. This made it difficult for John to see her—since he would have to wait till very late at night, until after their party, when the protector had left her—and he sometimes wasn't able to get to her till two or three in the morning. But, on the other hand, it made her very inexpensive, and John was able to enjoy her sumptuous apartment, listen to her built-in radio and drink the liqueurs and whiskeys with which her wine closet was abundantly supplied—all for nothing.

[A footnote in *What the Woman Lived*, the letters of Louise Bogan (ed. Ruth Limmer, 1973), tells us that EW was one of the first friends Miss Bogan made when she came to New York, in her early twenties. They remained friends (and later colleagues at *The New Yorker*) to the end. Miss Bogan dedicated her third volume of poems, *The Sleeping Fury*, to EW. She married Raymond Holden, mentioned below. EW characterized her early in 1924 as "a lady poet of remarkable achievement."]

Louise Bogan said that the poetry society had asked her to read before them. I asked her why she didn't do it. "Well, would you? Do you think it's the thing to do?" "Yes: why not?—if they offer you twenty-five dollars." "But they all come up and talk to you afterwards! What would you *say* to them?" Rolfe Humphries: "What did Shakespeare say to the horses?—'Whoa-oa! Hey, get over there!'"

John Amen [now a lawyer] on doing business in New York: "If somebody calls up and says, 'My God, my house is on fire!', you say, 'Well, you're a fool to let it catch fire!' And nobody ever thinks of doing anything that he's not held to in writing. Why, gosh!, if a person did the things people do in New York anywhere else, he could never get away with it—it would hurt his reputation—they'd say he wasn't a man of his word or something. But it doesn't make any difference here. They'd say, 'Why, you were a darn fool not to get it in writing!'" His firm had been defending the Consolidated Gas Company, in three successive suits, to get three successive gas taxes declared confiscatory.—"In other words, it's defending the interests."

Belle Gifford. They had had dinner at the Boyds' with Lawrence Langner—she had had a little flirtation with him at a ball once. "It was a little bit embarrassing because the last time we'd seen him had been just when Clem and I were having a big split-up. Clem knew that he'd been making up to me and we were all pretty drunk—I was sitting on a couch with Bob Chandler, and Tom Smith and that terrible man—he's an artist— oh, you know!—that goes to Bob Chandler's all the time—and they were accusing me of having bowlegs and I picked up my dress to show them I hadn't and Clem got awful mad and said, 'I don't mind your showing your legs in front of Tom Smith but I won't have you do it in front of that goddam bastard!'"

[Of Stravinsky]—"Oh, he's a *little* man!—I thought his music sounded like he was a big man.—Isn't it wonderful to think of that ugly little man with all those sweet sounds in him!" —Anecdotes of Paris: They met a couple on the boat—"We liked them and they liked us—and Sam, that was his name, Sam—they went to the Moulin Rouge and Galantière got a couple of tarts, as he called them, to come over to the table with us and we didn't know it but Sam fixed something up with them for afterwards—so when we started to come out, Sam and Clem stayed behind the screen and we kept waiting and waiting, and all of a sudden Mabel—she was a little quiet thing, you wouldn't think it of her—she flared up and got real mad and went back and dragged 'um out—Clem said they were just fixing up to have them do a Lesbian stunt upstairs. —But it just sort of spoiled every-thing—it happened just the day before we sailed—it was too bad." —They went to a peepshow: "If you saw much of it, that sort of stuff would spoil sex for you!"—She liked "Mr. Cummings."

Blond girl from Oklahoma. Lived for a long time in what was known as "the sticks"—the region wanted for farming but overgrown with timbers. The stories they'd tell yuh! It takes a long long time to get anything out of them. All they'll say is "Yes" and "No" and "I reckon." —The Indian married woman who could afford to take a lover because she was making $14 a day out of her oil well. The Indians and whites intermarried but you can't hardly speak to a Negro on the street. At the hotel, they are in a little outside room. The dining room there was too good for them. The hotel on its front windows had the flyspecks from the summer before and the cockroaches used to climb across the visitors' backs as soon as they sat down. The Indian that used to take his bread and his bottle of potato water to bed with him to keep them from freezing. I'll never forget how I tried to make bread once! I tried to get some regular kind of yeast—like Fleischmann's—but they only had one kind—Owl—and you'd have to put in about twelve cakes of it to get any results at all. Then I tried to knead it and I couldn't do anything with it—the bottom of the pan would just clink, yuh know, it was so big and weak—and then he took it and put it down on the floor and got down on his knees and went to it for all he was worth. —In the hotel they had big pans with ashes in them to spit in around the stove. —The country really looks wonderful but I couldn't stand the people. —"Oh, if a woman doesn't stay at home and mind the children and go to church, they'll almost tar and feather her! —They were all new homesteaders around there." — The Indian who used to be wearing the same collar when he had worn out three shirts—"I used to keep'um at a distance when I talked to'um. —I'd been in the hotel business myself and I thought I might be able to make some money giving them a few tips. They give me a dinner and then they stood around watching me all the time—they were watching to see how much I ate. I suppose if I'd been wise I'd have been careful and not eaten very much but I was so hungry that I didn't care. —I was born in Texas but my father moved to Oklahoma and set up as a doctor there. —I don't know whether he could ever give anything but calomel but he certainly gave plenty of that!"

Léonie Adams, Louise Bogan says, lives so much inside herself that she occasionally makes little remarks to herself. She said she was immune from love. She explained that if she got married, she thought she would have a great many children—if she began, she'd just go on having one after another.

[EW took an early interest in Miss Adams's poetry and apparently in Miss Adams, for Louise Bogan in a letter to Rolfe Humphries, December 27, 1925, writes: "Léonie informs us that the Great Wilson made some hearty passes at her, inviting her to stay at his house." Léonie Adams was then a delicate and articulate young woman, in her mid-twenties, recently graduated from Barnard, bird-like in gesture, brief and vivid in speech. Her lyric quality and her reticences appealed to EW. She later married the critic William Troy.]

Raymond Holden at Princeton was the victim of a form of Puritan-idealistic inhibition which made him think it dreadful to kiss or make love to a girl, but resulted in his evading this in imagination by imagining that doctors came to him and told him that having intercourse with the girl was the only thing which would save her life.

Follies rehearsal, March 9, 1925. The finale (*Rio Rita*)—long, many times repeated, often interrupted—a mission court with a bell in the gate surrounded by red-sandstone-effigied rock and purple cactus plants painted on the scenery; in the center a great square pillar with tall sombreroed girl posing on it—a group forms about it—twelve tall girls form a line at the front—Ziegfeld: "Five on one side and seven on the other! You've got two white ones together there!" —They explain it to the polite deaf Englishman. —"Just move over there between those other two ladies—we don't want two white ones together." —Ziegfeld: "Go over on the end, Gladys.

—That line's too straight. Have them pair off." —*I have a song I must be singing, Though a rope I should be swinging, But I've really got to get it off my chest, Though I'm not a butter and egg man from the West.* —*Oh, I would LIKE to CORRAL a very merry necessary little gal!* —The Tiller girls in orange sombreros with orange leggings and legs contrasting with white costumes—they make an exact line and fling their legs up in unison with such verve, with such flexibility. —"Are you going to do that tomorrow night?" The statuesque girl on the pedestal gets bored and begins doing a little shimmy. —Will Rogers ascends the pedestal and the girl sits down, letting one leg hang and hugging the other knee. —Will Rogers swings a lariat around the whole group, the Tiller girls turning on the outside in a direction contrary to the lasso. —They try the curtains again and again. —The curtain closes—the curtain opens and you're still where you were—the curtain closes and you close in. —Ziegfeld: "The first time you're still turning—the second time you're stopped." —Bathing girls. Ziegfeld: "I want the same kind of light as you've got on the group.—Keep the light off the scenery." Ann Pennington's waitress number—black dress, tray, red garters, red coral like a ribbon around the neck—her hair comes down. —Ziegfeld: "Well, make them put on their stockings right!—There's nothing to this costume but the stockings. [The girls laugh.] Darn right!" —Vivienne Segal, in a halt during a domestic sketch, stands against the light so that her full-thighed legs are outlined. The girls in the audience laugh and "Oh!"—"You think you're in the Haggin pictures?" —With her small-town kittenishness, she doesn't understand, retreats, holds her skirts about her legs. She tries to do a number in the center of the line of Tiller girls but they are too fast for her. She gives it up: "Well, they can have it!—I'm in the next number and have to make a quick change!" —Ziegfeld: "The girls are all right: it's the lights!" —"What's the idea of having one green chair and all the rest black?" —Ann Pennington: "They're not black."—(It's the spotlight.) —Ziegfeld's grayish hair, parted in the middle, brushed back in a double curve, soft white shirt, white handkerchief corner sticking out of breast pocket—not badly set up—wrinkled face. The old Jew—chews long cigar without smoking it. —Didn't "get" the comic supplement. —The Tiller girls in the dusky lobby falling together in groups of three or five, practicing their kicks and maneuvers, humming their refrain, their voices becoming girlish in the dark (like the Vassar juniors in spring singing their class song on the dusky campus). —The finale: the music has stopped on the Tiller girls' entrance and their voices singing their refrain sound foolish in the void. —People laugh, they stop. —"You come in on the second part of the refrain." —He sings the verse and *half the refrain.* —The Tiller girls getting flash-lighted together—"You can't take one Tiller girl—you've got to take them all." —

Ann Pennington amusing herself during a wait at the top of the Grand Staircase—in her silver valance body, her salmon tights and her tiny silver slippers. —The bee number—they come out of the hive with wings, and protruding black-and-orange-striped bee bodies equipped with limp stings on their bottoms. —A number designed by Bel Geddes in lilac blue and soft pale green. —Martha Lorber as the Circassian slave with her blond gold wig and in the audience in her light buff dressing gown close around her slender round figure and with her pale blond hair close about her head made small for the wig. —*I'm mad about Titina! I'm wild about Titina!*—rigid and glittering.

[These notes were used by EW to write "The Finale at the Follies," *The New Republic* (XLII, March 25, 1925, 125–26), reprinted in *The American Earthquake* (1958).]

Margaret Canby. She said that if a man so much as goes out and cracks the ice himself in a girl's apartment, they assume that he's her lover. —During a drunken party, Bonnie Glass got her into the bathroom and told her her troubles: she was living with a rich man who had left his wife for her but, unfortunately, in playing polo, he was hit by a mallet, so that he was slightly deranged and became very religious—he thought he had a call to serve God by saving the world from sin and, as she was the worst sinner he knew, he set out to convert her. He ceased to have any sexual relations with her and began to labor with her for her soul—a trying situation for her.

Mrs. Brown [blond girl from Oklahoma]. She had been married when she was fourteen—her husband was mean and cruel, he said he had Indian blood—"He never forgot a grudge, but it was him that always brought it up himself—I don't think he had any Indian blood. —His father was mean—that's why his wife left 'um, he was so mean—but he improved on his father's meanness. He was a teaser and when they grow up and don't get over it, it's pretty bad. The old man got kind of crazy one winter and tried to poison me. He'd sit around in the evening and say, 'John L. Sullivan's dead,' when he wasn't dead at all—and then he thought that I was a spy on 'um that his wife had sent—I guess he'd been up there so long alone brooding on his homestead that he finally went offuz head.—Well, anyway, one night he tried to poison me—strychnine they use for traps, you know—that night was a different night from the other nights—all the days were just the same but this day was a different day—he got up and went out for a walk after dinner instead of going right in for a nap like he usually did.—Well, anyway, at dinner, he offered me this piece of meat— deer meat—and I didn't want it but I wanted to be polite to the old man, so I waited till he'd went out and then put it back in the plate and in the evening he ate it himself and was *so* sick! But he knew what to do—I wouldn't have and might have died—but he ate a lot of lard. —Now he's my best friend—we write to each other all the time—he told me afterwards that he guessed he was queer that winter. —I had two children and the third died before it was born—a month before it was born—and poisoned me. And I wanted to die—I was so sick and my husband was such a mean monster—I couldn't remember anything—that was really terrible that muddled mind I had—and whenever anybody would ask me a question, it would be just like a big blank wall up in front of me—and I couldn't remember what I had to buy when I went to the store—I used to have to memorize them on my fingers—the doctor, Dr. Smiley, who was new up there then, came in and he felt right away what was the matter—and he said, 'You don't want to get well!' and I said, 'Oh, yes I do,' and he said, 'No you don't,' so then of course finally I had to admit that I didn't. —And he pled with me to try and get well, because he said he was new there, and if one of his patients died, they'd figure he wasn't any good, see. —So finally I got well—but when I went to court for the divorce, I couldn't answer any of the questions that were asked me—I'd just stand there like a dumb-ox. —When I first went up there I'd see all these wives of homesteaders with picket fences around them—Mrs. Shafer and Mrs. Huckaby and Mrs. Smith—and I resented that the wives always died but never the men—all except Huckaby and he had to be shot! —One woman got so desperate one winter when her husband was off on a spree that she killed her four children with the butcher knife and tried to get away with herself. It seemed as if it was hearing the cougar scream that she couldn't stand—they give an awful scream that just sends the shivers clear through you—just like a woman, you know. She tried to drown herself, but when she struck the cold water, it sort of knocked her sane again or something. The man who told me about it said that brought her to her senses. —He thought that was funny. —Only the baby survived. —I used to feel like I was sunk in a deep well—it's so close with the trees up all around you, you know, that you can hardly breathe—so hot in the daytime you can hardly stand it and so cold at night that you can hardly stand it."

The hotel: screen doors to the rooms—old grandpaw made advances to her—the real estate agent, who, when she refused his advances, sat out on the porch, just outside her room, and leaned forward in his chair and then wanged it back against the wall—the oilcloth she took off the table and burned—they never were able to figure out what had become of that oilcloth.

The Greenwich Village girl she knew in Seattle—a little Roumanian Jewess—she had painted fans and things like that—the first time I'd ever seen anything like that. —I lived with her when I was sick.

When she was a girl, they figured out that it would be a good thing to have me do the work and for me to get an education—and I did the work so well that they forgot about the education.

Elaine Orr. [She came from Troy, New York, inherited manufacturing money; was married first to Scofield Thayer of *The Dial*, then to Cummings, then to an Anglo-Irish M.P. named McDermott.] She came back to New York after her third marriage—she looked a little haggard because she had been sick but I thought seemed more attractive and more expansive—I thought her legs looked more mature. Wasn't it dreadful in New York everybody worrying so about money—she and her sisters quarreling over the china and cut glass [left by her mother] and neither of them really wanted them in the least—they'd probably never use them—they were in the most awful taste. —Dos Passos had had tea with her and had complained about the hotel—I told her about Cummings lying in the bath and imitating Dos—"Isn't it dweadful of me to lie here in this luxurious warm bath while human welations are being violated all over the countwy—stwikers are being shot down!" —I had asked if Dos still reacted like that—she said she thought a great many people reacted like that: Cummings thought that if you had more than ten cents there was something wrong with you. —She told about Cummings imitating "Sco" in Vienna receiving a visitor and giving orders to his German valet both at the same time—"Carl, another stick! Another stick!" —Cummings was the most conventional man in the world—"Don't ever be fooled by this idea of Cummings the rebel!"

[Early in 1924, EW wrote John Peale Bishop: "Cummings by the way, I understand, has come back to America, but I have not met him yet. I think that, after having been paid practically no attention to for many years, he is now rather in danger of being overrated. Believe me, that young man is very half baked and needs correction rather than encouragement. He has a genuine lyric gift but apparently no judgment, and so far as I can see, is still in a sophomore stage. Wallace Stevens's book, on the other hand, I thought remarkably successful in a limited way."

EW would be fond of Cummings, but always critical. As for Dos Passos, he liked his early work but found his drift to conservatism in later years unbearable and often wrote to his friend protesting against what he felt to be his a-historical irrationality. Dos Passos had a vivid memory of first meeting Edmund in 1922 in the offices of *Vanity Fair*, "a slight sandy-haired young man with a handsome clear profile. He wore a formal dark business suit." While waiting for the elevator, "Bunny gave an accent to the occasion by turning, with a perfectly straight face, a neat somersault."]

Cummings and Dos Passos. They had once taken a trip to Spain together. When we got to a town, Cummings said, I'd want to go out to the square or somewhere to see if I could find something [he meant a girl]. Dos would never go with me—he'd say, "I'll just stay here in the hotel, I think." One day I said to him: "Dos: don't you ever think about women?" No. "Don't you ever dream about sex?" No. What I went through with that man! He'd wake me up in the night groaning and throwing himself around in his sleep. I'd say, "What's the matter, Dos?" He'd say, "Why, I thought there were some beautiful wild swans flying overhead." One day I said, "You know, sometimes sex appears in dreams in very much disguised forms. You may be dreaming about sex without knowing it. Tell me one of your dreams— what did you dream about last night, for example?" He said, "Why, I dweamed I had a bunch of aspawagus and I was twying to give it to you." This had evidently stopped Cummings in his tracks.

He told me that on this trip, in spite of Dos's sympathy with the proletariat and his repudiation of the well-to-do world, they would always land in the best hotels. He said that Dos had an "expiated sweetness." "But this Big Boy tone that he takes when he writes!" He claimed that he never read Dos's books: they were all made up of externals.

[When I was married to Mary Blair and living at 3 Washington Square North, Charley Walker arrived in town and as usual wanted to stay with us. I told him I was married and had a baby, but he said he would sleep on the floor. It was difficult to discourage him; and though I was ill, had a fever and was lying in bed, it was impossible for me to prevent him from sitting down determinedly and reading to me in his emphatic way the first part of a labor novel he had written. This would have gone on indefinitely if I had not at last excused myself.]

Bernice Dewey. The smell of her light dress washed with Lux kept reminding me of "Fun with Soap Bubbles." —"This jaw's going to be preserved in the Natural History Museum, you know. [Hers, which, in spite of her prettiness, was unusually square.] —No: it's no use—I'm going to keep on looking the way I want to. There've been a great many complaints registered about my face—so no remarks." —The kind of girl that boys draw in the backs of their schoolbooks. A whole type of woman had culminated in her—the girl on a magazine cover—everybody's sweetheart. —I said that I remembered her eyes being wide apart—she said, "Yes, one on each side like a fish." [She had at one time been in the Follies and was telling me about it.] Dorothy Knapp in the Follies—virginity not a bad thing but then not such an awfully good thing, either. —The Follies girls don't make up in the street—in theory they don't—they're not supposed to. —Nothing ever goes wrong and people laugh, as happens with the Schuberts. —Mr. Whatshisname always got up after about a quarter of an hour and politely put his coat on. [This was a man in the bathing-suit

business, with whom she traveled around as a model and whom I sometimes found when I went to see her.]

Alec said that he felt as if Margaret Bishop had eaten up everything of
John but the mustache. Also, she sliced a little off John here and there, destroying him gradually but relentlessly—a little bit for being late to breakfast, etc.

May [1925]. The pale peach-silver sun dissolving the light green tree
fringe at the corner of Fifth Avenue and Washington Square. Breathing in
the rainy sidewalks of May.

New Canaan. Mr. Bartlett told a story about a married man in love with a
married lady—he got off the train at Stamford, in the evening, went to her
automobile; got in and threw his arms around her and kissed her—then
apologized: "Oh, I'm so sorry! I thought you were Mrs. Eaton!" Elinor's
[Elinor Wylie] attitude toward them—stolid, solid, uninteresting people.

Dos Passos. He said Cuthbert Wright was a creature who turned up in the
strangest places. First you saw a sort of mist, then Wright would materialize
like ectoplasm. (I remember his clammy flabby hand the only time I ever
met him.)

Cummings. "The man in the iron necktie!" (me)—"Well, I only hope to
God that when I come to die, it'll be said of me that I fell off a stone or something!" —Girl with her back to us in front of a drugstore, as we were walking up Lafayette Street—her dress blowing about her hips: "I guess if
anybody dropped a match, the whole block would burst into a blaze!" —
The girl on the bench in Washington Square Park: "Cylindrical!" —
When I gave him some of Léonie Adams's poems to read, he said: "This is
casting swirls before pine, you know. You know what I was thinking about
all that time: I was thinking about that cylindrical girl on the bench—
praying to God that she'd trip and fall as I passed!"—"It's all done with
mirrors!" [a favorite expression of his at this time].

Coney Island, early summer. Under the great wide white and buff of
Child's, like the Pennsylvania Station, with its high windows and bright
mosaics, one caught in the mirrors the reflection of girls in wide hats and
bright summer colors walking the boardwalk outside in the summer sun
that bleached whites whiter and blue and yellow white. —On the way
back, on the boat, there was a fresh sea wind, with the gay tinkling tune of a
harp and violin—black, black the shore and black the sea and sky.

Asbury Park, Fourth of July 1925. The girls were wearing long dresses and light coats lined with fur at the bottom and the men white knickerbocker trousers and sweaters checked tan and white. Hot dogs, dabbed with mustard from the common bowl with a little long-handled wooden trowel, and buttermilk; salt-water taffy, hot buttered popcorn. As day faded, the sands became palest buff and the ocean grayest blue, with the waves like white porcelain where they broke between—the moon was buff in the gray sky. As the sky darkened, the fireworks were started, and a rocket streamed violet and silver against the deepening gray—then it burst in brooches of red, gold and green, great bouquets that unfolded and shriveled, growing out of one another; the loud detonation of a cluster of white electric stars. Children held the bristling brass of their toy sparklers out to the enormous darkening sea. —Before night, little blond bob-haired girls and boys, in pink and yellow pinafores, slid squealing down the smooth bumpy slides in an interminable succession. —The last random pops and shots of the Fourth. —The smell of gunpowder.

New York. I saw the tightening sky, dull gray and yellow, distended with thunder.

Thesaurus for New Jersey article. Stagnant, rancid, etiolated; smoking and huddled factories; hot tennis in the morning—tinkling dinners in the evening; dirty wooden suburbs of Newark: dusty ailanthus leaves, shabby park, tacky, down-at-heels, threadbare, napless, boggy, soggy.

Tiny Tim [a Village character, who sold his candy in the speakeasies and restaurants]. Soul Candy—wide-brimmed Stetson hat and green suit to match the day—"Inspiration"—said to have made such a good thing of it (May 1923) that he is able to live uptown with his wife and children—some say he merely has a house in the country—has written philosophical pamphlets, which he produces and presents to you when sufficiently encouraged—never comes out of his character, even when engaging in serious conversation, as he did with us when speaking informatively on ants, scarabs, etc. —Said he was from Texas—evidently economizes on sugar—curious smiling expression which never betrayed his character. —Mottoes with each box: "Never be sure of a woman even if she has borne you a dozen children"—from *Poems, Proverbs and Parables of Timaeus.*

Jean Wright [Gorman]. When she had gone in to propitiate Herbert with a package of popcorn, as he lay, hurt and indignant, reading in bed—she came back comically, clumsily on tiptoe—"Well, I opened cold, as they say." He had said, "Well, you've got your nerve!" and that was all. When she had called him up and said she couldn't get back for dinner, he had said, "Then I won't have any dinner." —She asked George Hartman if Herbert had eaten anything. —Yes, he had eaten heartily a very savory stew made by George out of lamb and canned vegetable soup—afterwards, he had read George several episodes out of *Ulysses*.

Seabright. The large dark dining room at Panacci's, so much more prepossessing within than it looks from the outside—with its fresh clean tablecloths and its wide clean napkins folded in points and stuck in the large clear tumblers. We sat on a bench under a little shelter near the Beach Club: it was warm—the sky was as soft and dim as the soft dim sand, and the stars themselves were dim—the waves broke softly, the sea was obscure.

Rumson. The smell of hot blackened oiled roads mingled with honeysuckle—large green estates on either side, dark-shadowed with shrubbery and trees—grooms walking horses through the shadows along the smooth road—the regular wire fences, the well-kept hedges.

New Canaan. Great waves of dullness rolled back and forth through the room—one thought: "I must escape or I shall drown!"

Dick Maney, the press agent, said to Eakin: "Well, don't try to high-hat us, you animal-cracker from Pittsburgh!"

The empty sonority of the radio—a hollow yowling.

The sensual pleasure of peeling mushrooms.

Bodfish's story about the ironworker who turned female impersonator. He married a spiritualist, who thought that everybody was represented by a number—she had been looking for the number of the man she was to marry, and, meeting him (the ironworker), decided that it was he. It was announced that he was to sing at a church sociable in Boston for admission to which a nominal price of fifty cents was charged. The ironworker appeared in a woman's evening gown and sang a series of "old English ballads and roundelays" and other concert pieces. The audience were astounded but fascinated—it gave them *un frisson nouveau*. So successful did the performance turn out that it was repeated the following week at regular theater prices. When he went on to sing *I send thee a gift of roses,* however, and attempted to cast some artificial flowers into the audience, the wire stems got caught in his bodice, so that he had to keep pulling at them—like something in a dream, Bodfish said, when all your powers become paralyzed and you can't accomplish anything.

At Seabright. A buxom woman in a red bathing suit lying in the sand with her shoulders between a man's knees: he was stroking her arm passionately. John Amen said, "Those two are going to be in pieces in a minute!"

Little boy on tricycle with great energy backing off and riding full-tilt into other little boy on tricycle, then patting him energetically and repeatedly on his bare knee. —*Little girl* with bobbed fluffy brown hair, deeply browned and plump, dressed in knickerbockers, traveling stretched out along running board of automobile—she smiled readily at passers-by.

Atlantic Highlands. A garage man in corduroy trousers and the upper half of a bathing suit, from which brown arms bulged. —On the upper piazza of a "cabaret-restaurant," two tanned fishy girls with stringy bobbed hair and shreddy dresses, as if they soaked themselves habitually in the rank shallow water that lies between the mainland and the beach. —A green-blinded maroon summer cottage facing the breakwater of rocks, with crescents slit in the blinds of the first floor, a close row of pink and white petunias all around it and an old weather-worn children's swing on the porch. — Cottages rakishly designed as ships, with portholes and porches like decks. —Little sordid sandy sea-bleached bungalows, with people listlessly sitting about them in bathing suits.

Zelda used to say that hotel bedrooms excited her erotically.

The water silver fire behind the trees.

The remote moan of a train.

Sandlass's [Seabright bathing pavilion]. A flaxen-haired girl, with legs and arms burned salmon pink in a turquoise bathing suit—afterwards she put on an orange cap and went in the water, where she stayed for a long time, swimming like a seal—she did an excellent crawl. —A little girl in lavender, with a purple bathing cap, was marvelously adroit at plunging with the waves—she would dive over them just as they broke or, looking expertly over her shoulder, make a quick flight forward. —Turquoise, robin's-egg blue, vermilion with a canary-yellow belt. —A fish hawk flapping above the water in its businesslike way—first flapping, then gliding a moment—looking for fish—it makes a swift straight lethal drop when it sees one. —On the line of the horizon, flat against the sky, the white sails of a ship which seems to have almost the transparence of a phantom.

The ugly silly crude light-green *umbrella trees* which everyone plants on their front lawns at Red Bank, Oceanic and all along the coast.

At Sandlass's, the sound of a solo with piano accompaniment from the radio inside the wooden enclosure where the keys are given out and where candy and beach toys are sold—the sweet melody and the bright piano notes between, slightly scratchy and effaced in spots, as if it had been affected by the sand and bleached by the dry sea air. It pervaded the bathing place naturally, as if in harmony with the sea-seasoned color of the bathing clothes and the brilliance of summer dresses put on without subtleties after the swim.

Swimming. Wading out, each successive swelling wave lifts a new rim of chill about the body.

Marion Dell's account of the set of young married people in Paris whose characteristic was that they talked with extravagant freedom but with the attitude that they could be allowed to do so because they were all really all right.

The clear concrete white of the garage, in the morning, behind the dark-green clotted foliage of the trees. —In the evening, the yellow and white dresses of the women sitting on the steps of the house across the street, seen so clearly through the lucid summer twilight that thickens yet does not seem to tint the air.

John Amen and Marion [at Seabright—Marion Cleveland, who had been married to my friend Stanley Dell, was now divorced and about to marry John Amen, who had been two or three years behind me at college, but who afterwards became a close friend] *etc.* "Oh, Christ! it is the Inchcape Rock!"— "Well, I ought to be the most welcome guest you've ever had in this house [producing some bottles of Old Overholt]—there they are, little joy-berries every one!—No bed-whirling!—Nothing harsh about it! I woke up after a night of diverting dreams, as if I were being wafted down from paradise on a billowy cloud." —*Fantasia on letter writing* [we had a game of impersonating imaginary characters]: "Oh, yes: I always have a stenographer on the train with me—and I always have a stenographer at the theater—I have her in a seat right next to mine—so that any time when I cease to be interested in the play, I can turn around and say, 'Miss Dokes, take this.' I just drop the thread of the play and then later on I take it up again. I write to people all over the world—I just sent my first letter to Peru the other day—Peru and Bolivia! —I just write letters—I must write half a million letters in a year! Sometimes I don't say very much in them—I just say, 'Yours of the so and so received, yours very truly'—but it brings you into touch with people—into close touch with them! I'm able to get into touch in that way with perhaps two-thirds of all the people in the world—and those who can't read and write I reach by dictaphone records—I have a secretary for every language—very high-priced men, I have high-priced men for everything—I get the best people in every line.—Those who can't read and write and suffer from infectious diseases—like lepers. Oh, I have people with all kinds of infectious diseases!" —In late afternoon, outside, we saw the level sea of August that had already the colder blue of autumn and was dashed with some whitecaps—three bathers with coral limbs and dark suits stood against the blue, with their backs toward us, looking out at the sea. —"I get dead bodies for necrophiles. I'm perhaps the only person in the world who is occupied exclusively with that particular work." —"I thought you ran a chain of bawdy houses." —"Oh, no: I was just connected with one for a while, and that's how I got into this other work. It's usually just something that's done on the side, but I saw my chance for specializing, and now I have the largest, in fact, the only business of the kind in the world—I have branches all over. —('Oh, just what is your business, Mr. W.?') I must go back to my work—my clientele always become restive, as the business practically stops short in the summer when I take my vacation—the corpses don't keep at all in summer, you know—and the necrophiles get a little wild sometimes and very often commit crimes—it's simply a taste they have and when they can't satisfy it, they're likely to take it out in other ways—so I think it's just as well for me to go back." —"Yes, I know: it's a safety valve, I suppose—and I always say that a safety valve's a very good thing."

—The first moments of ecstatic abandon when you go in the water a little drunk—throw yourself to the waves. —Girl in green bathing suit stretched out on the sand: [JA] "Like to jump that before lunch—a little appetizer!" —The first cold, the earlier dark, the melancholy of the shore. The trains at Seabright blowing the racing days, the monstrous cottages once fashionable and admired, the racecourse overgrown with locust and ailanthus, where a record on the straight mile course was once made.

—Marion's dressing gown of Tyrian purple velvet, the pile of magazines, the plain glass pitchers from which we extracted the ice for our highballs, the oldfashioned screens fastened in the low windows, the white porches with their rocking chairs, the red carpets on the stairs and in the long halls, the neat but bleached-looking furniture of the seaside. —At Panacci's, while we were eating—rich dark clam chowder, slabs of fish with triangular pieces of lemon, well-grown but tasteless cobs of corn—we heard a woman playing a piano in the next room, which did not open into ours, a playing which began with jazz, then became troubled and desultory, finally lapsing altogether, till it commenced again in a soft strain of contented revery: MacDowell's *From an Indian Wigwam*.

—"That alcoholic pseudo-dip of yours—that alcoholic wallow!" — The first cold blue of autumn and the melancholy of the shore provoking thoughts not only of the end of summer, but of the pressure of time, the wavering of ambition, the disappointments of love—the period of life that approaches its close like the period of the year.

—*Aunt Caroline* took Kimmy [her grandson] on her knee and sang all the words of the *Songs of Yesterday* record: *Little Annie Rooney, Sweet Rosie*

O'Grady, The Bowery, The Sidewalks of New York, Yip-addy-i-ay, The Good Old Summertime. When he came to her house, he always insisted on bringing his own phonograph records with him—they were all cracked, but he said, "I don't mind." He was delighted at the way Aunt Caroline came out on the Yip! in *Yip-addy-i-ay.* He had a little pathetic look when he had to go to bed and couldn't play any more—he asked me to play a cheap mud-colored record called *Collegiate,* with a great bite broken out of it, using a loud needle, while he was being put to bed—I asked him why he liked it so much, and he said, "It's so nice where they sing." She let him stay up long enough to play *An Orange Grove in California* from the Music Box Revue. — She had always tried not to make her children and grandchildren do things she had hated herself when she was a child: staying alone in the dark, going to bed early in summer, etc.

Progress of a popular song (from fall in New York to summer throughout the country). Harlem cabarets, other cabarets, Reisenfeld's classical jazz, the Rascoes' private orchestra, the hand organs, the phonographs, the radio, the Webster Hall balls, other balls (college proms), men going home late at night whistling it on the street, picked out on Greenwich Village ukuleles, sung in late motor rides by boys and girls, in restaurants—hotel restaurants, Paul Whiteman and Lopez, vaudeville, played Sundays by girls at pianos from sheet music with small photographs on the cover, of both the composer and the person who first sang it—first sung in a popular musical comedy (introduced several times—at the end of the second act pathetically—and played as the audience are leaving the theater)—pervading the country through the movie pianists, danced to in private houses to the music of a phonograph—the Elks fair—thrown on the screen between the acts at the National Winter Garden Burlesque and sung by the male audience—Remey's Dancing Academy (decayed fairies).

Ted on radical Jew who lived with him and Jim in Russia. They would try to explain manners to him, and he would watch them at table like a hawk, catching them up on what he thought were breaches of their own code: "You didn't do so and so then!"

—There had been no blood on the snow at the time of the November revolution, because it wasn't snowing that day

—boorjewy—they would say, "You're boorjewy!"

Mary:
It's a shout.
I thot I was going to croak!
I want that in writing.
Try and find out!
sob-sister stuff

nebby—you dirty lizard
That's a pretty thought!
It's all applesauce to me!
old dames
Ices—Isis
I offered to take her over to Seabright on my handlebars: "You know, I
    come from Pittsburgh, the smoky city! I like to do things with a dash!"
I hope to tell you!
Of the coffee: "It lets you know when it's ready!"
You ran around like a hen on a hot griddle.
Hell's teeth—Christ's foot!

Popular Songs

> *Oh, my lovie came back!*
> *I feel so good I could rap on wood.*
> *Oh, jiminy gee! my lovie's come back to me!*
> *It was such a lonely old shack*
> *Till Santa Claus broke down the doors*
> *And brought me back*
> *My little used-to-be!*
> *I don't know where she hid or what she did—*
> *All I know she was breakin' my heart!*
> *When she returned, her kisses burned—*
> *Somebody else had made her terribly smart.*
> *Oh, my lovie came back!*
> *With six kids and a ⎱ Cadillac*
> *   a ⎰ broken back*
> *How busy I'll be!—My lovie's come back to me!*

When my sweetie walks down the street,
All the birds in the trees go tweety-tweet.

Oh, they call her Louisville Lou—
What that vampin' baby can do!
She's the most heart-breakinest,
Shimmy-shakinest
Gal you ever knew!
And when her taxi stops,
All the porters drop their mops—
Old black Joes that are old and bent
Pawn their crutches just to pay her rent . . .
Red hot mamma, turn your damper down!

You gotta love Mamma every night
Or you can't love Mamma at all!

[The following song was composed by Scott Fitzgerald, with some assistance from me. The third—and not so successful—stanza was contributed by me much later. A good deal of the effect of the song depended on the appropriate gestures that accompanied every line and on the impersonation of the dog lover who was supposed to be singing it. Scott always buttoned up his jacket and assumed an expression of imbecile earnestness. The curious thing was that the song somehow got around. Harl Cook and Paul Chavchavadze heard it in some nightclub, and I was astonished when I heard them sing it without knowing that Scott and I had composed it. It had been somewhat deformed in transmission. Scott and I discussed every line from the point of view of being sure to have it banal and inept enough. I violated this ideal by making the third stanza too clever. Dogs, for some reason I do not understand, always seemed to Scott somewhat comic.]

In sunny Africa they have the elephant
And in India they have the zebera—
Up in Canada the Rocky Mountain goat
And in Idaho the shoat
    (You've heard about it!)
But of all these animals
You will find the best of pals—
    Is!

    Dog, dog—I like a good dog—
    Towser or Bowser or Star—
    Clean sort of pleasure—
    A four-footed treasure—
    And faithful as few humans are!
    Here, Pup: put your paw up—
    Roll over dead like a log!
    Larger than a rat!
    More faithful than a cat!
      Dog! Dog! Dog!

The monkey makes us gay—
Tigers are byoo-ti-ful!
The patient horse, they say,
Drags heavy loads all day—
Up in the air we see our many feathered friends—
And for eggs we have the hens
    (They always lay them!)
But you may list or hark:
You'll never hear one bark!
    Like!

    Dog, dog—I like a good dog!
    Rover or Fido or Spot—

Clean sort of pleasure—
A four-footed treasure—
And loyal as humans are not!
Here, Pup: put your paw up—
Roll over dead like a log!
Bolder than a mouse!
More wholesome than a louse!
   Dog! Dog! Dog!

Tonsillitis: Two Dreams [December 1925]
Studies in the Effects of Tonsillar Inflammation on the Critical and Poetic Faculties

I. Rising Fever

I have come to a lunch at which I am to meet a number of eminent persons. We are sitting about a rectangular table; the place on my right is vacant. The guests seem uninteresting and wooden; I do not hear anything they are saying. Then the gentleman who is to be my neighbor finally appears. He is introduced to me as Mr. J. C. Squire. Mr. Squire appears strikingly different from the photographs I have seen of him: he is a gray-eyed light-haired young Englishman in a gray suit. I remember that I have had, a few years ago, a correspondence with Mr. Squire: he had written asking me to contribute an American letter to the *London Mercury*, and I had promised him one. My failure to fulfill this promise, though largely submerged during my waking life, has evidently remained on my conscience; for it now instantly comes to mind. I apologize to Mr. Squire for never having sent him the article. He looks blank, and I try to explain to him: "You wrote and asked me to send you a letter on contemporary American literature"; I tell him my name. But he has evidently quite forgotten, and he seems to apologize for the fact that the discussion of American literature is entirely out of his province: "You see, when I founded the *Mercury*, I intended it quite frankly to cover only a limited ground. My sympathies have always been those of the *fin de siècle*. So that the *Mercury* is quite frankly a *fin de siècle* affair, and I have deliberately kept it so." He is extremely polite; he smiles deprecatingly, as if over his hobby, his old-fashioned taste; but I perceive his complacent conviction that no other is possible. I try to make him see that is not the point; he wrote me himself, two years ago, inviting me to contribute a letter on contemporary American literature. He repeats his previous explanation, almost in the same words. I am silent in bewilderment. I am ready to allow the question of the letter to pass, but I do not know how to reply to his remarks on the *Mercury's fin de siècle* character—I summon the magazine before my mind, in the attempt to find some justification for this description: I see quite plainly the orange covers, the alternate pages of bibliographies and of essays on Thomas Hardy: these latter appear to my mental gaze as great square black seas of print. The figures of Wilde and of Dowson present themselves to my mind, and I try to find their relation to the *Mercury*. I have an impulse to ask him what the bibliographies have to do with the *fin de siècle;* and another to tell him that I consider the pages a great deal too wide. But I refrain, in reflecting that the first would be rude and the second irrelevant. At last, however, smiling genially, I challenge him: "Oh, come, Mr. Squire," I say, "the *Mercury's* hardly *fin de siècle*, is it?" "Yes," he replies, "I have kept it quite frankly a *fin de siècle* affair." The figures of Dowson and Wilde again float across my view; but I cannot connect them with Mr. Squire. Then it occurs to me, as the pages on Hardy present their solid masonry again, that the *Mercury* is perhaps *fin de siècle* in the sense that it has taken cognizance of no literary event of importance since the end of the century. I am completely baffled and balked. I realize that I cannot talk with Mr. Squire; our points of view have so little in common that words have practically lost their meanings. Yet other people understand him: he has begun to chat with the greatest ease and amiability with other people at the table, some of them English, no doubt. And his understanding with them has established an obstruction with which I am confronted, a wall of dullness I cannot penetrate but whose presence I must endure through the lunch. The guests are talking; but, as before, I do not hear what they say, I sit apart at my corner of the table. I glance to my left and observe that on that side the company has been enveloped in shadow. They have also ceased to talk; a lady, very awkwardly dressed, is solidifying into a monument unenlivened by even a face. The whole assembly, I know, in a moment, will have been blotted to a fog. But its obstructions, like a foggy block of granite, will continue to intrude upon me, half sleeping, half waking—yielding easily to my attempts to push it out of the bed, but returning with soft persistence, reappearing in a hundred forms, problems, tasks, interminably changing images, to be opposed, to be circumvented, to be refused, to be resolutely turned from, to be sloughed off, to be propitiated, to be casually brushed away, lest it stifle me or drive me mad.

II. *Convalescence*

We have been marching a long time, and our ranks are in considerable disorder. We are listless and indifferent. At last officials appear from the direction in which we are proceeding; our captain goes to confer with them and we fall out beside the road, which lies between wide green meadows. We are wearing uniforms of a deeper, but still very vivid, green, frogged across with vivid purple, our high helmets are green, too. The officers' uniforms are distinguished by frogs of a darker green. We are evidently dragoons, but some of the detachment stands taller than my own rather short stature. What a marvelous countryside! Beyond the fresh grassy meadows to our left, rises a screen of beautifully slender but excessively high trees, feather-dustered with leafy crests, against a sky both cloudy and clear. Refreshed by the vision of trees and fields, we begin singing the charming song, so popular at the time and place, of which the first line of the chorus runs, "Ahoy, ahoy! Sailor, ahoy!" But, after a moment, silvery voices begin answering us from the trees: when we have sung the first two ahoys, delicious feminine voices reply with the "Sailor, ahoy!" We begin to laugh; we are enchanted. Among the trees is a delightful town and it is the girls of the town who are playing with us. If we were only not serving as soldiers! If we were only free! At this moment, the captain raises his voice: "There's no use going on!" he says. "We were promised a large contingent, which should have joined us several days ago. When I complained, I was told they would meet us here. Now I find that no preparation of any kind has been made from this end of the line. The mission simply cannot be attempted with a mere handful of men" (there were only about a dozen of us) "and I refuse to undertake it! The government insisted upon this mission, and they have given us no support of any kind! I will not take the responsibility!" Our service is at end. Our hearts are filled with joy and freedom. In a new exhilaration, we tune the long "Ahoy, ahoy!" and the voices of the pale-haired maidens—we can see them now quite plainly, coming to the doors of generous white houses or loitering in the streets—with a seriousness of music beyond the mockery of sport—answer us as before with their silvery, "Sailor, ahoy!" Oh, what naturalness, what grace, in that carefree and lovely land! I realize that these young girls could speak or go as they pleased. For them, it can never be vulgar to sing responses to the soldiers. And they are coming out to meet us. Like California, I reflect, life so natural and so free—yet, with a refinement and a sensitive feeling which are like the silvery and cloudy effects of the wonderful varying sky, such effects as can only appear where there is moisture in the air.

We make our way across the meadows. Halfway, I meet a girl whom I know, a slim girl with pale straw-colored hair, for whom, when a boy, I conceived a passion. Before I have come close, I see her perform grotesque movements—high kicks, rotations of the abdomen—which I think not quite in good taste. But, as I approach, I realize that she is doing the exercises of the ballet. I express surprise; "Oh, yes," she answers. "I've been dancing for a year." I am perfectly satisfied, I am delighted, to find her there. I ask her if she will come out with me that evening; we are planning some charming, if rather vague, excursion. She consents, and I realize with rapture that the entanglements of her mother and her husband which in later years have estranged me from her have now been completely removed. I do not understand exactly why but it has something to do with the time of day: in the late afternoon she can go anywhere or do anything. As we walk along, I observe her full, her admirably rounded body, quite different from her old leanness, which, as she moves, molds the loose-hanging folds of her plain dress into forms of beauty.

But I must first wash up and shave my beard, which has grown unsightly in my three days' illness; and I must get rid of my uniform. I walk a little apart from her; I do not talk to her very much. For I am unwilling to appear to her now at these disadvantages. I hand her over to a friend, John Bishop, who is there in civilian clothes. I make my way straight to the bathroom, where I find the other men washing up. Changing my uniform for other clothes turns out a laborious process. Most of my clothes I have difficulty in finding and others I am obliged to borrow. But throughout the confusion, I am inexhaustibly amused by the conversation of my companions: each one is such a character, he is so interesting, so pungent or so witty! One is an Italian from Genoa. I am delighted by the richness of life—I am aware that it is one of those days when everything is felicitous. When John Bishop appears to make me hurry, for it is already growing late, I tell him the amusing things I have heard. I can hardly believe that it is not enough that I should suddenly be discharged from the army and meet Claire released from all ties on the same day, but that even in the washroom I should be delighted with such fascinating encounters. "We must have something to drink tonight," I tell John. "Why don't you try to find something while I finish." He has a conviction that it will not be necessary to go very far: the chauffeur outside will have some. I accompany him to the street. There is a large car drawn up to the curb in the late-afternoon sun. We ask the chauffeur if he has anything, and he at once produces some Scotch. I return to the lavatory, more delighted than ever. But a terrible fact now forces itself upon me: I have neither bathed nor shaved. I ask a young man, who seems a civilized college type, if he will lend me his razor. He amiably consents, but I stare at it in dismay: it is a Gillette, as I had hoped, but the top part, with the blade, is only about as large as my fingernail. Impossible to shave my three-day beard with this tiny razor! And then the bath, which means taking off all my clothes, which I have with such difficulty assembled and put on! Darkness is falling outside: the magic hour will soon be past, and it is only then that I can have Claire. John comes back to get me again. I decide that I shall have to give it up, that I shall have to wait until tomorrow. There is still a hindrance, an obstruction, which impedes me; it has prevented me from having Claire that night. I am still the victim of a sinister fate. But I look forward with a happy confidence to its eventual disappearance.

[This dream was no doubt a reversion to my frustrated state of mind before the too-long-delayed beginning of my active sexual life. I used to have ecstatic dreams of this kind—in which I usually imagined myself arriving at some marvelous seashore, where I found the most delightful people swimming. I first heard of psychoanalysis in a magazine article by Max Eastman, and Walter Hall at Princeton talked about it a little. It was given more weight for me by Kenneth Hayes Miller, when Morris Belknap brought him to see us. One evening, when Miller was talking about dreams, I told him about one of these seashore dreams that I had had not long before. He unexpectedly paid me what I took for a compliment by saying, "It is probably to your credit that you are the kind of person who could have a dream like that," or something of the kind. I never have such dreams any more. The dreams that leave the strongest impression on me are experiences of intense horror like the one introduced into *The Little Blue Light*.

I had a whole series of such illnesses. I remember one at 3 Washington Square North, when I read *The American* [Henry James] in bed; but I usually got off to Red Bank, where I knew I should be well taken care of, when I felt myself getting sick. It was at Red Bank that I had these two dreams. One of these illnesses—measles—was one of the most serious I have ever had. I think it was this case of measles that inspired the poem "Infection."]

Saranac [Visit to Saranac from Talcottville to see the Seldeses, who were staying on an island in Alice's father's camp]. So have I seen in Adirondack camps . . . But only the dark lake and the loon's cry. —They had got Bozo from the Bide-a-Wee Home, because you can get them free there—they are supposed to be guaranteed not to have anything the matter with them. But, in the first place, she turned out to be a bitch when they had thought they were getting a male dog, and then, after a month or so, it became plain that she was going to have puppies—they prevented her from crawling under the house and she had them one night while she was lying in the dining room with the Seldeses—they turned out to be all colors—one of them was pure white—Bozo herself had as many colors as a rag carpet—she had a white belly and evidently a touch of Irish terrier. Then she developed some kind of incurable mange, and they decided they would have to shoot her—they were afraid she would give it to the pups. She was going to be shot the next day, so they were especially kind to her. They had a cat, too. —The framed letter from Charles Evans Hughes to Alice's father—"My dear Commissioner—''—the Indian pictures—the stuffed fox on the mantelpiece—the stuffed owl suspended on a wire in a pose of flight—the deer's head (only one in a season but everybody broke the rule) —the Indian pictures—the framed legend—the roulette wheel and box of chips—*Lorna Doone, Beverly of Graustark, Midshipman Easy, Andersen's Fairy Tales* (dark blue and brown covers, heavily stamped with black complicated designs)—great stone fireplaces—a big map of northern New York hung in the upper hall. —The black lake—the thick vast silence drowning you in peace at night—the blue mountains with the white cottony mist rising from out of them—the long downpour of mountain rain—the guide boat—swimming in the black heavy water—there were two stakes to which the children had all had to be able to swim before they were allowed to go out in the guide boat—no one had been there for fifteen years— Alice, as she got on in her married life, matured as a lady of that particular sort, as different as possible from Gilbert. —She had that nice frank laugh which became freer and bolder—Mr. Hall (Alice's father) had bought twenty-five hundred acres but had never been able to sell much of it on account of Saranac's t.b. reputation—adultery of limited scope among the few camps. —The Villa Vera—they wanted to paint, "So's your Old man!" under it—a set of dark willow-pattern plates (a phonograph with the records of fifteen years ago).

I was whistling a theme from *Petrushka*, as I was getting up—Gilbert said that Cole Porter was going to have it put on his motor horn. —Alice was so tender to the pups.

Return of Ted Paramore. He called me up from Cramer's sanatorium at Sixty-third Street and Lexington Avenue. —As I drew near, I saw, framed in the open window above the entrance, a woman with her mouth held wide open, as if in an arrested roar. —Ted hadn't slept for forty-eight hours—had heebie jeebies, cold sweats, suicidal impulses between sleeping and waking—wanted to ask them to tie his foot, so he couldn't jump out of bed—had no money. —I asked him to tell me his story— "Well, what story do you want? I can tell almost any story." —Had a girl in Del Monte— "Oh, she was fine! She came and cooked for me and everything. And then she got drunk one day and married a hunchback—and when she came to, she was appalled. —She wrote me and said that he'd just given her a lot of money and she'd like to send me some. He was rich." —When the earthquake came, Ted and a friend had been drinking gin fizzes and they were just starting out to motor from Santa Barbara to Hollywood. "The friend said, 'Gee, look at that windstorm, Ted! Look at those chimneys swaying! Look at the tops of the trees!' But I said, 'Oh, that's just those gin fizzes.' But then I looked and I saw the chimneys blowing off. We were back to our house and there we found the whole family and the servants and everybody out on the lawn. And I said, 'Well, I guess we'll have to wait till this windstorm is over,' and Mother said, 'Windstorm! You're not going to Hollywood today! This is an earthquake.' —The car was just rattled back and forth on the road!"

Jimmy Gruen. He had run a gambling house and at one time he used to work with kept women, show them how to do their stuff—story about going to the man and explaining he was the girl's best friend—"Now I know that love is nothing," etc.—"How much does he want to give her? I'll give her twice as much!"—Girl in the cabaret he trained to ask for fifty cents to tip the colored woman in the ladies' room—you can make as much as three or four dollars a night that way.—"Midget Age-guessing Company—Pock-marked and Negro Midgets a Specialty—that last midget you sent me arrived in bad condition and is now in fact dead."

Mack Sennett, asked to dinner at Pasadena. Was originally a boiler-maker—white-haired now, red-faced and fat. He figured that he was the guest of honor and that he ought to arrive late. He came an hour late. The hostess said she hoped he'd forgive them for sitting down without him—he said, Oh, that was all right, he'd had dinner already. She asked him if he wouldn't sit down and he said, Oh, no, thanks, he'd stand up. So he stood up until they had finished. Then, attempting to bestir himself politely and help one of the ladies out of her chair, he knocked a vase off the mantelpiece.

Thoughts of a vigorous and violent man with a passive woman—dreams of lying in the arms of a charmingly sensitive woman, with whom he can share a tenderness which the present occasion lacks.

Summer 1925. Nude stockings (for Negroes, too), "pansy dresses, red dresses, wide floppy hats, chintzy dresses with flowered wallpaper figures, darkish blues and pinks, light coats with a border of fur along the bottom."

Anita Loos told Ted about the different make lines of different sorts of men—those who respected her purity.

National Winter Garden. Speech between the acts—someone had said, apropos of some risqué Broadway comedy, that when he wanted to hear "dubble-entenders," he would rather go to the National Winter Garden. "Because here's where you get burlesque as you like it, without any camouflage—sincere dubble-entenders."

Seward Collins fell in love with *Lee Morse* from her phonograph records.

—She liked the lugubrious sentimental records herself—and had written some of them herself—but everybody else liked the "hot ones."

Ukulele Ike announced songs: *You stole my wife, you horse-thief,* and, *I used to shower my sweetie with presents but it ain't gonta rain no more.* —*Who takes care of the caretaker's daughter, while the caretaker's busy takin' care?* —*Who makes the dressmaker's daughter, while the dressmaker makes the dress?* —*And for lovin', she's an oven.*—*Flamin' Mamie.*

On the back streets of suburban towns little girls in green hats are dancing the Charleston.

Lee Morse. Radio party. Barney Gallant's afterwards. Barney Gallant's rolling *r.*—"Waiterrs! Slaves!—Here, find out what they're drinking and give it to them—*sur la maison!*"—The Gertrude Hoffmann girls—the little fat one in red with hooked nose and black-line-penciled eyebrows. —"*Just an old-fashioned romance—Just a kiss and a sly glance—But where is another like me?*"—long-drawn, lugubrious, hoarse. —Her young Jewish manager— he thought the Poe play had been terrible, they had had Poe composing *The Raven* in a thunderstorm—with thunder and lightning and every-thing—really, it was laughable! —His wife, very handsome, had only just come in from Kansas City last January—had written her family that she'd either have to go back or get married—a great deal of poise, made a very good appearance. —Lee Morse was coy about singing, *Yessir, The Whaddyecall'em Blues* (Sew thought the latter uninspired). —She wanted to sing "an old-fashioned romance." When I said anything nice to her, she would grab me under the chin with her left hand. When, at the end of the evening, I began tossing the old-fashioned romance with Barney Gallant's Hungarian *r,* she grabbed me around the neck and said, "Old-fashioned omelette! Ha ha ha!"—Comic Toreador song when we first came in. — Barney said of some composition played, announcing to the audience, "This damn fool wrote this himself!" He sat beside our table and sighed, "Oh, Jesus!" over one of Lee's Negro spirituals. She began going on at great length about her father—a Methodist minister in the West—she had sung something which she believed him to have written—told both Alice Seldes and Mary that she hoped Sew would ask her to marry him, she didn't want to marry him, she wouldn't think of accepting, but she wanted him to ask her. Alice warned Seward not to breathe a word about marriage to her whatever he did. —Terrible undrinkable, unidentifiable liquor. Alice (ironically): "God, that's good! What is it, Sew?" "Pretty smooth!" "Going blind." Served in ginger-ale bottles. —Tom Smith left on curb-stone with last unattached whore: a middleaged lady in red. Uncertain whether he was waiting till others had gone, so as to take her home in a taxi by himself, or whether he was on the point of getting in with the others and leaving her flat.

Faint, sleepless, wraith-like, as if she might disappear any moment.

At Red Bank, while I was sick in December. That bleak blue rainy light throughout the day—the bare black branches against the bleak rainy blue.

Heard from a taxi driver and reported by Dorothy Parker: "Or I'll knock the red, white and blue Jesus outa yuh!"

Well-known actor's apartment (in which Leonora was staying). He had tried to make it Chinese, painted the woodwork black and orange; enormous bronze Chinese vase, with electric light inside, which supplied subdued illumination; early American clock; two enormous divans, covered with a rainbow of cushions; small, closely curtained windows; little boudoir off the sitting room; triple locks on the doors; Oriental copper ornament which stood on the floor and suggested a convenience for ladies; sets of Oscar Wilde and Stevenson, room completely dominated by three great portraits of actor, with the wires concealed by branches of artificial grapes; aquarium for goldfish with naked nymphs in attitudes of abandon among the gravel at the bottom and a bronze satyr rising from the middle; Oriental screen; white fur rug; two sumptuous cocktail sets; large Victrola.
The bedroom with its imperial canopied bed and a copy of *Who's Who in the Theatre* on the table—rather like a woman's bedroom. —In the bathroom, the pictures of his family. —The private telephone number: the first night I was there, three girls called up. —The apartment house: the cautious and confidential doorman. Sounds of hysteria, violence, merrymaking and love emanating from the various floors as we went up in the elevator. —Ice machine in the refrigerator.

Herman Oelrichs's apartment. Two telephones in the sitting room, so that if anybody called up about anything important while he was already talking, he would be sure not to miss it. Speakers in the bedroom, so that he could hear what was being said in the sitting room.
(First he tries to show off apartment, then as she takes a faintly ironic line about the goldfish, he takes the line of really not knowing anything about furniture, objets d'art, etc.—he had an interior decorator do it all, and no doubt he was badly swindled—"It's probably terrible, is it?" She has told him that she saw him once when she was a girl and he was on the road, and had fallen madly in love with him; he tries to appeal to her from that point of view—"It's I, Madeleine, it's your——!" —He tries violent passion and attempts to carry her to the divan, but gives out on the way and only just makes it—he explains that he is no good any more, an old man now—or,

worry about his work and his family affairs have worn him out, he has not had any sleep, etc.)

She (Leonora) had tried to call him at the McAlpin and could not get him. He told her he was registered under an assumed name—"Do you mean to say you were staying there with that girl under an assumed name!" —"Why, you didn't expect me to sign our own names, did you?" —She was piqued; she asked him what he could see in a girl like that. He said that he knew she was just a little dumbbell ("stand 'em on their heads, eh?"), but he'd got to that time of life where he really found her very satisfactory. —"She's just crazy about me, Leonora—all she wants in the world is just to be with me. She kisses my clothes."—Then he tried to work on her— talked dirty—became a simple unaffected child—became romantic —became friendly, told her about his family, showed her photographs of his daughters—talked dirty again. —She finally said it was six o'clock in the morning and he would have to go so that she could get some sleep.—"Oh, Leonora, how can I leave you and go back to that stupid little bitch? Here I've been caught up to the heights with you and when I go back to her, I'll feel debased, defiled! How can you send me away?" But she was obdurate; she bargained with him, however, that, if he would remain chaste during the week he was in Philadelphia, she might be kinder to him—"Of course, I only said that to get rid of him." He swore that he would be faithful to her and gave his word that, if he should slip, he would let her know.—No doubt, she enjoyed the feeling that she was inflicting a week's privation upon the little blonde. But Thursday he called her up from Philadelphia at two o'clock in the morning. He said, "Leonora! Leonora, I called you up to tell you I still love you—but I'm selling, Leonora, I'm sel-ling—I've got the most beautiful blonde here that I've ever seen in my life, and I can't keep my part of the bargain, Leonora!"

Leonora on the Jews. Of course, he didn't do like a dirty Jew lawyer would do" (her foot twitching on the couch)—social disadvantage in being a Jew, had married his wife for social position —Well, Barney Gallant kept the Jews out, anyway. I held her up on that by saying he was a Jew himself, wasn't he?—which put her under the necessity of making up a long justifi-cation. —When she had had some drinks, she said of somebody that she thought he was a Jew—"though I'm not sure—perhaps he's ambidextrous"—then, as some of her pretenses were suspended, she laughed. —The last time I saw her, she told me a Jewish story, imitating the Jew very badly. Her anti-Semitic talk annoyed me, because she seemed to be Jewish herself; but it may well have been true that she was Mexican.

On a previous occasion, she had explained to one of her admirers that she would not be able to see him. This, I suppose, had gratified me; but I was in for a disillusion. It turned out that she had been counting on me for high conversation. She wanted to talk in a goofy way about her emotions and philosophical concepts. I told her I couldn't do it. "Then why do you think I had you in my bed?" This affair did not last much longer.

Ted's anecdotes of Jimmy Gruen: "Why, he's hump-nutty!" —"Hump-nutty? Why, what do you mean?"—"Why, every time she sees him get a little bit gay, see—every time she hears him begin to sin or anything like that, she throws a piece of tail into him and knocks him silly again!" —A young newly married couple in a restaurant: "Look at her lookin' at him all starry-eyed. She don't yet know he's a bum hump!"

Florence O'Neill [the original of Daisy in my novel, but the story itself is invented—we were never lovers]. "We got plastered." —"Trying to ply me with liquor!—You'll be finding out my real name!" —In response to compliments, "I just eat that stuff up!"; hitting herself under the chin, "That sets me all up!" —"He's a twirp" —"The boyfriend's gone to the Mirador with some French dame tonight—when you realize that he's just a twirp!"—"I've got an awful yen for absinthe tonight." She had a tremendous appetite for drinking and dancing, having just spent two weeks of sobriety nursing.

1926 - 1930

The latter half of the 1920's was difficult for Edmund Wilson. He would remember "the first more or less exciting days in New York after the war"; but the excitement had subsided, and after a while Edmund discovered himself in a workaday world of editing and writing, a world fragmented for him by his having constantly to feed the hungry columns of the magazines. There is no more interesting reading, in the margin of his notebooks, than the small descriptive and critical New York pieces written between 1923 and 1928 which Edmund assembled as "The Follies" in *The American Earthquake* (1958). One is made aware how far and how deeply Edmund ranged—vaudeville, the circus, Stravinsky, Eddie Cantor, the look of Varick Street, the face of an old brownstone—or a panorama from a high-story window of the East Forties, "the monstrous carcass of the Grand Central Station and Palace, with its myriad skylights and its zinc-livid roofs, stretched out like a segmented sea-worm that is almost unrecognizable as a form of life. Beyond it rise the upright rectangles of drab raw yellow brick—yellows that are devoid of brilliance, browns that are never rich—perforated as if by a perforating machine." He possesses great precision of statement; and he follows his curiosity into nightclubs, bars, courtrooms, bookshops, and the paintings of Georgia O'Keeffe. Manhattan, in all its years of babbling journalism, never had so keen a mind and so sharp a pen survey its ephemera, down to Texas Guinan and Alice Lloyd.

Several years of this kind of writing, together with his larger critical essays, had their effect on Edmund Wilson. He was once again the lonely observer, working in a larger arena than his youthful days in Pottstown or Princeton. He was lonely in part because he had married an actress. Edmund's nights were long and he had to fill them. When he was ready at the end of the day for a drink, dinner, an evening's relaxation, he found himself instead "on the town." The town yielded him some fine writing; however, his vigils in bars were long, and his sense of isolation great. Mary Blair's career and Edmund's could not be reconciled. They separated wistfully, but both gave priority to their life work. They would remain friends even after their divorce in 1929.

Edmund's study of the metropolis extended to his study of America. He remained sanguine about its future; he believed in its newness and had a hope of its maturity out of its two centuries of innocence and rapacity. He

was struck by the fact that all the books of the twenties seemed to tell only
"what a terrible place America is" —Edith Wharton's *Age of Innocence*,
which had appeared in the early twenties; Sinclair Lewis's *Main Street* of the
mid-twenties; Van Wyck Brooks's *Ordeal of Mark Twain*; Mencken's continuing series of *Prejudices*. At that rate, he could say that only one great
book had been written to tell how somebody enjoyed America. This was
Leaves of Grass. Writing to Allen Tate in 1928, he said, "It is our high des-
tiny to step in and speak the true prophetic words to declining Europe." He
would swing forward and backward all his life: in Europe he was almost
belligerently American; in America he remained a quasi-European, certainly an intellectual cosmopolitan.

Years of writing for the periodicals changed the content of his notebooks.
He now begins to keep a record of his erotic life. He takes his notebooks
into his confidence—there is the erratic Katze, there is Winifred, there are
others, above all Anna, the dance-hall girl and waitress, with whom he has a
tender relation, and who touches him more than all the others. She was a
product of the slums; her husband was in prison; she had a kind of stoical
resignation to the hard facts of her life; and in her talk she transported
Edmund to a low-life Brooklyn world he could grasp, far removed though
it was from his own. Ultimately she would furnish him with the material
for "The Princess with the Golden Hair" in *Hecate County*. Edmund's erotic
candor was distinctly in the spirit of the time. James Joyce had defied custom
by using four-letter words; but even before D. H. Lawrence's sexual rhap-
sodies, Edmund was discovering the objective language—a mixture of the
crude and the delicate—to render erotic experience. In our present unbuttoned age his boldness may seem tame; what we should remember is that
what he wrote, in its truth to life and to himself, antedated the later avalanche of erotic writings that now colors the creative imagination of America.

The notebooks tell us very little of the novel Edmund began in 1926 or
1927. It was about his friendship and passion for Edna St. Vincent Millay.
He had written a few fine short stories, but had never attempted a long
work of fiction; and he was surprised to discover that this could be a quite
different enterprise from any other kind of writing. His first version of *I
Thought of Daisy* was set down rapidly. When he reread it, he saw he had
made a false start. The process of rewriting was long. He took the manuscript with him to California and there, in a beach cottage, rewrote the entire book into its final form. In the meantime he had begun work on a series
of long essays on the symbolists which would become *Axel's Castle*; and it is
amusing to find him writing to his editor Maxwell Perkins that this book,
"being literary criticism, is easier to do, and in the nature of a relief, from
Daisy." A novelist *de métier* would of course have said that *Daisy* was a relief

from criticism. Edmund was beginning to face the fact that he was more critic than novelist. A later letter to John Peale Bishop describes some of the problems he had with his novel. He could not give his Edna Millay character (Rita) "its true value, because if I had done so, it would have eclipsed in interest the part about Daisy at the end and brought about an anticlimax (the book was originally imagined from the Daisy end of it)." Also that, "once having written more or less real descriptions of Edna, I became self-conscious and began to handle the subject gingerly." The book was artificially conceived, he felt; "it was to be a pattern of ideas and all to take place, as to a great extent it does, on the plane of intelligence—and when I came to write the actual story, this had the effect of involving me in a certain amount of falsified psychology. I rewrote it to take the curse off it, but a certain amount of it was inherent in the thing which I was attempting to do."

The writing of *Daisy* and the planning of *Axel's Castle* represented for Wilson a determined attempt to seek the greater permanence of books; his only book publication had been the collaborative-ironic (and youthful) *Undertaker's Garland*; a small volume he called *Discordant Encounters*, in which he had put together certain imaginary conversations published in *The New Republic*; and *The Crime in the Whistler Room*. He was now in his thirties; his peers were bringing out book after book, and this made him all the more aware of the ephemeral nature of his own writings. Magazine publication meant there was "comparatively little I have written that has really been brought to completion." For this reason, "I set to work on my articles, verses, short stories, sketches, notebooks to try to get something more solid out of them." He wanted, he said, to put this material "into decent shape and get it off my hands, along with all the interests, ideas and emotions mixed up with it." In this he sketched the course he would ultimately follow all his working days.

This pressure to "produce", his unremitting work on his novel and his projected critical book, the stress of his tangled love affairs, brought the world tumbling in on him, as it had done at the moment of the war. He had said then that indecision terrified him. Now he suddenly had seizures of anxiety and panic. He had written with great accuracy, on first reading *The Waste Land*, that it was "nothing more nor less than a most distressingly moving account of Eliot's own agonized state of mind during the years which preceded his nervous breakdown. Never have the sufferings of a sensitive man in the modern city chained to some work which he hates and crucified on the vulgarity of his surroundings been so vividly set forth. It is certainly a cry *de profundis* if ever there was one—almost the cry of a man on the verge of insanity."

With certain important differences of temperament, this description fits

Edmund. He was surfeited with New York; he had a refinement of intellect which, if less delicate than Eliot's, still was at odds with his environment; and if Eliot's sexual life was seemingly dried up, Edmund's constituted a crisis of excess. Aside from his own account of what he called "a sort of nervous breakdown," which made him—like his father—instantly take refuge in a sanatorium, we have a revealing statement in a letter to John Bishop of October 4, 1929: "I'm trying to put my own affairs on a new basis—of which I'll write you later—and have had to go through a good deal that was emotionally harrowing, financially embarrassing and nervously devastating!" *Harrowing, devastating*—these words suggest the depths of Edmund's wounded state at this time. "I suppose," he added to Bishop, "that you and I have both got to the time of life where one has to take pretty desperate action or be choked in one's own toils."

Edmund's resilience and tenacity carried him through his black days and his nightmares. At the sanatorium he worked on *Axel's Castle*; and he left it to come to grips with his affairs at the sad ending of the 1920's. He breaks almost reluctantly with Anna (though he would return to her), breaks equally with the mysterious Winifred, decides to get his divorce, and will marry Margaret Canby, to whom he has been increasingly attracted, as his notes show.

What is striking on the intellectual side of these troubled and desolate years is Edmund's constant search for the meaning of art and the nature of literature. Part of this is related to his attempt to bring into focus the solipsism of the symbolists and the "stream of consciousness" of Joyce; another part is an actual questioning, doubtless out of his reading of Freud, of the relation between art and neurosis. Could a work of art, the world filtered through the mind of an individual, still be "reality," once it receives the imprint and color of that mind? Wasn't it a "fraud"? It made readers think they were touching the real, but they were in actuality receiving "realities" reflecting the artist's entire being. The subject obsesses him and overflows into his novel. "The author's work," wrote Edmund, "no matter how intelligent, elaborate (Proust) or rich and vigorous in imagination, always turns out to constitute a justification for some particular set of values, a making out a case against something or other in favor of something else." This inner debate—and he brings painting into question as well—points to the deepest quality of Edmund's later essays on nineteenth- and twentieth-century literary masters; they would address themselves always to the particular temperament, the particular "wound," the special forces which shape an author's operative thinking. In these sections of the notebooks we see foreshadowed his close and brilliant investigation of Dickens or Kipling—or Abraham Lincoln—and his questioning of the solipsists who "studied themselves, not other people: all the treasures, from their point of view, are to be found in solitary contemplation, not in any effort to grapple with the problems of general life." Edmund, writing this at the end of the jazz age, stood on the edge of his period of "social commitment." This would be a renewal of his wish to step outside the boundaries of himself, the shut-in world of his youth. He had initiated his readers into the word-worlds of the symbolists—Yeats and Joyce, Valéry and Gertrude Stein; so at the end of the thirties he would take his readers on a journey into the "acting" of history, to the crucial moment in our century when Lenin's sealed train arrived at the Finland Station.

Louisiana

New Orleans [March 1926]. From the hotel window, the dull chocolate and slate-lilac city with its high roofs and narrow windows, in the dim, damp light of March, and, beyond it, the muddy river.

Maidenhair ferns in front yards and wisteria vines on iron balconies—delicately fronded and foliated like the wrought-iron designs of the balconies—Louisiana—that perfume of Southern trees and plants in the air. —In the streets of the old French Quarter, that toasted smoky smell, much as I remember at Trèves—it must emanate from the masonry, particularly, perhaps, in damp weather.

Two Negroes walking down the street, singing the Charleston music together, with considerable elegance. —Some unidentifiable, invisible person whistling *Collegiate*, as we were getting out of the train, more softly, more melodiously, more roundly, than one ever hears it in the North.

The last vibration of a riverboat still beating in the air. Loud cries from the streets of newsboys and street venders. Not many harsh motor horns. The slight chime of the cathedral like a silver mosquito's whine. The high-pitched whining whistle of a steamboat.

Food. Deep-brown crayfish soup, with the bright red head and trunk of a crayfish floating in it, so rankly aromatic that it tastes like the smell of an old stable. —Chicken cooked, with mushrooms and gravy, in a sealed folder of brown paper, which is only sliced open by the waiter when the dish is set before you. Pompano in paper.

Beer on draught in an old-fashioned bar, with excellent hot pot-roast sandwiches. —Big barrel-shaped red-faced men, old bartenders and restaurant cashiers—the same type as the patrons whom they serve. —The sweet licorice taste—the iridescent exhilaration of absinthe frappé, crystal and pearl in green glasses. Saranac cocktails.

Green-gray oyster soup with white rice—coffee everywhere and at all times of day—the taste stained with chicory. —Oyster loaf.

The "exquisite diphthong" of *er* always verging, like ours, on *oi*, but never going over the border; the double tingle of the cathedral chimes telling the quarter hours; the tangle of nigger children's voices all about in the French Quarter.

Politeness—sentimentality—old romantic clichés.

Narrow windows and balconies, green lattices. —Iron cupids on balconies—slim pilasters.

The Lyonses. The magnificent wide coal-burning grate—the great lumps of coal that burn as soon as you touch a match to them—no steam heat: they needed it so seldom. —The garden—the night-blooming jasmine—so intoxicating that one of the guests threw them all out at once; buddleia; peonies won't grow, and they cheat on them, planting them over again the second season and pretending they have survived; sweet peas in abundance; the sprays of a climbing rosebush with small yellow roses. —The Labrador retriever and his bitch—"child-wife." "Do you want to be puddin'?" They get the dogs excited, working on them in relays. She felt as if she wanted to get drunk—she felt as if, if somebody had said, "Do you want to be puddin'?", she didn't know what she might have done. "I think the trouble with the other night was we dinun get drunk enough." This is my eighth Dodge: Sherwood Anderson's letter to Lyle Saxon printed in letters a foot high and pasted on the back of her car. —Her husband was a cotton broker. "Oh yes, you are!"—"Oh no, it isn't!" Her lovely voice and soft kind looks at her husband. Two bad paintings of her made her look Spanish—all in browns and reds. She collected first editions. They had odds and ends of beer, Scotch, curaçao, Sauterne and something that they had made cocktails out of. —She had a Belgian hunting griffon, who had pups by the retriever—they came out black, like him, but a little bit off. She gave them to six friends and made six enemies. —The bishop had sent word that he thought her niece ought to come around and be confirmed; she said she would if he wouldn't ask her anything, because she wouldn't know anything to answer. He probably wouldn't know anything to ask her—he'd just ask her, "Well, my dear, how's your aunt?" They had been scandalized because she had said that the convent life was delightful, because you went to church in the morning and then did what you pleased the rest of the day. —"Isn't that the most nigger-looking cake?"—so high, compact, heavily iced with chocolate and with a perfect dome of convexity on top. —"Well, Mr. Saxon, do you know that your Aunt Louise is sick?" —"How did you know it?" —"Haven't I got your cook?" —She had written him, "Maude is a fool—she keeps telling me not to exert myself—I presume she wants me to refrain from the Charleston." —Anderson was reported to have said that Mrs. Lyons looked like a Russian prostitute.

New Orleans. The live oaks lining great alleys, dripping gray Spanish moss. In the graveyards, the raised ficus—overgrown tombs which have warped or crumbled open and show the bones within. Along Coliseum Place, the slender spreading water oaks with translucent green-yellow little leaves and the dull dark solid green of the magnolia trees. Creepers of ficus and heliotrope-flowered banana. French alleys with a pavement between two strips of grass. Long thick shaggy grass grows under heavy shade trees.

The green doors, blinds and walls of two-storied houses, all shuttered up, turned away from the street. Acorn scrolleries and exquisite laces of wrought-iron balconies—slim columns—lattices—arrow-piked or crested railings—the barbs of iron torch flames.

The delicacy of the vines against the delicacy of the iron lace. Dead vines on rusted railings. Iron turned green with age.

The smell of vetiver. The fragrance of raw sugar, like honey, like a fresher and sweeter molasses.

The trains, the steamboat sounds, the whistling and songs from the street.

The stout stocky palm stems with horny *tignasses*. The dull gray-green cactus clumps.

Myrtle (a very young New Orleans prostitute): "Charity-ass, eh?—gives it away! —This fellow was drunk and he couldn't do anything—you know what I mean?—and he wanted his money back—and he tried to take it away from me, and I'd put it in my stocking, see. —Want your ass again? —When you jazz last?"—That rebellious, mulish, scornful look. —She had a guilty grin when I asked her if she liked her girlfriend a lot. — Hustlin'. —The police were picking all the girls up in Atlanta. —Her mother wanted her to come back to Elco for Christmas, but couldn't have her girlfriend. She said she would not have to think so much about pleasures and more of other things. She offered to send her the money—but Georgia wouldn't go. Georgia was Myrtle's real name. They called her Georgia because she was born on Washington's birthday. —The first time I saw her, she was anxious to get through with it as quickly and with as little sentimentality as possible. Wouldn't take off her clothes, didn't want me to take off mine, didn't want to be kissed for fear of disturbing her rouge (she didn't have any liquid indelible rouge, she afterwards told me), simply threw herself on her back across the bed with her feet hanging down at the side and pulled her skirts up over her stomach. After she had told me about her mother trying to get her to go home at Christmas, large tears came into her eyes. I wiped them away with the red quilt and they came again. I wiped them away again, and that was the end of it. —She had a pretty body, but said she was ugly—whenever I complimented her, she would say, "Yes!" with terrific sarcasm—some man had told her that she ought to be made over again. She had worked on the farm—her father had had one and she hadn't liked that; she had crudely formed feet, with a long big toe. —At home she used to go out to dances. She had been engaged to a man but he had been run into and killed by some drunken niggers in a truck while he was driving his Ford—"I'm sorry he was killed, but I'm glad I didn't marry him—you know what I mean." —Worked in a store in Atlanta, then was in Macon hustlin'. —Wanted to be married and be some*body*! —Used to play the organ in church and Sunday school—could only play *Yessir, That's Mah Baby* and one or two things like that on the piano. —"You hear what I'm tellin' yuh?"—"D'ye hear?"

"Turn me loose!—turn me loose!" —The dirty floor—green oilcloth—of the anteroom to the bathroom—the horrible stink of the broken closet, in which an unused condom floated. The green walls of the bedroom, covered in one place with names and dates and in others showing laths and plaster. The picture of Christ in the room below. —"My baby."— "Oh, you're laffin' at me!"—"Goddam, it's a pretty dress!" —She used to ride the plow when her brother was plowing—it wasn't any work but awful hot—Bobby used to have to water radishes and she had to carry the water in pails an awful long way. "That was the kick!" —They used to "kick" for everything. Myrtle called every kind of liquor "whiskey"—that was apparently the only name she knew. She opened the door to look across the street outside, from which the sound of some sort of horn sounded, had a sort of animal beauty.

Muddy breadth of the Mississippi and solid cement-colored Romanesque cathedral.

The elegance of the park, with its rearing equestrian statue—gracefully proportioned features—great green iron urn decorated with ram's-heads and frothing over with ferns—stalks of banana plants. Eighteenth-century elegance of Cabildo and corresponding building.

Vivid lines of orange clay brought out by rain between the bricks of narrow walks.

The incessant sound of mechanical pianos behind the shuttered windows of brothels.

The wood lace of an old riverboat.

The embroidery of New Orleans.

Old incredibly fancy bank buildings of the seventies, with twisted Byzantine columns still surviving on the chief business street.

The chattering sound of Creole French.

Old balcony-wreathed buildings.

Iron rabbits or sphinxes in the garden. The shrimp flower.

The light dresses of the girls in simple vivid colors—light greens and shrimp pinks—bright blues.

Screen doors and windows—banquettes—the gigantic mosquitoes.

The riverboats at the end of a street vista.

Furniture designed for monumental rooms: high, straight, smooth, mahogany wardrobes and beds; tall graceful vase-shaped cylinders for candles on high mantelpieces; immense lusters exfloreating into falling clusters of huge crystal *gouttes*.

The debris of the antique stores: green or red grapevine-garlanded goblets of Bohemian glass; gilt clocks encrusted with "allegories" under oval glass bells; china urns of the Empire ornamented with mythological groups.

Snoring of a riverboat—shivering moan.

The silver candlesticks, like tulips excessively tall, flowering in crystal bells, made to stand on high mantelpieces under high ceilings; the vast hanging candelabra showering clusters of crystal *gouttes*.

Lyle Saxon. "How 'bout yuh?"—"very proud and coquettish." —He pronounces *er*, as the New Yorkers do, verging on *oi*. —"The dreamiest bed—dreamiest mirror."—That whining note in beginning a friendly request—I remember that I had heard Walker Ellis and MacBarr do it at school.—Mrs. Bankhead was so awfully "old South." —"Ain' that the most old-time Southern speech you ever heard!" —"Come on: Cooley's got some money." —He used to raise one eyebrow. —"Cheerio, studio." —Boys who had been to coffeehouse in St. Louis Street, where waitress had said, "I'll do it two ways for a dollar." —"Just a jolly good-natured turn the evening had taken." —They had insisted he must come right away— the girls had been so clean!

Grace King [the writer, a historian of New Orleans]. She used "eat" for "eaten." They objected to having gentlemen smoke in the house. "He asked if he could smoke, and we said he could but might have known by the way we spoke that we didn't care to have him. If he had been a gentleman, he would have waited until he got outside." —Her sister had had a run-in with a taxi driver—she was very indignant about it. —Miss King used little French phrases like *gêné* and was even careful to pronounce *amateur diplomate* in the French way.

Anecdote about Joseph Hergesheimer, who had asked her whether she had bought her chandeliers or they had come with the house—she put him out. —She had met Lord de Tabley in England and a number of celebrities in France, had refused to go to a party given by the Princesse Madeleine, because she didn't approve of her. —"You have to take what you can get in Paris—the men and women there seem to be very much mixed up!" —Her nephew had enraged her when he had last come to dinner by referring to "the War of the Rebellion." —She had the face of one who had outlived sex but maintained, as men do, something of the interest which intellect gives—she suggested Renan a little. He was one of her great admirations—she had heard him lecture in Paris.

Florida real estate. They took prospective buyers on a special train out to a barren waste where it was proposed to sell them lots. Hastily thrown-together headquarters—indifferent lunch. But, after lunch, sudden eruption into room of real estate evangelist: he said there were three cardinal sins—fear, caution and delay—and gave them a sermon on those three heads. "And if Jesus Christ were alive today, he'd buy a lot right here!" —Inspirational effect on audience—several bought lots then and there. —When everybody else had gone, the promoter complimented the evangelist, who was mopping his brow like Billy Sunday: "That's a great line of bunk you've got there! You ought to make a lot of money out of it!" Evangelist: "Yes, it is. And I don't get paid half enough!"

Trip to New Iberia (I went out with Gene and Maria Jolas—Maria drove us). Little restaurant next to garage: EAT. —"Hello, peaches! Here's your car!" ("One more installment and it's ours. Maybe yes, maybe no.")

Curious town, like a fair, with merry-go-rounds and slides, coffee restaurants and soda fountains—all of a provisional summer character, light and made of boards.

That great gray skull of a plantation house against the gray stormy sky and the gray waters of the Teche, stripped of its columns and unpainted, so somber and dead-looking. Six Italian families had lived in it at once.

The delicious absinthe, drunk in front of the blazing fire, after the long trip in the damp, which had given us glowing faces.

The *café brûlot*, made in a chafing dish in the darkened room, manipulated with a spoon, a great display of blue and yellow flame, curling, blazing and dropping. Fine taste of coffee, brandy and spice.

The vivid feel of the garden after rain—red camellias in the middle of the square—statues of the four seasons, one at each corner: winter, old man wrapped in cloak; young boy; Ceres. Fountain.

Toile de Jouilly, with La Fontaine's wolf and lamb. Giant wardrobes and red-canopied beds. Tall silver candlesticks, like tulips, flowering in crystal. Transparent cylinders. Mid-nineteenth-century landscapes in watercolor. Set of Voltaire.

Boze's intelligent, sharply defined features contrasting with Hall's decomposing ones. Boze was the Negro servant, who—according to Anderson—together with his (Boze's) wife, completely ran Weeks Hall's life. There was certainly something rather sinister about the whole place.

Weeks Hall's and Walker Ellis's manner. Raising eyebrows—way of telling a story—elaborate modesty, "Of course, I don't know anything about it," etc.—smile, apparently genial and friendly, but actually arrogant and slightly offensive—manner with servants, "All right: that'll do, Boze, old man!" —Story about grandfather and horse—"Of course, there's not a word of truth in it." Discrepancy between his amusement at the story and ours. —Story about century plant—nigger wouldn't sell it to him:

"Everything in this yard came from the big yard"—wouldn't take my money, but said Hall could give him a cart (or something of the kind) that he wanted. Hall was glad to know that the old Negro woman in front of whose house we had picnicked on the road knew who he was—he wanted them all to know, but was hardly able to hope that they did. (He had inherited the place, I think, from an aunt.)

Weeks Hall's macaw, which he brought up and perched on the mantelpiece ("I thought you might find her amusing"). He would pull her tail at inappropriate moments in his own conversation, so that she would give a discordant squawk. When Mrs. Jolas told him not to torment her, he said, "Oh, she loves it, don't you, old girl?"

Type derived from Scofield Thayer and Hall. Collects early American bottles—tells about correspondence with museum official about loaning collection to museum—they would have packed them improperly—had them packed himself and accompanied truck in his car—"Now, if it had been a collection of pictures, or even of china—!" No letter of thanks after exhibition. —He only let people see it, in his own house, who he thought were worthy to see it; recounts letter which he has written, refusing to let people come. —Annoyance, elaborate but offensive manners—mannerisms; inferiority complex, delusions of persecution. —Hypochondriac: haven't been well for many months, sanatoriums, Hot Springs; hasn't been able to get himself in hand to finish poem or brochure or whatever. —Sometimes has to go to the Ambassador before they can turn somebody out at the Ritz to make room for him—complains of hideous suites at Ambassador—also, of overcharging him for serving meals in room. —Has eccentric and hypochondriac mother—they cannot be in a room together for five minutes without getting on each other's nerves. —Always thinks people are trying to get something out of him.

During flood, he (Weeks Hall) had to move to upper story of house.

The little Alabama girl on the train coming up—a cunning little blond girl, like a young Zelda Fitzgerald, coming back to school in the North after the Easter holidays—very smartly but not vulgarly dressed. Her drawling whining voice. She was with a girl who had evidently been visiting her for the holidays. They had a phonograph on which they played *Flamin' Mamie, Rolling Along,* etc. They asked the porter if it was all right to play it—her manner with the porter. She said to her friend, "If we can get the drawing room, we can play it all night." They got it later. —Gray stockings, dark blue coat. She changed her clothes several times.

> Roll 'em, girls—roll 'em,
> Go ahead and roll 'em—roll 'em down

show your pretty knees!
Roll 'em, girls—roll 'em,
Everybody roll 'em—roll 'em high or
    low just as you please!
Don't let people tell you that it's
    shockin'!
Keep your sweetie's picture in your stockin'!
Ha-ha-ha! Ha-ha-ha!
Give 'em all the Ha-ha!
Roll 'em, girlies—roll 'em—roll your own!
She's Flamin' Mamie—sure-fire vamp
Hottest baby in town!
She's a hard scorcher—she loves torture!
She's a gal that burns 'em down!

When it comes to lovin'—she's a human oven!
Awful funny—paper money—

New York

Just before I left for New Orleans (the first of March), walking out in the late afternoon and looking down at the sidewalk, I had the impression that the darkness of winter had lightened—though when I glanced up, I could not see that the streets were less gray or the air less subterranean than ever.

Florence: "You poor fish!"—"Well, I think that's very unjust!"—John Amen: "There's probably a good deal in it, though!"

Florence O'Neill. A friend of hers took us to a place under the pavement where they make punchino on a stove with lemon, rum and water; and then we encountered a friend of his, the son of a professor of economics, who brought over a little black-eyed, lowered-eyed Italian-looking man who, it seemed, was a prominent gangster—he kept saying something about fifteen dollars' worth of cigarettes—or fifteen cents' worth of cigarettes—discoursed at great length about the differences between Sing Sing and some other prison—at Sing Sing, they taught you a trade—"Like—you don't know any trade—well, at Sing Sing, they teach you to be a carpenter, or a shoemaker—they teach you a trade—but at the other prison they have this solitary confinement." He said several times, "Bleecker Street's going to be an arsenal!—Bleecker Street's going to be an arsenal!" —I was a little dazed with drink at the time—he also said something about Gerald Chapman, whose death had evidently stirred the underworld deeply. —He insisted we should go to a nightclub, which turned out to be deserted and very dull. —The other man who was with Florence told a long story about a wonderful man in Greenwich Village who had known everybody—the Vanderbilts and the Astors and everybody like that—and he was a friend of George Horace Lorimer at the same time. I said, "Everybody?" and then repeated it when he said, "You know who I mean by everybody," and tried to make it up by showing an interest and asking questions. Lorimer had wanted him to write his memoirs—I said, "He's writing his memoirs, then, is he?" He said, "Oh, no, he hasn't written a word—he's drunk all the time." But everybody went to see him—on account of his accident; he had been run into or something when drunk—face all mashed, terrible-looking. —We asked if he thought that would be an amusing place to go, then, and he said, "Why, yes—he usually gets sore late in the evening and throws everybody out"—he did this as the result of an inferiority complex. I said, "Suppose they refuse to be thrown out." He said, "Well, you know how it is, people usually don't want to stay when they're asked to go." Florence asked what his name was, and when she heard it again, said, "Oh, that fellow's a bum—he used to be our landlord!" —I finally left with Ted Leisen, who was drinking late, alone and the last person in the place, at Sam Schwarz's. —The point about the cigarettes was that you could get them at Sing Sing, but not at the other place. You were a fool to get sent up for six months to the other place, when you could spend a couple of years at Sing Sing.

Katze and Florence went out of the room and, after much laughter, came back with their dresses interchanged: Katze with the blue and Florence with the gray. —"Katze gets in the kindergarten class when she's had a few drinks."

Katze's thin but very pretty legs and her peculiar movements immediately recognizable as the originals of Franz Kuhlmann's drawings (which had appeared to me so seductive). When she came over to my table at Sam Schwarz's, while her companions were in the coatroom, she vibrated and fluttered like some quick young bird or animal.

The girls walking on the Avenue in twos, their white-stockinged legs and black-slippered feet pacing exactly together in a slow regular rhythm—almost self-hypnotizing dance. —A new shade of purplish flesh-pink.

The melodious murmur of boat whistles heard from a back room in Washington Square.

Man in telephone booth: "And this time make sump'n happen, will yuh?"
Unloading rusty bedsprings for a cheap second-hand shop.

Allison Armour. Refusing a drink, "I want to keep clear-eyed tonight!"—afterwards, drank abundantly. —"A Galahad with gall"—vastly delighted with this—"Idea of an ideal fellow"—wonderful title—thought up lots of good titles, but that was as far as he got.

Fort Girls. "Henry" (Henrietta) and "Pooks" (Louise). John Amen had sent a friend to Henry in Chicago—she had been impressed by "his strong white teeth."

Sex appeal, spring 1926. Florence and Katze had been sitting around at Franz Kuhlmann's and had finally decided that the men lacked sex appeal. —Joke in *New Yorker* about girl who wouldn't tip taxi driver because he didn't have sex appeal.

The girls doctored their hair with Golden Glint and other things of the kind, which gave it an unnatural and unusually rather ugly shade of bad brass—entirely different from that which appeared on the girls in the advertisements. —*Gentlemen Prefer Blondes*. —Girlfriend, boyfriend. —Hanging of Gerald Chapman. —Arrest of Mencken in Boston. —Skyscrapers. —Cold bleak April. —John Guinn catalogue for two dollars. —Raquel Meller. Circus in new Madison Square Garden. —Congressional debate on Prohibition. —Labor troubles in Passaic. —First number of *New Masses*. —Christian Gauss, Dean of Princeton and makes speech about not caring what students did, so long as they did it like gentlemen, also about "clean campus, clean town, clean country and clean state"—if the town wasn't "as dry as a bone and as clean as a hound's tooth" in a very short time, it would be the fault of the federal authorities. —Florida real estate boom said to be deflating. —Krutch's *Edgar Allan Poe* (impotence motif). —Living very cheap in France. —Nadir of franc. —Little thirty-dollar portable phonographs—Coon-Sanders Original Nighthawk Orchestra—Ned Horne and his Highhatters—Lee Morse and the Blue Grass Boys—too high, too fast, too nasal—punctuated by shots and explosions—cheap brown records, records made of mud—names in Spanish for South American circulation—"vocal refrain by Billy Murray"—breaks in, in middle of record—after that, the time is further jazzed in a more complicated fashion—kazoo squealings, sonorous beats of the bass hollow saxophone—speeded jingling-jangling trot—scratched scarred records piled on each other and scraped together—needles ruthlessly dropped on them when they are starting and turned off without the needles being lifted—needles never changed—after a short time, new needles and old get mixed up. —The old feeling of shame one used to have at some vulgar joke sung by a brazen voice. —"What? No women! What kind of a party is this? —Thanks for the terrible time!"—variation introduced in second verse by singing it as an Englishman was supposed to sing it—"What? None of the feminine sex?"—etc. —Some sweet shred of tune, simple and sentimental, like something out of an old-fashioned German song—rolled in on the ribbon with the syncopation, the jiggling, the explosions, the squealing, the glass crashes—from which the song derives the best of its enchantment—*The Village Blacksmith Owns the Village Now.*—"*Under a spreading chestnut tree, The Blacksmith used to stand; The Smith a mighty man is he, And he owns a lot of land!*" —Anvil chorus from *Il Trovatore* and accompaniment of motor horns—"*He used to go to church to pray, Now Sunday is his busy day!*" —They strike blurred and stammering stretches, where the thread has been worn off. —A few preliminary flourishes, then chorus, then verse played and chorus sung, then chorus played twice with refinements, cut off sharply after conventional final flourish.

—*Nize Baby*—North Pole—George Rylands—Alice Lloyd—All books commended on jackets by H. L. Mencken. —"Burn 'e, up"—"We've

heard that before!—Am I burnin' yuh up?" —Song *You* from *Sunny*. —
Stuart Sherman completely came over, changed his attitude reviewing
Ring Lardner; and reviewed by Van Wyck Brooks—*Albertine Disparue*. —
East Lynne—"No matter what she has done—remember she is my wife and
the mother of my child!"; *Two Orphans*; Mark Sullivan's *Our Times*. Proli-
fic manufacturer of imitation antique dogs and cows. —Vogue of Carl Van
Vechten. —Intimate Papers of Colonel House. —*The Shanghai Ges-
ture*—Sinclair Lewis refuses Pulitzer Prize; the flight of the *Norge*; English
General Strike; shooting of Chicago Assistant Prosecuting Attorney in car
with four gangsters—machine gun; Gilda Gray gone into the movies—
Aloha of the South Seas—surrealism; wrecking of Vanderbilt mansion.

Ted Paramore. Well, —— —— took a nose dive from the window of the
Rockefeller Hotel—he was at Princeton in your time—captain of the
tennis team. (I had forgotten him.) Question of marrying girl with Sex
Appeal. Tough line: "Why, there ain't nothin' in that! I had one o' them
girls once!" "You invite your best friend to dinner and the next time he
comes when you're away . . ." Irene had got married—she married the boy
of her heart—but had first tied up half the money of the man who had been
keeping her—she had prayed to the Virgin for his wife to die, but without
results—then she had tried the most newly canonized human saint. What
kind of a fellow had she married? —"Oh, he's just one of these dese-dem-
and-dose guys!" Leon Walker and his friends had stolen a piece of armor
from the Tower of London.

Jean. Looking down at me from the stair railing: "Got a new pair of
dogs?—do they bite?" [Dogs was slang for shoes.] —She had just bought a
little Japanese coat, a little too small for her and typical of the kind of clothes
she likes to wear: the plaid shirt with suspenders. Little white starched
clown's ruffs around her neck. Large shoes: thick legs and arms. Shiny black
hair which she would plaster down and be very much afraid of having dis-
urbed—*accrochecoeurs* on either side. —She never wanted to take off her hat
and seemed to identify her virtue with it. —Practicing the Charleston alone
with her phonograph. —When George Hartman (a friend who was living
with them) went out to have dinner with a lady and stayed away all night,
Jean scolded him and reduced him to the condition of a whipped schoolboy
the next morning—she said that Rolfe (George Hartman's police dog) had
kept coming into her room and waking her up all night. —Jean always
looked so ripe, smooth and clean.

The late spring of 1926. April seemed as cold and bleak when I got back
from New Orleans as March had when I left.
In the bathroom one day, as I had the window open, I seemed to feel from

the faintly lightening air outside the suggestion of summer freshness, when windows could always be left open and no difference be felt between outside and inside, which would have become one continuous soft ocean of air.

On April 21, going out in the afternoon, I found that summer had suddenly come. I rode uptown on the top of the bus and walked back from the Grand Central. Along Fifth Avenue, the people were still plying their way as if through the cold and the gray air; their faces were still bleak, boarded up and sharp, as if to cut their way through the city winter; they still had that air of callous masks made of some kind of inorganic material, as if they had been formed, like the horse's hoofs and the turtle's carapace, as a protection against environment. And they seemed stunned and taken unawares by the sudden change in the weather, hardly able to realize that they could permit themselves lighter clothes, an easier and more leisurely pace, and a little natural color.

The Gormans. Jean made uneasy by pornographic books—*Fanny Hill* and Frank Harris's autobiography. —Her sister, married to a naval officer in California: she didn't know any of the facts of life, didn't know anything about men at all—wanted to have her come to New York and to marry her off to George: that would be fixing up two weak sisters together. —She would pass into troubled and subdued periods when the question of her former love affair would come up, through his wife's finally getting a divorce to marry again and wanting her to allow herself to be named as co-respondent—would go to bed, refuse to go out, not want to see people. — Her appearance has changed greatly between the time when I first knew her and the present: she has become more robust, less artificial—less mascara, less mask (or rather, mascara and rouge less in evidence); somehow become more healthy: strapping round soft arms in evening dress (dark blue). I used to tell her she looked as if she had played on the college basketball team and she said she had. —"You're a hot momma, you are!", when she thought I had failed to look her up soon enough after coming back from New Orleans. —The Thursday evening sketch class, Herbert would always insist on showing me all his drawings, one by one: "What d'ye think of that? What d'ye think of that?" —Her confiscation of *Huckleberry Finn* intended for Mrs. Colum, her fury at the English sculptress's telling her that she had been told she wasn't beautiful but that she thought she was very beautiful, the effect on her of my burlesque scolding when I had come back from Hoboken with Bill Benét, when she had dressed up to go to L. Langner's party, and she came up to the Gormans' with a tall highball in her hand— George nobly drinking it up when I scolded her for appearing with it and she insisted upon giving it to us—Elinor's affiliations with the F. P. Adamses, the Warfields, the Hergesheimers, Cabells, Knopfs, Will Irwins,

Lawsons, Messners, Van Dorens, Van Vechtens—disapproving attitude of the Gormans—lunch at the Algonquin during which she paid no attention to them but was continually turning around toward the round table—eagerness to be mentioned by "columnists."

Ted Paramore. The girl he got away from Donald Douglas. —"She wasn't very good. She wasn't very pretty but she had a good body." —She finally made him feel so ashamed, however, that he gave her up: "She said, 'You make me feel as if I were on a barren plain whipped by a bitter wind!' —And I——!"—business of hanging his head in abasement. —But the first time he had been to see her, he was enormously set up the next morning—he came in to see me, beaming, and said it had restored his self-confidence. She had "made him breakfast and everything."

The afternoon of April 25, gray air but warm and summer-like—the windows open—the park outside.

Ted Paramore. No-Soap—the insane girl—thought she was a wonderful dancer and cutting Marilyn Miller out—daughter of a Yale professor—disappeared from party into bathroom; when he went to look for her, he heard sound of singing behind bathroom door; inside, he found her in the tub with all her clothes off, singing *"She was always blowing bubbles"* and waving spray around the room. —Wisecracking girls that he and Jimmy Gruen had at Hollywood—writing H. C. Witwer's comedies—"I don't like Harry Witwer; he cheats at limericks!" —Whenever they pulled a big gag, they would all three do a pratfall—girl whose bladder had been impaired by gin drinking and every time she laughed hard, she would wet herself—"An' I thought I was a big girl now!"—would leave the room and reappear in another dress—finally, came in in a bathing suit and said, "Now bring on your gags!"—Ted did a pratfall while shaking cocktails and the cocktail shaker exploded all over the room—Jimmy Gruen fell out of his chair.

The pale blue thin-clouded sky of April lightening after rain, in the early afternoon, over the gray asphalt pallors of Waverly Place, bluing with its reflection.

Party in Throck's apartment [Cleon Throckmorton, scene designer for the Provincetown Players]. I came in and found the room full of people whom I took at first to be the cast of *Orpheus.* I went over to Catherine Throckmorton and we sat down together—she was just drunk enough to be partly speechless and to have assumed, as she often does under those circumstances, a bogus foreign accent—when I asked her who the people were, she gave me a long burlesque story to the effect that Throck used to teach a Sunday school class in Washington and that one of his Boy Scouts had arrived in town and called him up and asked if he could have a party in his apartment. She said that they had been so scared at first that they wouldn't come out of the bedroom. Actually, they were young boys and girls from vaude- ville—he said that one of them had claimed to know him. They had brought their own sandwiches, which were solid and thick and wrapped in oiled tissue paper, and their own sherry and port in large glass jars. The party was being given for a very pretty girl—a brunette in a green and gray dress and gray stockings and black shoes with round toes and light tan ton- gues. It was her birthday. She chewed gum the whole evening. Their danc- ing was wonderful—a boy threw a girl over his shoulder—a little English girl in green with an accent mainly American did the Charleston with her partner, exploding in wooden angular motions in all directions, with tremendous vigor. Said, afterwards, "I'm tired.—Are you in the show business?" She had been on the stage three years. They did squatting Russian dances and tried the Charleston on their knees. Music supplied by Throck's radio, which he had built himself (he explained that the best radio feature had all been patented by different companies, so that there wasn't a single radio on the market which was as good as possible, and it was only the government or a private individual, making his own, who could have one) —"I don't believe you, but say it again!" —Big blond girl in red, with thick red lips, who lolled around on the couch and in the Morris chair (They kept losing their shoes—either the boys would playfully steal them or they would drop them off themselves when they were lying on the couch or in a chair.) They sat around embracing each other—the girls would lie down on the couch together—or one with her head in the other's lap. — There was a toe dancer, but she "didn't have her shoes." —When the brun- ette went to the bathroom, her man insisted upon following her in —Finally, she put on her big-brimmed bonnet hat that matched her dress and, after doing a very quick walking one-step with her man—"See us taking a walk?"—went away with him. —One boy was a sort of grownup choirboy type with yellow curly hair and blue eyes. They all drank the wine and ate all the sandwiches, till there was nothing left but messes of tissue paper, unassimilable crusts and empty glass jars.

George Cram Cook's daughter [Nilla, who was also there—she had been living, like her father, in Greece]. I told her about seeing her on the beach when I was at Truro with Edna [Millay]—she said that she had had the most tremendous admiration for Edna then—she had never read any of her poetry, but, as the Cooks had lived in the next house to the Millays, Edna's discarded lovers had been in the habit of coming over to their house and mooning around, and she thought that she must be a wonderful person to have all those men breaking their hearts for her. —She talked very loud and put her face very close to mine. She wore, or was wearing, her hair down and frequently threw back her head to show her throat. (Catherine said, "She is without an anchor.") —Edna led to Sappho—she had read Sappho in Greek, she said—and she thought that Edna was really more important. —Homer more compact than Plato—the *Symposium*, the *Republic*, cited "and thick burned the funeral fires" in the opening of the *Iliad*— Sophocles—Euripides was the end—Homer and Theocritus—spoke modern Greek and pronounced ancient like modern—had attended ceremonies of the Greek Church and when you heard them, you knew how ancient Greek had been pronounced—Eleusinian mysteries—passionate indignation and scorn, when I ventured to suggest that the pronunciation couldn't have been determined by the religious rites. —"Oh, yes, the music!" —Greece more alive than any other country today except America, and there was where the hope of the future lay, and she was going back there to work—when the moment came—she had been in love and that had prevented her, and she was still—but when the day came, she would go! —She had had three years of Sanskrit, but she couldn't remember the characters—they didn't write the vowels. She wanted to learn Russian, but first she wanted to learn Chinese. There was China and there was Greece, but between them was India. —The Kamasutra ought to be taught in the schools, instead of these books by women doctors! —Missolonghi, where Byron died (they had lived near there). —She didn't like the French, knew nothing about them: it was an opinion taken over from her father— everything was art, the art of cooking, the art of love—they thought they were civilized, but really they only cared for the flesh. —She became very loud, showing off, sang *Don't go out tonight, dear father*, etc. (of which she knew all the words), at the top of her voice—to which the vaudeville people listened in polite silence, with an occasional appreciative laugh. — Did the *Robson and Gilpin Blues* (Throck supplying a tom-tom effect). — Reminiscences of the Provincetown Follies of the summer before—Bobby Edwards's songs—one song about antique dealers—*"boys from Boston— pottery, crockery—Chippendale, Hop-and skip-endale—if you really want to please us, buy a plaster of—Paris Jesus!"*—little gavotte between dances—*"Halitosis! Acidosis! We're young O'Neillians out on a spree!—We write plays on prostitution—And pollution!"* —She shouted, "I'm free-ee-ee!" and one of the vaudeville boys from the corner said, "So are the slaves!" Then she began reading Keats aloud to somebody, sitting on the chest against the farther wall, and was so much ravished by it that she reeled over and fell on the couch: "Oh, is the cathedral at Seventy-second Street open now? I want to go there!" —Perhaps her poses were suggested partly by the idea of Edna—she said that this was the only party she had been to in a long time where none of her lovers had been present. —She pulled up her skirt to show where she had been scratched on the thigh. —She said, "You know, you'd be quite nice, if you hadn't said that about the French!" (Poor "Gig" Cook had been part professor, part Messiah and part drunken bum.) She had a prejudice against the French, but sometimes the people she had formed the strongest prejudices against, she had known individuals among them with whom she had felt strongest bonds, from whom she had gotten something intensely fine—she had had a prejudice against priests, but a priest on the boat she had been on had done something so wonderful for her—she had been going to jump overboard (in some sort of exaltation) and he had prevented her—he had caught her, but he had held her in such a way against the movement of the waves that it was just as if she had jumped in the water—he had been wonderful!—she had been engaged to a Greek poet—he was a great poet—he had been translated into seven languages.

Ring Lardner's line about the Fitzgeralds: "Scott is a novelist and Zelda is a novelty."

Reaching home, he found copulating in front of his windows two of the thin and threadbare city cats which so often kept him from sleep with howling of damned souls: unwilling to intrude on lovers and remembering what he had heard of the pain involved in the insertion of the male penis-bone, he waited until the male had detached himself and then drove them both away.

Ghastly party that Ted and I gave on May Day. "I've got enough stuff here for a brawl that'll bring out four fire companies:—punch bowl as big as a man!" —Nobody came: Don Douglas's puns and their effect on Florence Arrival of Gropper, Wolf, et al. The macaw, bird of ill omen which sounded the note of doom in a harsh discordant cry which "sent a shudder through the whole room"—my attempts to shut the bathroom door while the macaw was perched on it. —Some of the girls came back upstairs and plundered the china closet in the hall, stealing pretzels, coffee and cups and saucers. Ted's altercation with the landlady, whom he called by her first name—"My name's not Mary: it's Mrs. Bilbur!"—He thought Florence wanted to get away to another party down in the Village, so he got her "all cock-eyed and berles," so that she had to spend the night. —I went to bed with my garters on.

That vague and charming feeling of coming to (no doubt a dose of aspirin contributed to these sensations), after having been drunk the night before very late in the day—of going out and finding the warm May day, the people out on the Avenue in their Sunday clothes and riding on top of the buses; of lying inside and hearing, from behind the lowered shades, where a bright sun comes in through a hole, the cries of children playing in the street and the sound of boat whistles. We leave the windows up during the day and the shades up at night: we don't need to shut ourselves up any longer. —At night, the park in a warm obscurity plaited with the bright pearls of lamps, the taxis moving on their errands—they seem more genial, more attractive now—the first soft mysteries of the city summer.

Central Park. The muddy lake full of sunken paper, on which men and girls row in boats—the great gray walls of rock, the bald turf—beyond, the unequal and disagreeably colored buildings of Eighth Avenue—the trees putting on their thin green foliage did not much help the scene: all the color seems discordant. Driving at night: cold and rather windy—rough parties in automobiles, women with their legs on seat backs—walled all around by the uptown buildings as the victoria swung around the black asphalt curves of the labyrinth, different dark skyscrapers were brought into view—office buildings, hotels, apartment houses—Fisk Tires.

Florence and Ted. "Florence and I get along just lousy, don't we, Florence?—I thought that your boyfriend gave us an exceptionally sour reception." —Gin and ginger ale; gin and White Rock; gin and plain water from the bathroom; plain gin. —The great abyss, the great vacuum out the window of 142 West Forty-fourth Street, great raw black spaces gaping for a solid tight-fitting new building to rush in and fill them. —When Florence cut her wrist on the spaghetti can, the doctor who was summoned said, "If it's attempted suicide, I'll have to report it to the police, you know." When he told me she might not be able to use her fingers, she was filled with remorse and virtuous resolves—she'd just been such a fool, she'd be more considerate of people in the future, she did those things and felt like a tramp afterwards. —At dinner, after a long silence, she looked up and jerked the corners of her mouth up with her fingers. —She thought that all the people she'd been amusing with wisecracks ought to come around and amuse her.

About Ted. "Why does he always want to wash dishes?—and go around emptying ashtrays—making everybody self-conscious? —Why does he go off and drink by himself? —We found him wolfing down a couple of straight gins behind the screen—why can't he drink with everybody else?" —She told Mary that she had done it (cut her wrist) because she had got tired of the traffic going in and out of the room. —When I asked her if she had been trying to commit suicide, she pursed her lips scornfully and shook her head. —"Did you think I took one of Henry's razor blades and gave myself a gash?" —Ted's hectic and unnatural overdoing of his amiability, helpfulness and jazz high spirits, which, even when he was sober, gave people the impression that he was drunk. —His trip to Buffalo and Detroit, getting an engagement to write a prospectus in Buffalo and selling some articles to the Detroit *Athletic News* —His masochistic tendencies, letting Florence and Leisen spend the night in his apartment—lending them his silk pajamas—they said they were going to sit up and read—he lay awake and listened to them—Florence said she never saw anything spurt like the blood, when she cut her wrist—it went way across the room—it was as if all the blood in her body were in her wrist—she thought she would have bled to death in a few minutes. Leisen held her hand up and went to the phone to call the doctor, still grabbing her wrist, then he put a tourniquet on it. —The afternoon when Ted and I were in her room, she had that slightly haggard look in which her complexion seemed tarnished and her hair rather muddy than reddish; when I took her to dinner two days after, however, she had got back her clear pink skin and her pretty coral lips, under her little round bell hat. —When she was dressing in the bathroom, she asked me to play the phonograph, while she . . . —She had lost her job with the Scandals—she had got notes to come to the first three rehearsals, but not to the fourth.

About Katze (Florence speaking): "I hate to disillusion you, but I don't think you've got a chance. She's always having third acts—where you or I would just laugh." (She had her hand in a black silk sling made from a scarf.) When I protested that she was jumping at conclusions: "You were all steamed up about her." —Lemon and lime cocktails that tasted like turpentine, so that only Florence and I could drink them. Leisen, who was dead drunk, threw the rest of his away on the hearthstone. —"Well, what a flop *you* turned out to be!" etc. —I noticed that Leisen, over the telephone, had begun to talk a little like Florence, or she had begun to talk a little like him. —Just as Mrs. Barton (afterwards married to Cummings) had got to look like Elaine Orr and to talk like Cummings.

Morning after; plying to and from New Republic. A broken phonograph record and ashes on the floor—warm day, messy sweaty feeling of feet not in shoes, vagueness and inadequacy to life—the shifting and chuting of a load of bricks on Twentieth Street, the air gritty with brick dust—babies lying as if dead in their baby carriages, asleep in the heat—little burned or syphilitic girl always playing on Twenty-first Street—pretty and healthy black-haired Italian girl sitting reading in a doorway.

Enjoying Elinor Wylie's apartment in Bank Street, where I lived for a few weeks that summer while she was away—in Europe. Ruth Warfield's posing to Elinor about her indifference to possessions—just a piano and a few scores she likes, etc. [Ruth Warfield left a bourgeois husband, was first Don Stewart's girl, then Dos's, then married the conductor Alexander Smallens.] Melancholy consequent on drinking neither coffee nor alcohol in evening. — Riding to Bank Street, at evening in a taxi: one short vista of low red brick fronts would present the sober and compact appearance of the past; but the next would be sordid, dingy, hard and dark—the New York that is all about us. —When I came in and found the shades down and the windows closed and the balls of tissue paper lying about, when I saw on the shelves and the table great accumulation of books which Elinor had drawn on for her novel (*Orphan Angel*), I almost envied her and Bill, almost considered that she was fortunate in life. In the closed-up order of the room I could smell the cabin of a steamer. —To people my solitude.

Katze at the Millays' party. She went into the front room, where they were almost alone, with rather a good-looking boy with abundant blond hair, and there sprawled in a large armchair with her long white-stockinged legs and her thin arms thrown about like the legs of a young colt. She was dressed in black and wore a large white gardenia on her shoulder and her evening dress slipping down on one side showed the gardenia-white skin of her neck. She was a little drunk and kept trying to talk French, and she had just been to see *The Importance of Being Earnest*, so that, when I asked her to come to the theater, she kept saying, "That would be quite, quite charming!"

Norma Millay's yellow maid, who sang, *Oh, tell me how long must I wait*, and other blues, at the party. She offered to sing *A Good Man is Hard to Find*, if they would give her a little extra money. She said she wouldn't sing at colored joints, but only at white people's parties like this.

Ted and Margaret at dinner, at the French restaurant at 154 West Fifty-fourth Street, the day she had just come back from Europe on her way to Santa Barbara—both looking their best, he serious, deliberate, in good health, dressed in a dark blue suit with a garnet tie, which, on my advice, solicited by himself (as he had had doubts of the one which he had first put on), he had substituted for a rather unhappily harmonized one of ordinary brown, blue and purple stripes, at great pains to give the impression, in connection with mailing letters, sending a suit home from the Yale Club and other business, of being *très affairé*; she with a new and very pretty orangy-pink dress and hat from Paris, which brought out her orangy-pink California color, much fresher and clearer than when she had left, after living for a time in New York. Contrast between Ted's more juvenile and gala phrases, in connection with his work, etc., and his tone in discussing with Margaret the news of Santa Barbara society—Ed and Miriam are married, Prince Hopkins is taking a huge château ("Why, what are you doing here? Don't you know that nobody but social radicals dine with the Hopkinses"): "Well, they married that little girl to a foreign nobleman," "Yes, they certainly did," "Did Edith really commit suicide," "I don't know." —Ted told about giving Donald Douglas a package of condoms for his birthday—he was tickled to death and went around showing them to everybody at the Harvard Club—("blowing them up").

No, do spend the night here—I won't molest you—much as I should like to.

Across the wide court from the study at 68 Bank Street, the bright brick red of a single front in the late afternoon sun, against which the leaf shadows cast by an ailanthus tree showed distinct and dark and, to the left, against the gray sky, the white clothes hung out on the roof, so meager, so clear and so bright.

Mother, Gauss, etc. I thought of them always in connection with myself, admirable insofar as they contributed to or promoted my own career; but, of course, to them I seemed only an incident or an element in theirs.

There were pink geraniums in a window, a tortoiseshell cat on a fence—with an abundance of ailanthus trees at one end of the court—children playing in the yards.

Songs: Thanks for the buggy ride—thanks for the buggy ride—I had a wonderful time!—I wish I was in Peoria—in Peoria tu-night! You talk about your Sweetie and I'll talk about my Sweetie (final chorus, after prolonged talking passage, in which they sing against each other). *—Sitting on top of the world—Paddlin' Madeleine, sweet, sweet paddlin' Madeleine home. —*Irving Berlin's *At Peace with the World and You*, written after his marriage to Ellin Mackay. *Show me the way to go home—I'm tired and I wanta go to bed—I had a little drink about an hour ago and it's gone right to my head . . . —You'll always hear me singin' this song*, etc.

June. A great shaded sheet of diamond projected across the sky at the end of the street—or the dropping red-golden sun like some summer fruit just ripened. —That marvelous cool June, with winds strong enough to blow off straw hats, that succeeded the horrible hot spell of the summer before.

Helen Westley [the well-known actress associated with the Theatre Guild], that old vulture, fattening her soul on other people's humiliation and discomfiture. —She suddenly began working, dressing carefully and making up, as if, now that she was getting really old, she had begun to think for the first time of taking pains to appear attractive.

Little Francis Dell liked John Amen and me because we were "so silly." (Elaine McDermott's little girl liked Dos Passos, because she liked the way he giggled.) She would not answer all questions or reply to all remarks.

Run-in with little boys in the Park—there was the rumpus—pum-pum! I
said she was a baby and couldn't ride a bicycle.

Katze: "I haven't the foggiest! I haven't the slightest! We're not on
speaking."

Dos Passos's version of *Australian girls are very fine girls*—keep away! keep
away! keep away! (apropos of Bernice Dewey).

They had torn down the whole corner of old houses at Fifth Avenue and
Washington Mews, and one saw looking over the Mews the square compact little back windows of the top floors of the Washington Square houses
and the chimney pots under the blue June sky, as if one suddenly had a
glimpse into the low and open provincial New York of the last century, a
city with the summer sun and air and the free spaces of a small town, where
the multiplied rectangular windows and bulk in cubic feet of the red
middle-class mansions of Washington Square were the tallest and the most
impressive structures to be seen.

John Amen: "I haven't read this letter over, so it's probably cockeyed.
—That's the most cockeyed contract I ever saw."

First warm day of summer rain—one got wet and perspired at the same
time.

Visitor's entrance of Tombs. (A West Indian presser's boy had robbed our
apartment and stolen some of Mary's clothes. He was caught and I went to
see him in jail.) From Lafayette to White Street: a high building with a
great raw blank side and at the front a fire escape of rather curious design,
which, when looked at from below and at an angle to the façade of the
building, became vertiginous and sickening—beside it, a corrugated iron
shed facing on a gritty yard and sheltering a few cheap cars—a dreary
disused shop with panes broken in the loft windows and, below, a sign
Popcorn and Candy, rendered obscure by a rusty stove and some other
pieces of junk, themselves apparently representing an abandoned business;
at the top of the front steps, defaced and out-of-date posters for burlesque
shows, the election of assemblymen and sheriffs and obscure steamboat
excursions; on the corner, a Bail Bonds sign—as if the whole side of the
block had been blighted by the proximity of the prison.

Waiting in the telephone-booth-like compartment to talk to the prisoner—glimpse of American pie face, with round spectacles, on front
page of rolled morning *World*—appearance of prisoner behind grating
on other side of slot, like some effect in a play or moving picture—people shouting across all at once—before appearance of prisoners,
loud voice of policeman or warden: "Give it to me, *please*!", with the

"please" prolonged and expanded like the roar of a lion at feeding time.

Cold June. The Plaza rose from Fifth Avenue like some high white sea cliff, and the whole scene, in a pale setting sun, had a certain bleakness of marine skies—the statue of Sherman, at the entrance to the Park, showed a spiny and black silhouette.

Mr. Croly. When I asked him, in the lobby of the Algonquin, what sort of a place he'd like to go for dinner, he said, "I'm not particular," and when, at 154 West Fifty-fourth Street, I asked him what sort of wine he'd like, he said, "I'm not particular." —His face, which is capable, in the *New Republic* office, of becoming a heavy sallow mask, is at other times as sensitive as a brook which streams stumbling over stones. When anything was said that hurt him by reason of his misunderstanding it (from his natural humility and gentleness), his face would wear for some moments the expression of a child trying to keep from crying. —His gentlemanliness about Hackett—who, he said, had made more sacrifices for *The New Republic* than anybody else, because by nature he was the most independent, the one least fitted to work for a group. When he spoke of Lippmann's defection to the *World*, a look of pain passed over his face—yet he couldn't be blamed when they had offered him more money. The vulgarity and bad accent of the occasional British Labour guest at lunch also gave him suppressed pain—this reaction was evidently a heritage from the British background of his parents.

First conventional hot June day—the hot haze in Washington Square Park, dulling the full-blown bushes and trees.

Lying in bed, I heard some phonograph or guitar playing the *Merry Widow Waltz*, through which rang some city sound of steam whistle or motor horn, and, carried back to a Vienna of twenty years ago, I could see only the whores of public dance halls, as unromantic and rudimentary as those of today in their different clothes and accompanied by their different music, dancing in slippers of a different model, but soiled and worn.

Peggy [John Amen's mistress, described above, kept by somebody she didn't care for. When John and Marion decided to marry, John suggested that I might take her on; but she was not the kind of looking girl I like—though her appearance had something in common with Marion's, so she was evidently a type that John did like—but she did not interest me]. When I asked her if she could go out the next night, after I had had to call off *The Merry World*, she said, "Not any more this week," and when I called up Tappé's (she was a model at Tappé's) and asked for "Miss Tompkins," the girl, after inquiry, replied that "Peggy" had left and wouldn't be in "any more this afternoon." —Blond girlfriend Pat, who entered into romantic telephone relations with a young man from Alabama "who wrote a little,"

by accident in getting connected with a busy wire. She was just ripe for a
romance in her life, but when she made an appointment to meet him in the
Park, where he was in the habit of going riding, she was bitterly dis-
appointed. Both she and Peggy thought him somehow most unpleasant and
unreassuring—they didn't like the color of his eyes, which, so far as I could
gather, were a pale gooseberry green. They parted with promises to look
each other up, but had never communicated since. —Peggy's bare floor,
with couch, outlook over the long radiator onto Lexington Avenue,
phonograph, brown black radio horn, pile of *Cosmopolitans*, Maxfield Par-
rishes and Remingtons—I had expected divans, varicolored cushions, a fur
rug, batiks on the walls, goldfish and a heavy atmosphere of perfume and
cigarette smoke. —Peggy and I were dressed [formal]; Pat's boyfriend was
not—which, perhaps, had the effect of making Pat a little haughty and cold
when we met them at the theater. —Peggy's innocent and rather weak pale
gray eyes and her wry smile on one side of her mouth, as if the result of long
and rather sour experience. Her hair waved and parted like the wigs on
dressmakers' dummies or like the photographs of elegant English women in
the London illustrated papers. No wisecracks, no penetration, just a safe, refined line. She is the slim type which I suppose is fashionable now. I had
expected a black-haired, black-eyed girl, rather big, amiable, able, deep-
voiced (from my telephone conversation with her) and common. —On the
way up in the E1, having had a couple of drinks before I started, I was transported into an ecstasy of enthusiasm thinking of A. N. Whitehead—
crystalline abstract thought—a world of events continually progressing
into novelty—enjoyed it far more than Peggy.

Princeton reunion [EW inserted here that this was "the last I ever attended." He was forgetting that he attended the fortieth reunion in 1956, when
Princeton gave him an honorary degree.] The look of the setting sun, hanging yellow right above the west side of Washington Square, reminded me
of the late spring sunsets over the wide spaces of the campus, and in the taxi-
cab, the smell of the cushions reminded me of the smell of leather chairs in
dormitory rooms. —At New Brunswick, the soft sight of the Raritan with
round lights strung along the bridge in the gray-blue and gray-green of
evening. —Getting out at Princeton Junction, the sweet smell of the wide
meadows, of hay not yet cut, as if I had smelled the country and the summer
for the first time. —Gauss's account of students drinking, whoring, gambling, getting killed in motor accidents, setting fire to haystacks in the fields
and making bonfires on Blair Tower. —Gilly Pitcairn drinking at Charter
Club—"My wife's got a lot of sense—she's got a lot of sense!" —I thought
at first he said "sex," and congratulated him—battle of politeness over beds,
based on misapprehension on Gilly's part that there was only one—he

finally rushed off and slept in the library, and I couldn't get him to come back. —Parker McComas: "Hey-ho! lack-a-day! Here today and gone to-morrow!—If any—*if any!*—Well, it won't be long now!—What are you going to do?—take a buggy ride?" ("Here today and gone tomorrow" inspired by Bob Hyle's suddenly losing his lunch, after lying for some time apparently quietly sleeping on the bed.) Parker kept kicking over the gin—they would always scold him and put it back in the same place. —(Boy from another club who had been in the night before—I kept saying that I didn't know there was anybody in the club who could play the piano except Cy Seymour and John Wyeth.) —1911 grad in orange and black Spanish costume who came in with a glass in his hand in a humor of high contentment—the great thing about it was everybody drinking, that was the thing to do—hundreds of men came thousands of miles to re-union—1911: their permanent costumes, strongly made—"Now you go ahead and go to sleep, don't let me bother you," at intervals. —I stood in the upper center window with a glass in my hand and looked out on the wide oval scene, the flat green baseball field speckled with blue, orange and red costumes under the tender blue sky washed laterally across with thin unsolid clouds, into the light of the cool and delicate afternoon, the white tabby-cat tigers of snow, with their soft contours and shallow shadows, gave the effect of melting; a wonderful cluster of balloons, orange chiefly, with a few red and green—a pearly one in the hands of a child. —The nig-gers gathered at the gates—the boys on the field-house roof. —The Parade: Earl Carroll's bathtub—about three classes had the same joke—a nigger from town—a thin man with glasses from whose bathtub another man pre-tended to fill and drink bottles of beer. "Gentlemen Prefer Bonds—Others Sell Insurance." —George Darcy limply towering and drooping at the head of '16. —The dignified and interesting aspect of the classes of the '70's—the oldest graduate, Dr. Baker, rector emeritus of Trinity drawn first in a carriage. (The drunk whose bottle broke in his pocket between the halves—he stood gravely taking the pieces out, one by one—also his money, wet dollar bills—put them all on the ground, then began picking up the pieces of glass by mistake for the money, and putting them back in his pocket.) "What game?—with Harvard?—No, Pennsylvania's playing Purdue.—What victory?—We won a great moral victory in the seventh inning—didn't you see?" "Gee, Bob Hyle's sick as hell!" Everybody expressed concern—no one made a move to do anything—they finally de-cided to call the boy when they went down, and get him to clean it up—went on drinking. Conversation with Scotch boy: Man who starved to death—Scotchman who rode in pay-as-you-leave car. Buttons told a story about the origin of the Charleston—we encouraged him to tell other sto-ries—Scotch persistency and cockiness. —Bill Kalts. —Ralph Hinchman,

Sterling Carter, Arthur Jackson, and I lay on the bank beside Prospect—the iron fence banked with ivy which must have been tangling it since Witherspoon's time—the clear air, the late bright light—the birds flying from tree to tree so low that we could see their bobbin bodies with their legs folded along them—balloons traveling south—the first a dark speck moving slowly as if with hesitancy—the second a beautiful red bead sailing fast with a steady wind. —Tried to get them to come down to the club and have a little drink—"That isn't much of a temptation." Ralph: "I guess *you* better have one, Bunny." —Ralph continually looking at his watch, worrying about trains. —The silver sun melting the firs on the President's lawn. —Moore Gates and Wilton Lloyd-Smith, faces hardened in the direction of the iron and the rectangular. Trying to get Arthur to drink a bottle of beer by telling him it was sarsaparilla—he smelled it, however, first: "Aren't you cold already, without drinking something cold." —Parker McComas falling out of bed—we lifted him back in, after dropping him on the floor several times—dark American-Spanish fellow in bed next to me who said that when he heard the crash, he looked up and saw a great scar on the wall above his bed and said to himself, "That's where he fell!" —Calliope playing Triangle tunes of 1905—"Floating headquarters of 1915." —Empty bottles of ginger ale and White Rock standing around the next morning—half-filled highball glasses, stale. Frank Robert's swollen red coarsened amiable face under the three-cornered hat—his voice coarsened and hoarsened from choir leading. —*Lunch at the Gausses'* with the Gauss children, lovely blond girls, different shades of blond hair—greater freedom with parents away—Natalie's lilac dress with her golden hair and lighter lavender stockings—the others in white—Hildegarde reproved by Natalie for saying, "Where at?"—controversy on the subject—the wide mahogany table, white tablecloth, old-fashioned silverware, tall, slender, graceful pepper and salt shakers—looking from the dining room into the sitting room, the liquid luminosity of the indoor light—translucent, softly ruffled white curtains—a gilt mirror—spaciousness. —Old songs revived at reunion: *"Shut the door, they're coming through the window"*—perfect expression of blotto state of mind, attempt to grapple with imperfectly apprehended problems, forces working against one Press Club man's description of grads who arrived in his rooms—his roommate said, "Come right over! there's an old grad here with a big valise for drinking, with separate compartments for cracked ice and for orange juice and everything!"—but, by the time he got there, the valise was gone and only the grad left asleep on the bed—when, late at night, the roommate tried to get him to move, the grad said, "Why don't you get in with me?"—and when the fellow said there wasn't room, the grad said, "Tch-tch-tch!"

Afternoon with Marion. At the entrance to Westlands, I heard a song of the silver-whistling bird like water blown in a silver tube—the lawn with its trees, the garden and the servants' quarters in the sun—Dr. Preston and his swarming bees (he was Mrs. Cleveland's second husband)—putting on his bee clothes—Marion said, like some sort of super-drinking suit—he had an even more amusing one with a green veil—"The woggle bug" (Preston's spectacles)—"The bees don't like me as well as they do George—he never pinches them." The attitude toward Preston of the Cleveland children was always ironically humorous. —Dear McClenahan. —Allison Armour's creaseless trousers: "I don't feel very *spruce*"—his fine and sudden waggery in saying goodbye to McClenahan, grasping him by the lapels—"which would be exceedingly agreeable for me." —Esther's English accent, short quick way of speaking (Esther Cleveland had married an Englishman named Bosanquith and lived in England)—her insatiable appetite for tennis—"It's like some drug" —If the other person is a few minutes late, "Oh, dear! they can't stand it." (Marion must have said this.) —Fresh clean little children being taken by nurses in and out of the house. —The Russells—Doug Russell's way of talking, like Bill Mackie, only much worse—red face, swollen with sport more than drinking.—Marietta Russell, slender and pretty in a thin way and with a patrician blond charm—charming way of speaking very quickly, rather vague, but with perfect assurance and never making an error—reclining on the summer chintz bed—chair on springs—long legs and long feet in white summer shoes. —Swimming pool with copper-sulphate blue-green water—no towels, had to dry in the sun—ladies reclined on bank. —Tea: Russell took (Howard) Cox and me into the pantry to "look at pictures" of sailboats and yachts which he had painted himself—highballs. —Veiled marble bust on pedestal in hall, great vase, volumes of Shakespeare in bookcase—on side table in front of window, a row of perfectly untouched, uncut French books, Pierre de Coulevain, etc. —"Forgot to ask you if you'd have any tea." —They were "so vague—they always just sit around like that—they never show any initiative. They almost drive Howard crazy when he stays there." (Marion): "Is this house very old?" Cox: "No: I don't think it's old at all." He always had an incipient grin. Elderly lady who came to tea. —Handsome deep dark blue roadster. —Photographs of children on table; portraits. —Cox sat around with his coat off and ate grass. —The look of Mrs. Russell's gray eyes when you scrutinized her closely, as if the female vitality of her so feminine features lapsed easily, leaving a face devoid of sex which might have been an old woman's, which might have been a man's—no doubt her father looked like that. But how slender, smart and lovely she looked coming down the stairs across the hall, her pink figure and white legs perfectly, naturally posing and moving against the dark background, in the high frame, which just easily contained her.

Gauss (indicating the automobiles on Nassau Street): "When you have all that power at your command!—Look at one of those things! See how fast that one's going!"

Bank Street. At night the moon embedded in the pane, like a bright flaw of pearl in dull blue glass. —The deep blue of June dawn, through which the deep red and green of brick walls and trees are brightening—the emergence from indigo of bright colors through the brightening blue. —The final falling away of the blue veils and the freshness of even the shabby yellows of the poor apartment houses in the first distinct light of day. —The leaves of the common ailanthus trees swaying flexible clusters washed fresh by the first slight libation of spring light. —The child always crying in the back yard. —Music: highbrow piano and jazz accordion. —Appetizing smell of dinners cooking in the late afternoon.

Lloyd-Smith, with his litter of little foxes—perhaps I did him an injustice—made some not unintelligent observations when I met him on the campus, he had gone into McCosh Hall and sat smoking a cigarette alone. —Marjorie Fleming, whom he had married, a California heiress, was pretty, healthy and honest, they might produce some very fine children—especially if they derived from latent cells referring themselves to Wilton's grandfather or uncle.

Idea for wedding or some serious occasion on the part of the Algonquinites—FPA, etc.—everybody pulling practical jokes and wisecracks. Picture puzzles, poker and puns. FPA's wedding, after which they had all sat up playing cards all night.

Abyss of depression caused by calling up girl, finding the line busy for a considerable length of time and finally, when it is free, finding she doesn't answer.

Bank Street. The darkening sky of a June day, where the air still seems clear below and the houses, the windows, the trees maintain all their distinctness. —The remote unmenacing rumble of thunder—it will rain a little or pass off. —The pianist playing the music of some impressionist composer—wandering, seriously disporting himself in the treble in some light lingering in water or some wind-ruffled garden of Debussy—the metallic wavering and shimmer.

Effect of the declining sun over the buildings of the West Side—pale and grand in wild gray clouds, like the sun in some illustration of Doré for Dante or Milton—it made me think that I ought to be seeing it after some country thundershower or some storm at sea.

Howard Cox. He said he had passed a very dull weekend at the Russells'. "What's Mrs. Russell like?"—"Just like that?"—"Yes, but not so good."—"There's a possibility she might be better."—"Yes, but when you come to try to talk to her, she's just blah." —He said that he was sure Russell had no soul. —Anecdote about his quarrel with Fitz, just as he was preparing to go to his house and bring the little girl a present—they were drinking at some bar in Paris. He had said suddenly, "I could sleep with Zelda any time I wanted to." —Afterwards couldn't imagine what on earth had made him, felt terribly about it just as soon as he'd said it. Actually—my own comment—Zelda was not so loose nor Howard so dangerous as this implied. He was envious of Scott, I suppose, and the drinks had brought this to the surface.

Katze. We sat on couch from immediately after a late breakfast until just before dinnertime and drank almost a quart of sherry and half a bottle of Scotch. We sang, hummed and whistled Raquel Meller's *Violetera* and *Flor del Mal* with great enjoyment. She had her ash-brown dust-gray hair brushed in a new way, parted in the middle, so that it made rounded bangs over her eyes and brought out their roundness, their largeness and their softness. She told me that she was built like her mother, who had small bones, but that her eyes were like her father's—he was an arrogant, imperious and intolerant German type, and her mother had lately divorced him. It made me think how beautiful eyes were produced—not by happy matches necessarily. —"I think I'm about to pass into a recline—I mean a decline." —"Mr. Dooflecker." (Cummings used to call Mrs. McCormick "Mrs. Doodlebug." Mrs. McCormick was the janitor's wife at 3 Washington Square North.) Katze had been to the Metropolitan and seen a Nativity of Greco and gone off afterwards to a tea in a great state of exaltation. A man said to her, "You're far too young to pose," and she had replied, "You're far too old to tell me so"—because, she explained to me, she thought he had got past the age when one is capable of feeling the kind of enthusiasms which move people to pose. —Favorite expression: "Not so hot." —"Just be sweet to me: I'm so tired. —I'm so silly when I'm sleepy; you have no idea." —She talked about her parents in the impudent dramatic way that clever young people do, especially when they have them on their minds: she said that her father was intellectual and mother sentimental: she read Schiller, who was an awfully sentimental writer; "Mother is quite beautiful, you know." Franz used to say to her *"Schlaf schön,"* when he left her at her door at night. —Her young girlish way of lowering her eyes with an air of anguish, when I asked her what had happened to her affair with the man she said she had loved—he had been "so sensitive"—a long time ago—she wasn't in love with anybody now. I asked her how long ago it had been, and she said a year and a half. —She shook her head and snorted, "Br-r-ri," and then said, "Isn't that cute?" —During the Greta Nissen ballet: "Look at the paste on his face!"—"For no reason at all—as a matter of fact." —Trouble at school—put a cracker and a piece of pie on the desk of the teacher, who was always eating—boy who had crush on her and did all her chemistry for her, so that, when it came to examinations, she didn't know anything about it and flunked. —In the delicatessen store, in flowered pink and white summer dress and big hat, so much more becoming to her than the little ones. Her meager and high-beginning calves—long ankles—long neck. —"That's probably because I had a grandfather who was a baron or something of the sort—not that I think that sort of thing's particularly important.

[*My moment of anti-Semitism*. I laid siege to Katze for a long time, but could never completely get her away from Franz. I finally told her that I thought they were both Jewish, and Katze, quite justifiably, said this was in bad taste. Not that I had no real reason for assuming that they were Jewish, and that, even if I had known they were, it would not have improved my position with Katze. I am not at all proud of this, but I include it as an instance of the depth from which such a reaction can spring. I regard it as an example of the way in which a purely superstitious idea—that the Jews were responsible for executing Jesus—instilled into one's unconscious, may irrationally influence behavior. I was moved by the same stupid instinct as a Russian friend of mine, a pianist, who claimed that his concerts had been thwarted by a conspiracy of Jewish musicians or as Céline when he thought that production of his plays had been blocked by the Jewish dramatists.]

Henrietta Fort at Marion's. The roof garden. Henrietta in the dark, with big black hat of the kind that has just become fashionable, and handsome white legs with knees crossed. Singing the old songs. Cute song from old Follies, in which the wife answers "Umhumm" to the husband's questions, that she and Pooks (Louise) used to sing together, they had it down fine. One day, they spent a good deal of time learning a new song to sing to John, and when they sang it to him, he didn't like it. Their father approved of the Eddie Cantor song, *"And they call it dancing, dancing, that's all,"* apparently under the impression that it was a satire. Charley Arrott came to visit them and remained for weeks—it was he who first brought John around. He and Charley spent all their time at the Fort house, staying up till the early hours of the morning every night, to the great scandal of the father. —*At the Devil's Ball, Papa Love Mamma, That Spanish Dancer from Madrid.* —*"You can easily see she's not my mother"* had been sung to her without any relation to anything that had gone before, but by an uninteresting man in Detroit. —*"That wonderful moment—when you and I forgot what 'no' meant."*

Taxi ride to dinner with Marion and John. We found part of a newspaper, including the radio section, in the cab. John's frantic diving for the market reports. Tearing up the paper and throwing it around. Wadding it into balls and pelting one another's straw hats. —John playing a maniac: "Not normal! It's quite normal! . . . No: it's not quite normal." John had got a piece of excelsior stuck in his throat. —"You can easily see she's not my father, 'cuz my father's more refined.—You can easily see she's not my sister, 'cuz my sister's got a beautiful face.—She's just a good little kid, who remembers what she did. —She's Winny the Whitewash Man!"—John's idiot laughter.

Fast taxi ride through New York streets when you are drunk: impression that you are plunging through all obstacles at exhilaratingly giddy speed; nothing can interfere with your progress: woman with German police dog, American Railway Express truck, other and inferior taxicabs; ripping your way through traffic and El posts.

Fifth Avenue on a hot July night. Coming down on the bus, one moves through the gray hot heavy air, in which the taxis, the victorias and the buses seem to be embedded, muted and subdued, and which is seen condensing more and more thickly toward the end of the vista of the Avenue until, as the sky deepens from gray to indigo, the prospect becomes completely obscured by a sooty atmospheric fog, through which the white globes of the street lamps show dimly. Just as we get to the Square, an unexpected and delightful breeze—the stagnant hot bilgy smell of the river.

Marion said that she had never read any of Howard Cox's stories, but she knew that they were this sort of thing: "Now so-and-so was a bold young man, but this was beyond him."

Seabright in July. A thin moving platform of glass—lucid water over the gray sand. I put my hand, sweaty from my face, in the water, as if I should be washing it fresh, and then tasted, when I wiped my face with it, that, instead of being freshened, it was seasoned with cleaner salt. —The sun dulled and the waves turned dark with the look of a mid-ocean sea, so different from the white curling crests and the shining blues and greens of the surf; and, presently, against the gray sky, appeared a small army dirigible, like the glassy iron-silver ovoid of a shark or a whale as we see them hanging stuffed in museums. It moved slowly toward the shore till, passing before and above us, we could see the number and the letters painted on it and the little black men in the car, one of them waving his arm. There were fins on its smaller end and, behind it, a small American flag, stretched out in the wind like a little steerer, and from its chin trailed a rope like a feeler. It tilted up, moving all in one piece, and moved off along the shore above the sea. —A girl in a green cap and a gray bathing suit with gray stockings and

shiny black blunt-toed shoes, which she kicked off on the sand, after she had
been sitting there awhile, went into the water. She was well filled out and
swam quite competently. Her gray bathing suit became like a skin over her
solid torso and molded her broad flat breasts, revealing the nipples as dark
dots. This, as I later found out, was the beach for the rich people's servants,
who were sometimes in their bathing suits unrecognizably better looking.
—An engulfed sea crab, a purplish grainy gray, like the sand as one saw it
through the water. I skimmed him out with a rusty wad of tin and put him
over on one side in the shelter of a little breakwater which separates the
Pavilion from the Beach Club.

View from inside Child's. A harmony in tender darkened tints framed in the
zinc-white rectangular window, above the middle of which Child's was
written in zinc-white letters backwards and at the bottom of which showed
the nickel-silver of the buttercake griddle and an even pile of white plates.
The girl who made the buttercakes (she was standing picking her teeth,
with one white-stockinged ankle crossed over the other and resting on its
toe) was dressed in a light plain green which harmonized with the green
trees outside and the blue-gray twilight of the rainy afternoon, jeweled
with red and green taxi lights, to which a woman's purple umbrella passing
the window contributed a new and still harmonious note of watercolor.

Olympic Burlesque on Fourteenth Street. "Say, don't look at me! I can't play
when you look at me! Why, you've got a face that only a mother could
love! If I had a dog that looked like you, I'd shoot'um." —The comedians,
a large man in a straw hat with a wide common mouth of white teeth, like
the fake sets in a cheap dentist's window, and two nondescript funny men,
one of them a solemn German Jewish type, did their stuff with a bass drum
and cymbals, which they banged, as they marched around, after every verse
of their comic song, against a background of the Monte Carlo Spaghetti
House, Ed Pinaud's Hair Tonic, the Cobin Dancing Academy, The D. & S.
Pants Shop, the White Rats Tonsorial Parlors. —"I'm going to jump off the
Brooklyn Bridge!"—"Don't do that! You'll get the water all dirty!" —
The girls came down the runways, which were like hollow bowling alleys,
with the electric lights along the edge all directly on them: some blond and
wrinkled, others ugly little fat black-haired Jewesses—perhaps the best-
looking girl was of curious shape, a young amiable attractive smile of the
California type, but disproportionately long legs and enormously thick
thighs (California also, perhaps); she couldn't do much shimmying but was
otherwise a great success. The blond leader with her muscular stringy straddling legs: her look of strain while going through the final convulsions of
the orgasm dance—in one number she appeared in a garment like a pink

flannel undershirt with a flannel ribbon tied around her waist, presently she untied the ribbon, revealing the contours of her crotch through the shirt—standing in the wings, waiting to go on, she looked charming with soft deep shadows marking her eyes and the lower part of her face so that she looked like a pretty blond kitten. —One featured woman appeared in a costume consisting of several large white feathers and, at the final spasm of the orgasm, made a significant gesture with her white feather fan, putting it behind and pushing it outward between her legs. "If you're looking for a big-time mamma, here's your opportunity!" —In one number they fished from the runway with pretzels hung from fishing rods—the leader had a small lemon. —Sitting on the side, I could see the legs and arms of the big chorus girl thrown shamblingly about from behind the wings, as she was practicing Charleston steps or something of the kind. —The audience of men, who sat with their coats off, watch stolidly through the girl numbers and then surprise one by breaking into sudden and loud applause as soon as the chorus have left the stage—there are always half a dozen encores to every song. —In a burlesque show, there is always some comic sketch in which a magic bottle or something of the kind is introduced—in this case they had a magic box, which, when powder was squirted from it on some victim, compelled him to do whatever one wanted: first, the man with the straw hat proved its efficacy by making one of the comedians give him his watch and sold it for five dollars to the other comedian, who then got the five dollars back; then the possessor made one of the girls give him a kiss, an embrace, and finally undress piece by piece—big curtain! —"Next week we are going to have a new act by Jimmy Schwarz—Jimmy Schwarz is verry verry funny. You saw him with the cymbals tonight. Verry verry funny. —And we are going to have a special number—the Masked Dancer. She is called the Masked Dancer because she wears a mask, and, believe me, boys, she's some dancer! Now, the Masked Dancer has been a sensation in San Francisco, and Mr. Rausch has secured her, at great expense, to appear at the Olympic for a week. She's some dancer, boys! I thank you."

Late afternoon sky after rain: white pearly banks of solid light, rifted with a crack of red; and, above them, a great canopy of cloud, yellow-rusted.

The Follies, July 1926 (moved to the Globe Theatre and produced under a different name). Tableaux: "The Bride." "Silver and Flame. An arrangement by Ben Ali Haggin." Song: *When the Shaker Plays a Cocktail Tune*, by Gene Buck; song: *I Want a Girl to Call My Own*, by Gene Buck; law skit by J. P. McEvoy—man is up for murder, "I'll tell you what happened, Judge," scene in which he is trying to read paper and all his family come in Charlestoning, he shoots them all, the judge lets him off; song: *Henry Be Mine*, by

Gene Buck; James Barton's drunken act, fixed ginny stare produced by
painting eyeballs on his eyelids, passes through various stages of friendliness
quarrelsomeness, etc., sings, tries to start a fight and swings himself down
numb and paralyzed fingers, held stiffly, like claws, "I've got something
nice to tell you!" He is almost too realistically gruesome to be amusing.
He's down in program as Mickey, the Monster. "A Little Café in Paris: A
Stewed Rich American, Andrew Tombey—His Ball and Chain, Edna
Leedom—The Absinthe Lady, Little Marie, Montmarte Rose, A Boy from
the Big Parade": another sour sketch by McEvoy—Rae Dooley as a little
girl on a railroad train makes so much trouble that the long-suffering conductor finally throws her out the window: *Florida, the Moon and You*, by
Gene Buck; finale: The moonbeam blonde, Claire Luce, lowered in a
revolving silver globe whose surface sends a play on the backdrop of red
and green sparks of light; she passes later through a series of slow naked
poses, while the show girls with enormous white headdresses of various
combinations of peacock feathers, each outtopping and outdazzling the last,
advance one by one to the front. (This is the year when, owing to the Earl
Carroll scandal and the attempt to suppress The Bunk of '26, Ziegfeld advertised that all the girls in his show would positively appear clothed—one
of the features was, therefore, a chorus in garments like thin silk pajamas cut
to hang loosely with flaring bottoms about the ankles and to cling tightly
about the thighs, as if they were wet with perspiration; and in another number they wore trousers which had diamond triangles on the crotches.)
—Treasures from the East, a Venetian Fantasy by E. A. Haggin: a girl from
Siam, a girl from China, a girl from Korea, a girl from Greece, Venetian
Ladies, Venetian Boys (both girls); *Every Little Thing You Do*, by Gene
Buck; Comic Dance by Barton and Rae Dooley; songs by Edna Leedom,
that great big pretty bediamond-and-pearled American Blonde grinding
her comic songs, full of wisecracks, out through white teeth; Greta Nissen
in an Oriental Pantomime of her own creation called Mlle Bluebeard: her
beautiful body, in conventional Oriental costume with beads around her
breasts, etc., sumptuous thighs and legs, tilted, slightly squinting, provocative Swedish eyes—lures first lover into death chamber, where a series of
papier-mâché heads are seen hanging, he sticks his head out the door and she
cuts it off with a scimitar, after pushing it carefully out the door, in the
further course of her incessant leisurely dance, with one of her very modern
European-shod feet—the second lover suffers a like fate, he sits about gloat-
ing fatuously over the irresistible queen. (Katze: "Look at the paste on his
face!") Moran and Mack; song: *Wasn't it nice? wasn't it sweet? wasn't it good?*
by Gene Buck—girls in summery Palm Beach costumes, with wide hats
and pink dresses (it is in such numbers as this that Ziegfeld excels, as Franz
says, in making his chorus look like "lydies"); scene by Gene Buck: *Rip's*

Birthday Party—Rip Van Winkle comes back, and there pass before him Lulu Belle, Peggy Joyce, Irving Berlin and Ellin Mackay, Raquel Meller, Cinderella, Peaches Browning and Countess Cathcart —Ziegfeld is said to have spent all his money on the Follies productions, so that Erlanger finally refused to let him lease the New Amsterdam Theatre any more. Rather melancholy effects of seeing the great framed display of former Follies beauties, which used to stand at the top of the stairway in the New Amsterdam, moved to the outside lobby of the Globe, where it is lost away from its setting and reduced to the status of a vaudeville advertisement, moved about with the show and deprived of the dignity of its former historical interest in its relation to an institution. —I forgot to include in her place the little rowdy jazzing girl, straight dark bobbed hair, bright smile of complete teeth, Charleston steps at breakneck speed, gathering up short skirts.

Those solid masses of white light at sunset, like crystal at once opaque and clear; the tender surfaces of gray above them.

Getting into New York by the Liberty Street ferry on a rainy day—a blotting of gray over everything, behind which the strong heavy colors of summer showed dark and dull—the green of trees in the Square, the red of the house fronts on the north side. Coming up, the ruddy roasted dark walls of factories overtowering and standing out among the lower buildings—in a window of which one would see a livid but acrid and flint-like lime-green light. And the red and green lamps on the backs of taxis had a similar jewel-like look.

Coming home down Broadway at night, as he passed under the windows of some nightclub, he was sprayed profusely with some cold evacuation of liquid from the second floor and thought at once of a nickel-silver cocktail shaker which it had been found advisable for some reason or other to empty. But, looking up, he beheld the drawn sallow face of a gentleman whose drinks had not agreed with him. With energy and virile disgust, he tried to wipe off his shoulder and his knee with his handkerchief. —Stripping off his contaminated clothes, he disclosed the white double box of his breast, which he admired in the glass. "Some *bastard vomited* on me!"—he stung her with the words like masculine stabs.

The fashion of large black hats that folded about the ears, like bonnets, and half concealed the face, with mysterious and provocative effect. The two girls at Thirty-fourth Street and Sixth Avenue, both in black, with white stockings and these black hats—the face of one was easy to be seen, Jewish and plain; that of the other hidden in her hat, as if from bashfulness—she was pretty, with a nose like Belle Gifford's and a deeper stronger voice than one expected—she was apparently governed by the other and always waited for her to make decisions on any proposition. At the same time, boyish bobs are fashionable, and you have a regular type of little girl who, with a bob, simply seems to tie her dress around the waist with a boyish leather belt. The little girl of this type at the Tango Gardens—the first night, I thought her slight, slender-legged, shrewd, gray-eyed and matter-of-fact. The next night, I found her amiable, honest and with a ready simple smile and I observed that her body was ample and thick—it was perhaps the bob, the dress and her black round-nosed slippers with a strap across the instep, of a model that looks old-fashioned but is now popular, which gave her the effect of being slight. —When she disappeared in the middle of the evening, at the instance, apparently, of the ticket taker, she came back with a different pair of shoes—light coffee brown.

Marie. I picked her up somewhere in the Forties or Fifties coming out of a hotel. We just looked at one another and began to talk. Looking out into the hot, the smothered summer night, the dark greenery of the park (Washington Square Park), its benches loaded with slowed and muted swarms of human beings, hundreds of them stupidly swarming in the night so close to my spacious empty room, my comparatively so much cooler apartment, just across the street, dirty, sweaty, giving out the sounds of life, but obscured by the darkness and restrained and keyed down by the heat. —When I first saw her on the street, I thought her whore-broken, hard-boiled—her dissatisfied, disagreeable look, as if she smelled a bad smell: but when I came to talk to her, I learned that her father was supposed to have come from Barcelona, and saw that her hands were strong, broad and thick, her fingers blunt and large. She had a simplicity and feminine gentleness under her hard-boiled New York manner. —When she came to the apartment, I was amazed to see how much younger she looked and how much handsomer. She had the large soft tragic eyes (with the "nose all over my face" and the thick red sensual lips which she worked into vulgar grimaces as she talked) of the Italian whores and peasant women of whom the Renaissance painters made madonnas. She told me about her brother in jail in Brooklyn, falsely accused of rape—this kid who had him indicted hadn't yet appeared for a trial, the boy she had been going with and who had been jealous of Marie's brother who had made all the trouble—she had retained a lawyer who was supposed to be very good, having got somebody off in some well-known case (well-known in the tabloid dailies)—she had given him everything she had, $350 (her tactful way of asking for money).

A gray day at the shore—it was going to rain—sky and sea were both gray—a few gulls above the water—dry smell of salt dust in the nostrils above the breaking crests. —The next day, the girl on the sand whom I took at first for a boy—she had glossy black hair, boyish-bobbed, and wore a white shirt tucked inside a pair of black trunks like a boy—I first recognized her as a girl by the way she held her cigarette—her feminine gesture moving the upper half of her arm toward her body—later I saw the low roundness of her breasts. —A young boy and girl playing ball across one of the lifelines in the surf, she a blonde in a turquoise bathing suit and with her tanned summer skin not quite continuous with the edge of the slip at the shoulders and thighs.

Vision in the streets of a thousand girls resurrecting themselves in the afternoon from dark and messy rooms, unornamented, poorly furnished, and putting on their white stockings, their black bonnet hats, their chemises, their flowered chiffon dresses, and emerging, like butterflies from cocoons, enchanting and romantic creatures to exert their magic in the streets, to wander and draw men's glances.

A child's voice from the summer street, nasal and shrill, but working the charm of some popular song with a subtle and fascinating deviating melody which it follows accurately through and repeats.

Reflections on the natural stultified life of nonthinking and nonfeeling, of the laziness of bodily processes fulfilling their functions and the mind drifting among random memories and images, giving wide berth to one's problems and tasks. From this condition, how rarely and with what effort we raise ourselves to compose a picture of experience which invests it with some sort of intensity and insists for it upon some pattern! So that literature and art cannot truly represent life, even when they attribute to it the character I have suggested above—because, in doing so, they imply that this character is somehow a defection, an abnormality, and that the attitude, the state of feeling, the kind of activity, represented by the statement itself is the actual reality. Literature is the crystallization of the consciousness at the extreme points of man's self-consciousness and self-expressive impulse coinciding.

All of literature gives a false view of life, because it is the obverse of the reality—the artist fills in the holes in his character or experience by the fabrication of imaginary spiritual material.

First of all, the artist, in his productions, distorts life in a certain direction, manufactures for it a false face—then the reader, who is likely to be deceived into believing, erroneously, that life is really like that for the author and is therefore capable of being made so for others, tries in action to realize the picture which the artist had invented for the purpose precisely of supplying something which he has failed to find. In the end, the impossibilities of the system conspicuously appear, and the model is discarded, with the result that the reader abuses the writer for having misrepresented things.

The point is that the readers of books *lean*, as if upon something unquestionably real and strong, upon what, for the author, was merely a comforting and quite conscious falsification of life, as his own experience has disconcertingly presented it to him, a sort of euphemism made in the hope, which no one knows better than he to be ill-founded, that, by putting such and such a face on things, he can actually give them that character—in subjecting the whole of his experience to the coloring and pattern of his own temperament, he forgets for a moment the real unknowable world in this extension of his own immediate consciousness to fill—as, by an illusion, it seems to do—the whole landscape of experience. To the reader, it seems as if this inverted world were perhaps the real world which he has himself been looking for and, for the time being, he may accept it.

One of Ted Paramore's songs:

Oh, your mother is in bed,
And your father is dead.
There ain't nobody at all,
Turn down the lights in the hall,
But don't hurry, because we've got lots of time.

Oh, twist it around,
And fling it up and down,
Oh, how I love that sound,
Just like a cow's foot in wet ground!

Oh, the clock was striking one,
Oh, yes, the clock was striking one,
We had just begun
To have a little fun. —And we didn't hurry,
'Cause we had lots of time.

Oh, the clock was striking two,
I said, "Let's try something new,
Just to see what we can do."

Oh, the clock was striking three,
Oh, yes, the clock was striking three,
I took my baby on my knee,
Just to see what we could see.
But we didn't hurry, etc.

Oh, the clock was striking four,
Oh, yes, the clock was striking four.
I was afraid that she'd get sore,
But she called for more and more.

The clock was striking five,
I was more dead than alive!

I said, "How can I contrive
To ring the bell at five?"

The clock was striking six,
Oh, yes, the clock was striking six,
I said, "Come, bring out all your tricks,
'Cause I'm in an awful fix.
And please hurry,
'Cause we haven't got much time."

The clock was striking nine,
Oh, yes, the clock was striking nine,
I said, "A little sleep would go fine,
    You get in your bed and I'll get in mine."

Old Uncle Joe, the Jelly-Roll King,
Has got a hump on his back from shakin' that thing!
Prince of Wales, son of a King
Fell off his horse from shakin' that thing!

Two saxophone players went to bed—
Shook that thing till they both fell dead!

Oh, shake that thing! Shake that thing!
I'm tired tellin' you to shake that thing!

This song was sung everywhere in New Orleans when I was there but in the North a recording was not permitted. [Sherwood] Anderson, who had been celebrating Mardi Gras, somewhat shocked some respectable company by bursting in on them and singing it without inhibitions.

Late July sky. In the asphalt sky of summer, the sun burnt a blunt point of white light, like the blinding violet-livid torch with which an engineer attacks an exhumed pipe—it suffused the clouds with no dissolving color, but merely cut out those which encroached upon it with a sharp wiry edge of copper. —At another time (crossing Abingdon Square), however, I saw exquisite pearly marblings softly rufous, as if from some infusion of iron. —The boys playing ball in the streets on the way, the handball court—little boy with spectacles, who wasn't allowed by a bigger little boy and two robuster little girls to participate, cried in a hoarse loud passionate voice: "You son of a bitch!" —Another little boy, playfully (perhaps in the course of some game): "I'll put you all in jail!" —Those recurring red backdrops to streets—the labyrinth of the Village—one feels lost in it and yet secure, as if it were a sort of asylum in the summer.

Marie. She was broad and had olive skin when she took off her bandeau, disclosed large full breasts of which the nipples were spread from pregnancy—she was marked all the way down from the navel to the pubes with a long straight dent which gave her bronze and anatomical look of Dürer's women—her cunt, however, seemed to be small. She would not, the first time, respond very heartily, but, the second, would wet herself and bite my tongue, and when I had finished, I could feel her vagina throbbing power-fully. —Thrust naked cock up into those obscure and meaty regions. After-wards, she lay with the cover pulled over her up to the breasts, which were thus left bare.

—Her sister Loretta—her mother was very beautiful and had been mar-ried three times. She had been married at fifteen to a man who was just a beast—she only stayed with him a few months. (She came from Brooklyn and said "bersterous" [boisterous], etc.) Brought up in a convent—all that about the nuns was the bunk—Father James used to kiss her every morning when she came to open the gate for him. He used to kiss her awful hard, too—he didn't stick his tongue in her mouth, but she used to begin to tingle all over: "It was an awful passionate kiss." Finally, one day, she said, "Father James, don't you know that that's a sin?"—He stunned her with some technicality that she didn't understand. —They had told her that she was ruined and she'd have to get married. —They asked her to stay and work at the convent, but her mother had said, "Be a servant!" "I didn't care whether I was a servant or not." —Her sisters were married and had child-ren—they didn't know anything at all, which was rather annoying and made it hard to talk to them. —She had been a model for Neysa McMein (I saw in her then the 100 percent Americanized gypsy and Indian girls that Neysa McMein had been doing for magazine covers), who paid her $3 an hour—Miss McMein was temperamental, sometimes she was nice, and other times, instead of just saying, "Won't you turn your head a little?", she'd say sharply, "Can't you pose?" She worked, also, for a wholesale dress manufacturer, posing. —She said it was always her luck to get somebody who was married or engaged. "Then, I get the bum's air, huh?" —At the restaurant on Sixth Avenue. Just before I sent her home: "I'm getting irrit-able now."

—She had the large opaque glassy black eyes and curving overhanging brows of a grimacing Japanese mask when she glared (as she ordinarily did in public); but was capable of being appealed to through amiability, so as to melt into a delightful cunning good-natured smile of the eyes. —Evening at her apartment in 105th Street (really the apartment of the woman through whom she operated as a call girl): incredible department-store newness, spotlessness and stiffness of her room, with its tapestry, its dressing table, its crinolined china lampshade figures, its pink electric light (above the bed) with a dangling silken cord, its wide bed (filling most of the room), on which the pale raspberry silk cover looked as if it had been put on like a coat of shellac—her collection of dresses and underclothes, all carefully folded and laid away. She carefully hung her dress (and my suit) in the closet. Professional prostitute manner and line brought on by my dullness and lack of interest: "Why, you little rascal!—Come on, let's have a party!" When I explained that I was feeling languid: "You know why: because it was an effort!" —Her album: costume balls, studio parties, camping. Her artist friend's portrait of her, in the magazine-illustration manner; and the pictures of her cunning little nieces on the bureau. Photograph of herself as a very young girl, with her dark eyes, big dark mouth and dark hair webbing out in all directions—she thought that picture was a great joke: "I took the comb and teased it, y' know. —I thought that looked swell." —Reestablishment of cordial and playful relations.

After she had gone, that hot night, I read (this must have been one of the times she came to see me in Thirteenth Street), shoving my mind along against lassitude with effort but not without pleasure (if one can speak of pleasure at a time when the capacity for pleasure of any kind seems all to have been spent), a page-and-a-half paragraph of Matthew Arnold; and sank into sleep. In the morning, I seemed still sunk in the heavy atmosphere of heat and the satiation of my energies, a kind of dull animal contentment.

—She knew when people appreciated her and when they just wanted her for a purpose—the latter class she would just get rid of.

At the climax of a bout, being drunk and thinking I was performing particularly successfully, I discovered that my cock had slipped out and that she was trying to put it back in again.

—"Tryin' to show me a good time?" —She used to call me Jack by mistake. [I had no real girl then, thought constantly of sex, was never really satisfied till I came to know Anna. In *I Thought of Daisy*, I have the hero finally satisfied by the character based on Florence, but actually I never slept with her. My relations with Katze, though I was very much fascinated by her, were unsatisfactory, too.]

Hot August days. Gray haze filling and blurring vistas, as if asphalt and buildings were vaporizing under the pressure of the heat. —A white truck horse, with head lowered like a lizard, stupefied and sleeping, with its eyelids closed, in the sun, while the driver piles up a mountain of boxes on the dray. —Little lost crying Jewish child in police station—large equable impassive detective in his shirtsleeves holding her—"They mostly always cry when they come here." —Old obsolete-looking beer saloon on Katze's corner—discolored blue Pilsner sign—windows, some of them without blinds and the blinds of the others, always hanging open, deslatted—they gaped on a dark and inconceivably sordid interior.

The New Jersey shore, etc. Fully developed, heavily tanned girl and boy in bathing suits in delivery wagon—like Ford. —Straight slender-legged Swedish-looking blond girl in red bathing suit with sharpish nose, gray eyes, boyish-bobbed pale hair, well-developed pretty girl's breasts which were yet not excessive for her tall slim figure—unabashed independent manner and gaze, serious, except when talking to friend, when she had a fine smile—proud. —Little children at Monmouth Beach in orange and pale green bathing suits, like flavors of lime and orange drops or bottled soft drinks. —Shredded seaweed swimming like spinach in the surf and when we got out, sticking to one's body in green transparent flakes. —A churning and crashing of wreckage—sticks and boards—by much too strong inhuman gray-green-colored waves breaking on the bias, which made swimming impossible and standing in the surf uncertain and uncomfortable. The rusty keys and locks of the humble and obscure bathing pavilion—and torn towels five cents extra—no separate men's and women's sides—between a wicked-looking breakwater and a limit.

Rosalind. Her sharp peremptory way of calling "Stella!" —When the telephone standing in the hall was broken: "Have that fixed! Have that fixed!" —When Mother went off to Talcottville early in the morning, standing up in bed in nightgown and seeing car out of window: "What's dis? What's dis?" (Little black eyes contrasting with pale [cotton] nightgown.) —At river: sun, boats, fish (minnows playing in water—"two fish"); swallow ("around and around and around"); inquired about noises of riverboat—"What's down there?"—"What's in 'ere?"—"That's enough—go home now!"—Rosalind transformed, after being sick in hospital, by boyish bob. —Delight in knowing names of things: toes—knees—two knees—two toes; house—cows—two cows: smiling with ecstatic satisfaction. —Repeats things like "Glad to see her" and "Had a nice time" obediently but without giving the impression of knowing what they mean.

Evening of an overcast day which had brought coolness after a spell of heat. The night air coming in through the screened window with the sharp icy coldness of ice water drunk on a sweaty hot day—a soft moisture congealing in the air, not so formidable as rain, a gentle mist—the look of the white garage, blue sky and green trees and the hedge from the windows of the sun parlor—soft brightness of blues and greens—freshness in dimness. The rose-or-orange satisfactory unsubtle American light of the interior of a small new cottage warm in the mist close of day.

The shore. A girl in mauve or old-rose bathing suit with carpet-like flower patterns, of which the purplish tint in rose balanced beautifully with the pinkish tint in purple tan of her skin. —Two girls on the sand: one, a straw-haired blonde, so deeply tanned that her skin seemed to have been thickened like leather, in a dark blue bathing suit, and, when she went into the water, a very businesslike-looking blue cap which fastened down over her ears and spoiled her good looks; and the other, a girl with wide (but not round) dark eyes, a mouthful of large white teeth between lips of deep mauve, a dark skin of a purplish plum, a red bathing suit and a red cap: they lay back stretching out their legs and bodies on the sand, propping up their heads and shoulders a little with their arms (John Amen: "Jump those!"), spreading their full thighs and irresistibly drawing attention to the sumptuous cunts between them. The flaccid, the stringy and the fat. —On a gray day of rough uninviting waves, the neutral-tinted dishwater drawing back its thin and dingy shreds of suds.

The sun seen like a bright silver coal through an even pile of ashes— which give the forests in the distance on the night an added darkness and bluish depth.

A cat run over by an automobile on the Oceanic road (concrete with stripe of tar down the middle and flattened out like a tiger-rug of fur and blood, in which only recognizable feature was a small series of ribs).

Katze. Her body in her new thin black dress as she lay in the armchair with her feet in another chair, *en faisant valoir* her breast and thighs and crotch. She went to sleep, and I carried her in and put her on my bed, kissing her voraciously but respectably on her beautiful neck and on her feet at the low instep of her shoe, before I left her.
　　—Her appearance at lunch—she had had dinner with her mother the night before, and her mother had talked to her for hours and got her all upset. She had gone home and "wept and howled." She looked all the better for having been harrowed—her hair was a little disheveled and her great black eyes were blazing like nothing I have ever seen before in my life—like a deer's but much more intense, a much higher power of deep blackness. —Her almost a little ridiculous ready debutante politeness when I would leave her at the door and thank her for coming to the show: "It was awfully nice of you to drag me along!" —She suspected, when she first began it, that *Vathek* might be meant to be funny, but she had remembered that I had spoken of it in my letter as an "improving romance."

Dos Passos's voice over the telephone, faltering, groping like his purblind eyes: "Well—well, what are you doing—what are you doing today?" — Oh literature: painting was in a very bad way, too—but in painting there were certain fundamental difficulties that had to be overcome—whereas anybody could go in for literature—you didn't even have to be able to write, because you could dictate. —There was a good deal of the "Ain't it awful, Mabel" attitude about Kyd (Thomas). —He had gone to the Chekhov plays (Moscow Art Theater) and "wept buckets" over *The Cherry Orchard*.

Dos Passos. When we were drinking in Red Bank and I stopped halfway n some tactless sentence (about *Manhattan Transfer*) after a pause of several econds, he said, "That unfinished sentence is filling the room in great :oils!" —His look at Aunt Caroline, half turned at the door, before I intro-luced him to her. —She said, "Well, I'll see you at the [Beach] Club." I aid to Dos, when she had left, that we were *not* going to the club, of which I vas no longer a member. "I know," he said. "I was alarmed: I think those olaces pollute the water for miles!" —He had told me once that he could arely get through reviews of his books: he always found his mind wander-ng. He said that Albert J. Nock hadn't done "a stroke of work" over his ook on Jefferson, and that he much preferred reading an old-fashioned Life nd Letters to a smart modern biography. —That too-softness (Elinor Wylie once said about him that there was "something about him that was oft that ought to be hard") set off, or rather, retrieved, by an intransigent, oo insistently asserted independence. —He said that his play *The Garbage Man* was "very infantile," contained the remains of a very early idea. —He rought Rosalind a little doll. —Held up by cyclone at South Amboy, nearly driven crazy by the smell of cooking blown across the racks"—"wicked little boy who kept jeering at us, 'You'll get there to-ight—not!'" —His prolonged almost hysterical laugh over my breaking he high-low bulb string in his room—when I said to Stella, "I did that, and : broke." —His flat limp old hat and his musette bag, with a rolled-up ainting in it, of which I could only see that it was red. He had told me once hat Bernice Dewey was like a mechanical toy.

[I had begun reading *Manhattan Transfer* at the Princeton reunion de-cribed above. I had marched in with my class to the ball game. When it egan, I left the bleachers and went back to the club to read. I was amazed nd made rather envious by what seemed to me the wonderful handling, in he first fifty pages, of the New York of the period of my childhood. Dos 'assos was, so far as I knew, the first American novelist to make the people f our generation talk as they actually did.]

Movie news film. Motorcycles driving up impossible grades, leaping, skid-ing furiously, throwing their riders, swaying in a headlong rush; motor-oat race, with the boats like waterbugs nose to nose, to the music of a diculous little dance; wonderful slow-motion diving pictures of girls, irning beautifully in the air in molded recumbent postures and sending up slowly condensing cloud of spray after they have slipped into the water; tching a giant sawfish, shown in proportions which made it look like an ichthyosaurus; Gertrude Ederle at Atlantic Highlands sitting on the steps of her father's house playing a ukulele—her father, a German butcher, collarless and in his shirtsleeves, and her mother to match: it is the silence of the picture and the music of the movie piano which give the sight its dramatic value, despite its utter commonplaceness, Gertrude not even being pretty—afterwards much more impressive in her vigorous lithe overhead stroke and lifting her head like a seal to have her food fed to her from a rowboat.

August 21–22. The dark green leaves against gray-silver sky. —The rain from the gray-silver sky, as if it were being momentarily shaken. That feeling of indoors in the country on rainy summer days (reminding me of the Knoxes, when we used to sit indoors and play anagrams). A comfortable damp within doors, a wet by no means formidable outside—the summer wind of rain stirring the low sound of surf in the trees—blowing rain about the trees and gardens, darkening tennis matches, swimming and motoring for a moment, after which the brilliant glare will reappear and the bright sun-broken surfaces of Seabright dry out again in a single night—a flurry of wind and wet and darkness to be comfortably, amusingly endured for the refreshment of the great lawns, which will have revived their green tomorrow.

Doremuses' back porch. "You remember Bill Lippincott?—Well!" (nodding toward little Joan).

Katze. "Mother used to take me up to the Mall—I wanted to play in the streets, you know—but she wanted me to be highest and play in the Mall—all the other little girls used to have their nurses, and they used to see Mother and ask me, 'Is that your nurse?'—and I'd be so mortified! and I couldn't be friends with them any more!" —Her story about the attempt to send her to a Catholic school—somebody slapped her face and she wouldn't stand for it—it all seems to have ended very painfully.

She asked me to kiss her in the most public place of our whole ride—Fifth Avenue and Twenty-third Street.

When we started out and she had just had her first drinks, she ran on about the Catholic school, their kindness to horses—she really felt more sensitive about animals than about human beings; Goethe and Nietzsche—drinking out of glasses in Central Park, giving the driver a drink—attracting attention (envious and admiring?) of people in buses, going up Fifth Avenue.

Mysterious ringing telephone when I plunged into darkness of apartment in order to get glasses to drink out of.

She admired the water at night, with lights reflected in it.

"You do appreciate my neck!"—"I admire your persistency—in putting yourself in proximity with Miss Szabo [herself]!'"—(Unexpectedly) "I'm just getting into a state where I'd like to have you make love to me."

The impression her body gives of being made of tender and fine material. Her small slender fingers ("You may kiss our hand!")—Her shoes in her room that looked so like her feet.

"Don't you think this is rather unconventional?" (when I was holding her legs or something).

MacDonald (when he came to see me at Red Bank). Frank MacDonald of Princeton. The semi-stagnant wash of gossip, anecdote and book talk that goes on with him continually, without direction or aim. Anecdotes I have heard him tell over ten years. —Addiction to the East: his father had been a missionary in Siam trying to convert emirs, caliphs, etc., to chastity—they didn't understand what he was talking about. —When he got them to accept Christ, he merely got them to add another god to the Buddhistic pantheon. —I asked what went on in Afghanistan: "Oh, they're very remarkable physically!" —Frantic prejudice in favor of the Japanese as against the Chinese (due to his having served in the Japanese embassy under his old friend Roland Morris). —Firm stand against freshman jerseys—told Hibben he'd resign. Freshmen, in my time in college, had to wear black jerseys, and little black caps. He didn't like this, because it spoiled their good looks. —Row with women who lived above him in apartment—complained to Hibben, after women had complained to him. —Wrote letters to two boys congratulating them on marriage of girl (she was rich and pseudo-artistic and traveling in the East) with whom they have been in love but whom MacDonald regarded as a very objectionable character, because she had "the heart of a whore but not nerve enough to do anything about it." —Ralph Pomeroy (the rector of the Episcopal church at Princeton) lecturing Teddy Brown on chastity until he felt that he wanted to "go out and get a girl right away." —MacDonald's addiction to coffee—always in a nervous, uncertain, excited condition of caffeine intoxication. —Always changing apartments and having bookshelves specially built—gave one of his books to the Nassau Club, but afterwards went and got it back. — Stories in which he always scores with the most tremendous dignity. — Always owes a great deal of money in Princeton and can only walk on one side of Nassau Street.

Early September. The afternoon light of summer losing its warmth and appearing paler behind the trees of Washington Square Park, whose green had begun to have that coppery look of the foliage of autumn and, later, against the pale rusty sunset, looked rustier and duller.

September. Looking out, at 7:30, after the shades have been pulled down, into the black clear silhouette of the park, the trees and south side of the square, in which the lamps and a red taxi light are so sharp, under the clear cold blackening blue of the September sky. The blackness, the bareness, the clearness of September.

Perth Amboy. The smooth steel of the bay, like a blade which the haze of the horizon seemed to thin and make more sharp—under the pale blue sky.

Coming back from visit to Sandy (I was concentrating on the sights from the window in order to keep my mind off poor Sandy). Those coy artificially ivy-grown flavorlessly Moorish concrete hotels, with red crenelated tile roofs; those spick-and-span banks and post offices, which seem to exist only in relation to the colony of commuters; those pink brick houses, shining with glass, which have just been neatly knocked together, and others still in scaffolding and plaster, before the light wrapper of brick has been fitted on them. Paint signs, lawn-seed signs, stations with long green roofs growing from a single row of stalls over a neat and narrow platform, where motors wait for weekend parties, a town composed of the new low buildings of lumber companies, milk distributors, light suburban-looking but sober factories. Light electric trains with bright frescoes of Lux and tomato soup advertisements and wicker seats—a stream still running over brown translucent shallows and fringed with green rushes but contradicted by the orderly straight new streets of suburban shops or houses which often ran along them—a new smooth light-blue suburban sky. The Botanical Gardens—the streets of the upper hundreds, the light but even less colorful sections of uptown apartment houses, still spaced but tending to coagulate and form solid blocks; between them there will presently be no space any longer and the breathing of the buildings will seem to have ceased—Heavy Hardware—Universal Sheet Metal Works—Fairmount—bathtubs, washtubs, sinks and lavatories—valves and fittings—Morrisania—a tunnel or two—redder and more professional-looking factories—Melrose (the train seems to stop every two minutes)—motor oils and greases—Forgelight Iron Works—Metropolitan Carpet Cleaning Co.—baths and swimming pools—fireproof partitions—lighting fixtures and metal novelties: We Make Them—flue pipe; sewer pipe; terra-cotta blocks; gypsum blocks—the Harlem River, with dingy, extensive and unconciliable factories—the city: cheap hotels, Coca-Cola signs (defaced on the sides of brick apartment houses)—cheap red brick of a bad rose—El stations bridging street vistas—General Outdoor Advertising Co.—Beech-Nut Gum—clothes hung out pillows and bedclothes stuffed out narrow window—Grand Central tunnel—close tunnel smell.

John Amen's birthday, etc. Louise Homer and the Fort girls over movie

pervert incident—"Was he asleep?" Louise: "I think not." "But I don't
understand!" Henry: "Well, there are many unique fellows in this world!"

They came down to her Washington Square apartment and stayed till
seven. Louise sat on the windowsill and attracted the attention of a late
reveler, who had to be discouraged. She threw the remains of her sandwich
on the floor and left her silver vanity box on the windowsill. They sang *Forsaken, forsaken, forsaken am I* over and over again (at my request)—they had
learned it on their West Indian trip. —Louise had only a few days in New
York and wanted to keep awake all the time. (She cried a little when she
finally went back to Chicago.) Enthusiasm for the discipline and high ideals
of the Hill School imbibed from Pete Connor. She looks so different from
when I had seen her at Swampscott—her hooked, rather long nose—more
grown up, with more grownup way of doing her hair—but her dear little
three-cornered black eyes. Both girls dress so well: Louise's dark evening
gown; Henrietta's big chrysanthemum. —Louise kicked off her shoes
(which were new) sitting on the windowsill—made some deprecating
remark about "ending up like this after a respectable party." Henrietta's
clear skin and gaze and her wonderful "strong white teeth." Henrietta said
that Marion "understood everything," and Louise replied that she understood everything too well, that she was too perfect. —Louise doing the
Charleston at the party, with her hair, which she had evidently let grow
long, flying and flapping (putting out of joint the nose of the "technically
perfect" Charlestoning girl at the party, who, they both agreed, was *assom-
mante*). Their enchanting awkwardness—Henrietta's lisp—John: "You
sort of get to like it, after a while." Capacity for drinking. Louise going to
sleep on my bed; when Henrietta woke her up, she thought she was at home
and had only "to go just across the street." Louise a little scornful of my re-
sources for entertaining them.

Ted Paramore telegraphed Florence that he had sailed with a gold-
mounted velvet-lined Pulmotor for a traveling companion. —Postcard
from Berlin: "Next week I'll be in London. Don't miss it!" —Florence,
when Katze showed the imitation pearls she had just bought: "Let's take her
out and hock her!"

Ted Paramore's story about Don Stewart in Paris: "Ted: there's a new
Christ coming in America!" —Ted doing his stuff in Olympia bar—big hit
first time, but next time he was thrown out. —Place in Paris where women
waited on table, etc., naked—one of them was sitting quietly sewing. One
of them picked up a franc with her cunt. Another, after rejecting his various
offers, said, "I'll bet I can give you a new sensation," and squirted her breast
in his face.

Katze. Hearing someone drunkenly chanting in the park, she shuddered and said it put her back in her ether dream (on the occasion of an abortion, as it later turned out). —Her caginess in Washington Square in keeping to the chairs. Once when I carried her to the couch—we had both been drinking—she succumbed completely till I began to address myself to her bloomers, when she made me stop—"Why?" —"Because we're both being foolish—we're neither of us in earnest." —When Franz got himself invited one night, she came in through the bathroom to the kitchen—so pretty, so electric, so cute, *toute frétillante*—when I kissed her, however, in the kitchen, I noticed that she took it rather uncordially, as if the consciousness of Franz's presence restrained her.

The girl, with something of the prostitute's resentful stare, who was always collecting money to go home in a taxi to her aunt on Long Island (the last train had gone) or, when her circumstances were better known and a more serious appeal was needed, for an abortion about which her father mustn't know. —One high-minded little girl, whose innocence they had all been worrying about protecting, did have an abortion and had to be helped out.

Katze's European *jeune fille* respect for her mother and her opinions and prejudices—her violin and needlework—her silverpoint—her fondness for and appreciation of lace. Her impossible manners—when she would "thank you very much" in such a way as to be positively insulting—and then, after I had had my great talk with her about Gerald, and urged her to try to be a little more gracious, her excessive unnatural regret expressed over trivial misfortunes of mine—her infuriating "Oh, no's!" when invited to do something on a night for which she had already made an interesting engagement.

—"Made of hairpins." —"Your woodchuck cheeks and your shoe-button eyes."

—Toward the End: I used to say, "You're so sweet!" or "You're such a darling!", when I was taking her home in a taxi or when she was on my couch, but I didn't mean it—I felt strongly, at the same time, that that was just what she was not.

The Rupture—Gerald Jenks (an English friend then studying at Harvard Law School): Her look of a cornered angry ferret hunted to her lair when I went to her house and found her coming downstairs the morning she broke her breakfast date with me. I made her go back to her room, held her by both arms when she wanted to go, etc. We glared at each other (though, on these occasions, as later that morning when I left her at the subway entrance she had a way of tending, as if involuntarily, to grin, which detracted from their seriousness as final ruptures—even though she might have told me that she disliked me so much that she didn't want to see me, etc.). She then became self-conscious and said, "Don't talk like that! Oh, don't talk like that!" She looked so dreadful that my impression of her had the effect on me afterwards of really making me like her less. I would remember how she had stolen the glass vase from the taxi and, another time, torn up the driver's card with his photograph on it—how she had made me come to see her at inconvenient times of day, etc.

The taxi the night of Elinor's party—my heaving the bag of rubbish, which looked so much heavier and more formidable than it really was, at Ted and Florence's window. —When she came to my house before she went to Boston (the night before), when she was lying on the couch and I had been kissing her, I saw her face, with the ordinary consciousness of her expression and her make-up relaxed, so that I saw—and loved—the woman, so soft and unmasked, as one sees a woman one is married to in her nightgown in bed—her soft, bare and unadorned cheeks and neck and her eyes looking out like a child's. All women have these moments—when we have seen them thus, we know that we have seen them as feminine beings, helpless and naïve—with a woman whom we want to love us, we may feel, in this connection, a sort of satisfaction of triumph, yet we are stirred by a deep tenderness and pity, and irresistible masculine impulse to protect, to play the husband to the wife—so wives who have just had babies lie with their heads on their sides on the pillows—so the mother of puppies looks slabbed out on the straw on the cellar floor, thumping her tail, perhaps. Here, even with a perverse, self-centered and cruel girl like Katze, in the midst of however sensual and cynical a love affair, we are stirred by a deep unexpected feeling of an entirely different sort—a feeling which may lead us to marry a girl of whom, at the beginning, we have never thought seriously as a wife and which, at any rate, with however unamiable the girl, makes us, in the sequel, respect her confidence, protect her reputation and lend her money when she is in debt.

After the party at Elinor's, where we had both drunk a good deal, we came over to my apartment and lay beside each other on the couch—her sudden inexplicable crying—I made long serious and no doubt infelicitously phrased speeches, and I was too drunken and too preoccupied with what I was saying to have the sense to find out what was the matter. The only other time I saw her cry, I think, was when Franz, at her house, had said something harsh to her over the telephone—I had been able to be tender with her after that: she had been so gentle and sweet.

Tremendous effect on me of Gerald's letter to her: "I understand you so well," etc.—explaining, just as I might once have done, how badly people might behave when they were very much in love. —I saw all my adoration of Edna over again, how I had "understood" and forgiven her everything, how I had seen her simply as a creature too noble, too courageous and too brilliant for the ordinary mind. I thought that Gerald was deeply in love with her, and would ask Katze to marry him—I a little overencouraged her in her hopes about him, I fear—I lectured her on what she ought to do if she married him—I said that she and the rest of the Villagers led the lives of outlaws—an observation which made a great impression on her. She told me, on another day, that she had been thinking about it since; that it was true, that if they all died down here, no one would ever know or care. My lecture seemed to have an almost Girl Scoutish inspirational effect. I felt very virtuous, wise and glowing afterwards—no doubt, I had really behaved very foolishly and, as it were, gushingly. I found that I tended to develop with her a tone of "Ah, my dear child"—which got on my own nerves and which certainly must have got on hers. I had never felt older than a woman before—all the women I had known had been my own age. I began to realize what it meant to have missed the war—she asked me why I thought the Germans ought not to have won—and I realized also the tragedy (of *Le Misanthrope*) of love between people of different ages. I was beginning to think of getting myself in hand and putting my house in order and accomplishing work which I had begun to feel was long overdue, whereas she still felt that she had infinite possibilities—of love affairs and matches—before her, and the idea of going out to a party where she might meet new people, and perhaps her fate, excited her beyond the anxieties of any situation and was irresistible to her, at a time when I was no longer tempted by the parties of the journalistic and Greenwich Village world and indeed usually regarded them with horror—sorry to be so hard up for society and so demoralized as to go, and usually ashamed and regretful afterwards. —Also, she took love affairs, in some respects, more seriously than I and, in other respects, less so. She went on the principle, as I had once done, of "All for Love," whereas I went on the principle, of which I had once not felt the force, of "Love, let us be true to another, for the world that seems," etc. (I once told her that she didn't know a line of poetry from an old piece of kindling wood.)

Visit to New Preston. Florence had developed great muscles—fine-looking in her outdoor walking clothes: knickerbockers, muffler, knitted cap. — Walk to neighboring village for gin—hair-raising stories she told me on the way back—I said that she must find Ted (Leisen) a relief after John (O'Donnell), but she said that, to tell the truth, she didn't find much difference between them, though she did find that she got along better with Ted. It was the gin that carried us back: we drank it raw on the way. She said that she'd learned that you had to take people's defects with their qualities. — Drinking gin raw on the back porch that night, looking out on the frozen winter landscape, I thought: How different from my early visits to Washington (Connecticut).

When Florence and Ted came back to New York, they called me up, and I went to see them at the "young Smiths'." They were drunk, and from what they said over the phone, I couldn't make out where they were, whether in a restaurant, a private apartment or a speakeasy. I found them plastered—Florence with tousled hair and her mickiest face—Ted said she looked like a French whore. The host was in the bedroom and the hostess in the bathroom. Florence had insulted the hostess. Everything was a mess—sandwich crusts and oiled paper, ginger ale and gin bottles, but nothing left to drink.

The night when I took Florence out and talked to her about Katze—went to my house afterwards—I sat in the chair and Florence lay on the day bed—till I came over and lay beside her, we were rather sleepy—it was such a relief after Katze: easier understanding, nervousness allayed. When I kissed her with my tongue and held her breast with my right hand while I kissed her, she would say, "Oh, I've seen that done!—seen *that* done, too!" Her breasts were not full like her buttocks, but, though not low, hung a little. "What a lover *you* turned out to be!" She was worried about Ted getting home and not being able to get in, so finally left, though, "I guess that we could get in anyway—climb in the window." In taxi, on way back: "We'll do better next time, won't we?"

But next time was a bad one. Jeanette's, Henry de Wolf. During dinner (to Henry): "You understand you're just along to show us the place—you leave right afterwards!" (Jeanette's: the Lesbians, with their nauseating language, the *cabinet particulier*, with its haircloth-covered sofa between the kitchen and the dining room.) Henry's mustache—Florence's "yes-man"—their line when together. "I've been rejected by an expert!" This time it was I who was plastered. Florence had some sort of reaction and insisted on being taken home.

When Ted Leisen got a job, he bought her some new clothes: how smart she looked with her brown dress, carmined lips and brown hat. They had at last been married.

It was sometime before this, however, that I took her to Peter's and she told me about her family. On the first night I took her out after she got back to New York, she had told me about her father's trying to rape her. (I reminded her of this, "Oh, did I tell you that? I must have been pretty plastered to tell you that. I've only told about three people that.") That was one reason she didn't feel more warmly toward her family. She had done an awful lot of reading and was very romantic when a girl. I had thought her scornful of literature, because she had always been scornful of poetry—"Oh, don't read me any poetry—John used to read me *The Oxford Book of English Verse* all the time! —To hell with what the poet said!" —She had spent a good deal of time in Newfoundland—really came from up there: Scotch-Irish Canadian, the healthy wholesome farmer's wife at the bottom of the New York twirp—reason why she had taken to New Preston—one of her family up there had married a duke—she always thought there must have been something wrong with the duke: syphilitic or something. —"Now that I've belittled my family for you!" (Her family would be very much upset if they knew she was living with men—reason she didn't write.)

Her deep-going cracks when she was drunk: I didn't offer to marry people; my gestures so definite beside Ted's; living with Ted just like living with another woman, on account of noticing make-up, etc.; all she wanted was a nice man to bear her children (older than she was, brighter than she was). Her interpretation of her dreams: Arthur (her first husband) coming after her with a knife—the first time she had told me about it, she told me as if it were true; second time, she knew that it was a dream, afraid that he was "going to try to play the husband." Her understanding of unequal love: when I was telling her about Ted Paramore and Margaret: "And can't a woman do that when she's got a man in that position!" —She always referred to Arthur as "the ox" or "my ox"—just wanted a man who wouldn't turn away after the first pretty ankle he saw. When she was sober and was reminded of these utterances, she always took the attitude that she must have been maudlin. —John a "witch burner." —She said of me, in connection with my not dancing: "You probably read too much."

Her story about Arnold Daly in Paris: He took her out to lunch and asked her if she wouldn't be his little sweetheart; he said, "Think, when you go to the theater and see me on the stage, you can say to yourself, 'I have had a love affair with Arnold Daly!'" —When I went to see them on Thirty-fourth Street, did I think that she and Ted were getting to look alike?—She had got so that her conscience would let her read in the morning, she would wake up and reach for a book. —Ted and John both had typical little-men complexes—didn't have the necessary rod of iron. She would have "starved for dirt" (with John) if it hadn't been for Ted.

Time I met her just coming out of Thirty-fourth Street bookstore, pale, not made up much, thin fragile fingers and legs. —At Peter's motorcycle trip from Pittsburgh to Atlantic City, she on the handlebars, six accidents. —"I don't know what it's all about at all" (when he had complimented her on her intelligence). —She had run wild in Paris, because Arthur was going with a French girl, so that people wouldn't say, "That poor Mrs. O'Neill," etc., but think that she was as gay as he was. She had sworn to go through with this if it cost her her life (she and Ted)—unhappy all the time—horrible nightmares about burning houses, from which she fled, and then afterwards felt that she had behaved badly—usually could figure out dreams, but couldn't figure out these—dreams in which she had gone out with Arthur on a lawn and met a red-haired girl, for whom he fell, etc., which afterwards came true. I saw tears in her eyes when she was talking about how she didn't know what to think or do now—"business of twisting handkerchief"—she was very good when she was talking about how she didn't know whether she had ever been happy. —In taxi, we discussed her habit of always keeping her eyes open when she kissed (she had told me, on a previous occasion, that nobody had ever bitten her)—liked to look at the lobe of an ear of somebody she liked—said she wasn't putting her head on my shoulder just because she was drunk, when I accused her of this—she liked to do her own necking, kissed me on cheeks (very few girls do this)—when I gathered her legs over my knees: "No groping! Mustn't pass the line marked off!" —Her coolness like her pale eyes, skin and hair, when Golden Glint wore off, I saw her pale straw-colored Yarmouth hair—bottle of ginger ale she found in taxi.

Night when she came over to my house from Franz's: If she deserted Ted when he was down, if she went off with anybody else, she would lose her self-respect. When Ted finally arrived, she pretended to have passed out; then she woke up later and began to cry, with a tousled crybaby child's face, and said, "It wasn't my fault!"

Florence at Clark and McCullough, criticizing the dancing: Egyptian dancer, finally carried out stiff as a board—"She ought to have an apple in her mouth!" Of woman at movies who went through extremely clumsy pantomime while other woman was singing: "Old Gerty Goof herself!" —At *Rio Rita*, she told me about Elsie Behrens, who had come over from Germany only a few years ago and yet learned all the steps so much more quickly than the other girls that she would teach them to them herself—"Look at Elsie Behrens: pep in every movement!" We left after the first act that night. She invited me to take my dress shirt off at my apartment, didn't see how men could stand those things, supposed it was like high heels; reminded me we hadn't any time to lose, then when I tried to make love to her: "You kill me in your sheik role!"—although she had said also: "Remember I'm only here for a limited engagement." —Then: "I believe you're afraid!"

Ted Leisen's engineering turn for automobiles and machinery; his wretched handwriting and his excellent clear printing.

Her big forehead, a little too big for her small thin fingers and calves—her way of talking, so much like Scott Fitzgerald—curiously unfeminine (for such a feminine person) resemblance to Daniel Webster or someone of the kind, when her nose was edged, mouth straight and unsmiling, eyes puffy and haggard. How cute and sweet she was, the night that Ted Paramore came to Thirty-fifth and Lexington—with no stockings and a sort of a cinnamon-pink dress, not drinking much, following his jokes and my remarks with her eyes and face—humor, wit, shyness, embarrassment—I never saw her so sensitively responsive or so *jeune fille*.

Ted made me spend the night with him—acquiring booze at the Yale Club—my conversation with the bartender (formerly at Sherry's): luxury of Sherry's, bar dissimulated behind mirrors—bartender at Princeton Club not from Sherry's: "Very polite but I don't think he was ever at Sherry's"—being polite seemed to be one of the principal virtues of a bartender in a high-class bar—I noticed that he took the bad language Ted used to him with great dignity and tact—had made a bet that Ted's show would run two months. —Ted's suspiciousness and ill-nature—unnatural high spirits and East high hand with violinist next morning (a degenerate revival of the easy genial bullying manner of the old West, which he had inherited).

Ted's play. The dowager, so tactful, so shrewd and dignified, who behaved in such a knowing manner, but proved to know nothing whatever that was important. —The bomb at the end of the second act, when the corpse falls out of the safe, during the thunderstorm—taken out at one time, specially put back, the night we went, for Florence's benefit. They had cut all explanations in Boston—I saw the play twice, but never understood who lived in the house—constant serving of drinks—detective outwitted with knockout drops—lights out at end of the first act and people jumping in through the window and shooting—"I wish that we could have given the bank messenger a line so that people would have known who he was— he was shot without a peep." "Why didn't you?" "He was a member of Equity." —My argument with him at the Gormans': "Why, you're just a stupid oaf! *Of course*, it was explained!"

In the role of successful Broadway producer, besieged by all sorts of people. His apartment: the bedroom, with its wide and elegant Wanamaker bed, its Wanamaker eighteenth-century pictures on the wall and the floor carpeted with tabloids—the kitchen full of orange peels and potted flowers sent him by admirers—the faded lilies in the sitting room—the black-covered divan—the picture of Glen Hunter—the sets of Kipling and O. Henry—the bootlegger who said that, if you got anything from them, you'd always know it was pure. Ted, in his overimportant—or important malapropos—state, engaged in long conversation with bootlegger out in hall—later, at Gormans', sang *Who'll bite your neck?, Hushabye, dollies—your Daddy's in the Follies!, Take me back to North Dakota, Frankie and Johnny, The Monkey-Gland Blues.* —His original phonetic transcription of the Lord's Prayer into French—he had carried over the mistakes in the typewritten part: it looked like Basque or Czech.

His friend (long before all this) who always had everything arranged:

"Now, I'll call you up at 8:15, and you can get a white taxi," etc. —About Earl Carroll's *Vanities*: "You just go to him and say you want a girl, and he says, 'Well, do you want one that's hard to make, or only pretty hard to make, or do you want a pushover?'"

Jean, when I met her on the street: she was a little *gênée*—she explained that she had just had her hair cut and was covered with "feathers." —She came back all athletic, tanned and unglamorous—then she got sick—then, during the winter, she drank too much and went out too much—Elinor— she (Jean) generally looked badly, except when some love-making and mischief had given her an *oeil espiègle*. Her perforated French shoes, black shiny leather with blunt toes.

Scene over Herbert's reading aloud passage from *Two Virginities* (a novel of his) about "the lick where the beasts go down"—Jo Mather's look at Herbert.

Jo Mather. Her diving and swimming; her shyness, but sudden loud way of talking, attractive, launching the words with all her natural force at you from her long full lips and her strong white set of teeth. How well she looked, how one felt her health and strength, when she came in, in furs, from the cold—how smart in her rather athletic way—didn't beglamour you at once with the perfume of her prettiness when she first came in, as a very pretty woman will do; but one felt, after a while, that smartness and her vigorous sexual attraction.

The Ernest Boyds, seen at Peter's sitting till late at night; then, the next day, heard about them as having been at the *New Yorker* party. His brown dinner jacket with velvet lapels: "Next time, Ernest, please dress!"

D. and T. D. had got, since I last saw her, something of that dried-up, businesslike, lean, unromantic look of the masculine Lesbian—and T., whom I remembered from Mary's absinthe party as very smart, attractive and insolent—especially with men—had become pasty and lusterless and had the helpless passivity and docility of the feminine Lesbian—spoke so softly, said such mildly cute things, and dropped her eyes when men talked to her. —D.'s signs of discontent with her situation, but she couldn't leave T. flat. Whereas she had *affiched* her tastes in Paris when I knew her and before she had actually crossed the line, and had always been talking about attractive women (a tendency still instinctively contradicted by protestations that she was not a Lesbian and telling me with indignation and disgust a story about being approached by the chambermaid at the hotel)—she now showed embarrassment when people talked about Lesbians in her presence and was perhaps altogether, like T., shyer than before.

The value, the significance, the magic which a phrase, an expression or a remark seems to acquire for us when we have heard it from the lips of someone whom we have loved or admired—"He isn't funny—just thinks he is" (Bernice Dewey). "What with the lack of solidity of the foundation and the craziness of the superstructure, a more insecure edifice could not well be imagined" (Kemp Smith on Jung as having made use of Freud to build on in *The Golden Bough*).

Dorothy Parker. When I first saw her after she had come back from abroad, she looked fat and bloated, puffy-eyed—"Why dontcha ever come to see me, yuh damn fool?"—her bobbing of her hair seemed to figure her emergence from her good conventional stage, though it looked then, in one of those ragged bobs, a little unraveled, ropy. The two nights when I took her out and went with her to Tony's. Paroxysmarvelous city. Embezzle woman in the world! Scrantoknow you're appreciated (Scranton)—Dorothy thought they were not right unless the word began the sentence. —"Do you mind going up to Tony's?" [It was inevitable that she should insist on going to one of their regular hangouts: they didn't know how to get along with anybody but one another.] "Mr. Benchley is sunk tonight, and I promised I'd go up there and see him" (it was one of their affectations that she always called him Mr. Benchley)—his girl and awful little whore, unfaithful to him, made him give her money (Mrs. Benchley busy with children's tonsils), he was getting worse and worse in debt (his syndicate stuff began to show it—overdrafts on Scarsdale bank), he would rush out to Chicago, where the mistress was playing, to lecture; the girl had been a waitress, then on the stage, he had met her in Music Box Revue; he would say, "She enters the room like a duchess!" —When I finally met her, she was quite a pretty blonde with thick ankles, who, however, I thought, had something of that hard-eyed prostitute stare, the result of there being no coherence or purpose in a woman's emotional life. —We drank a great many Tom Collinses. When we first came in, we had found Benchley, with his red grossening face, leaning against the wall in the hall—talk of going down to the cellar to sing—he had got to a point where he no longer went at all to plays he reviewed for *Life*—(Fred Allen had begun to disapprove of him.)—Mosses from an Old Manse; Benchley: "Mosses from an Old Nance." Don Stewart's line (at a party of Elinor Wylie's): "Hemingway is finished!—Fitz is finished!—he's been steadily getting worse and worse!—Dos is finished!"

Dorothy Parker: "Mother is awful dependent—Mother can hardly read them herself." —Her excessive flattery, which always inspired me with misgivings. —"I am cheap—you know that!" —Her desire for a child:

"You've made another person"—combined with her cruel and disgusting jokes, her enjoyment of Peter Arno's Whoops Sisters pictures in *The New Yorker*: they throw the little boy down the drain: "Whoops, dearie, don't he float!" —Benchley's joke on the ship about throwing the children's life preservers overboard—also, his looking over the side of the ship when they were sailing: "God, what a night to go out in the storm!—and I wouldn't mind if the crew wasn't yellow!" That was the time he and Dorothy crossed with Hemingway, who, one of them told me, ostentatiously took saltpeter at table during the voyage in order to keep his sexual appetites under control—in the hospital—the little boy who marched up and down the halls with horseshoes, and then they operated on him and nothing more was heard(she told me about this when I went to see her in the hospital—she always referred to Rosalind dotingly as "it"). Vicomte who sent her an anthology of French poetry and a turtle—"You can have it till two o'clock"—the turtle finally ran away. —The happiness girl who taught her rug weaving. She got thin; her intelligence and sensibility came back into her eyes. —I asked how Benchley was: "They're getting the room across the hall ready for him." He would come in, she said, and say that he didn't know what to do about moving out of the Shelton—he owed them a lot of money, but he had to move, couldn't afford it, yet couldn't bring himself to the point of getting out.

Dorothy in doubt as to whether to accept a job as drama critic on the *Telegram*: "What would Lincoln have done?"

Benchley, saying goodbye to me: "Well, come in to use us when you're passing through Fall River!" —Drumming with fingers on table at Tony's—he stopped when people at opposite table indicated disapproval. "All right, then: I'll stop!" he said that he said to himself. "*But the day will come* when you'll come to me on your knees and *ask* me to drum!!!"

Dorothy went to old English folk-song concert with Thornton Wilder: "I was up to my chin in derry-down-derries. They came [the singers] and sat down at a table, and I kept expecting them to deal!" "Did you tell that to Wilder?" "Yes; but he didn't pay much attention to it. He said that there was a great new interest being taken in madrigals. I hadn't known about that."

[Edna St. Vincent Millay had married in July 1923, after her return from Europe, a Dutch coffee importer, Eugen Boissevain. EW saw her at rare intervals before the occasion described below. He says, in his later memoir, he remembered calling on her in "the tiny little house in Bedford Street," where the couple lived before they moved to the country. We have a record of that visit in a letter to John Bishop of January 15, 1924: "I saw Edna the other day for the first time since her marriage. She summoned me

around and I waited upon her in her little house in Bedford Street (buried in
the bowels of the Village). The operation she had during the summer on her
intestines—for congenital stoppages—was apparently really rather serious
and she doesn't look terribly well yet. I found her drinking gin and reading
William Morris on the top floor of her house, all alone and with really an
air of having allowed herself at last to be attended to and put away and forbidden to see people. Her husband takes good care of her and her lousy rout
of followers has been banished. —She is calmer than she used to be—and I
really felt for a moment as if I were visiting a sort of voluntary prisoner who
had crept away and given herself up to other people's kindness. —Then she
told me she was about to start on a month's reading tour which, so far as I
can find out, is to take in all the important cities east of Chicago! And she is
going all alone. 'I must keep clear of the people I know,' she said, 'in the
cities that I visit'—but—! She can never be caged for long, I know—never,
never. —I think the necessity for the question had something to do with her
marriage and her partial helplessness since then with her withdrawal from
the world. —Her husband came in before I left. He seemed a very nice
honest fellow—he is a Dutch importer, you know, a little older than she
and not, I think, overwhelmingly clever. She was at pains to tell me, as if she
were on the defensive at having married a businessman, how irresponsible
he really was—'just like me'—but I am sure he is the steadiest importer in
the world. —We are planning a grand party for her and you and me,
detached from our respective husbands and wives, when you come back. —
She left today on her tour."]

Feb. 19, 1927: Edna in New York [at the time of *The King's Henchman*,
Edna's play made into an opera by Deems Taylor and produced at the
Metropolitan]. Our formal dinner across a too-wide table drinking
Boissevain's whiskey and sauterne. He tactfully withdrew with a book
called *Wine, Women and War* and came back at 10:15 sharp. She inquired
about *New Republic*—I resented this piece of politeness—I saw her wince
and the collapse for a moment of her manner: nervous, trembling, worried
and dismayed—the new slang, too (which she didn't know)—like her
never having heard of Hart Crane, "The Master of Us All." —"I'm not a
pathetic figure—I'm not!" "Whoever said you were?" —I had previously
talked her into an enthusiasm for the country, then talked her out of it—I
now talked her into it again—she told me about her feeling about trees, etc.
I had said what a wonderful thing land was. —"I love life—I love every
moment of it! —I love sitting here talking to you, having that sleet beating
on the window." —Her photographs of their Indian trip, and now her
beads and things from New Mexico—she had come to think a lot about
posterity, the Benéts said. —Boissevain seemed to feel a certain satisfaction

in finding something that was at least relatively critical among the reviews—had heard of and thought of nothing else for so long but "that Henchman." —"You know, Bunny," Edna said, "what satisfaction I must feel—it really means something!—to get that wreath [with red, white and blue ribbons and *The King's Henchman* in large gilt letters] out of the Metropolitan!" Boissevain had said it was probably a property—they would be furious at her having taken it. —He said, "Do you know what this is, my dear? It's Scotch"—so she didn't drink it. —Boissevain on the headwaiter, who had said that the guests at the hotel nowadays were synthetic *nouveaux riches*: "*Il n'y a aucune joie à être maître d'hôtel!*"

She was all burning and lit up when I came in, quite different from her paleness and brittleness when I had seen her in bed the winter before, and she put her arms around me and kissed me, leaving Boissevain behind in the bedroom, and it was I who was too stiff and unresponsive.

The time in Bedford St. when I had found her reading the big paint catalogue, with its wonderful colors and names.

Big engraving of Boston in Provincetown museum, made in 1857. The city steel-silvery on the water under the clearing and gigantic clouds of one of those mid-nineteenth-century heavens—the fine steely needles of church spires and masts, the few smoking chimneys, the State House, the docks raying out from the town, the square-rigged ships in the harbor, the old-fashioned side-paddle steamboat, the boys and men in long breeches and high curved-brimmed hats with crowns like truncated cones—not otherwise than Rogue Riderhood and What's-his-name Hexam on the Thames of Dickens, of which the gloom of the wharf, the fishermen's baskets and the floating barrel reminded us—and, above all, that dark somber zone which streaks and stains the water—that gloom of the nineteenth century—as to which we wonder about its connection with the innocence and naïveté of the men and boys in the boats.

Cummings, at Bob Chandler's party, pulling the tablecloth and all the dishes off the long refreshment table: lobster salad, sandwiches and all—because, when he had got drunk, his nose was put out of joint by the attention paid Jimmy Watt's burlesque Russian dance.

Aimee Semple McPherson: "Girls—I can't tell you how *lovely* Jesus has been to me!—I said to Jesus, 'If I hope and pray, will you do the rest?'—and Jesus said, 'Of course I will!'"

[In this and subsequent entries EW seems obsessed by the question of the nature of the imagination as a falsifier of literature; he is haunted by a feeling that literature distorts life and is a projection of the often tortured fantasy world of the writer. Apparently during this period he was deeply concerned with Freud's writings on art and neurosis; but no less with the question of the representation of reality in imaginative works of art. It will be noticed that in his ruminations he includes painting as well. There are many improvisations on this theme. He would arrive at a synthesis in *I Thought of Daisy*. But he is also considering the nature of the symbolist movement and the subjective writers he would treat in *Axel's Castle*, a book on which he worked while he was writing his novel.]

Literature. The author's work no matter how intelligent, elaborate (Proust) or rich and vigorous in imagination, always turns out to constitute a justification for some particular set of values, a making out a case against something or other in favor of something else, a melodrama in which, even if the hero is actually defeated, he is morally triumphant—and the hero may not be a person or persons but merely certain qualities or tendencies. The effort of the author has thus been concentrated on making life look as if it justified his own ideals—that is, his own desires—and it is the indestructible impulse to make his experience, disappointing in actuality, wear a different and more satisfactory aspect, which has provided the motive power to carry him through his book. When his work is done, he may feel reassured, half believing that what he has written, because he has asserted it and it has been printed and read by people who assume that the author had some divine revelation of the truth and adopt an attitude toward him based on that assumption—that what he has written must be true.

A ship at Seabright or, on the Shrewsbury, two sailboats, one behind the other but not quite even, so that they had the appearance of one of those small white butterflies perched on the water with closed wings, below the dimmed green ridge of the opposite shore and above the treetops and branching weeds of the river slope in the foreground, against a ground of silver-gray water. What the artist would do to these scenes would be, in the first case, to blur the surrounding colors of the buildings which framed the ship, so that they would harmonize with it and the sky and sea, to gratify some favorite vein of his own, or, in the second, to soften the distinct and prosaic details of the houses, trees and private docks of the opposite shore, which, even on that misty day, had some of the vulgarity and ugliness of vegetation and human habitations in August (unless, of course, he was someone like Botticelli or the Douanier Rousseau, who makes everything clear and distinct, so that he incised all the dim lines of the wet day to match the sharpness of the white sails against the water, and brought out the details of the opposite shore with indefatigable industry). He would thus substitute a corrected spectacle for the real one, which, for him, as for everyone else, was only beautiful by reason of the harmonies it *suggested*. He has merely selected something which suggests the sort of harmonies that happen to be sympathetic to his temperament, and modified it in such a way as to please him still more.

Matthew Arnold, writing critical essays, and editing selections from Wordsworth and Byron, introduced lines of poetry he liked—and out of their context—in a setting which, being an alien prose, could not betray them—lines such as he himself would like to have written, but, owing to his defective gift, never, even in his best poems, did—his dead impotent spot in his pulpiteering repetitions.

Opposite of view elaborated here—that is to say, of conventional, official view—according to which great artists are extra-human: "It was about this time that X decided that a history of so-and-so should be written" or "decided to produce a new form." —Running into the ground, by modern biographical criticism, of human-all-too-human view.

The great writer's notes, carefully preserved and published after his death (Baudelaire, Chekhov, Butler), though they may have been merely mechanical and meaningless jottings, the products of an instinct to write in its most rudimentary habitual twitchings, like the instinctive defensive or predatory gestures of the lowest forms of life.

How books carry the stamp of the barbarous ages which produced them: the gallows and the flogging block in Pope and in Swift.

Forms of words, never really understood by the original writers, become incantations.

The new anomalies and accidents of life continually being assimilated by the artistic faculty—immediately seized upon and encrusted, rendered symmetrical and iridescent, like the oyster's pearl—until, when the oysters have died and only their work remains, the annals of the human race, instead of a succession of casualties, take on the appearance of a string of pearls. The whole literary and artistic process merely the type of all human activity, which tends inevitably toward the ordering of the disorderly, the harmonizing of the inharmonious, the decoration of the graceless.

Yet this continual tireless attempt to assimilate experience into art may be only a small beginning at some great assimilation of the universe by humanity.

In connection with the readers of literature; the collectors of first editions, the tendency to make reading, which should be a field absolutely open to all, into a luxury and an exclusive privilege.

Slang
Not much of a help (Florence)
What a guy *he* turned out to be!
What an oil can *you* turned out to be! (Katze)
The old army game
A pushover
A setup
Not so good—not so hot—pretty hot
To get a break—a good break
—*and* how!
all wet
and were *they* embarrassed!
Am *I* dirty?
Shake a mean leg, etc.
The sticks

[Mary Blair and I had separated. I had found it impossible to be married to an actress. She was always at the theater at night and I was out on the town. I took Rosalind down to my mother's and went to live alone at 229 West Thirteenth Street in one room with a bathroom. I formed the habit of taking very long weekends at my mother's in Red Bank, where I could be quiet and see Rosalind.]

Glassware. Carboys—gourd-shaped and bottle-shaped—glass rolling pins (they used to fill them with cold water)—bull's-eyes from transoms—log-cabin whiskey bottles (they were given to everybody who voted for Harrison)—whiskey bottles with American eagles on them—Indian bottles for Indian bitters.

The hidden effects of the war. The men who have been rendered unstable and erratic by their war experience are like those who—like Fred Murphy, for example, who had been blown up in a tank (brother of Gerald and Esther)—were badly shot up and then put together by some surgeons, to survive for only a few years in the constant fear and danger of collapse. When I met Fred Murphy at dinner, I thought him supercilious and didn't like him, because he kept contracting his eyebrows as if he were in pain. He was but I didn't know it.

Amens and Forts. Disapproval of Amens's friends—that bounder (from Dallas) Dick Knight—John had detested him at first, but afterwards got to like him—John growing more and more like him every day—the household becoming impregnated with the atmosphere of the tabloids—they subscribed to the *Graphic*. —Howard Cox and I—and the Amens themselves—looking forward to hilarious and congenial parties—then John's necessity for achieving success lowering Marion's and his own standards—John's opinions became more conservative and intolerant—on Felix Frankfurter, on Sacco and Vanzetti. Their social career—the Deering Howes'—Howard Cox's disapproval of them—his constant moral indignation, viewing with alarm, disapproval—of the Amens, Fitzgeralds, newspaper reporters, etc. He came from Utica, New York. Quarrels with Marion's friends. His terrible break with the Fitzgeralds—didn't know he was capable of such a thing—made him sick for months afterwards (the incident mentioned above). Marion's friends—Billy Liston, the painter, always drunk, always boasted of being able to get theater tickets free, intimate friend of the King of Spain, under suspicion of homo-interest in Howard Cox, always promising to take Henrietta to *Rio Rita*, etc. —Girl who lived in hotel, who always came up to get a cocktail, but always coyly refused it at first—Marion thought that, though she perhaps hadn't had much experience, she was "really quite sophisticated," "without your really being able to see how she got so," but it was she whom Howard Cox was continually shocking. —Marion's old conventional stuffy well-to-do middle-class milieu creeping back in on her after she made such a desperate effort to put it behind her, had so violently rebelled against it. —Taming and housebreaking of Louise—she now approved of steadiness and responsible behaviour—thinning profile, aquiline nose, wore black toque which accentuated it, hiding her pretty part and the dark loops above either brow. —Howard's "evangelism," as Marion called it—a little on the Frederick Townsend Martin side. —Dick Knight as a supernatural apparition, a warning, a limiting case of what John's bad manners might get to be. —Knight's liking so much Howard and me, who disliked him—his awe before Howard's apartment on Sixty-sixth Street—Marion's attempt—a little deliberate and forced—to catch the tone of light banter of an attractive woman of the world—she never could quite manage it—for the same reason, no doubt, that she could, in general, only manage kindly and tactful personal criticisms when we played the game of written insults—though she could be quite crudely hard in making sport of the Hall-Mills murder and the Snyder case, or even occasionally in a single insult or two (in the game) when her kindliness and her tact were temporarily suspended—of Henrietta: "She had a sister and it seems she missed her."—Louise and Henrietta found that they did not sing so well together this time. —What had become of that jolly spirit of boys and girls together—the college prom, the Hill School or of drinking at Marion's old apartment, where everyone was at loose ends and everyone's position ambiguous? I remembered how Louise had sat on my windowsill at Washington Square singing *Forsaken*—like college—like camping—like school, like all our American youth. We turned out to have known all the same people—we almost took common friends for granted though we had never heard one another mention them—the space between us seemed naturally to fill up with these unmentioned common recollections and relations as soon as the first few had been specifically discussed. It took me back and refreshed me and made me feel again about people—*about all those people*—what I used to feel about them, and what I had never felt about the Village people or about the literary people I had known in New York—Cole Porter—we both knew the words of his songs for the Yale smokers.

Apparitions of monstrous people seen on the streets in May—a huge lumbering man with a high head and bone-rimmed glasses and a chinless long-necked lumbering woman—like brontosauruses.

The popular shows, like "Broadway" and the Scandals, at the end of the season—a little stale, too smooth, too mechanical, with a tendency to be underplayed—the Scandals looked so tawdry when one saw it at the end of its run and sober.

Ann Pennington. Her straddling legs with their tiny feet in diamonded slippers—her woman's breasts and her ecstatic red mouth and little girl's long hair with a bow—*Black Bottom. —Team* (two sailors, like two rubes who used to be with the Follies) of which one, the older one, more or less stood by, while the other does unexpected clogging with slapping flat shoes, slips, slides, collapses on his back, makes sudden disappearances between the curtains, stalking withdrawals into the wings, as if his legs had acquired a certain momentum and carried him away—flat-sole-slapping dance while partner is trying to deliver a speech—"fresh-faced boy"—somersaults turning in air on head as if on ball-and-socket.

Katze. In telephone booth—against the dark background, toned by the dirty glass, with her maroon dress and the high red color of her brownish cheeks contrasting with her deep large dark eyes shining out of their shadow, she suggested the shadows and rich color of a Rembrandt. —Gerald had said that she had the eyes of a cow and the face of a bee. —She was always under a sort of nervous pressure, I noticed it again dining with her for the first time after so long, at the Algonquin—she accused me of being "preoccupied" or "in a bad mood" when I was merely extremely calm and sober. —Her intense solid grasp of the objective world, her terrible objective eye—I felt it again at the Scandals, as she has once noticed and commented upon, without drawing any generalities from them, all the buildings and the changes, especially, it seems to me, the inanimate sights—on the way where she lived on Twelfth Street. —Her eye for fabrics and new clothes—would always comment, though Zitty (her sister Zita, the actress) had told her not to, on new shirts, newly shined shoes—would comment on good material. —She admired the back of what I thought was

a very plain woman with a very bad figure in the lobby between the acts.
—Her appreciation of the women in the revues—she seemed to have a
special taste for blondes (she had said of the little blonde in the *American
Tragedy*, "These blondes ruin me!")—criticism of their figures—admired
the show girls with great plumed headdresses. —Recurrence of the Raquel
Meller motifs. —Walking with my hand under her arm on the street, I used
to feel her full fleshy breasts—which were so unexpected on her wiry
body—which gave out surprising warmth even through her dress against
my hand—they redeemed with a kind of animal heat and fecundity whatever was of hard and metallic finish about her, whatever it was that made
her sometimes seem like a charming and costly bronze and which used to
make me feel at one estranged stage of our relations, when I would take her
to dinner at Charles's, as if I had acquired some precious and desirable *objet
d'art* rather than as if I were having dinner with a human companion whom I
liked and desired. —Her persistency in trying to do everything herself that
she saw other people do, in insisting upon competing—calling attention to
herself, refusing to pay attention to other people, interrupting, on the subject of her painting, when there were artists and writers around. This was
connected with that ungracious and self-centered side of her, which had
made her say that that was "sentimentality" when I told her how she ought
to talk to Franz, when she broke with him—say that she had loved him and
been very happy with him and was sorry that things hadn't worked out,
sorry for all the trouble she'd caused him, etc. She said that it would never
have occurred to her to say that, but she told me afterwards that she had said
to him everything I had recommended.

Bernice Dewey going to the Snyder trial, then coming back and hypnotiz-
ing her alligator, which she kept in the tub and which Dos Passos said was
rather limp from having been hypnotized so much. —How musical and
sweet her voice sounded through the door when I went to her apartment on
Madison Avenue.

Julian Street at Princeton talked about his Ovaltine in the vein of the people
in the American advertisements—"An Ovaltine addict. Yes, sir, I like my
Ovaltine!"

Oh, Ernest—unspeakably dull musical comedy made out of *Importance of
Being Earnest*, with director of dancing who had singular and rather clumsy,
though somewhat obscene, ideas. Girl puts up her foot so that he takes it in
his hand, then puts up other foot, hooking it over the ankle of the first—
they kiss. Chorus of maids with long stockings and old-fashioned drawers
who crouched down and put their legs over each other's heads.

[In the notebooks of the 1920's EW's "proletarian" mistress is alluded to most often as Milly; later he uses the name Frances. In *Memoirs of Hecate County*, in the tale of "The Princess with the Golden Hair," she is called Anna. In order to avoid creating the impression these were different women, and in the interest of consistency, the name Anna is used here throughout. All three names were fictitious. EW became involved in this relation—one of his happiest—in 1927. It was a new experience for him to be taken behind the scenes of "low life" in Brooklyn reported to him in Anna's talk. What is equally interesting—in the light of the notoriety of *Lady Chatterley's Lover*, published in 1928—is that Edmund seeks, before D. H. Lawrence, and more realistically, less rhapsodically, to set down the realities of erotic experience. *Lady Chatterley* created the precedent, however, which gave EW the idea that he might publish in America *his* representation of sexual mores of the Eastern seaboard. *Memoirs of Hecate County* became equally notorious, was banned and for the first time attracted a wider public to EW than he had hitherto had. *Hecate County* was, he said, "my favorite among my books—I have never understood why the people who interest themselves in my books never pay any attention." He was referring here to the fact that certain of his readers continued to take Wilson the critic seriously and ignored Wilson the storyteller.]

Feeling of the season's being over—it was no doubt my malady [I had caught gonorrhea from Anna, of which more later] that made me feel so—the songs in the Scandals (*Lucky Day, And the Girl Was Me, Black Bottom, Never Saw the Sun Shinin' so Bright*), which I had been hearing all winter, made me feel that the play was over and that we had laid off for the summer—I was so out of love now with Katze—I didn't even try to get her to come to Thirteenth Street after the show, but told the taxi driver to go to her house—she meant almost nothing to me sitting beside me in the theater—I sometimes wished for a more comfortable person with more repose. —I remembered how we had gone to the Winter Garden, in evening clothes, drunk, excited and formal just about a year ago.

A woman on the Red Bank train, sitting on the arm of a seat and impeding the progress of passengers through the aisle, chewing gum and gesturing with a lean hand like her lean figure and face: "His stummick's always troublin'um!"

Coming into Red Bank (mid-May), the sharp-outlined sunlit summer look of the street beyond the railroad gates—the cars, the low shops, the garages in the whitening stronger sun.

Elaine McDermott on the subject of Liza Abbott's second marriage—Liza had married a young French artist and they didn't have much money. Elaine told Mary that, when you want to call on her, you ought not to wear black clothes, because you always get your clothes covered with dust.

Somebody capable of considerable brutality in his personal relations whose sensibilities are tortured by a fine phonograph record played with a blunt needle, which he imagines scratching wider grooves, as it trails, like a chisel, little shavings of wax.

How the war—by fettering our activity and attention to inhuman, úninteresting things, to the deliberate, methodical, relentless machinery of destruction—now made us appreciate human things, the commonest human fellowship. With what relief, what delight, one turned from the guns, the drill or the discipline, to the good nature of a comrade, the satisfaction of a bottle of wine, the irreverent jokes of the army. I never loved humanity so deeply and sincerely before and I never expect to again—this, in spite of the fact that I had begun by detesting most of my fellow soldiers individually and that I continued, even when I felt sympathy with them, to entertain a low opinion of their integrity, their intelligence and their personal charm. —These thoughts were all suggested by seeing the procession of guns being moved to the border—*"and the caissons go rolling along"*—in the movie *Spread Eagle*.

[Stark Young, poet and novelist, was drama critic of *The New Republic*. George Soule wrote on economic affairs for the same journal.]

Stark Young (a Southerner) on the New Englanders. About George Soule: "Well, I don't think he's worryin' about any of us." —About the New Englanders in general: he didn't wonder they had to preach to them about service—otherwise, they'd all eat each other up—o' course, you have to teach 'em manners—otherwise, they'd push the old ladies off into the gutters—what they call teachin' manners, in the South they'd just call not bein' a hog. —Story about Sam Eliot, who wrote him a letter asking if he wouldn't review a college play—couldn't pay him for what he wrote—couldn't put him up, but knew he could easily find a place to sleep at Amherst, which was near—not to come over weekend, because they were more likely to sell tickets then, but come Friday.

At Ruddigore, which I hadn't seen since the days when I was first working on *Vanity Fair*, in the same theater, there was a moment when it hardly seemed to me that I could be quite a different person, seven years older—when it seemed to me that everything was the same, that I was the same—when the glamour and the vagueness and the mystery of the past had disappeared, and life seemed its same immediate, unarranged, unartistic, unbeglamoured, natural self that I had first known when, as a boy, I had enjoyed going to Gilbert and Sullivan (with some elements of the production of which I was usually dissatisfied), and before my intelligence and my imagination had fully possessed themselves of the world, lending interest to the prosaic by assigning to it a significance (in a whole so much larger and all-inclusive than anything I had then grasped) and dramatizing the commonplace in character and incident by interpreting according to my fuller experience both of others and of myself. (Everything was more mysterious to me then, but, on the other hand, there were great areas of life which seemed to me utterly uninteresting because I had no real insight into them.)

Dr. Geiringer (the doctor to whom I went to cure my gonorrhea). "I used to say to my classes, if any of you tells me on the examination that silver nitrate cures gonorrhea, I'll flunk him. —If you're ever in doubt as to whether to use silver nitrate or not, don't use it at all. —It's like a chisel—you know, in the hands of a sculptor, it'll take a piece of marble and make a beautiful statue out of it—but in the hands of somebody else, they'll just make an awful mess of it." —He was a Viennese and had a Viennese gaiety and intelligence underneath his barrel-shaped Germanic figure and his black-shaving heavy-jowled face. —On the subject of "the curt individual" who comes in and says, "I've just got a little strain, Doctor"—when you tell him it's the clap, he says, "Oh, no, Doctor—she's a *nice* little girl!"—his faith in human nature is shaken (looks shocked). —One of those despondent individuals came in one morning even more despondent than usual—he had knocked up a girl, wanted an abortion—then he knocked up her sister—I said, "Here, get out of this office—you're breaking my heart!" Boy who got gonorrhea in the war, had to lie to his wife, etc.—prizefighter—"Keep your pecker in your pants"—but she had made a pass at him. —"No cunt worth bothering about." —Story about old chief at Postgraduate Hospital—young man who waited on table at summer resort and "just caught a chill"—"Does it sneeze?—Does it cough? etc.—Well, I guess we'll have to call it the clap." —Stories about hard guys: "What's the matter with you?—I was just thinkin' that must have been some puddle where you dropped your crumb!" —Sailor who got chancroid ulcer from a Dahomey African princess—"a specialty of the royal family"—"If you come back again, I'll cut it off!"

G——T——'s legs in her dress of the fashionable kind which seems (draped) caught up in front, so as to leave in the skirt, as it were, a curtained doorway of which the angle draws the eye, as to a cynosure, toward the just-concealed cunt.

Margaret Canby. Ted's marriage—her sciatica—going around with a cane. —At *Daisy Waterman's* (she had been Margaret's father's mistress): the framed drawings of her when she was younger—just after the days of the

Floradora Sextette, no doubt—a straight-nosed clean-browed girl of the Gibson period, with straight dark hair—in the distinct straight lines of the drawings, queenly, straight-backed, haughty-necked, dignified, almost austere—now frowning a little, haggard and lean, her straight nose turning to a keen dog's muzzle, her eyebrows drawn in with an eyebrow pencil till they look entirely artificial. Her line over the telephone to her present recreant lover—who had got drunk at the races at Belmont Park and said he had broken down twice on the way back—"the old army game"—"Oh, you're in Flushing, are you? Well, I think it would be a fine thing if you both got drowned.—Bring the girls along!" —Margaret's account of the circus dance at Santa Barbara—there was a tent, the floor was covered with sawdust and everybody was given a clown costume and everybody looked alike—with their faces painted white—they ate scrambled eggs off bare board tables, sitting on long board benches—they had wanted to have everybody enter the dining hall by a chute, but the country club wouldn't let them—Margaret had evidently been rather impressed by their "carrying it out in every detail." —Her (Margaret's) sister Camilla; the man and woman who were living together in perfect happiness—his wife was insane, etc. She broke the household up because they were "living in sin," had the man put in jail, etc. —Italian (?) man and woman living together in Pennsylvania industrial town, where her (Camilla's) husband had had his parish before getting his fashionable California one—great quantities of children by early marriages and something like six more of their own—living in sin, but so poor and with so many children that she decided not to make trouble. Margaret said that she couldn't "make him out." (All the Scotch Presbyterianism of Margaret's Canadian mother was concentrated in Camilla.)

John and Marion. John so amiable that I realized it must have been the situation resulting from Louise's visit that had made him rude and bad-tempered. —Marion's coy delicacy about the Deering Howes' yacht—a large motorboat in which they were going up the Hudson and up through the St. Lawrence. —John greeting me with burlesque exclamations over Lindbergh (who had just flown the Atlantic): "Don't you think Charlie Lindbergh ought to be made ambassador?—I hope you're going to give up your apartment to him—and the *New Republic* office!" —John on Sacco and Vanzetti—impossible to know whether they had had a fair trial without going through all the evidence.

Benchley's telegram to Charley Brackett in Paris: "Has Lindbergh arrived yet? He left here a week ago." —Brackett's reply: "Do you mean George Lindbergh?"

Margaret Canby's conventional unconventionality—her reaction toward the romance of *The Barker*—indignant at the father who didn't want his son to marry sideshow girl—hoped girl wouldn't give him up—at end of Second Act: "How *can* they end it?—Yet it leaves you in suspense," etc. — Margaret always thought that pregnancy was so surprising—seemed so silly that you should start a baby growing by an act of that kind—never could get over how funny it seemed.

Resemblance between Lindbergh and Veblen, the mathematician [not Thorstein: his cousin (I think) at Princeton]. Blond blue-eyed tall skinny Scandinavians, naturally well-bred, detached, with accurate and durable intellects, capable of carrying through difficult operations with easy and single-minded tenacity, Lindbergh didn't smoke and drank neither alcohol nor coffee, and Veblen sat around, in his cool clean way, offering me tea and Coke, but not taking any himself.

Looking out through the window at Red Bank (June 25), I saw the white gawky and graceful figure of a girl moving across the wide black open doorway of a new white garage, just framed in the green fronds of summer trees.

Marion's visit, with Mrs. Headley (a former nurse), among the first families of the Bronx. She found they all said "bunked" for "bumped" and other things which she had formerly supposed were peculiar to Mrs. Headley. —They had one maid and helped out in the kitchen themselves—got the tenses of their verbs wrong. Doctor who took drugs and drove car through hedge onto lawn of one of them—smashed pane of glass and "probably knocked over some of the iron deer"—couldn't sue him because everybody would say what did a woman in her position want to sue a poor man like Dr.—— for—would *not* have the car taken out front way because it would involve destroying several little trees—wanted to take it apart, but finally had to sacrifice trees. Talked much about obstetrical casualties—one of them went in for charity—helping delinquent children—said, on parting with Marion, that she would like so much to take her to court sometime—had on one occasion seen little boy eating out of garbage can—thought he must be actually hungry, because, you know, "adults will eat out of garbage cans for effect."

Just beyond Red Bank, in late May [1927] when I slept past my station on the train—out the window the bright signs, red roofs, white walls, green foliage.

In the first week of early June in New York, I was walking among those old-fashioned crisscrossed streets—Barrow, Grove, etc.—I could smell the faintly saline, the mildly rank smell of the river, as if it had invaded the streets of the lower butt of the island, now that the people had left for the summer—for Woodstock, for Provincetown—I was looking for Fitzy (Eleanor Fitzgerald) [the manager of the Provincetown Players] on Barrow Street, but, in an unfamiliar deserted square, ran into Harold McGee, who sent me to Grove—he knew the way, I did not. —That *cavernous old house*, where Fitzy, Stark Young, Dorothea Nolan and Djuna Barnes once all lived at the same time—with its wastes and stretches of linoleum, its steep staircases and rambling halls, its balustrades, its broken skeleton hatrack in a marble-framed niche, its high square-topped radiators, its enormous vestibule doors, its mysterious inside windows covered over with cloths from within, the desolation of its corridors, the interminable and exhausting climbs of stairs, the yellow plaster and yellow woodwork, the smell of bathrooms, the sound of dripping bathtubs and defective toilets. Fitzy still trying to make the Provincetown Players go, to get it started by July 1 for next year, raise money, pay bills (she had got so she could tell the bill collectors when they came to her own apartment—because they came early in the morning and knocked with the knock of a stranger)—she was so tired—her little place in the country.

Idea of character (in play, perhaps) like Carl Van Doren, heavy "civilized" (should he go in for this word?) type of renegade college professor—makes love to wife of other literary man, putting whole thing on wholesome, serious, reasonable "civilized" basis—he tells her how fond he is of his wife—she is the mother of his children and he has been very happy with her—just as much as, he is sure, she loves her husband, but he believes that it is possible to love more than one person, we have different sides of our character which everybody doesn't bring into play, etc., etc.

Trip to Coney Island with Florence [which EW incorporated in *I Thought of Daisy*]. She said she had begun taking separate remedies for all her different ailments—kidneys (back), eyes, etc. —I said she was tanned. —"No—just sallow—very thin hair." —"No, it's cute." We bought sandwiches and ginger ale—went straight to upper deck and sat on bench—drank Scotch out of paper cups—Florence's lipstick (the very best—sort of a mauve—woman in store where she bought moccasins inquired about it)—I had kept her waiting in Brevoort writing note: "Well, the first twenty-five years of my life I spent in the Brevoort Hotel. —I felt as if I'd been married to you twenty years, when you were sitting there writing that letter." —Said she felt "pretty sassy"—I felt depressed—thought of coming into New York in the morning on the *North Carolina* (coming back after the war on a U.S. cruiser) (smell of white boat paint in sun)—I tried to talk about it, but she several times steered me off—sitting under ventilators—"warm for fanny"—"drinking in the wind keeps you sober"—the two hot dogs that

were blown overboard when the boy tried to be smart for her benefit—"First time I've known that to happen!" —When the boat stopped,
we felt the heat, standing in the sun, everything very quiet, she said that,
when the wind stopped, she began to reel—going down steps, down the
long pier to the boardwalk. Noah's Ark, intermittent fog horn, the ark
swinging from side to side—fisherman, elephant, HANK shaking his bars.
Drink in frankfurter place—postcards: American flag with silver tinsel in-
scription—"I thought of you at Coney Island." —"I'm going to be dirty—
X marks my room." —Glazed photographic card of foreign-looking
couple about to kiss—"I am Waiting to Hear from you"—bathing beauties—man touching hat to "goopy" girls. —Waxworks: Snyder murder
and Lindbergh—she had "never seen but one corpse," an aunt—rolling-
ball game—bored Jap so by continuing to fire off snake and make him put it
back—"Now, don't pull that," he would admonish her—poker hand,
shooting gallery (candles, ducks), throwing rings around clocks and baby
dolls in chemises—won a mouth organ, a miniature roulette wheel and a
pistol which shot a snake with a spring inside. —Her dilemma over the girl
who engaged her in conversation in the shop—chummy at first, but afterwards, as girl grew more familiar, she became superior and a little sharp,
suggested our going if girl wasn't going to find the right size—walked
across park to Brighton Hotel—drinks there: Arthur had taken her there
when he ran away with her, first time she ever got drunk, manager plied her
with champagne, little black dress that buttoned up back and every time she
danced, they unbuttoned another button, you know how men are when
they've got a girl that's kind of cute and they're trying to get her tight. I
asked her again if she had ever been in love—no: didn't worry about it, but
just woke up sometimes with that "ache in your armpits"—outside, the
sea—sky was becoming deeper and deeper blue with the globes of the
boardwalk becoming yellower and yellower against it—I: "Have you seen
how blue it's getting?" etc.—Florence: "Yes: I've seen that." —How her
father had burst in on them with a detective and asked if she'd slept with
Arthur, she said no—Arthur knew I wasn't crazy about him, so we just
rolled over and went to sleep.—Well, if you knew Arthur, you'd understand—he's not like you and he's not like Ted[Leisen], etc.—everybody's
different—Arthur had the reputation of being the wildest fellow in Pittsburgh. —We took a chair on the boardwalk—I tried to kiss her—"Wait:
When the time comes, I'll neck you right—later." —I said I'd feel much
better, if she'd let me kiss her—"Do you feel much better?" "Yes." —Blue
Moon—rather luxurious, rich-looking rugs and things—dinner in large,
almost deserted dining room next to a slightly open window—I thought of
ocean voyages—she had two orders of clam cocktails, followed by lobster—I had bluefish—we sat long (till about 10:30) after dinner—then left

and she went to the toilet in a cheap lunchroom—"Have to go to about eighteen ladies' rooms"—came out, having shot seafood dinner—"the smell of that place"—went into Noah's Ark afterwards: "shimmy stairs," electric current; my support of her, solicitude about her health, afraid that it was much better outside than inside—my solemn feeling of tenderness for her while we were going through it; on happier occasions and earlier in the evening, it might all have been deliriously gay—shrieking girls, etc. —Luna Park closed—bus—ineffectual attempts to get drink—sitting on bench beside sea—she worked out the first part of *Nearer, My God, to Thee* on the mouth organ—too brownish artificial sand—regular winking light-house—lights and gray steamers along line of gray water in the afternoon made me think of summers in Europe—Adelaide Knox coming back from England—Henry James and Edith Wharton, etc. —How I had seen the lights of Coney Island tarnishing the water with their brassy light and shuddered at the idea of America—(would have had fun under happier circumstances somewhere on my native Jersey coast)—where I could have seen her blond head on those pale sands where so many other little blondes spent the summer. She, unlike them, so truly interesting—surf balls, rusty bathhouse keys, etc.—I thought that I wanted to embrace her all the way back in the taxi—she had remembered how I had kissed her at the Throckmortons' when she had come out on the landing as I was going. The place was closed up, chilling: automata no longer human, posters of wild men folded over—she had never seen freaks—her mother hadn't let her—inquired if they weren't all fakes. —Her French phrases and European references—home in bus—jolting and baneful hiccups—she told me about her father, he had been first to design certain kinds of trucks, they had things on the front and sirens that you turned on by just pulling a string—ruined by being indicted for manslaughter, he and another man had hit each other (both's fault) when father was coming out of garage; man killed and father in hospital for a month—they had never been able to get over the idea that she ought to marry somebody rich. —We got a taxi at Madison Square (the sour smell of the city) and she left the mouth organ in taxi—she had composed songs while taking baths—one was comic, one sentimental. —So perfectly a girl whom I might have lived next door to—I might have told her that I loved her, for it was true, but was afraid it would cheapen the situation—we were like children in that childish place, and no doubt that was partly what we had in common which gave us an American fellow-feeling and solidarity—both had had our childhood in the era of Roosevelt, whom we had seen in the waxworks, his charming sympathy with his children and his cognate success with the American public—let down from the tense pitches of passion and suffering, of high effort, we had arrived at this simple normal (so banal) level of friendly and national solidarity, people of the same country and the same race, almost of the same family and the same house, the home-earth from which works, as well as children, sprouted—she and I—of different stocks—acted upon by the climate, etc., merged at last in the same race and ready to fertilize one another. —I was sorry that she had bad dreams and that she had just thrown up. —When I left her with a kiss at her house, I felt, though dead-tired and sick with the hiccups, a deep satisfaction and, as it were, disappointment.

How well she looked in those short tight skirts that cut off their legs just above the knees. —Failure to respond properly to my "Gee, I'm a clever guy!" —"Gee, I think I appreciate women awfully well!" —When she had appeared at the window and said, "We don't want any," with her smile. —"You have the worst-looking nails I've ever seen—they look just like mechanics' nails except that the mechanics' nails are dirty." —"I think that words like dear and darling were just invented for bed, don't you?" — Ted Leisen spent most of his time kissing her hands—which I had not thought particularly beautiful. —She complimented me on my gray socks, which matched my suit but which my mother had given me, and she said she liked the way my socks went with my clothes—most people's socks didn't have anything to do with the rest of their clothes.

Aviators [Charles Lindbergh had made his historic New York–Paris flight May 20–21, 1927]. *Lindbergh's* speeches about his receptions, London bobbies, etc.—letter from Hemingway: "Isn't it fine what the American embassy's doing for Lindbergh. It's as if they'd caught an angel that talks like Coolidge," etc. —"America has no better friend than France," as if he had learned a piece. —On Photofilm: the barking of the regular army officer, which he was not able entirely to divest of the gasping of the schoolboy who has been obliged to speak a piece—"Thank you!"—amid the canned cheers of the crowds, already stale. —And breast the trans-atlantic sleet. —But, when we saw him alight from his Washington plane, in his aviator's suit, climb into a car, speed to an amphibian, clamber into the amphibian and make it soar from the ground, then land in the water among the milling pandemonium of river craft (rejecting the offers to help him into the tug of the newspapermen, whom he suspected)—one had a striking impression of a new sort of genius, of a thorough mastery of a new medium, a complete, sure and unostentatious virtuosity.

Commander Byrd at the Harvard Club. "All the old stuffed shirts of the Har-vard Club paraded in and sat down in front rows"—Byrd appeared with a glass in one hand and a cocktail shaker in the other—"And so they started out, those two brave men, and they got lost in the fog—there they were," etc.—"Only an aviator knows what that means," etc.—They turned out the lights and began the pictures—a dead and ominous silence. (Byrd's very grand people in Virginia, according to Aunt Susan [Wilson]—it was the descendant of Byrd "who built Westover"—his brother was the governor—they had very simple ways of doing things—somebody rang the doorbell—the governor's wife had said, "Don't you really think that you occupy a position now where you ought to let the servants answer the bell!" —"Oh, but it's just old so-and-so!" —Addressed his brother [who made use of no governor's staff] as "Your Excellency" at ceremonies in Richmond—"Thank you, Your Excellency," with a smirk, for glass of water.) —"Some gentlemen think I can't finish my speech"—the lights are turned on again—the audience with "tears streaming down their cheeks"—the pictures commence—Byrd makes them help him up on table—wavering billiard cue—"Extreme northernmost town of the whole world!"—"The brave explorers—the intrepid airmen"—he would look around at the audience and smirk and say, "That's all the bunk!"

That cigarette poster: a young man in a dress suit with a great carnivorous mastiff jaw and his mouth open (a big canine paw holding cigarette) as if he were about to devour the succulent neck, cheeks and shoulders of the molasses-haired girl in décolleté beside him. In taking off her evening wrap, he peeled it down, as if she were a human fruit being skinned to be eaten—"No harshness—not a bit of bite." —The slatted backside of a sign.

The successive wringings for blank-verse dye of the Elizabethan dish-cloth with its deep and gorgeous stain of Shakespeare and, at other stages, with the butterfly-wing brightness (vivid but thin) of Marlowe and of the poison green and yellow of Webster, till, with Otway, there is no color left. Even Tourneur's sullen cindery dinginess was a precious dye diversified with dry yellow.

Aunt Susan (Wilson visiting us in Red Bank): snobbish people at Ashe-ville, North Carolina, who felt that they were ruined if Mrs. Vanderbilt failed to ask them to a function—well, we say, "That's North Carolina"—populated by descendants of people who had got into trouble else-where—the Botany Bay of the colonies—"Madam, I come from the valley of humility between two mountain peaks of conceit." —"Oh, you come from North Carolina, suh!" —In Alabama, her sister had observed, on a visit, that the women were in the habit of going from one house to another in their dressing gowns—and that they ate no kind of bread except soda bis-cuits—with too much soda in them. —Woodrow Wilson: Aunt Susan was sixteen and vastly impressed by him—he used to come often to the house—his speeches on Gladstone and Bright—she used to tremble so when she held the hymn book with him that she could hardly keep hold of the book—on occasion of unveiling of her father's bust, he changed sides with his companion, when he was marching in the procession, as he came near the platform, so that he could pass up to where the Raleighs were sitting—he shook hands with the family and said, "I see that my inspiration is here." —She had been in the habit of listening to his speeches with her eyes fixed on his face, drinking in every word. He was considered remarkable (his only rival was William Cabell Bruce) but hadn't many friends— though the "intellectuals" liked him. —Grant's great-granddaughter, the little Princess Cantacuzene—"General Grant," "Mr. Jefferson"—her father was able to tell where any student came from in Virginia as soon as he heard his name, or, if he said he came from New England or the West, he would say, "Well, your grandfather must have come from whatever county it was in Virginia." —She seemed rather startled when I told her what Allen Tate had said about how everything would have been very different if the South had won the war. As I went on complimenting the South, she finally made an attempt to be gracious about New York, telling me how fine Fifth Avenue was, comparing it to Paris and disparaging Paris. —"Judge" scolded and reproached her for not having let him know that Minor was coming to West Virginia—that part of West Virginia that was practically in Virginia. —North Carolina was a very wonderful state: industry, people very thrifty and everything like that, gettin' rich, and she didn't mind people gettin' rich so long as they didn't talk too much about it.

Provincetown

[Aside from short visits, this was my first real summer at Provincetown. I stayed at Mrs. Mayo's on Commercial Street, read *Moby Dick*, looked for a place to bring Rosalind and Stella, went around with John Francis, who, though professionally a real estate man, discouraged clients from taking any of the houses he showed them. Then a wire came from Jimmy Light that he could not stay in O'Neill's house, as he had expected to do, and that I could have it. I moved in at Peaked Hill. O'Neill gave up Provincetown when he and Agnes were divorced and he gave it to his son by his first marriage, from whom he was renting it. He came to see me at one point—later on, I think, when I was living there with Margaret—very serious-minded—a little on the heavy side.]

Provincetown. That dull linoleum-blue sky over the dull red-brick factory buildings of Boston, like the colors and child's-block-like shapes of a child's picture book, coming into Boston, struck a chill in my soul.

Coming into Provincetown, exquisite delicacy of mother-of-pearl sea thinning to a fragile shelly blade along the shallow shore—a sort of iridescence of violet, blue and green—a few gulls.

Provincetown, June 20 [1927]. "Full of fairies that keep antique shops"—"The Anchorite," with its pseudo-stained glass (ecclesiastical) in the door—that soft and plumy gray-white sky, the wide westward gold such as one sees aboard ship—the lavender-ashy harbor, so fresh and lovely, full of little craft, less lavender and more ashy as the evening fell—a large clear star in the dark above the eaves of a clear white house. Excellent mackerel fried in butter and some kind of sweet oyster soup—old captain in hotel—talk of swordfish at so much a pound—clean sea-washed olive but not ruddy-tanned or swarthy slight Portuguese, black-eyed, not often handsome, nor the women beautiful, but a scrubby growth like the dune weed of the northern sand—a pretty black-eyed baby who smiled, in the arms of a weather-seasoned woman talking to another weather-seasoned woman. —I recognized the spire of the church, among roofs, that Charles Demuth had painted—the green-looking, high, dark, ominous house about which there had been some strange story that delighted O'Neill had been put into excellent shape and changed into a historical museum. —Harry Kemp on forgotten English poets, drunk and inconsequent, discouragement

261

with study of literature—"dozens of dumb artists—literary people gone"—John Francis's gentle, appealing voice and gentlemanliness (an eccentric real estate agent)—painted wooden figurehead of woman with head thrown up and one hand clasping wreath across breast over doorstep shelter of yellow house, sunk like an old water-logged ship in a dooryard of long uncut grass, with an old woman sitting at the window—"a drink distilled from the sand on the sand dunes." —Episcopal Church of St. Mary's of the Harbor, singing *Holy, Holy, Though the darkness hide thee*, in the clean evening in the little cabin-church with the minister in his white surplice.

The sun of late afternoon glowing silver in a sky lightly iron-shadowed above a white house whose dark-blue blinds respond to the shadows of the sky—a Chinese-white house with bright lettuce-green shutters. —A fine white house with a low white fence, braided in, of long flattened rectangles latticed with diagonals, behind which the clear evening light showing the leaves of the trees on the lawn like precise silhouetted green lace, all delicate and in the flat; light-green shutters on high slender white houses, vaulted gold canary cages in windows—Pete Carr (the Carrs were two brothers who had a cart that we depended on for transferring baggage) knew better how to talk to O'Neill's guests than Dick—neither ever seemed to get married—"kept bachelor's hall" in house with radio and round sanded receptacle for tobacco juice; man who was frightened of black snake, woman who took adder by the tail and snapped its head right off. Bright blues of bachelor's-buttons, oranges, vermilions of nasturtiums, reds of poppies, deep yellows with brown-orange centers of those small sunflower-looking flowers, such bright primary colors against the meager greenery and the pale sandy soil, and the white houses.

Florence. Her voice on the telephone—"people who hear me say that it's the most terrible thing they ever heard."

Ted hates dirty stories, you know.

Women who say, "Oh, God!" (hoarsely).

She used to read Compton Mackenzie and think he was swell.

When I removed the cat from the chair: "Well, what could be kinder than that?"

At Coney Island: "I suppose you think I called Ted up and told him I was having a rotten time—well, I didn't."

I said I felt in New York as if I were in a cage of wild animals—well, she had been feeling that way.

My father was fit to be tied—when she went to Boston, during the war, as a telegraph operator.

"I don't know what it's all about."

[Hazel Ufford was commended to John Peale Bishop by Edmund during

the following year as "a girl who lived near me last summer, when I was
living in O'Neill's old coast-guard station near Provincetown. She is very
young and very pretty, and she has quite a remarkable literary gift, as yet in
rather an immature state." Bishop was then residing in Paris and Hazel
Ufford was planning a trip abroad.]

Hazel Hawthorne (Ufford) (She was still married to Ufford and they had a
shack at Peaked Hill) had her children call her Hazel, and their grandmother "grand-Hazel." The grandmother had been a minister's wife, her
thinning face, her way of saying "little"—"You mustn't hurt the sand
flea." "Why not?" "You mustn't hurt any little living thing." (Susan
Glaspell had said about Roger that that was "kind of a nice story, too.")
When Hazel came with friends to look at the house: "Oh, Edmund, do you
mind if we just take a peek upstairs?" —Husband's sermon on the Ten
Commandments—giving the trustees what they wanted, "Crash! another
commandment rent the firmament!" —Abel's blood crying from the
ground—have to give the old people what they wanted on the subject of
immortality or set up as an authority on social reform, etc., about which he
actually knew nothing. Had gotten into trouble at Durham (University of
New Hampshire) for giving student drink, so was a little afraid to take a
drink I offered him while we were waiting at the station. —Roger wanted
me to meet his sister—not at all the sort of girl you would expect of a minister's wife with six children—his eternal helpfulness—his eternal boat—its
"center pressure," which he hadn't had right—throwing skates and squids
back into the sea. —Hazel's (and Ufford's) preoccupation with a body
which had been devoured by sand fleas and with misfortunes of George (the
good-looking coast guard), who had taken her on patrol, but afterwards
come down with clap, caught from the wife of a Portuguese at the station,
to whom he had perfectly assured access by reason of the fact that he knew
that, when he was on liberty, the husband was safe at the station. Both
caught the clap and were confined to the hospital, where they "learned to
know each other better." Roger deplored George's downfall—a good kid,
but didn't have any sense—could have mixed with the nice people of the
town, but now the scandal was all over. —Her way of saying, "Hello-oh"
said Fanny, sticking her pretty little head in at the door). (There was an
atmosphere about Hazel and Roger of rather goody-goody old-fashioned
New England stories.)

Gormans (who had been staying with me). Herbert's delighted relief over
my fight with Jean over Carl Van Doren—I could hear it in his voice when
he talked to her that evening—and he lay in the long wicker chair and
wrote a poem—a poem to her, no doubt, or a satire on me. His reproaching
me (I take it) for loss of dignity. He always called Jean "Babe." Herbert's

complacent twitting me on the excellent Scotch of Carl Van Doren's he had drunk the night before.

Susan Glaspell, etc. "Something kind of nice between them," etc. —Dramatist friend who had formula: three points—condition at the beginning of play, "which grows"—obstacle at end of second act, which is removed by surprise—ditto at end of third act. —"About our age—you know, there's the young thing, and then there's the middle-aged thing, and then there's the older thing—and then, after that, there's just mumbling and shaking the cane—this way."

Provincetown. After a night of rain, that marvelously clear morning—with all the flies and mosquitoes blown away—with the sea brightest deepest green and purple, choppy with green waves, which, when their shapes dissolved into the wobbling water of the shore, became so clear that you could look straight down to the yellow sand of the bottom and see a blue or greenish stone or a large white clam shell. —On hot midsummer days the ocean was hazy and gray and at night a dry cherry-colored billiard ball, without radiance or sunset stainings, would descend into the leaden sea and leave the sky scarcely less leaden—at night, the stars would be dimmed.

Florence. Vitreous seaweed—Mack Sennett bathing girl of vintage of 1915—*Priscilla, Priscilla, she smells like vanilla, she keeps the mosquitoes away!*— her thin bird-like legs below the knee—the vivid system of blue veins from her Charley horse—she had drunk so much to keep herself going in *Louis XIV* that she finally got some sort of d.t.'s and saw a horse sitting beside her bed, leering at her, with its hoofs, which were painted blue, on its knees— she told herself that it couldn't be real, but he seemed so—until they gave her a great big drink of something bitter and she went to sleep.

—high-keyed and gala the day she arrived in Provincetown—we're all high-keyed and you're quiet and sober—her rompers—her color began to come back the next day.

—"I dreamed last night that you'd fallen in love with a redheaded pajukis" ("That last's just the usual applesauce—better than saying 'I love you'").

—her father used to get drunk and come home and sit on the edge of the bed and hold directors' meetings: "I used to think it was funny, but my mother would be so worried!"

—She didn't know why her hair had turned pink—so long ago, didn't remember what color it had originally been—just mouse-color, I guess— they put white henna on it when they bleached it for *Louis XIV* and she had been reviving it with peroxide and orange juice every once in a while ever since.

—first time she'd met Ted, she went over to him and said, "I feel more at home with you than anybody else I've ever met!" —He just grinned— showed a good deal of discrimination.

—Feet not much use for dancing—too small to hold her upright.

—missed more performances in *Louis XIV* than anybody else in company (independence of girl whose father had had money).

—"if I ever get my beak in that coffee!"

—"the kind of girl men fail to remember—it rankles, don't you hear it rankling?"

—weeping because she'd decided she had no future.

—men—"I hate 'em, anyway—just one thought in their heads twenty-four hours out of the day—leering and ogling and pinching and pawing— grasping and pushing!"

John Francis. Fox said you saw the John Francis sign on all the houses—"you got kind of dazzled." —His father had been a fine strong upstanding man—he passed his boyhood on the farm—timid—believed in ghosts—moved tables—ghost followed him upstairs—never knew what houses he had—"asleep most of the time," prospective tenant said—John Francis himself said he didn't see how a man could look himself in the face after putting a lying ad like the other real estate man's in the paper—half Portuguese, half Irish (Irish mother landed in wreck)—grocery store always out of stock—said I seemed like a lonely young man—couldn't furnish house and get it in order in time—nice educated couple who had bought house but almost immediately got divorced—"'Sacco and Vanzetti must die!'—wasn't that an awful thing to shout out loud like that!"— gunboat in harbor for celebration—what did they want to have a great big boat like that to go out and kill people for?—soft, whiny voice—they thought anybody was rich up there—he didn't see much of the world, but was probably not so badly off—he worried about the meaning of life— intellectual son—read Thomas Mann, Hemingway, *The Dial*—voted the Communist ticket (only person in town who did)—asked if son would go to the city: "Will hasn't the money to leave town!"

Exquisite fragile kiss of the sea at Peaked Hill at night after a fine day. — Wild-eyed looks of brown pebble-mottled skates being washed up on the shore, where at dusk their white-sided floppings are seen.—Rich wine-stained rug-patterned medusas. —Sand fleas lit up with phosphorus.

[EW traveled to Boston from Provincetown at the moment of the final efforts by libertarians in behalf of the condemned anarchists, Sacco and Vanzetti. He went actually to see friends; but the drama of the celebrated case, the tense atmosphere, the tragic overtones of every step in the appeal, the arrest of liberals on the Common, impinged heavily on EW's feelings and colored the mood of his entire stay. The notes he set down of his impressions first at the country club, then his various lively sociabilities with the Fort sisters, Louise and Henrietta, friends of the lawyer John Amen, their talk of pollution—"condemned clams," of boiling lobsters alive, a quip about men from Rumpelmayer's, the international caterers (and actually an allusion to a phrase on the first page of Virginia Woolf's *Mrs. Dalloway*), coalesced in EW's mind into a masterly story of the "high ironic." He published it as "Lobsters for Supper" in *The New Republic*, September 28, 1927, and renamed it "The Men from Rumpelmayer's" when he included it in *The American Earthquake* (1958). Of its time and place, the story must be read in the context of the judicial rigidities and the grimness of Boston at the time.

Direct expression of his opinion of the Sacco and Vanzetti case is to be found in a letter written a year later (October 22, 1928) to John Peale Bishop, who was living abroad. EW told Bishop: "You were too far away at the time to appreciate properly either its [the case's] importance or its interest. It revealed the whole anatomy of American life, with all its classes, professions and points of view and all their relations, and it raised almost every fundamental question of our political and social system. It did this, furthermore, in an unexpectedly dramatic fashion. As Dos Passos said, it was, during the last days before the executions, as if, by some fairy-tale spell, all the different kinds of Americans, eminent and obscure, had suddenly, in a short burst of intensified life, been compelled to reveal their true characters in a heightened exaggerated form."]

Boston Harbor. First the big square frame houses, set too big and too bare on some dullish dark-green island—then the stony rime against the water, red buildings like institutions, the factory chimneys, and kind of bell tower—Boston before us under a setting sun of industrial red copper, metal-edging a bulk of rain cloud filling the sky to the left and overcoming the still limpid blue of earliest fall, the old-fashioned-looking boats—but the gloom on the waters was of Sacco and Vanzetti, not the nineteenth-century upholstery obscuration of a landscape which somehow made it profounder and richer, but merely dulling, the further denuding of a level and uniform metallic surface, pricked and spiked by the buoys and ship masts—the dumb immobile unthundering storm, like some great blank immovable menace, the blank menace not merely of some disaster to humanity, but of the negation of humanity itself. —I shouldn't have thought of the Boston Harbor of the picture —hard-blowing, but unsultry wind.

Visit to Fort girls at Boston, August 16–18. Provincetown Harbor—canoe with long-legged handsome barefooted boy with fine square long phalanges, in white pants with girl, who took the forward paddle and looked something like him—the darkening summer light (darkening with a threatened storm)—against which the white bright sail of a boat, the light-houses, like snowy-white pages, and the lessening disappearing land—the departure, the girls (with their Charleston stockinged legs from town and their boyish bobbed hair), who walked out to see the boat off—the bobbin-headed gulls, the straight tanned sea-hardened officers, New England-looking and -talking, who told the canoers to look out and, when we reached Boston, the boys who handled the rope, "All right." The fortifica-tions and factories—the horizontal apocalyptic shafts from the clouds over Boston—provincial old-fashioned pulling of the ship to dock—the line of axis down the pier—it was lucky the boat was late because the girls had just got there in time—Henry's white straw shoes with red strands interwoven, light straw-colored stockings, blue- and red-flowered straw-colored shirt, lightish-blue close-fitting jersey, pinkish-violet scarf around neck, clear skin, clear tanned ruddy color—Louise in yellow jersey and golf shoes, with band around hair. —Percy Wendell's apartment—little cannon ball of Harvard, 1913, football team—had studied medicine, but had coached team at Lehigh—they always played *Down the Field for Harvard*—*for Har-vard wins today*, when he came into restaurants—pale blank blue eyes most of the time tightened to slits—getting bald, blond toothbrush mustache—apartment with picture of Apollo and the Muses—book with proceedings of Porcellian Club dinner inscribed with handwriting like Phil Littell's, bronzes and chairs with covers over them—fine old desk, bureaux and tables—gray used bachelor's bed in bedroom—old-fashioned bathroom, so unlike New York—"Got terribly sensitive": lay awake all night over Louise's calling him bestial, but he always tried to show off strength when drunk (had swung some girl around his head and landed her, so that she had hurt her skull, against grate)—"Don't be fast!"—Hotel Ritz rathskeller—"If I didn't know you girls well, I wouldn't take you here." —Enormously wide table—grotesque cockeyed fresco of masks—*Wein ung, Wein alt*—"This man is suffering! (Help! help!)"—Waiter suggested turning on electric fan—afterwards, I tried to order another chicken sand-wich—waiter called attention resolutely to two halves which had not been eaten—did I want to drive by the prison where Sacco and Vanzetti were? —Louise's wonderful driving—*Hard to Get, Gerty, Tea for Two, Forsaken, he Wouldn't Do What I Wanted Her To*—"brisket you around"—rpentine cocktails with lime juice and a deep-red petal of snap-ragon—country club where I stayed seen across golf links, with music and ight pouring out till it seemed merely a kind of lit-up square banner of the ind carried in parades—a floating steamboat palace—Louise disgraced erself with the steward (we couldn't get into the house). Solid comfort of country club—slatted doors that let in the air, bathroom with nobody else in it—in the morning, from the bathroom window, the grounds, a little like the view from the back porch of one of the Princeton clubs, with the dark trees seen through thick air—the haze-darkened air of a darkish damp of one of those days past mid-August when one already foretells the fall—and from the bedroom window, the dimmed mist-damped tennis courts where slender girls (still the Boston girls) with gray coats watched the tennis, and elsewhere the players with gray and brownish coats watched from the benches, the girls distinguishable only by their whitish crossed legs—the sounds, subdued and rather sparse, of the game—"I might be testy in the morning—a snack [the ginger-ale bottle of gin]—a tasty snack"—(tonic, it seems, is a Boston word for pop). They drove me into Boston after a breakfast in the big deserted country-club dining room: the slender-runged comb-backed chairs, the lightly spring-flowered chintz, the wheel of magazines (John Held's covers) on the sitting-room table—while I was waiting for them, I heard a girl, just come in from the tennis court, order three sarsaparillas with cream. —The amusement park, the Thunderbolt, some quite grotesque and amusing Grimm-brothers shooting galleries and fun parlors populated with papier-mâché gnomes—the lobster- and crab-meat-selling booths, with their long shelves of different-colored pop—the funny dull muddy stagnant-rank shore—the clams were all condemned between Revere Beach and Nahant—taxi motto: "Always alert—nobody hurt." —The Bellevue, Louisburg Square, Clarendon Street—girls were now asleep—a gallon of alcohol, "The old oaken bucket," Wendell manipulated it against his biceps and with his thumb in the little round hole of the handle—on the way back to Beach Bluffs: How different Swampscott looked—quite prosaic, suburban, inhabited—the 'bile, which they always depended upon, had by her mother been taken away from them that night—"I can be happy, I can be sad, it all depends on gin." —*The pretty girl who gets a kiss and runs and tells her mother—Oh landlord, fill the flowing bowl*—He passed around the bowl of crab meat with the fork—boxing passes, "just in fun"—if anyone were found fault with, just in the mood to knock somebody down who gives any trouble—"Have the men from Rumpelmayer's come?"—cold, dull, thick cold of water on muddy shallow beach—"You haven't got anything to do but think—Death, that's the only thing definite—you want something definite—how can you get anything definite?" —He was in Boston for some mysterious reason—they didn't know why he didn't want people not to know that he was there—wouldn't go to any club—some member of his own set whom he didn't like and didn't want to meet—it was a question of taking a lease on a house for two years. —Oh, well, he could see how he felt—wouldn't make much on it otherwise—What was that anyhow (the two girls dancing together at the Bass Point House), did you ever see anything like it?—what was it?—if you put one man on the team, you have to put the other, too—but who are you going to lean on?—I can't lean on you—I wish I were married!—pretty slim tall Irish cigarette girl, black dress, light gray stockings, expensive curly-bobbed head, gray eyes, one-sided little smile while getting us cigarettes—sitting with legs crossed in coatroom, reading, I saw her bangs—half view, as I was going out around side of coatroom door. —(*Marion's* party at Southampton where she thought afterwards she had been so dull and hadn't talked—man she had sat next to at dinner, with whom she had talked about people they knew, until he mentioned somebody she didn't know—when, she fancied, his whole manner changed.) Leaving Percy Wendell at his mother's in Nahant (white old-fashioned, porchless New England house)—he "crashed" upstairs, came back to say that he couldn't come with us. —Louise's Boston boy-friend who had taken her, drunk, to some scandalous places in Paris—"You were a da'n good little spo't"—the Ma'shes—Their brother, to tell the truth, had turned cheap on them—they never mentioned him—but there was a picture of him—he married an Atlanta girl and called her honey—I could see what they were like from that—the next morning, Louise's baby breaking his leg—she said they treated her superciliously at the hospi-tal—Wendell said that everybody in Boston was like that. —When I bought the paper with the news of the Supreme Court's refusal of writ of error (or whatever—you only had to look at the pictures of the Justices—nothing in the paper but bare announcement and ads), he said "refused" as if he were rather shyly sorry. —The lobsters—look out for that now!—They had holes in the bag for air—she did want to see—"will it excite your appetite?—I have to do this—I like to eat 'em, though!"—all the butter was melted for the lobsters—thick slices of bread—glass jar with some dried peanut butter in the bottom—more alcohol—the old oaken bucket—view out window of clock tower (grimly reddish) and down straight vistas across the bridge ("What's all this architecture?"), the white classical façade and long low classical-modern-mechanical length of Boston Tech.—Tarzan of the Apes—he had to withdraw to eat the claws, legs, etc.—his salmon casting. *Forsaken, forsaken*—apparently moved to mention it by an association of ideas arising from *How to get Gerty, that doggone hard-to-get gal*—eating and drinking, but?—her front hall's as cold as an ice-cream freezer—she will go out, but she won't give in—Wendell's blue-banded unbecoming yellowish panama and his blue car—he was nervous that morning—"I'm in no mood to sit still!"—I complimented the girls on their white teeth, bright eyes and clear skins—Henrietta said, "It's just the inclemency of the weather"—the repulsive, touching, bespeckled, pale-haired and -eyed Irish waitresses who brought me an all-white-meat

chicken sandwich with giblet gravy and three poor inch-long banana frit-
ters (30¢) in that awful upstairs South Station restaurant reached by an elevator where it's terribly difficult to get hold of the operator—while I, daze-
minded and -eyed with alcohol, read that full-page *World* editorial about
Sacco and Vanzetti [they were executed August 23, 1927]: to make room
for it, the weather had been crowded out onto another page—the cartoon
of Massachusetts between Justice and Death—the arrest of Powers Hapgood on the Common—"I am innocent of these two harms" [Vanzetti's
words] (reason why Henrietta thought Vanzetti guiltless)—on the train, at
a station, the autumnal soft low sound of voices in wet weather on a late and
earlier-darkening afternoon, in mackintoshes and dark capes, greeting one
another, with cars waiting behind, at summer resorts on the lower end of
the Cape—I was getting sober—it made me feel lonely—the close of the
American summer at well-to-do summer resorts of the whole country
—and driving back with the girls at night, the street lamp in the dark-green
damp darkness of late summer, and just turning fall, seen through the
slightly dimming dustiness of the windshield—the street lamp—yellow—
of the prosperous American suburb, seen through the American young
people's windshield of all the country—austere long-roofed white houses,
the houses of the seacoast, in the darkening day, and then a long lovely strip
of silver, under the cloudless graying sky, which I presently perceived was
the sea—the black ponds and rivers of New England, beautiful, dense—
precious effects, seen from the uncomfortable, too-close-together and hard-
black-leather-upholstered seats of the smoker.—At Peaked Hill, I found the
sea turned cold and sheeted with the iron-blue tinsel of fall.

Wire from the girls: "Come at once. Rumpelmayer's men are draining
the old oaken bucket. Forsaken."

Little Johnny (Ufford) with his hoarse little passionate voice which broke
into high forced squeaks like that of a person with a cold—his contention
with June as to whether or not a certain block of wood was to be allowed to
float out to sea, he wanting to let it drift away and she to keep it—but, one
afternoon, when he had come back, after being separated from Nancy, he
kissed her little bare arms and stomach with the most astonishing
fervor—"Oh, Nancy!" and then paid June the same affectionate—or
scarcely less affectionate—attentions. —I heard June reading aloud to
Johnny in the next room with her little child's lugubrious voice.

Gray misty sea—with fog and warm dry-misty weather—the waves got
gummed together—they couldn't even break—instead of breaking, they
stuck to the shore and stopped the movement of the waves behind, which
then, could only helplessly, foolishly, heave—dead-fishy stinks, brown

soupy scum in the water—water brimming uglily up beach—dull greenish water.

Going out to the bootlegger's barn, past the misty graveyard—the trees about the dark mass of the house, ink-velveted silhouettes blotted on gray.

Harry Kemp wanted to go to St. Pierre islands, where they bring you wine in milk bottles every morning, but he didn't know what to do with his cat—would desert a child without compunction, but couldn't abandon a cat. His wife, when she left the cat with him, had known that it would keep him domestic even though she was getting a divorce.

Nobel's wife (Miss Provincetown) (Nobel was another coast guard) had announced her intention of taking on every man in the station—she was behind in her book for the Christmas club.

Ufford. Hippopotamuses are easily teased—he had seen an elephant in the next cage to one putting its trunk in the hippopotamus's mouth. The hippopotamus would snap his jaws shut and the elephant would snatch out its trunk—the elephant was so perfectly sure of its stuff. Here were these great rows of teeth ready to shut to crush it!

Dudley Digges's story about Moore and Yeats (the Diggeses came out to see me at Peaked Hill): *Diarmuid and Granya*, first written in English by Yeats—then translated into French by Moore, then into Irish by Douglas Hyde, then into English by Lady Gregory. —Moore went to Paris—Yeats to Sligo—telegrams, Moore to Yeats: "Put more lust into Granya!" —It was finally played by a company of English actors, which included Walter Hampden—they read all the Syngian lines with strong English accents:—"It's myself heard her say." Hampden, asked what it was like, had forgotten except that it was a "very painful experience."

Provincetown. That infinitely delicate fine wrought-ironwork filigree, metallic and foliate, against the brilliant clearness of the blue and white diamond-summer sky—in thin diamond sheets, cloudy and clear blue.

Harry Kemp. Went to a party at Provincetown where they had absinthe cocktails—got drunk, wrote everybody poems, offered hostess to write her a poem, if she would give him another drink—thunderstorm: he offered to conjure it away—hocus-pocus with candles, knelt down, went all around the house—storm actually stopped—he threatened to bring it back unless they gave him another drink.

Dawn today—the sea so smooth, such faint and tender blue and, in the light-blue sky above, a few clouds tinting delicately pink like shells—the faint surf fringing the silk of the sea with a light swish and a little silver.

Provincetown street. Girl to boy in house: "You were so snooty—we called up when we went by in the car, but you didn't answer."

—Those sneakered girl's feet—the American afternoon of all the country—they spoke to me with an unmistakable flavor—some largeness and crudeness of the life of youth which then seemed to me poetic and strange.

The Hapgoods. One brother had stayed behind in the factory and finally taken to democratizing the business—Norman and Hutchins were horrified—Susan Glaspell tried to kid Hutch Hapgood about it—but he said, "I can't joke about it—it touches me too closely."

Harry Kemp said that on the days when Frank Shay was sober, he couldn't make his motor bookshop go, and on the days when it would go, he was drunk.

The Italian landlords in the Village used to give restaurant keepers short-term leases, then when the place had been equipped and the business built up, turn out the tenants and run the restaurant themselves.

Man who used to take his family to live in haunted houses, because the rents were always so low.

Brawl that Polly Halliday and Frank Shay got into—knowing the technique of disorderly Village parties, she had thrown herself on Frank; but the host, "believing in the equality of the sexes," hit her and cut her lip.—When one of the guests, just driving off, tried to tell the host that he thought he behaved badly, the latter smashed him one in the jaw.

Harry Kemp. Story about Jack O'Brien and Fitzsimmons—Jack O'Brien knocked out Fitzsimmons—but Fitzsimmons was old then—Jack found out that Fitzsimmons's mother and father were in the poorhouse in Ballyrat in Australia, and when the fight began, he said, "You know where I'm going to send yuh?"—"Where are yuh going to send me, Jack?"—"I'm going to send you right back to Ballyrat to join your old man and your old woman in the poorhouse!"—Harry Kemp had said, "Well, don't you think that was kind of a mean thing to do, Jack?"—Jack said, "Well, yuh know: I just thought of that! I guess it was!"—Somebody began a fight with the gentlemanly Tunney by saying, "You oughtn'ta be a prizefighter, yuh fuck—yuh ought to be a bootblack!"—and again, when he was being presented to some hard-boiled old prizefighter, the latter said, "I'll get you next!" etc.

Harry Kemp would just get ready to put his cat in a bag and drop him in the water, when the cat would come and put her paw on his arm and he'd say, "No, by God, you darn old bugger—I'll stick by ye!"

His vanity kept him from working with a group. —He was a mountebank—but couldn't be a showman in a big way—because he didn't *believe* in putting things over in a big way—he believed in doing them in a small way and having something big come out of them—like O'Neill out of the Provincetown Players. —He used to go around to the restaurants with a cowbell to get people to come to his show—his wife didn't approve of this. —On one occasion he became so much preoccupied with other things that he forgot to send out announcements and there were only three people there the opening night.

Anecdote about O'Neill—had had such difficulty establishing contact with him—so thought him offish and, coming out to the beach one day, Harry decided to pass him by, simply saying, "Hello," and without any attempt to engage him in conversation—so he went on the beach and sat down and presently heard this pat-pat-pat like a big St. Bernard dog—O'Neill said, "You know, I'd have liked to be a prizefighter, too—but I got a blow once that loosened all my teeth."

Harry Kemp said that what had kept Jimmy Light from ever being a great producer was the fact that he tried to make the actresses. —In the old days—no Jewish angels to be flattered—if they had money, they spent it all on the production—if anybody came along who didn't get along with the group, they didn't bother with him.

New York

Hortense Alden. I think all marriages are incongruous, but I think that one (Jimmy Light and his wife) is particularly incongruous—(Why?)—becau᷐ he's an Anglo-Saxon—and she's (shrugging)—oh, I dono!—Oriental Western—That's not really an English accent, you know! (she had a stage-flapper accent herself). —Penetration of the Jews at detecting each other's impostures and hypocrisy and gratification in exposing them.

Bingham, the Industrial Psychologist. His live-eyed partially desiccated wife, not entirely devoid of charm—he himself a little bald colorless man, with a lifeless sucked-in mouth and little dead holes of eyes—his precise professional speech: "Well, I think there's nothing to consider about that." (I was trying to rent his house.) When I asked Mary about him: "Well, he gave me 100 in Psychology, when I hadn't opened a book, and I know there must have been some reason."

At early evening in New York, a girl standing at a doorway on the street beside a man, with her arm behind her in a square American angle, so that she could hold his hand.

A legless man with his trunk in a leather case dragging himself along with his hands in a great pair of dirty yellow leather gloves—crossing the road at the feet of the traffic and lifting himself up the curb, while people watched him smiling.

Dorothy Parker. Had the mumps—Don Stewart, Marc Connelly and Benchley had been there in the afternoon—Don had been "screeching": "I *will* touch you!—I *will* show you that I'm your friend!" to the amazement of the doctor—Benchley had been drunk, to her knowledge, for eleven weeks—he was "in all different pieces"—he had written a musical comedy and they had massacred it so that he wouldn't go near it. —Marc Connelly had been drowning his cares because his play had been a flop—"I like soft burlesque for breakfast—Atwater Kent be the Atlantic."

I had got to know Anna at the Tango Gardens, a cheap dance hall on Fourteenth Street.

Anna. Stepfather a big, fat, awful-looking guy—we were measurin' ourselves—we have a lotta fun when I'm not sore at'um. —We were measurin' ourselves and it's as big aroun' his thigh as it is around my waist—I'm 34 aroun' the waist, see, and he's 34 aroun' the thigh—an' my mother supports'um—she gives'um money!—he was arrested along with my husband—they found'um in a stolen car—he got five years and Sam only got one—When I think of my mother cuddlin' up to'um!—when I go past the door of her room and see her cuddlin' up to'um in bed—I could just go in and smack her—Honestly it's an awful thing to say, but I'd rather have my mother dead than livin' with a guy like that! (He was Russian; she was Ukrainian.)

The party—christening her sister's baby—a big time—$200 worth of liquor—alcohol—all kinds of drinks—fellow in love with her—but she would'un even give'um a tumble, see—he follows me aroun' and looks at me—they kidded her about him—he's just crazy for one thing, I suppose, and after he got that, he would'un care anything about me any more—at the party he'd sit beside her and say, oh, Anna, let me hold your arm and when somebody would come up to dance with her, he'd say, "You can't dance with her!"—"Can't dance with her, Jesus!"—Italians, Jews, don't you know what they all were. —When I asked her if she thought of me: "Yes, always." —They made her do all the cooking, sleep in the base-ment—mother brought stepfather breakfast in bed—never did that for her—when she had been pregnant—the stepfather had been too much for her father-in-law's family. —The boy who bothered her—she just gave him an awfully strong drink and he was out like a light.

White soft skin of face with a little pinkness—wet red mouth—passionate for so soft and frail a girl—blind kisses—nothing but those wet meeting mouths.

Horrors of the street. Pretty young mother with dirty homely baby in baby carriage.

Negro girl with gruesome rush of teeth to the front.

I saw a man standing against the brick wall of a lunchroom, and it seemed to me at first that he had no head, his cap was pulled so far down over his eyes that it looked like a decapitated neck, and his body was unusually short.

Man on street with too narrow face and head too narrow and pinched-in at temples—like a wooden head which had accidentally or purposely been carved in the wrong proportions.

At Seabright, blond girl in light blue bathing suit lying on face on sand, with bath towel over her buttocks. —Little tow-haired girl in thick black sweater with an almost collegiate neck, examining a handful of shells.

Rosalind's little German box of blocks, which Mother bought her for ten cents—so simple and so attractive—the true German taste for toys—thin plain wood box with sliding cover, on which appeared four colored pictures of buildings, with little pine trees and palm trees set around them, which could be constructed with the blocks and into which were compactly packed the carefully proportioned square strips half this width, the special beams stained brown and intended to diversify and distinguish the monuments created, the small cork-like green nubbins of pillars, the slim-legged arch with the square top upon which further constructions could be erected, the red arch with the round back, the little solid half circle that made a useful ornament—each of these last sawed neatly out of the one before, so that no wood had been wasted and all fitted compactly into the box—and, finally, most elaborate and, as it were, luxurious and interesting, a little section of stream to be used when one of the arches was made to span a river—deep indigo blue and curled with five corrugated waves like a tiny washing board—economy, propriety, proportion—a droll and impeccable taste—simplicity and beauty. —Another German toy, also very cheap—say a quarter—the rooster that came out and crowed when you unlatched the door of the coop—American toys—such as that cat in Boston—often so ugly one won't buy them.

Baby in baby carriage perched on ledge of subway construction—child on roller skates who falls—women crowd around agonizedly crying child—abnormally fat woman, dropsical perhaps, with gray loose wispy hair, lifting garbage pail.

A thin beak-nosed woman with head turned to one side seemed to me to have a twisted neck.

Cummings on Sacco and Vanzetti. I asked him what A. Lawrence Lowell was like: "Well, he was one of my father's greatest friends!—he goes around everywhere with a little poodle whose balls trail on the ground and make the letter H.—that's what he's like!—I've known several of these young men who are being groomed—groomed is the word!—for big positions—First, their teeth go—then they wear glasses—then, you mightn't believe it, but it's really so!—they have to be seen at certain places on Fifth Avenue, at certain times, with a silk hat!—and if they do that and are always on hand and make calls and suck pricks—after a while somebody dies, and they stand up and put on their silk hats and take out their pricks, and, if they've been good, they get the job.—When Henry dies, you get to be Lee, and when Lee dies, you become Higginson! There's a kind of collar he [Lowell] wears that's part of the tradition—my father was supposed to be part of the tradition, too, but he dressed like a gentleman—he wore a wing collar—but Lowell wears a kind of a thing that's just wrapped around his neck, and there's a kind of little black bow tie that they have to wear with it that gets way up on one side under their coat—Mrs. Royce will say, 'Now, Josiah, you've forgotten your necktie!' and he'll say, 'Well-well-well-well!—so I have!—what a wonderful thing it is to have a woman around!'—so they wrap this old dried condom around their necks—and their Adam's apple falls out—you were speaking of old with-ered hollyhocks—well, Lowell has a neck like that—there's something indecent about it!—it's like the man standing in the street corner—he says to the cop, 'Am I pissing?'—and the cop says, 'No'—and he says, 'Well, I ought to be—my fly's open!'

"You've no idea how many wives are turning cute on their husbands this year—[Is that so?]—Why, you never saw anything like it!—You'll see Mr. and Mrs. X walking together one day, arm in arm, and then the next day you'll come along and the woods will be all cut down and the under-growth cleared away—and signs up, Don't Litter!' "

Anna. She thought she was oiling the sewing machine—oiling it all up nice, you know—and it had some kind of glue—mucilage—oh, it's all stuck up now!—you ought to heard my mother!—her mother was Ukrainian and spoke a lot of other languages, too—her sister never drank nor nothing—she could have married lots of fellows with money, but when this greaseball came along, she was just wild about'um [an Italian]—her stepfather had tried to get in bed with her one night—Sam must be crazy—he'd take a cat, you know, and put it up on a wall and tie a rope around its neck so that if it jumped it'd hang itself and then of course it would jump and he'd stand there and laugh to see it hang itself—and he'd roll off the roof right into the snow in the wintertime—you know—oh, I'm tellin' you, he must have been cuckoo.

They scorned her at Oswego (where her husband's parents lived) because she didn't play bridge—his high-hat aunt from Long Island—his uncle's a pretty big man—didja ever hear ov'um?—seen in car—he was lovin' it up with his aunt in the front seat—puttin' his hands all over her—I was calling her all the worst names I could think of—in the back seat—you know—but she was too drunk to hear me—he got $100 from her—she was too drunk to know what he was doing—his father and brother made love to her when they were drunk—high-hatted her when they were sober—

It was the stepfather who got five years with Sam the first time he was arrested—the man who'd had the speakeasy that the stepfather afterwards owned and where Anna now tried working for a night and got disgus'ed—used to write poetry and he leff some of the poetry when he leff—he did'un look the kind that would write—he was a big husky guy.

October 15—she would have to begin giving the tenants heat—

difficulty of getting a dispossession paper—tenants paid up, however, so
that she was saved the trouble— She was afraid of that damn furnace—when the pressure would begin to go up and up—once when it
began to go up and up, she had to rush out of the house and get one of the
neighbors in to fix it—she was afraid it would blow up the house!

She had loved Sam more than me but Sam didn't throw her the way I
did—she used to kiss'um all over just the way I did her—I don't believe
there was an inch of his body I didn't kiss!—I don't suppose he minded it.
Sam's was longer than mine, but it hurts nice—you know what I mean?—
the doctor had said she was very passionate, wasn't she? because the opening
of her womb was so small—her cousin did'un care anything about it, but
she did it every night because her husband liked it, you know—she thought
her cunt (I never heard her use the word, she always called it "it") was an
awful-lookin' thing—didn't know about her clitoris—washed it but didn't
look at it—didn't mind a man's—when Sam used to make me touch it, I'd
pull my hand away quick, you know, but I'd get the thrill of my life—one
night they came back drunk, and Sam made her kiss it, etc., and she did it all
night and liked it, too—that was the reason why, when Sam was in jail, you
know, he thought I couldn't be faithful to'um—because I was so passionate—but it was true: I loved Sam so that I didn't want to do it with anybody
else—there was one boy I saw that would throw me because he looked so
much like Sam, and I used to dance with'um, and I thought if he ever kissed
me I'd just pass away—I'd think about'um—and then he took me out inuz
car and kissed me, and I didn't like it at all: I was just disgus'ed and made'um
take me home.

When she came, she'd get a sensation like a thrill that would go through
her from her toes, all through her body, you know what I mean? and she'd
want to scratch and bite—I don't know where I am or anything—didn't
feel the semen, didn't feel herself putting out anything—and (when we
were together) I doan wantcha to go, but if you keep on, it makes me nervous—like me, she enjoyed it more the second time than the first—had had
a dream about me—"What did you dream?"—"What d'ye think? I
dreamed we were doin' it on the sofa at home and my sister came in and
said, 'I guess you needed it pretty bad'"—she had wanted a lovin' so much
once during the summer that she couldn't sleep—she had used to let boys
take her home and then love it up in the hall, but she had never done it with
any of them—"Oh, how I love to love it up when I'm drunk!—because I
have to love somebody to do anything with them, anyhow."

They had lived all over, she had used to ride a bicycle when she was
young—that was the kind of thing they'd do—ride bicycles around (they
worked fast)—her letter and handwriting—Sam so clever that he'd got off
when the stepfather got five years—how Sam had beaten her up when she

came out of the hospital because he thought she'd been flirting with the young doctors, who all clustered around to watch when her doctor examined her, in the ward behind the screen—"He's crazy, I'm tellin yuh!"—he had told her he was an auto salesman, but what he did was steal cars. Where did he live?—"Doan ask me! he lives all aroun'—lives with his friends." —Driving drunk, man had asked him directions for going somewhere or something of the kind from the street. Anna had tried to disentangle Sam's drunken part of the talk from the other man's—she had tried to take over the conversation herself, Sam had knocked her down with the baby in her arms—loved'um just the same—was thinking the other day that she had only taken up with me to spite Sam—he'd bring other women home—can yuh beat it! Arrested for drunken driving—waiting in garage, tried to stick up garage man—carrying concealed weapons—would have gotten off through showing his Burns badge—but it was she who gave him away in court, told about the forged check he had made her write in his uncle's name—then they called up Burns and asked about um—I think it was Monday night and that it was while waiting for Burns that he stuck a man up. —Uncle and aunt, they're finished with'um, would'un do anything to help'um—afterwards she was tormented by conscience, hoped he wouldn't get too long a sentence—when she came home and told her family about it, they congratulated her.

Her worry about the child in Oswego, when his family had put her in a home—later on, desperate to get her back, she cried about it, thought how she had hit her and knocked her down—if she could only get her back, she'd never do that again!

The time she and her mother had gone to Coney Island and let themselves be picked up by two men who took them for sisters. —It was fine with her mother when her stepfather and sister went there. —Her mother liked to step out sometimes herself, yuh know.

Her pale little passionate face in the half light with that mouth moist, and always ready, more like a sexual organ than a mouth, felt the tongue plunging into it almost like intercourse—liked to cuddle up at night—cuddled up with her mother when she slept with her—her mother would push her away—I don't know what I do to her. —Responds so easily with that rhythmic movement—quickly catches rhythm—to any stimulation—("Well, do you want me to bite it off?")

She had had three teeth excavated, but didn't have enough money to get them filled.

I asked her where she liked best to be kissed—"I like it all!"—never had been kissed except on the face by Sam—at first resisted being kissed on neck, breasts, etc. (her coquetry one night, when I tried to take down her chemise: "only one")—"Don't you like it?"—"In a way!"—They were sitting around talking once—"You know, when we're sitting aroun' talking like that, we'll say anything! and my cousin and the rest of them were telling about where their husbands would kiss them, and Sam said [mimicking his heavy masculine declaration]: 'I never kiss my wife anywhere but on the mouth!'"

Her soft little face with its white tender skin and its shadows, as she was sitting half upright on the bed, with the bathroom door half open, her eyelids lowered at my compliments—her round and attractive legs from under the short skirt of her pale blue dress, rather snappily draped. —She had borrowed $80 from her friend Doris in order to buy the dress (wouldn't think it cost $80, would you?) with its dim gold and red transparent skirt (that's transparent velvet, yuh know—the latest thing), which was so smartly short and contrasted so with her white stockings that it made me want to put my hand on her solidly crossed thighs—her bloomers, worn by calculation when I first saw her—"I wear them on purpose—when I'd go out with a boy, you know, and he'd try to put his hand up my clothes—when they touch your skin, they go wild."

I didn't like her habit of not washing herself after intercourse ("To hell with that!")—Odor associated with Tango Gardens—garlicky breath, which I liked—bad breath after night out, smell smothered with cigarettes—she wouldn't drink if you were watching her—her hair falling back in that womanly fashion—unaffected by bobbed hair—head hanging off edge of couch, "Sweetheart!"—deep husky city voice in amorous bed—"Oh, don't!—Oh, yes!—What did you say?"—straining back with the pillow under her buttocks—my part rendered unsatisfactory and imperfect with condoms, especially so after the first time—only difference for her was that it "didn't slip as easy"—her shyness, modesty, gentleness—"I don't know what you call them: I call them balls"—sliding her hand under my bathrobe—she'd have to know me a long time before she'd do with me what she used to do with Sam—"only whores do that, you'll think I'm a perver' whore!"—I didn't like her pinching me under my chin—Sam hadn't liked it either.

Had once been all nice and plump—"my scrawny neck"—skinny—not pretty any more—they didn't like her any more at the Tango Gardens—didn't think she was pretty at home.

Little cunt rather far back and not capaciously opening, very little hair, but more than there had been since she'd been shaved at the hospital. —The strains of the melody of coming prolonged in moanings over her neck.

How she and her cousin had measured their husbands' cocks—when Sam came out of jail, they must have done it for twenty-four hours—he hadn't had any for a year and a half—the bed creaked so they had to put the mattress on the floor. —"Well, for heaven's sake! I was only seventeen when I

was first married—I wanted to go to sleep on the couch, but my mother—
she was right in the next room—heard me and Sam arguing, and she said,
'Go in, Anna: don't be foolish, go to bed!'—so finally went to bed
with 'um, but I rolled myself up in the blanket. —He'd just kiss me and then
he'd go right to it." —Her family kept rubbing it in to her that she was the
kind of girl who'd never be able to get another man.

A long slow meditative process with lapsings and pauses—"Shall I
come?"—"Yes—no—just as you want—I don't care!"—I came three
times then!—a man only comes just once and then it's all over!—Wanted
to do something so ba'ly. —Pretty in her white pajamas with blouse
open—pale skin, eyes which were softened and looked dark, yellowy hair.

Climax of fellatio, that light infinitely soft and sweet caress. —Sometimes, afterwards, I would see her face coarsened by sensuality and weari-
ness—I thought then that human flesh could look like clay.

She used to sleep curled up to fit my back and with my cock in her
hand—she had always slept that way with Sam. Couldn't go to sleep unless,
etc. —When I had her naked and her little middle elevated by pillow—the
little narrow lozenge of her cunt, which had such a slight lining of hair,
seeming charming, with her rather slender legs and feet extended and
drooping wide. —I used to stroke it and caress it with my tongue—it was
so pretty it would make me linger and preoccupy me, so that I almost forgot
to do anything else.

Red Bank—first of subnormally warm November. Coming out at night into
glass door, into the air in which cold crispness was beginning to be felt, as
when the first ice splinters web a pond, and the outside vestibule framed in
white, where the pale daisy-like cosmos and a rose from which I caught a
chilly fragrance had been set in vases for the night—outside, the chilling air,
the lawn glittering with the wet of autumn rain, the pavement lightly dappled with leaves—all a delicious delicacy of iciness, thin glass and silver-
leaf, fall-leaf fragrance.

Lyle Saxon's story about the fellow whose girl kept on eatin' an apple all
the time he was friggin' her. —Edna, when I told her of this, said it ought to
be illustrated and called "Deflowered."

Gill Wylie's story about football coach at school who scolded boy,
during game, for *slugging*—boy slugged him back, gave him a black eye—
the coach didn't do anything to him for it. The Old Man's (coach's) act:
"Who dye think yuh are? A prima donna? Who told yuh yuh could be so
indegoddampendent?"

Going into the deserted library at the Charter Club, the night of the
Princeton–Ohio game—the shut-up autumn room—a whiff of undergra-

duate days—Scott Fitzgerald—all dark save for the big-shaded, dark-shaded lamps throwing thinning circles on the table and one end of the couch—the dark woodwork, the mulberry carpet—the furniture all turned about, grouped for twos and fours, the rounded-out seat on the couch, the faint tobacco smell with the college smell of the woodwork—heavy furniture, upholstered and oak—the matches and cigarettes on the floor—I went in: the faint and rare smothered spark of the cold fire and the sound of the phonograph, remote, coming up from the dark lounge below (*Sundown*)—there was a pint whiskey bottle lying in it. —A thousand emptied college rooms, from which the girls and men had gone—I felt in it the more complete and definite desertion of commencement. —It brought me back at first to the thing itself, then made me melancholy.

—**A** bit of cracker—a wet towel on the floor outside the shower room.

—**Party** downstairs: had run out of drinks—Who would go to **Kingston**?—wonder if they can go to dance without dressing—girls eager to do something but boys letting them down—boy finally confesses he'd go, but hasn't any money—girl plays piano a little and rather well—they play with the club cat, girl says he has sad eyes "from living in this club"—it is cold, the boys also stall on building a fire—again propose going to the dance: girl says, "I'll bet my last tail feather they won't let us in!"—boy replies, "You lost that last tail feather long ago!"—girls look at all the magazines: *Spur, Theatre, Judge*—finally begin pairing off—there are three boys and only two girls—probably that was the trouble all the time. —They had also suggested sliding down the banisters—but "everybody has to start at the top." —The sound of a girl's nice laughter—slow—as they were going.

—The boy said of cats, "They have those whiskers so that they won't bump into things in the dark, you know."

The girl said: "Yes, did you ever cut them off?—I used to cut off all my cat's whiskers."

—In the bathroom, all the sheaf of attached towels taken from the shelf and piled up in a great bulging white damp clump at the bottom of the bent rod.

—That prolonged, very well played music—went on and on—I didn't know why—Chopin—

—haunted, in library, by idea that I was keeping them from petting there—I heard him, I thought, pretending to escort her to the bathroom. The girl said: "Is there a toilet up here?—Well, if there's not, there will be soon!"—"Then, go down again—It must be down below."

Pomegranates I had purchased for Katze, thinking they would be good subjects for pictures. Kept them a day in my room and they began to deliquesce—all syrupy and slimy on the outside. When I had brought them back the next night and picked one up to eat it, my fingers sank into it—I ate two over the wastebasket—they were bright slimy red inside and rather sickeningly sweet. When I picked up the paper bag to throw it, with the last one, into the wastebasket, it fell through the soaked paper onto the floor with a dull wet squash.

"Burn your clothes, kid! This is heaven!"

"It smells on ice!"

Florence at Barrow Street—elaborate and delicious dinners cooked by Ted Leisen—her hair was washed and beautifully blond, her skin much pinker than usual; she wore a blond soft blue scarf with white dapplings—the way she would comically go into the kitchen or start off along the hall to the theater with me, clumsily heavily stamping and shuffling.

That cold night we went out to walk the dog, after Florence had come back and found the key with a note signed P. I. Q. U. E. from Ted—it was very cold and bracing when I kissed her at the door, it was a delicious light cold and faintly moist kiss—like the flowers in the glass porch at Red Bank.

"Mad money" (if she had to walk home)—she spoke about her negative attitude nowadays—she didn't want to have too good a time on account of what would happen afterwards—the French Club—the man with the exciting concertina, which reminded her of her days in Paris—*On fait ça en douce sur les fortifications*.

How she had been dressed in the little hoopskirt in *Sunny*, with curls and everything, and had looked so sweet that Henry de Wolf said he felt as if he'd like to smack her down.

In those days, the Notre Dame boys had broken the glass of the show pictures outside the theater and stolen her photograph and put it in the college magazine.

Anna. Fucking in the afternoon with her dress on—different from anything else—rank satisfactory smell—peculiar zest, on these hurried occasions, added by shoes and stockings and dress, which would be discouraging and undesirable at a regular rendezvous at night.

Her aunt had commented on the fact that she hadn't had no bumps or black eyes since Sam left, but here she was with two black eyes again, when Doris had been drunk and she hit her head against the wall of the toilet and Doris had struck out at her.

She was so sweet the night I read her poetry: "Will I understand it? I'm so dumb!" I read her Yeats's "Never Give All the Heart":

> He that made this knows all the cost,
> For he gave all his heart and lost.

I asked her what she thought it meant, and she said at first that she knew but couldn't explain it—then said, "Like me with Sam, for instance!"

Edna [Millay]. She seemed well and normal again, almost robust—no make-up, a dreary white-flecked gray dress, which, however, she insisted, had come from a very expensive and good place. Her hands and feet and ankles were so much larger than they used to be that I could hardly believe they were the same ones I had loved. Nor did her throat seem so beautiful—I think her putting on flesh had spoiled its contour—and her mouth, which seemed thicker than it used to, revealed two big square front teeth.

She liked that story about Joe Cook and the shower of which he had boasted that it didn't get you wet—I said that it was just like life, as she had said about the mantelpiece at Sixteenth Street in the old days. —Her servant, who had read books and asked of scrubbing the bathtub, "But is this beautiful?" or something of the sort. —When I remarked with a nuance of scandal, that [A. E.] Housman was homosexual, she said, "All nice people are, I think."

Julius's, December 1927 [I was writing the essay on Yeats in *Axel's Castle* and used to go there when I had finished working, very late at night. It was a more or less horrible bar, which sold Prohibition beer, but was the only place open all night]. Crowd, extraordinary pictures, Mabel Normand, etc.—amiable bartender, with old-fashioned sweetness and geniality, rose complexion, toothbrush mustache and black oiled curly hair—disagreeable assistant, who gypped me on two beers ("That'll be a dollar!")—stuffed alligator as big as a horse, posed sprawling against the mirror. Free lunch.

Polly Halliday presently emerged from a crowd where I'd thought I knew nobody—she seemed to know everybody; knew old man with big black shoe-string bow tie and beard, who turned out to be editor of an Anarchist paper (Hippolyte Havel). Cecil Fiske (Agnes O'Neill's sister) also appeared in corner—red-eyed, very drunk, indiscriminately amorous, but still with her pre-Raphaelite hair. —Her husband—I couldn't tell whether he was the same one I had seen before with Hemingway in the cab, who had merely shaved his beard and acquired a Hemingway line—as he told me how much he admired Hemingway, when I mentioned him, and kept saying, "Have another drink!" and then not ordering any. He treated her abominably—said, "Did you ever see any low Irish worse than that"—and abandoned her completely. He kept wanting to drink to Herman Melville: "Drink to the same man!"

Anarchist (HH): "Morse Lovett and all those nice boys might just as well be writing for an anarchist paper!" —Of W. Z. Foster: "He's an intellectual!"; of Mike Gold: "He's an intellectual!" —"The Socialists, the Communists, the Anarchists! they can't write a single sentence!" I had said that Anarchists must be having a big boom now—but he replied that they weren't, because *we* were writing so many articles: —A Babbitt in the corner asked him whether he wanted to see people killed, or something of the sort. He clasped his forehead and gasped—I explained that an Anarchist wasn't necessarily a person who wanted to blow up other people—great difficulties: Anarchist disgusted, wandered off, wandered back and sat turned away from the table, looking into his spectacles. Babbitt: "I can ask her questions [Polly H.] and she'll answer them. Why can't he?" I tried to explain. "Somebody mistakes you for a clothier when you're really a banker." He replied, "I want to find out! I've talked with Democrats, Republicans, Socialists." Havel: "Why don't you read our literature?" "Who the hell wants to read your literature?" —Horrible-looking man, faded hair and pale eyes, incredibly wide mouth—looked more like an ape than anyone else I had ever seen, when he said, "Newton Baker wrote a lot of articles!" Havel had said that once *The Atlantic Monthly* had had a certain prestige in Europe, had represented a certain culture, etc.; now America had no standards. When the Babbitt made this retort, Havel's attitude was, "What's your idea in bringing that up?" —But later he complained (the ape man), when I saw him in the urinal, that that was the trouble with New York, or any place in America, for that matter: that you couldn't find interesting people to talk to, people who knew anything.

Great scrap afterwards between Irishman and Fiske: former didn't believe that latter was, as he asserted, Irish—an Irishman come from Ohio—began challenging each other on ancestry, etc. —When I had asked Cecil about Agnes (O'Neill): "Yes, I've got to see her and Gene during Christmas week, damn it!"—or something of the sort. —Fiske's boastful New Englandism: three kinds of Yankees and nutmeg Yankees. "Which are you?" "You think I'm drunk!" I thought at one stage of the proceedings, when Havel asked me to take care of Polly (after he had told me that he had got her off of Ward's Island), that he was going to leave her on my hands, but he stuck to her quite decently to the end.

Obnoxious man in golf stockings, who was said to have been a judge, whom I called the Duke and who seemed to be dead set to get a girl. When he tried to waylay Polly Halliday, she said that she was my wife. His apologies, his insistence on joining us. (I'd never seen Julius's so crowded.)

Cecil's losing and finding her hat and losing it again. —Departure of Babbitt and his wife and Irish friend. Polly Halliday wanted a cigarette—I had only four cents left and tried to borrow one. Finally, wife of Babbitt—who had hitherto taken no part in the conversation and was no doubt rather miffed by her husband's preoccupation with Polly and Cecil—proffered one, hoping, as she said, that the next time *they* wouldn't have any cigarettes so that Polly could pay them back. The look of Polly's teeth and eyes.

Literature as the result of continual stress and strain in the universal organism—when the whole organism has, as it were, been reimagined and re-created so as to eliminate stress and strain; then art will have become unnecessary, because the whole universe will be a work of art and the "creative" energies of humanity will be merely occupied in its advancement (this last situation is inconceivable as, as I have stated it, nonsensical).

The artist's conception of what he is going to produce is something far less personal than what results—because he is really, in reimagining things, striving toward a completeness which is beyond the powers of the individual human being—and the artist's mannerisms, his strongly marked style, which his admirers particularly savor, may really, from the point of view of his ambition and his first conception, represent merely the limitations of habit, the lapse into the line of least resistance, the regretted but inescapable stigmata—like a can tied to a dog's tail—of his physical peculiarities, his family failings and the limitations of his nation and race. —If he has been successful, it will, to be sure, be true that he has introduced a harmony among these, that he has made them play their part in the production of some kind of generally appreciable beauty—but, on the other hand, this process may be effected on any level, however low, of idiosyncrasy or limitation, and a work equally perfect—though not of equal range or general importance—may be produced; the aesthetic impulse—like any other manifestation of life—finds the means of adapting itself, of surviving, even in the most unfavorable environment. —It is therefore ridiculous to say that a trifle that is perfect has the same value as a great epic or a symphony. There is an analogy between the Shakespeare or the Dante, who has such a comprehensive view of life and can do so many different things with his art, and man among the other animals.

Don't forget history—Burke, G. B. Shaw, immediately, in their pamphlets, painting the coating of reason and art over contemporary events and thereby reassuring people (Burke on the French Revolution, Shaw's *Commonsense about the War*). When things happen, they do not seem to happen in the world of literature—except in that cultivated conversation which is a form of literature—but in a barbarous animal world, bloody, ignoble, uncontrollable—we must at once adopt an attitude toward them, whether comic, tragic or scientifically detached—we must divert our fellows from simply groping or from becoming panic-stricken, like people staring at a street accident or stampeding out of a burning theater—and that attitude is embodied in literature.

Philosophy and Logic—also Scholarship—e.g., Verrall: —One says this position is open to certain serious objections, or this position presents certain serious difficulties—merely a dignified and pompous way of expressing one's abject ignorance and the ludicrous puerile inadequacy of the only accounts one can give of the conditions of our existence. —The primary difficulties of Logic: the further one pursues truth, the less certainty one has to be content with it—Russell, in his preface to *Principles of Mathematics*, says that the book originally had been provoked by his attempt to deal with more abstract principles than it was possible for ordinary language to handle—the limitations and dubious aspects of this method—the Whitehead–Russell taste for paradox. (Whitehead on Bradley's "mistake" in his logic: If B is to the left of A, and C is to the left of B; then C is to the left of A.)

And writers who were noted for *sober judgment*!—I remembered that such small reputation as I had achieved was apparently based on the supposed sober judgment of a few literary articles and reviews—yet, except when I was writing about literature, nobody could have worse judgment and I—I was invariably either treating occasions of importance either too casually or too flippantly or extravagantly overdoing other occasions which were intrinsically trivial—disgracefully underestimating or grotesquely overstating—and the sober judgment which, by an effort, I was sometimes able to muster in print was nothing more than compensation for the disappointments and humiliations of a life which never hit the mark or suited the means to the end.

The readers of books—vicarious experience.

The moralists, indulging like Shaw in the ignoble pleasure of making other people feel small, and, if like Mencken, they realize the scandal of this, but still feel the need to scold in the merely different form of the same thing which consists in making people who do this feel small, by denouncing intolerance, the imputation of motives and moral indignation itself.

The basic impossibility of a common denominator between pain and tranquillity—a discord which art tries to resolve.

A writer strains desperately to express something definitely and all that results is incomplete sketches and inconsecutive fragments—which, after his death, are inordinately prized for their personal flavor.

The great convention of all literature which we learn with effort and to which we deliberately ascend from the turbid chaos of life.

Movements dominated by catchwords and jargon, which relieve their adherents from the labor of thinking.

Our incapacity for escaping in our novels and plays from a form which is itself determined by the character of our reproductive activities—either working up to a climax toward the end and then slowly subsiding, like a Greek drama, or working up to a climax and then stopping, like a modern one.

Men and women writers so closely identified, each with its separate sex, that it is almost impossible to judge them together—each functions, even as an artist, so completely within the sphere of influence of its sex—tied to that stake and only circulating about it within a narrow radius—so that I hardly knew how to estimate the merits of Christina Rossetti, in relation, say, to Yeats, or those of Jane Austen to Turgenev.

Examples of authors: Housman putting all his sensitive and affectionate heart into sixty or seventy slight lyrics and spending all the rest of his intellect on the reconstruction of the Latin text of a poet inferior to himself and all the rest of his passion upon the excoriation of obscure scholars who have happened not to distinguish themselves in his own field.—(His ungracious public reference at Cambridge to his predecessor—"scarcely touched the fringes of his subject"—Gates's story about the boy at Winchester who asked him about "cannot see the record cut": "You will notice that the cutting of the record is enumerated among the unpleasant things which will happen to the athlete after death—perhaps this will help you to understand the meaning of the poem."—"If Mr. X is unable to understand what I have written in my book, he will not be able to understand what I do not intend to say." —The schoolmaster seen in these letters—the petulance of the schoolmaster.)

Plato's cold fishy side, from his homosexuality.

Works of art perhaps the product of notes excreted, under pressure of quite other interests and emotions, by the necessity of turning the mind to something else, something that could be objectively viewed—something (the work) put together from these fragments.

Confused language of symbols taken and applied literally. —Writers derive from one another, not only by imitating each other's style, technique and ideas in easily recognizable fashions, but also by catching from one another points of view and effects which they put so completely in terms of their own style and temperament that it is impossible for the reader to detect whence the original suggestion has come. Thus, what seems from the outside a significant movement—a case of a number of different people all arriving at the same ideas and forms independently of one another—may really be only a case of all except the first following the line of least resistance—so that they present the spectacle of a rippled and shadowed field of grain, over which a wind is passing, or rather, of a standing file of dominoes of which the first has been knocked over.

Incommensurability of literatures of different periods, countries, classes, kinds of men (practical versus aesthetic) and sexes—errors of attempts to put the arts, which depend merely upon our various senses, which depend upon the kind of environment, the environment of the world, to which we have had to adjust ourselves and conform—Clive Bell trying to base painting upon the analogy with music—the symbolists doing the same thing with poetry, and the critics of the school of Eliot, with their horror of politics, propaganda, popularity and journalism, becoming philosophical and abstract, Allen Tate finding fault with Keats for giving in to the emancipatory views of his time(!)—Eliot insisting upon "skipping" the generation of "Wells, Shaw, Strachey and Hemingway"(!) doing the same sort of thing in another way—though they insisted upon "amoral interest" (and found Baudelaire important for this reason—Eliot took his Christianity so seriously)—Varèse's geometrical ideas about his music (he named one composition "Integrale" after the calculus).

The English and the Classics: What they made of them, read into them—Verrall and Gilbert Murray on Euripides—a writer like Aeschylus or Sappho seems to us all the grander and stronger because we do not know precisely what he means—as often happens when we begin reading a foreign language, it may be that things we admire especially as examples of the author's genius are merely formulas or clichés of idea or art.

Literature is merely the result of our rude collisions with reality, whose repercussions, when we have withdrawn into the shelter of ourselves, we try to explain, justify, harmonize, spin into an orderly pattern in the smooth resuming current of a thought which for a moment has been shattered and torn by them—they become mere colors and forms which can soothe and amuse the placidity of other minds or which, in the press of circumstances or actions, can superinduce that state of reflective detachment—for even the highest excitement of imaginative vision *is* a state of reflection and detachment. —Literature is a long process of neutralizing these shocks, mitigating the crude and barbarous, treachery, murder, unrequited love (anomalies must be included as well as crimes)—the constant, never-forestalled outbreaks of our barbarous nature and the accidents of the internal maladjustments of our situation as a part of the universe—we lend them, in art, the logic of our reason and the harmony of our imagination—reason and imagination, like leucocytes accumulating themselves at the place where the infection, in the physical system, has occurred, they rush at once to the breach and, ingesting the alien elements, are discharged in the form of art—so we are able to laugh at or to weep at these casualties, relieving, in the one case, our worried intelligence and, in the other, our balked emotions (through the operation of the aesthetic process, whatever that is), and the wound is presently healed. —Thus, only the works of art—which, like the phagocytes, have really ingested the hostile bacteria, the source of the inflammation, the disturbance of the system's equilibrium—are important and valuable; there must be a struggle with real hostile bacteria, the constantly recurring enemies of the organism. —The produced works of art themselves, which, in a sense, like the white cells, are dead, can never by themselves, i.e., by merely being contemplated, set up the inflammation which evokes the live leucocytes. —It is only by reinfecting the reader—in the case of literature, with a milder form of infection—that works of art may produce more works of art; the puzzled intellect and the baffled emotions are caught over from the work of art and, also, since the works of art are but human, as the leucocytes are—that is, imperfect agents to perform what they are attempting—they exhibit in their own form and texture the anomalies and the tragedies and vices which are inherent in every part of the organism (the great Whiteheadian organism of which the works of art are but parts like the beings that produce them). If these anomalies, etc., are strongly felt—that is, if the critic, having already been invaded by the measles, the diphtheria, the tuberculosis or the syphilis of maladjustment and suffering, is further infected by works of art (to which he perhaps prefers to confine himself rather than risk the more serious, and perhaps for him fatal, infection of life itself)—he may himself produce further works of art. —The analogy, of course, does not hold all along the line and one must not attempt to sustain it absurdly.

The social scenes of *Education Sentimentale*, in which Frédéric is shown rather helpless and stupid among people who are up to all sorts of things which he isn't in on—these effects were imitated by Henry James, as Virgil's effects in the VIth Book of the *Aeneid*—Deiphobus, Palinurus—haunted Dante and were reproduced by him—the former in certain characters of the *Inferno*, the latter in Buonconte.

New York from Liberty Street ferry, November 25. The city through the glass front doors of the ferryboat—the downtown buildings were merely the insubstantial lights of windows—like a cloth irregularly worn held up in front of a light—then when one went outside, like an insubstantial structure of bright yellow wire—or rather, best of all, like the weave of a Wellsbach chimney almost burnt out—erected in the air—a tinselly glitter—insubstantial block, the weight of stone and steel all abolished.

[E. E. Cummings had been married to Elaine Orr; the wedding EW describes was his marriage in 1927 to Ann Barton, which ended in divorce.]

The Cummings Wedding. Dos with his withered bachelor's but-

ton—drinking at Hoboken—they had been stewed for days—married in
what they called "the church of the Holy Zebra"—Dos had put them
through it—Cummings had taken several baths, one after the other: he had
felt his arms and legs getting numb, as if they weren't there—Ann went to
sleep and slept for days and couldn't wake up—awful moment just before
ceremony (Cummings's mother and sister were there) when, after everything had been most nonchalant and amiable, they all suddenly began snapping at one another.

The sad German band—we had them come to the table and play the
wedding march. —Cummings looked unusually washed and well and carried things off with an excellent easy distinguished manner. —Talking
about evening before: somebody had said they didn't like women with thin
arms and legs—Dos had got up, flapping his arms, and said, "I haven't got
thin arms!"—"I don't remember this sudden change of sex," he now said,
when twitted about this by Cummings. "I was a little besotted—just a bit
sodden." —Dos and the orange bitters (in the Cummings apartment, which
had been Ann's): they made his bowels move, and in the bathroom he sang
an aria from some opera. Cummings asked him if he was all right, was afraid
he sang because he was suffering—"Oh, no: just sheer lightness of heart!"

Ann's story about the man who lost his legs in the war, shot his unfaithful
wife and got away on his stumps—wooden legs—fastened his socks up
with thumbtacks—went to a vaudeville show in Montreal and saw a performing bear. When the trainer challenged someone to come up on the
stage and go into the cage with the bear, he walked up, entered the cage,
held down the bear's head and let her bite his wooden legs. The legs became
a part of the act—the man had money but, Ann said, was "adventurous."
But the bear became neurotic: she had only been taught to do those certain
stunts. He finally had to give up the act.

Sound of birds singing, which seemed to emanate—at the restaurant—from an ornamental cluster of glass grapes: "It's those grapes!"
On our way out, we identified it as coming from an aquarium of goldfish
(small and red in dark block of water, decorated with deep green leaves of
plants).

Anna. Her aunt had taken a great interest in her, she had been the only one
of the family her aunt had cared for, but her aunt had a cancer, so Anna
wouldn't go near her. —"I feel awful when I think about it now—how she
wanted to see me so bad and I wouldn't go near her, you know." —Her
mother and aunts had been born in Stanislau in Galicia: her mother spoke
Polish and Yiddish (almost as well as Ukrainian) and her Ukrainian aunt
had a voice and sang at benefit banquets—all the Ukraines would be there
and they'd all dress up, you know, to go—none of her family went, because

they didn't have the clothes—Anna was afraid to see her aunt now, because none of the family went—her grandfather had hated her mother, probably because she'd run off with her father—her grandfather had had money at home, one of the best houses in town, but had lost it all.

Anna and her sister had been put in a home from two to four. They were spanked by the sisters every night. When she got out, she had to work so hard with her mother that she never had a chance to have any fun, washed dishes from the time she was twelve—mother and stepfather used to fight every night—then they'd always make up again in the morning—but Anna would go to bed, you know, crying and praying—and at school she'd always be thinking so much about this that she couldn't put her mind on what she was doing—but they used to ride bicycles around—picture of her when she was at the sisters' home—great big eyes—I don't know what's become of 'um—and my pug nose—(I said it looked cute)—yes, it was—but the clothes! I cerunly looked like an orphan. Mother wanted to move up to Broadway and 125th Street—wanted to get bootlegger stepfather away from his friends—Anna thought that her mother was getting a little cuckoo.

They had lived among Jews and Anna had a Polish girlfriend from whom she learned a lot of Polish—but she'd lost her Ukrainian at the home—and when she came out, she was so bashful that she wouldn't learn to speak it—she'd just look at her mother and not say anything—she always had to say, "Momma, momma" every time to her mother and couldn't address her as "you." —Her mother heard her say to her aunt, "She's gone out and come in furious"—Anna didn't know what it was all about, you know. —Ukraines don't like the Russians.

The time, when she was at the other dance place, that they wrecked it on New Year's Eve—"Oh, they had the boss standin' on his head—givin' exhibitions and everything!"

How lovely she looked in the dull light of the half dark—her eyes Slavic and rich and deep with shadows and her mouth rich and dark red—I was looking up at her from below—her little cheeks and neck and chin looked so soft (they were actually pasty and dry from too much drinking and her eyes green and with irises too close together)—I was gentle and slow with her tonight and she responded at the spasm with intensity, pinching my back or arm, as she hasn't done in some time. (The other afternoon, how pretty and pinky-white smooth soft skin of her thighs looked above her clean white stockings, under her nice light-blue dress, which she now had just cleaned.) When she first came tonight, however, and I looked at her from the middle of the room, the light-blue dress gave her little eyes a forget-me-not look. —Her attitude when I tell her anything is this: "Ye-e-es!"

The night when she had on a red dress and I was drunk and kissed her, just rubbing my mouth against her wet lips, again and again, till it was almost like some kind of intercourse—meaty effect like lips below.

Katze. Franz had committed suicide: When Ted Leisen broke the news of Franz's death, he made wisecracks, said, "Franz has done himself in." She had never heard the expression before, but knew what he meant—had pretty much known before he said anything. At first, thought about what he must have gone through the twenty minutes before he did it—then thought about how he must have looked—then thought about what he might have done if he had lived. —Her sister was coming to live with her—she dreamed about Franz every night. —Her tactics about Helpmann already just what they had been about Franz. She looked quite beautiful, dressed in red, eyes made up and made to slant. —I said I was glad to see her—she said that she didn't know whether she was glad to see me or not.

First part of dinner awful: I felt physically sick; we drank a lot. She told me about Franz's getting into trouble in the army and being stood up before a firing squad—he used to say that he wasn't afraid of anything after that. His sister had drunk poison before his eyes, when he was a boy. He had sat up one night with Katze—slept in a chair all night, for fear she would kill herself, which she had had no idea of doing. —When I first went to get her, she hesitated several seconds before saying, in connection with the doorbell's having been out of order: "The night—that Franz died." She said that she felt gay tonight—kept conversation away from Franz for some time, but any road would have led back to it—Ted Leisen, as it happened, brought her back to the subject, by way of his wisecracks. —Concertina in French Club—we talked about Franz, half drunk, to the sound of the concertina. Ted Leisen kept calling up for Helpmann, just like Franz in the old days when Katze was with me. She was ashamed to admit that there was anything between her and Helpmann, or that she wanted to go to the Leisens' because he was there—said she was at liberty to sit in French Club all night, but kept putting on gloves and saying, "Let's go!"

Cummings at French Club. "This is Dos's idea of heaven!": women who looked like Foxy Grandpa, etc. —"Evewybody's so fwank and fwee!" (Cummings: mimicking Dos Passos.)

Helpmann looked a little like Noël Coward and greatly admired him, wanted to write plays. He said that when he drank too much, he was likely to become "very homosexual" and get into trouble with the police. When I took him to Julius's one night, there was a chunky Indian in an overcoat, with a sugar-loaf-looking hat that was too small for him and stood on the top of his head. Helpmann said, "Who is that man? I like that man!" I thought he was joking; but when we were taking a taxi and the Indian was leaving at the same time, he seemed reluctant to go away and craned out, as I was shutting the door, crying out, "I like that man!"

Margaret. Her father had come from Philadelphia; her grandfather had made money in coal (which, for Margaret, was now giving out). Her father had had softening of the brain. Daisy Waterman, his second wife, never knew him when he was himself—she talks to Margaret about "your dad." Daisy had been a girl in the Haymarket and had been one of the original Floradora quartet—"a little above the kept-woman class." —Margaret's uncle had invested in $10,000 worth of fireworks and set them off in the Bois de Boulogne, and then killed himself. (Dorothy Parker said, when I told her about this: "And those bum French fireworks—probably about only a fourth of them went off!") An aunt used to sit at her window and drop ink on people in the street.

The woman in Paris who wore those great goofy French rings and then used to pick her teeth, flashing the rings all around the room.

The orthophonic record we bought on upper Broadway—we had heard the music emanating from one of those long-distance horns above the door of the shop—we thought it sounded rather like Gershwin in his more serious vein, but when we got it home, we discovered that it was a monstrosity: *Creole Love Call, Black and Tan Fantasy*—"Bla—bla—bla!—I'll never believe in God again, never believe in anything again." Margaret suggested pasting poem about mother love and Bethlehem on it and sending it to Ted. I had bought Mallarmé's *Coup de dés* and *Igitur* at a little bookshop next door to Margaret's apartment.

Margaret was living in a green apartment belonging to Wanda Lyons and her sister—phonograph in bedroom—low luxurious bed—on walls, passionate women in attitudes of abandonment—in bathrooms, pictures of little boys pissing—kitchenette with glass folding doors opening out into living room, convenient for drinks. Looked through Sargent catalogue sitting on divan which let you down so low that it was as much as you could do to get up again. The girls were in Palm Beach—they had left a timid little Scotch terrier bitch.

Dorothy Parker. Embezzle woman in the world. —The rams—the little mean men—the little old man who went around to the nightclubs and nobody knew who he was—Benchley's badger—Marc Connelly's three little owls that roosted in his mouth: of course, they were awfully little, but he didn't like having them there—the other day they tried to bring home a house guest.

Benchley's telegram from the boat: "Oh, dear, Oh, dear. Fred." His going to the Morris Plan to get a loan—large dreary room, with wretched-looking people sitting around smoothing their hats, you know—threw his knee out of joint going in—while waiting, he sat down and read a letter from his girl, announcing, from London, that she had another lover.

Dorothy said she was going on the wagon—Marc Connelly said he knew somebody who'd done this and it hadn't made a bit of difference. She'd been drunk with Benchley the night before and at one moment put her hand to her forehead and said, "No, I guess that was a false dawn!" — Benchley had thought he was talking to Don Stewart [Donald Ogden Stewart], who was standing by his bed, but it turned out that he wasn't there! Marc Connelly had said, "False Don!"

Marc Connelly explaining to me about Walter Winchell: "The main stem"—"girl trouble." The kind of thing he'd write, for instance: "Poe couldn't hold his giggle water."

She began talking in an, as it were, deliberately quiet way and not looking toward me, a little as Ann Barton does.

Anna. She had on a brown dress, borrowed, I guess, from her sister, bluntish new shiny black shoes—her eyes looked darker than usual and her color ruddier. For the first time, I think, we both went to bed naked, and she spent the rest of the evening, and even when I had turned the lights on and brought her a ham-and-egg sandwich, naked and with the bedclothes simply pulled up over her breasts. Her hair looked redder, too. She laughed so over the story about Margaret's uncle and the fireworks. "Know any more stories?" Sam used to drop paper bags full of water down behind her when she was leaving the dancing school—"that crazy husband of mine." —He just used to roll on and off: but he was different with other women—"he'd love 'em up, you know." —Once he kept on with her for three-quarters of an hour—the clock happened to be close by and she couldn't help noticin'—she didn't know whether he could'un come or did'un want to—but she must have come about twelve times.

The aunt had never forgiven her for the fact that her own daughter had been in love with Sam and Anna had married him. The cousin disappeared after this and was never heard of afterwards (she turned up later married to Walter Polyakov). —Drunken party where the girls were floppin' in the bathtub and everything. —Suburban party at Hackensack, where the men took the girls out in the cars—when one of the wives tried to stop her husband: "We're just goin' for a ride!" "Yes: ride for ride!"

Once, after she was married to Sam, he had introduced her somewhere as just a girl—when somebody asked him if he wasn't married to her, he said no, he was just livin' with me, he wasn't married to me, see—that hurt.

Her sister's child had pneumonia—"Poor little thing—it's har'ly five months." —Had to get up to collect the tenants' rent early the next morning, so that she could take it to her mother without sister's getting it.

She was so cute, she would keep looking up at me to see whether I was looking at her. When, after we had finished making love the second time, I came back from the bathroom and put my arms around her in bed and told her that I'd be so happy with her—when I lay over on my back, and she touched me several times lightly on the cock.

Middletown. I saw, from the window of the train, the dim vision of the little station, its lamps hardly warming the wet mid-February dusk and with its sign illuminated dimly, standing rather high on its embankment and suggesting, in its soft rural cordiality, old-fashioned country journeys and meetings, buggies muddy from sloppy roads, a communicative stationmaster, driving up the wet road through a hedge which enclosed an estate—so far from New York, so far, even, from the modern suburban amenity and enterprise of Red Bank.

Edna [Millay], when she summoned me up to the Vanderbilt to talk about her bobolink poem: "You mean you think it sounds like Mary Carolyn Davies!"—I said that, when she had written *Second April*, she had been under so many kinds of pressure that people who read her poems hardly thought about them as literature at all, there had been an element of panic about them. She said, "Yes, and I still want to knock 'em cold!" For two cents, she would tear up the bobolink poem and not let the *Delineator* have it. Boissevain soliciting an unfavorable opinion of her sister Kathleen's book—his attitude far too protective—said that her later work was "more objective."

She looked quite beautiful, very high pink flush, brown dress which brought out her color.

Anna. She went up to Oswego—her husband was supposed to be dying of a blood clot on the brain—but afterwards recovered—when I had asked her what had been the matter with him. "They did'un want to tell me, see—he wasn't hardly conscious" when she first arrived, but he later went out and got drunk and came back and knocked her down and kicked her between the legs and made a big cut and was trampling on her face—"I was all black and blue and then he tried to beat up his father and they called the police."

The sister had married a man who afterwards turned out to be married and she had some children and she came back home and she treated the children terrible, she knocked them unconscious—and she'd begun to take dope—and she never did that before—and she'd scream and yell and curse—and she'd make Anna stay with her—"I want Anna!"—"And I'd stay with her and keep her quiet, see." She threatened to kill the children—the old mother was crazy and the stepfather was sort of crazy—and the elder brother was just disgusted. When she was just getting on the train to leave, Sam arrived and grabbed her pocketbook and said, "I'll meet you at Syracuse—cash in your ticket from Syracuse to New York!" —She went to a cheap hotel in Syracuse, $2 a day, and he just sent somebody with the pocketbook, from which he'd extracted $10.

Waiting on table at her mother's at 125th Street—people did'un tip her because they knew she was the daughter of the person who ran it. — Worried for fear her little girl would wake up at night at sister's at Fifth Street (East Side) and want her. Wasn't the sister there? "Yes, but she doesn't know her, see." —Her mother was crazy about the baby. —She got so nervous whenever she got excited—had nervous headaches—said "hoddly" for "hardly."

Sam liked her sister and it upset him to see her come back home in this condition. —Also, he used to go on about Anna having gone with men while he was away—would ask her who she'd been with. —Stepfather used to try to sleep with her and her mother finally got jealous and thought that when she got sick, he had knocked her up—she called her a whore in Ukrainian—"and oh, that sounds terrible in Ukrainian, you know!"

—That black shadowy mite at the end of a street, which, with its tiny twinkling legs under its larger rounder bulk, swells and, drawing nearer and nearer, increases to a girl.

When Sam came back and called her up, she took the baby and disappeared.

Margaret. Her skin was so smooth—she seemed so smooth and soft after Anna, with her hard high bones—her own hard pointed chin (sticking in my back)—the gray in her hair—her amiable face—her Scotch matter-of-factness and composure, occasionally broken by some severe remark—surprise at seeing her blush—powder which removed odor—discrepancy between ordinary manner and way of talking and passionate enjoyment (groaning)—strong neck and back from horseback riding, etc.—small feet contrasting with rather thick torso—small hands, but with rather blunt thickish fingers.

Her father chasing her mother and the children in a carriage, firing at them through the carriage top. —He took her to *Pif, Paf, Pouf* when she was a little girl—she was dressed in a Peter Thompson suit and her father thought she ought to be dressed better—he bought her a hat with a large ostrich plume in it. He took her to lunch with Daisy at her own request—he was very constrained. Daisy had originally been at the Haymarket—beyond that, nothing was known.

—Indian who said, "Damn splendid."

Her sudden departure for Europe. Cunning French shoes: gray blunt-toed, with butterfly bows, gray dappled with silver in a very curious way, which made her look awfully cute, as the shoes were a size too big, and a little larger, and consequently in better proportion, than the small pointed ones she ordinarily wore. She said that she didn't want to become a complication for me, that I had handed her her hat and coat, that she was beginning to miss me and that that was one reason she thought she ought to go. One last *étreinte*—it had almost the violence of some accident from which it took a long time to extricate ourselves—a muscular crushing embrace—we lay stunned when it was over—I could hardly get my arm out from under her back—she was apparently stopping her mouth with her hand to keep herself from shrieking. "I don't want to go very much!" I told her that she was the best woman drinking companion I had ever known—she said, "I'm a Western girl!" When I said how sorry I was about not having been able to give her a better time, about having had her come down late to my house, etc., I was astonished to see tears come into her eyes—she looked away and said, "I'm very tired" (she had previously said, "Look out: you'll have me in tears"). I looked at myself in the glass and said that I looked like an old ruined chestnut worm. "Well, who are you arguing with? I never said you were an Adonis."

At the best, we had some difficulty checking up on her traveling companion's trunk, because they couldn't seem to make up their minds whether they were going to Cherbourg or Southampton (there were two places where baggage was attended to). —The long-stemmed roses—the palatial stateroom.

The last time I had seen her before, after a tender and graceful leave-taking on my way to the bathroom, I had fallen backwards off that treacherous unenclosed soft low bed, as slippery as a snowdrift, and landed on my head, without, however—due, no doubt, to the anesthetic effects of the drinks I had had—getting hurt at all.

Winifred. Her little moth-flutterings and rabbit-startings, her soft tender cheeks, arms and neck, her little vibrating limbs, seized with the tremor of fear and excitement when I embraced her—"You mustn't mind if I'm frightened"—nervously, spasmodically contracted—it hurt a little, but not much or long, because when I asked her later whether it had hurt, she said that she was sorry that she'd said it hurt. Her little pansy or violet face, with its touch of Spanish sensuality that made me desire her. Her obedience and readiness, in spite of her fear. Her little whispered exclamations, begun and not finished unless I urged her, and not always then: "It seems very strange! I don't understand! . . . I'm not sure it's right to make love! . . . You don't know me!" I asked her what it was that I didn't know about her, and she said, "Not any one thing"—but she nodded that she did think she knew *me*. I thought how people always felt so when they were first in love. She talked as if not to me but to herself—she said that in her family they all talked to themselves, sometimes went for days without speaking to one another—she used to have long conversations with herself, "and very good conversations, too."—She was so sweet, so dear.

Leon Walker about girl: "Oh, I made her and she's no good!—she's got breasts like oranges in a Christmas stocking!"

Memories of Margaret. "Pretty as green paint—cute as a bug's ear."
Story about *ex-Follies girl*, kept by some man for seven years—pretty as green paint—said she'd had fourteen abortions—discussed her lovers fully, how they worked out, whether they were any good or not—told of girl who had missed chances of marriage by allowing herself to be found by fiancé, who was bringing friend around to see her, sitting on W. C., reading the funny paper with the bathtub full of champagne. —Margaret: "Well, I think that was rather a good thing to do, Sunday afternoon being what it is. —But she *ruined* her *marriage*!" —About things that amused her, Margaret would say, no matter how subtle or remarkable it might be, "It's silly!" or "It's inane!"—or about sensational or merely unconventional things, "It's perfectly mad!"

On the way to Chatham, New York, May 19; going out to see Edna and Boisse-vain (they had sent me a telegram). The widening landscape of upstate with its dark hills blurred with mist, above and below, misted with the blossoms of fruit trees—Boston Corners, Copake Falls—long roads leading over hills, little red cabins and white houses, enormous dark tarnished barns, the loose meshes of blackish stone fences, the thick-bristled hirsute hills, the little faded rural hotels opposite the stations—the wet gray day superimposed on the freshest greenness of spring—upright gritty seats in the train, faded maroon plush—the clapboarded buildings of New York State—desolate yellow freight cars strewn along the route—timbery swamps rank with green skunk-cabbage leaves, dark ponds and streams with a dark smooth luster even under the rain, a pasture of dirty sheep (yellowed, tarnished like the apple blossoms), two bony white horses grazing in a faraway field—the foam of the blossoms so dulled—Hillsdale, Philmont—a growth of squarish whitish houses in the bowl of a valley like the growth of skunk cabbage in the swamp.

At Austerlitz, the sultry overcast weather that seemed to be brooding, like a mother bird, over the beauties of the spring—the birds themselves seemed subdued (and Edna said that she imagined the farm hands, also "ominously silent," perched away with their heads under their wings), the little pink fruit-tree buds about to burst into flower.

The big hill whose green dense tree foliage, stitched with white distinct birch, seemed densely, elaborately woven and all on one flat surface, like a tapestry.

The dandelions on a lawn as thick as grated egg on spinach. —The deep crude yellow of the "winking May buds" in the marsh.

Boissevain planted a border of pansies and then went all to pieces, began singing Cockney songs at the top of his voice—oiled the lawn mower and stopped. —We all had a drink. Decided we wouldn't go for a walk.

Edna playing the Beethoven sonata in the afternoon.

Several grades of apple wine—and apple brandy—ranging from citron to the cruder amber.

German police dog which, when Boissevain had scolded her, would, in a condition of Freudian paralysis, drag herself into the room, as if unable to use her hind legs, bumping into chairs.

Margaret back from Paris. When I went to meet her at the boat, I thought first, as I was approaching the white paling that enclosed the space reserved for the landing of the passengers, those two white strips with black rests at the bottom, nailed on to lean against the fence in such a way as to support it, were the legs of a young girl with a smart slim figure leaning with her back against the paling and her feet pushed forward so as to prop her.

The days when we embrace many and love none.

Raymond (Holden): explaining that there had been much more terrible wars than the last war, because there had been wars in which a greater proportion of the nation had been killed, etc.

Louise (Bogan) and Winifred. Both told me at different times that they thought it was better, or more interesting, to fall in love with a person than to fall in love with just a member of the other sex.

Mid-June: Seven Bridge Road (New Jersey). Those tongues of low grassy land extending into the still shallow reedy water—I went out to the end of one—saw, behind me, a large house with its grounds extending out, almost islanded by the water—and in front of me the land in a strip, where, above the deep full blue of the water, the cream-colored cottages showed, among green of the bank, in clear relief, and where a gas tank, dimmed by the distance, had acquired a certain beauty of dulled metallic luster. It smelled rank of the river there, and there were a few big water birds that seemed to dangle long legs and to fly flappingly, like some kind of heron.

Anna. Perfect feeling of possessing her completely—arms all the way around her slim little figure—tongue in her soft little mouth—legs which I make her put over mine finally throwing her soft little cunt forward and up into place—she is melting into me, as I, from my loins, will finally [melt] into her—I possess, I partly absorb her—the rose flush of her little woman's face, of the face of a woman being loved—and, after the climax, she looks so dear, when I kiss her, when she looks at me with love, with the look of having been happy with me. —I had uncovered the little pink and reddish bud of one of her breasts in a space between her chemise and the ribbon of some other garment, and kissed it and pulled it with my lips—the nipple began to stand up—I kissed her white little thighs, above the stockings and below the skirt of the chemise. When I thrust my bigger thumb into her, she winced with pleasure and pain—it was her throwing her legs over mine that brought the passage straight into place. The slim and white beauty of her body so delightful to find underneath her dullish and shabby clothes. — Her kisses, the passionate appetite with which she holds her mouth under mine for pressure of kiss after kiss, when I rub my lips against her mouth, which is growing moist, when I thrust my tongue between her lips. They receive it and lovingly detain it. —The time before, the cool moisture of her lips when she has bent lower for fellatio, so delightful, so curiously different from the warm and mucilaginous moisture of ordinary inter- course—the incredible-feeling caress, gently up and down, until the delightful brimming swelling of pleasure seems to make it flow really in waves which fill her darling woman's mouth. —In taking hold of my cock and my balls, she had a gentleness, reluctance and timidity which, as well as the way she rubbed over the glans and below, gave the whole thing a de- licious and as it were tantalizing, lightness, only satisfied, completed, by the fullness and the richness of the final flow. —Feeling about woman after this. A little tarnished, a little degraded, the man a little embarrassed, feels a little bit differently about her mouth, but affectionately kisses her. So natural to a woman, but always seems a little strange to a man, and hence has a special fascination.

Taxi ride. Idea for couple riding in taxi, sordid conversation, the emana- tion of sordid New York life, with, on the left at the same time, along Sixth or Seventh Avenue, the furnace of the sunset making molten the recurring blinding vistas down the spokes of the cross streets.

Princeton, June 22–23. Damp darkish days, but cool not muggy and that lovely rich velveted effect over everything—the irregular attractive slopes or the Matthewses' back yard framed among the light walls of wooden houses and just planted by Mrs. Matthews, Tom's mother, with shrubs. The new house, with its white sides artificially smudged in places so as to give it the effect of being old—Julie regretted that Negroes lived in the house

beyond the back yard—she was pretty and her legs had an unexpected attractive thickness in comparison with her small head and the rather thin
upper part of her body—also in flat white sneakers—in the evening, when
she had made up a little, given a little warmer color to the rather pale tints of
her face, she wore black shoes with white stockings. —Coming back at
night, a bush of white roses seemed foaming over the wall, in the darkness
and dripping richly, in its petals, on the pavement below. —The young
fellow, '24, who had gone in for physics—nice clean young Princetonian,
nice clean physical entities: H_2, Ryskind's constant—he was measuring
molecules in gases under various pressures. When Tom Matthews woke
him up—"It's a quarter to nine." —"Is that positively true?" "Yes: that's
definitely true." —"That Tom says it's quarter to nine." —Regular
Princeton line of those days: When Julie admired his blue tie, "Isn't that an
unusually attractive tie?" —Tom Matthews said he had had a rotten morning—John Miles said he had had a wonderful morning—"Would you like
me to tell you about it or would it depress you?" —Later, "I wish you'd let
me tell you about my morning—just a little bit." —"All right—just a
little." —"Well, in the first place, I had four German magazines—and I
looked through 'em so that I saw there was nothing in 'em"—"I've been
thinking about old age—I suppose the thing to do is just to say, 'Well,
damn it, I *am* going to finish this story,' and just go ahead and finish it and
then get up and go downstairs."

As soon as the Matthewses had gone and the maids thought I was alone,
they burst into loud and raucous song, singing, humming, whistling, *That's
Love* or something of the kind. The maid at once went into the kitchen and
had a loud emphatic dialogue with the cook: "I do all the sweeping and you
get all the gin!" or something.

When I first came in, in the evening, he was lying on his back on the
floor, with a glass in his hand.

John Miles and Julie's brother had gone over to Asbury Park one night
during reunion and John had gone in swimming naked—he had encountered a girl on the boardwalk and said, "Get away, pretty girl, I'm going
swimming!" She had reported him to the police—he had insisted on getting all the sand out from between his toes—which had "rather irritated"
the policeman. The friend was lying on the sand with the gin bottle clasped
to his breast. In jail—the night's catch, seven people, man and woman who
had been fighting on corner, said they were not married, came from Hoboken; old man who had been dancing on pavement with bare feet. They had
been very jolly in the jail, asking which button to press when you wanted a
whiskey and soda. In court, the next morning, he had raised a great laugh

by saying he was a professor of physics. The judge: "Well, you'll need one before you get through"—fined $15—only had $13—companion had to raise the rest.

Self-limiting character of that kind of life—Princeton suburban younger people—intelligence, tolerance, curiosity, imagination, courage, only just goes so far, then it naturally thins out and desists, leaving them, though free in appearance, in reality immured.

Tom Matthews: complaining of old tennis balls—"But why should the ——s have bum tennis balls?" "Oh, it's just like these rich people who always have very poor gin!" —Drinks at lunch—did he think they'd better have them, if they were going to play tennis?—"But *what* tennis!"

Mother's expressions:
wild as a hawk
crazy as a June bug
old coot
you're a high one!

Ted. Frisco's wisecrack to the effect that Chicago had gotten so tough that they'd shoot your girls right out from under you.

Gene Buck's nigger accent acquired from Jewish comedians—he was really an Irishman from Detroit. On the Fitzgeralds: "If you want to get your furniture antiqued up, you want to get the Fitzgeralds in—they'll antique it up in a single night—why, they'll put their own wormholes in the furniture with cigarette ends!"

Beautiful red-haired girl whom Belasco had been stringing along for a make—told Ted that she didn't know why she was telling him all this, but he seemed to understand—"God took away my mother, but he sent me Belasco!"

Anna. Working at Schrafft's at $1 a day with tips—$20 a week. The skilled girls could make $50 a week. She looked as if she had been working, eyes protruding as if hard-taxed and face a little hardened. She left the baby at the nursery in the morning and had to be back by six to get her. Terrifically hot day in mid-July—I had waked up with rivulets of sweat rolling off my forehead on the pillow. She was wearing almost nothing—she showed me her little thighs bare all the way up—she had on, under her pink shirtwaist, only a little chemise.

She was wearing a pink shirtwaist, and white pleated skirt with some kind of yellow flower on it and nice white stockings with her old blunt black shoes. The mother had left her stepfather—and he had turned the place into a regular speakeasy with girls and everything—"they pulled down all the blinds at ten o'clock and I don't know what they do." I asked if the girls were terrible and she answered, "Yes, they're terrible—what I mean—terrible!" One of them had explained to her that she got $3 a man ($6 an hour—she thought)—Anna was so foolish, you know, to work when she could do the way *she* did (here, as she went on, I saw Anna's nice fine humor begin to come out from under her hardened unfortunate surface, the result of having got up early in the morning, come to see me and gone to work) in order to earn her $15 in a couple of hours every night. I asked if the girls had been pretty—"I'm telling you, each one is worse than the other." One night they had a big fuss—the man gave one of the girls $5 and tried to get back $2 change—they had a big rumpus and threw the girl out. —Anna complained of her heart, which she said hurt her awful sometimes—I suppose she had to be on her feet too much at Schrafft's.

Seabright beach. Pretty girl in rather a Germanic way, with plain white bathing-suit upper, belt and red trunks with white stripe down side—she had smiling darkish brown eyes and very white skin; her movements with her legs, first lying on her back and holding one knee up, with the thighs rather apart, her head on the man's chest; then turning over toward me, so, as it were, to expose the pretty nest of the lap creased deep between well-rounded thighs—her movements with her legs were voluptuous. In the water, she swam beautifully and as if it were a natural element: she had a slow easy and elastic crawl. —They were one of those couples who do a certain amount of petting on the beach, he putting his arm around her, etc. Another couple: the girl would slip her hand under the man's bathing suit and caress his back.

Beautiful young blond slender girl, with plainer tanned mother and sister—they were sewing and reading on the beach—she would stand with her very long slender white legs apart, with movements unconstrained and unself-conscious, or rather with the calm assurance of the consciousness of beauty. Her shoulders, reddened with sunburn, were narrow, her low but properly developed, not flat, breasts beneath her white swimming shirt— she wore a belt and dark-blue trunks. Her towhair was bobbed straight off all around—there was something a little Swedish about her narrowish eyes, her pointed nose and V-shaped mouth, which was vivid and sharp against her blondness, perhaps by the aid of rouge. At last, when she was done with her sewing, she got up and put on a white wrap, broidered with a pattern of blue—she only put her arms half in, then stood, with her feet wide apart, looking out at the sea with the wrap billowing out behind her shoulders in the wind.

Gruesome sights of the New York streets. The little boy who put the younger child's doll under the wheels of a commercial truck which was standing beside the curb—the little child began to cry—I picked up the doll, itself a naked headless carcass, and gave it back to the child. A vast and very good-humored-looking woman, who seemed to be emerging from a basement, said, "You mustn't put that there!"

Little boy with atrophied undeveloped legs crawling down the steps and over the curb like a spider.

Sandy. When I came in, he was looking out the window and offered me his hand from behind. Nice gray Brooks suit—mussed; face at last profoundly changed: thinner, harder, grayer, more mature and more staring. Difficulty of talking—long painful stalls—would tend to respond naturally to easy natural questions, but often only after long silences or pauses of muttering, pulling himself finally together and mustering his old humorous charming manner—as, when I asked what sort of people the other inmates were, he replied, brightening with momentarily smiling eyes: "Some are criminal, but not all," as if he had been saying—as he did once when I went to see him—"I was a dirty Cottage politician.—Some of the Cottage men were dirty politicians, but not all." All the time he was standing up, looking at himself in the mirror, grimacing, talking to himself: "There isn't very much money—not much money!" "That country streak we all have" (he meant the Talcottville background); "Are you divorced yet?" (cheerfully, as if this were to be taken for granted); Adelaide Champollion (after André's death): she needed somebody to "make a fuss over her." (He came out now with rather shrewd insight in a way that he wouldn't have done when sane.)

I said it was a beautiful country—the green slope, beyond the barred windows, was all golden-green in the late afternoon sun of September. He said, after one of those pauses: "It's no good for farming, though—it's too rocky." —Began muttering again: the newspaper; "Yes, that's what I want"; history—the asylum library: "The history of things is as bad as the things themselves. Life's all right if you can stand it"—his politeness again, implying; "But I never could!"

Just settle down to jail. His privileges had been taken away—movies—he was still violent. —I will tell them at home that he doesn't suffer, but I can see in his face that he does. —I said, "You were always better dressed than I was." He said, "Do you still get your suits at Brooks?" I said, "Yes." "You really ought to have a tailor." I had admired his tie, and, looking in the glass, he adjusted it—it was an orange and red striped one—so that it bulged out, knotted exactly and neatly at the soft collar, as I never could make my ties do.

The last thing he'd been able to read was E. A. Robinson's *Tristram*. He'd kept muttering things that I'd try not to pay attention to. —The attendant knocked at the door—I said, "Come in"—he said, "It's 4:30." I said to Sandy, "It's time for me to go." He said quickly and emphatically, "Yes, it's time for you to go!" and went off down the corridor. —The attendant told me, when I questioned him at the door, that he wasn't so violent, that the cases in the ward were just ordinary—that it was pretty hard to keep him tidy.

Red Bank, October 12. Going down the other side of Prospect Hill on my bicycle, to the left the autumn landscape where the barns showed a red almost as soft, and unlike the sharp bright red of clear air, as the deep red of the petals of a rose—or rather, like the cheeks of a Baldwin apple otherwise green, as did the great red stain of a tree still around the stain, and exactly matching the color of the barns, above which the bushy leafage of a tree, at once faded and enriched, where the irregular high grass and clumps of shrubs and trees seemed interesting, as if somehow with the autumn they seemed to conceal some special life, vegetable, animal or human?—the impression was indistinctly blended—ended in the rough dense or feathery treetops, through which a window of a house behind the trees glittered silver from the top of the hill—it glittered as I rode, extinguished now and then by the trees; and to the left of the road stood the white bole and crooked limbs of an old buttonwood tree, still green but dying at the top from a fish hawk's nest, while on the right the reddened leaves of poison ivy wound around the trunk of a tree that was dead.

Mid-October in Red Bank. From the window in front of white October-cold-washed garage, a hydrant as red as a gladiolus, with a canary-yellow top.

Cutting across from Rumson to Oceanic on my bicycle, a little dim-eyed, plunging in a dream through the clear medium of air, rich autumnal shade from the wall of undergrowth and trees of some estate beside the road and the deep golden stripes of autumn sun.

On the side steps, the colors vivid and clear through the late autumn afternoon.

Late on an October night, leaving the Gormans' on Twelfth Street, against the high black flight of stairs of one of those comparatively old-fashioned houses, a man and woman, he in a dark fall coat, black like the background of steps, and she in brown, handsome and tall, with her head turned away from him, yet both in an amorous pose. New York of my own today against that old brown stone.

Anna. Sam said, "I learn' tuh hannle 'em quick."
Her look, having her painful monthlies, with her evening dress all torn—

black velvet below, and above, that brassy patterned blouse, deep-stained with rose, that matched her bronze-red hair—and passionate lips and cheeks inflamed—and unexpected ready words, when I asked: "Won't you love me?"—"Uh-huh!"—that sweet melodious scream.

"You'd never look at me again if you could see my sister" (I had said that I thought I'd go and call on her family)—she wasn't quite bright or something—"I think it was because my mother used to beat her—she used to hit her in the head something awful."

Calm way in which she took all her misfortunes—it made her ashamed, evidently, to have me sympathize with her. Once when I had said something about how unfortunate she was, she said, "Oh, I'm not so bad off—I'm happy now!" I asked her why. "Because I'm sure I don't love my husband any more." I said I thought she'd been sure of that for some time. "No: just in the last four months or so. I was never sure before."

Sam was all diseased, had grown terribly thin—couldn't have any place to stay—probably didn't get anything much to eat—knew all the people who kept speakeasies and would bum drinks off them—always drunk—said, as it were, hopefully, that she didn't think he'd last long. —Finally wanted her to hustle for 'um. Alex threw 'um out.

Girls in apartment house caused great scandal—gave all the men the clap. Place about to be pulled, but crisis averted by girls' moving out. Woman who slandered Anna, said she wanted to lay every man in the house. Her mother was worried and told her to move out.

Her attachment to her mother—got homesick for her when she went to stay in Oswego—that was the reason she'd come back.

"I wanted affection—I suppose that's why I went so crazy about Sam."

Feeling of doing it without condom, after doing it with one so long—crude, animal, meaty, more intimate.

Second time, partially atrophied by drinking, long hard pull—she comes two or three times before I do—the way she looks after being fucked for twenty minutes or so—brown-looking eyes as intimate as an animal's—ordinary expression of face gone with makeup—as naked and unstudied, as unthinking as rest of body. —Finally did it behind and came.

Night when we had come in and found people there—we had both been drinking—according to what is probably a general principle, we enjoyed it more, as, after the difficulties circumvented, we were finally together alone, we lay in each other's arms, she with her dress on (she was having her monthlies) and I in my underclothes. It seemed to make us want each other more. Feeling of her dear body in its silk-feeling dress in my bare arms.

My departure for California. As I was packing and the room was all bare: "I don't like to see you go." I had never felt before that she cared much about me. Lizzie was waiting, as she had made her do before, like a good little girl, on the steps of the house across the street. Lizzie wouldn't talk to me when we all started out in the cab together, but gave me a nasty look. I said that she had handsome eyes—"She's got wicked eyes!—she's got her daddy's eyes!"—very black, a little slanting and rather Italian-looking. Lizzie presently stood up, however, and attentively looked out of the window all the rest of the way. She seemed fat and well fed, and Anna had tried to dress her nicely—little kid-topped buttoned black shoes. Anna herself had on white stockings and new rather blunt-toed rough-finished black shoes, which made her feet and legs look very pretty—but she was thin and pale from the continual loss of blood of her too-long-protracted monthlies. "Don't be afraid to put your arm around me." I said that I hadn't on account of Lizzie. "She's looking out of the window," said Anna. (The family had been kidding Anna about her new papa—"They talk about me and kid me all the time, y'know, when I'm there.") She pressed close against me: "I don't see why you go so far away!—You're the only person who's ever been nice to me!" She kissed me harder and more fervently than I had ever known her to do on her own initiative, holding me tight. —And I had never heard her talk so before.

When I gave her the $50 bill, she sat, as if stupefied, on the day bed, and said, as if I had given her a blow, almost as if her surprise were painful, "I didn't think you'd ever do that!"

California

[EW had become increasingly attached to Margaret Canby, to whom there are many earlier allusions in these pages; and his trip to California was in effect a visit to her. He stayed in a beachhouse near her home and here rewrote the greater part of *I Thought of Daisy*. He also was gathering together certain poems; both books were to be published by Scribner's. To Maxwell Perkins, his editor, EW wrote: "I have a little house here on the beach and have done nothing but read, write and swim. The weather is beautiful and all the days are exactly alike. The calm Pacific spaces are excellent for work—I always feel cramped in New York. But if you stayed out here very long, you would probably cease to write anything, because you would cease to think—it isn't necessary out here and the natives regard it as morbid."

Earlier in the year he had written Perkins (June 9, 1928) when he was working on *Daisy* at Red Bank: "It is the sort of thing that has to come off completely or it is likely to be impossible. I mean that, from beginning to end, I have made characters and incidents and situations subordinate to a set of ideas about life and literature, and unless the ideas are really put over, unless they are made interesting enough to compensate the reader for what he is missing in action and emotion, for what he ordinarily gets in a novel, the whole performance will fail."]

Santa Barbara, October–December 1928
On a bright rather cold December day, the banks of sheer white clouds behind the tops of the mountains are seen outlined against the sheer blue sky, and the markings of the mountains themselves, though patternless, are as distinct as the markings of tan on dark on the back of a snake.

This fat pillowing of clouds behind the heads of the mountains, on one curious evening, turned tan itself in the sunset and looked like something solid, stuffed and made of light leather—they were not, on this occasion, behind the mountains' heads, I guess, but covered the tops of the mountains, which were lost in them.

The white card tower of the new town hall, built since the earthquake, plaquing its flat square surfaces against the flat blue sky.

The lovely watercolor effect of everything in Southern California—the flowers: purple bougainvillaeas, acacias, lion's-tails like tiny packs of firecrackers—beauty of a fall day when this Californian sun is given a slight smack of coldness and the clarity of the colors of sky, grass, trees and houses is slightly heightened. The dresses of the women have this water-color quality, too—blues, reds, garnets—worn easily, without smartness—a view of schoolchildren at recess—these colors seem so prettily and easily washed on, they grow wild like the flowers.

Blue and orange of the inside of my beachhouse—its heavy, beautifully woven Indian blankets, on which the bright sun would fall in the mornings, when I would awake feeling their weight—the cold of the night had been dispelled—white walls—Indian oven fireplaces—window seats which, much to our surprise, turned out to have very comfortable cushions—an Indian bird of red clay—an elk dance, colored drawing—an effaced Spanish saint with seven swords through her heart—a little German angel bearing a candlestick—the sea-gray window-seat cushions—the red-tiled floor, with its red and brown on white Indian rugs.

The colors both soft and bright—in late afternoon, the blues washed along the mountains. —Pale writhen trunks of trees, cork-light, woven in the tapestry drop of not very bright green. —At Margaret's family's old place, against the green screen of the drive, a great spray of Japanesy yellow flowers among the broom bristles of needle-like stiff leaves.

The fuming, the awakened voice of the slue, bringing the rains down from the mountains, heard at night going home along the beach.

Syphons in a paper bag—turned one on in taking it out of the car—"Those syphons are hissing like snakes."

Paul Dougherty spoke of monotony of California—"You think if you could only see a cloud shadow, you know!" —But at Carmel the sea was more interesting—an occasional volcanic wave.

Santa Barbara to Los Angeles. Ventura—the big white Californian court-house revealed by the vista of a street on an elevated site. —The distant hill-side, against the pale winter sky (mid-December), its gray-green surface mottled by paler markings of dirt showing through in the bald places and dotted with the small pearl-silver cylinders of some kind of gas or oil tanks. —Rabbitries: sign in silhouette of rabbit, duck and chicken. Mike's Tavern; Poinsettia Lunch. Red poinsettias—their flimsy and lovely red flowers. Barbecue lunchrooms—an atmosphere of festivity and plenty—all kinds of fancy places to eat: Trading Post, Uncle Tom's Cabin (a very large one), Old Stage-Coach Inn, Swiss Chalet, Indian Wigwam—colored pampas grass—an element of the factitious and theatrical which begins almost as soon as one leaves Santa Barbara. Blue and light yellow gasoline stations—blue and white signs—Avocado Acres, Walnut Acres—walnut groves—compact and prickly effect of even-growing bunches of fine wrought-iron branches on short straight stalks—a sort of energy in their round immobility—the palms, on the other hand, have irritating personalities—they are somehow not what one expects of trees, but give the impression, like sea anemones or molluscs, of being too rudimentary a form of life—they lack personalities—they vegetate where they are rooted, unaffected by the wind. —The Canejo Grade—Migs taking the dangerous curves with masterly dash. [Migs was a close friend of Margaret's. They had run a hat shop together.] —On the trip before, Margaret was always having to wait for long trucks—the kind in several sections—slowly transporting pipes—truckloads of beans—the beanfields. —Lion farms. —The speckled hills, round and dry. —Real estate developments: fantastic headquarters of real estate companies: one of them a sort of gnomes' castle, with a high Nurembergian roof, which looked as if it had come out of a comic drawing. — Movie constructions on a distant hill. —A great, brightly painted wooden sign, covered with comic figures, which looked like the façade to some amusement park, but which, behind it, had nothing apparently—merely some private houses—the whole fantastic approach to Hollywood. The French Village—the little bogus villas and castles in the hills—the houses; on both sides of the street probably the most absurd series of residences in the world—a doorway shaped like the entrance to a tent and in the same house, I think, a silver statue in bas-relief—Hollywood-Byzantine. —The goofy plaster statues advertising things: which is the goofiest?—the bellboy with the suitcases and the idiotic grin—the Joan of Arc of the Hotel Normandie—the old Southern gentleman with the wide trousers, beard and mustache, advertising coffee—the rather weird silver dancing couple—the rooster—the mother and child with the cow, who have become discolored so that, instead of looking wholesome and reassuring, they have a somewhat sinister appearance, the mother looking more like a witch. —The big orange booth shaped like an orange—the ice-cream-cone booth, with four enormous and phallic papier-mâché ice-cream cones at the corners, pink, chocolate and white. Fantasy reaches its climax in Los Angeles itself in a curious way—high white building as one goes up a hill, undoubtedly merely an office building, not actually built, but drawn for fancy or funny effect—everything seems papier-mâché. —Pickford and Fairbanks's former residence—fountain and white lions—"They've got everything!"

The day I arrived, as I left the Nevinses' house (a good example of a fancy and attractive Southern Californian house), the sky above the palm trees and the white Los Angeles houses was streaming diamond in a bright brief Pacific day end—we had had some drinks—my moments of elation.

The man who dressed as a little old woman, asked motorists to give him a ride and then held them up.

Eucalyptus Avenue, where the tall sparse plumes meet overhead.

The restaurant where you pay a certain amount for lunch and then get all you want to eat of enchilada, goulash, spaghetti, stuffed tomatoes, pâté de foie gras, glazed tongue, glazed lamb, glazed beef, salads (hot red Spanish sauces and purple ripe olives), rolls and cornbread fingers, eggs with chopped-up chicken à la king, like all entrées, in a chafing dish—ravioli—pickle sauce, eggs stuffed with anchovies, coffee in glasses, French pastry, strawberry cake with glazed, deadly-looking strawberries rather like the decorations of the restaurant itself (the Victor Hugo), where a long carpeted staircase led to a luxuriously curtained interior—mirrors, Empire ornaments, birds of paradise behind white looped window curtains—we commanded the room from a raised and carpeted dais which ran along the walls.

Santa Barbara Beach. When I first arrived, the soft spaced explosions of the waves, which seemed ineffectual—later on, they seemed to crash and smack the beach with intolerable force. —A lizard that looked like Ted. —A white condom floating on the surf. —The constant twinkling line of lights at Carpenteria—and the twinkling of the stars in that quarter. —The dead coots and cormorants, with necks bent under the breasts turned up or with necks snapped off or with only the whitened vertebrae, divested of flesh and feathers, trailing on the beach. Dead rats—gophers. Large gulls—when you go near them, they merely walk a little way and stop again. The black coots that live on sand crabs and get so fat that they are overbalanced by their breasts and can't get enough leverage either to walk or fly—they can only flap on their long black feet, straining with helpless ridiculous wings. The pelicans. Sandpipers scooting along the beach. The sea pigeons, smaller than a gull. The empty carapaces of sea crawfish—langoustes. Opalescent abalone shells. At Sandyland, the opalescent sea crawling on the long shallow beach. The killdeer. The sandpipers—like Tiller girls, they perform evolutions in perfect unison: all make for the waves, then all right turn, then all stop and simultaneously stick their bills in the sand—then, if alarmed, all together rise and fly, making a white flock of exact cuneiform carats, against the sand or the sky.

The dogs on the beach—making the rounds—bulldog, wolf dog, Scotty, mongrels—the last very humble. The English whippet trainer—two whippets and a whippet pup—the pup thicker-limbed and clumsy, but soon grew to the whippet slenderness—one could see the change in a month—the grown whippets running to the trainer, undulations of yellow against the pale brown sand—the trainer, always trim, always fit, looking neither to right nor left, knowing his place, never speaking or nodding to any of the people on the beach, not speaking even when spoken to by people who saw him every day and thought that they should salute him—

so that they finally gave up attempting to. —The people passing on horse-back or breaking horses in—they would pass, fine silhouettes of brown against the blue sea—the coffee-colored horse.

The glass weed. The hummingbirds. The glass-weed-like wild spinach, with its bright and beautiful purple flower, at Sandyland. The kelp—from the Coast Highway, a roughish dull band of tan on the gleaming surface of the sea—the kelp ropes, with their amber leaves of Corinthian columns. Bobby Dalton (he ran the Miramar Hotel) on the kelp—the mayor who had lived a few blocks away from the beach and who suddenly discovered that the beach was covered with kelp—he said that Santa Barbara would have such a beautiful beach if the kelp were removed—so he had men with wagons go down and set to work removing it—he didn't know that that kelp had been there off and on for thousands of years—that it would come and then it would all disappear. The stalks of kelp with a great green-ish-yellow bulb at the base—like the scepters of Tritons or like squids. The big spongy brown bunches of nests. —The long Miramar pier—every day Bobby Dalton and the guests at Miramar would walk out to the end of it and look around.

The chillyhawk, hovering motionless, ready to drop on an insect. Two cormorants or gulls flying together. The cormorant Margaret and I saw on our way to Sandyland, posed on the edge of an oil well, beside an impassive gull, which remained after the other had flown, with flapper wings ex-tended, evidently watching a fish—it stood so for some time without fly-ing, then put off from its perch and flew low over the waves, flapping its wings a little while, then gliding in its low straight line, as if it were coasting on a bicycle. The pelicans and the cormorants reminded me of Louisiana, going down to Grand Isle.

Dawn at Carpenteria, with the answering pink and blue of sea and sky (the pink against the blue sky a little cheap and ugly—too pretty) with the mountain in the middle. Swimming at sunset—how soft the islands lie—Santa Cruz and Santa Rosa—on the dreamy misted horizon. The sun makes the water pink against its own blue, and the islands are blue against the sun's pink, against the western sky. An earthly paradise—a little soft and cloy-ing—the seascapes are bonbons for the eye.

The lobster fishers with their boat. The elderly man camping, building a fire, apparently living in a crevice of the cliff. The remains—the rusted twisted skeleton—of the motorcar that fell over the cliff. The sluice from the cliff where the baby was thrown down. The occasional boats—one of them represented a small company which had undertaken to extract iodine from the kelp, but had never particularly prospered. The children—the cunning little twins, "cute as bugs' ears." Old ladies passing, taking regular constitutionals.

Santa Barbara Beach. The boom of guns—the rumbling up of caissons—crash or rattle of musketry. —The long shattering crunch on the shore—even these more violent manifestations, as a result of their following on each other at vacant intervals, have a featureless quality—they do not speak.

In December, for the first time, on a day when the rain set in, it got a gray wintry look—Santa Cruz and Santa Rosa even managed to seem bleak. —The empty sound of the Pacific.

In the midst of the steady uneventful downpour on the roof, of a rainy night in December, a sudden crash on the roof: Margaret said, "A real spell of hail—hurry!—it's the first in years." —Then, as suddenly, after the brief onset, spare single stones—then faint and soft and mild, almost dying away—then brushing harder, falling faster—relenting—banging heart-ily— blown up and down, fast and soft—crashing, sprinkling, more or less brisk—merging with the rainfall, setting in, forgotten.

The two girls at Santa Barbara who committed suicide.

Steve Gates. Used to throw plates around the room to relieve his pent-up feelings about Paula. When she divorced him, another woman married and fleeced him. When we met him at dinner at the Cortijo, he said in his nice gentle low-voiced way that he was done with women. We said that we were going to the movies—he inquired what we were going to see: Lon Chaney in *West of Zanzibar*—and when we told him, he remarked that he would like to see that himself. He said that he had just seen *Plastered in Paris*, and that Sammy Cohen got pretty tiresome after a while—he spoke of movie films with gentle childlike seriousness.

Hollywood. Dorothy Parker's story about John Gilbert's projected film: he and beautiful girl dragging themselves through African jungle, dead with thirst—she finally offers him her beautiful white body for the last drink in the canteen— "Can you imagine anything he'd want less?" The gag was that finally they found a sparkling cascade, which turned out to be diamonds.

Wilson Mizner's big idea for a story about a rich man who couldn't buy happiness—he finally threw two thousand dollars at the dog and the dog wouldn't have anything to do with'um.

Insolence of hotel employees—"You're damn lucky to get into this joint at all!—Is this the Crane girl?" Mizner summoned the manager and said "I've got a hell of a big belch, Frank." The manager later sent up flowers.

The last thing I heard as I was leaving was Mizner sitting on the floor telling them about somebody who had one of the best heads in Hollywood but was a *drug addict*! (He was a drug addict himself and was all hopped-up on this occasion. I did not find him amusing, nor did Dorothy Parker.)

Ed Freeman. Rich himself, but took all Jane's money and wouldn't even let her have enough to go to see her sister, when her sister was sick. He was jealous—would call her up beforehand at women's parties to make sure there were no men there. Kept her completely in subjection. Indignation of all the other women. Advised Margaret to pick up driftwood. He economized on cocktails— "Do you want a large dividend or a small dividend?" Would call up beforehand and ask whether she was coming, so that he'd know how many cocktails to make.

The Miramar. Old-fashioned Californian hotel—dark low-ceilinged interiors—screen doors—old ladies and gentlemen sitting around—library where each guest left a volume or two—always a fire in the fireplace in the darkish room, full of mission furniture.

Our walk to Sandyland—we started off tight—I talked furiously. The elaborate and rather far-reaching system of interrelated oil wells, with their feelers for sub-sea-bottom oil, quietly moving up and down—a few shacks where the operators lived—against the sky like a Pennell drawing. The stretch of sheltered beach, walled around with yellow rocks. We sat down on a log and had lunch and had some more swigs out of the whiskey pint bottle full of cocktails mixed with grapefruit juice. The stone wall looked as if it had been made of the stage rocks in the old Metropolitan productions of Wagner's *Ring*. The real estate development—a tract where everything was sloppy, in process of being suburbanized, always a lot of tacky Fords. Margaret in her brown bathing suit, becoming to her and pretty against the brownish yellow rocks and pale brown sand—she had a jersey that went over it of a slightly warmer purplier brown—the bathing suit had an irregular streaked design—her plump little figure in her bathing suit with her pretty legs—plump round thighs and small bony-toed feet. We went out low tide and came back high tide. The birds and other things seemed to take on a new interest and value. Her prehistoric black bathing suit at Sandyland—when I tried to hook it over her shoulder, all the little rusted hooks and eyes broke off. She finally tied it, and when she went surfboarding in it, it exposed her pink bottom. Holes in the porch where she had practiced pistol-shooting as a girl. Opalescent slow sea—bigger waves breaking only far out—more primitive, wilder, more lonely. The dark bare-wood inside of the beach-house—it was grown around with wild purple-flowered spinach, with its coarse beach-grown foliage, flame purple blossoms. The background of rugose blackened hills, the rampart. I watched her sliding the surfboard along the shallow beach following the wave's white hem, till it faded in the sand—the long rollers. —On the way back, clambering on the smooth stones, where the waves were already breaking—I looked back once and saw the pale yellow cliff powdering into the pale blue ocean behind us, where night was soon to fall. She remembered, when we went back the next day, that the day before, when we were tight, we had felt sorry for ourselves because we didn't have enough to drink, we had declared that the next time we came we would bring two bottles of cocktails— "Well, you're not tight today"—"I didn't think I was yesterday either." Stepped on her toes and hurt them badly when I tried to kiss her, stopping her, standing among the stones, on our strenuous but exalted return. I kept saying that I didn't know whether I had told her how much I liked her, how fond I was of her, etc. —Our cocktails, greenish liquid, in green teacups. Her blue and white rubber beach shoes. Her short figure standing sturdily with bare legs among the stones against the Californian cliffs. Her breasts showing solid though sallow, with nipples plain, under her wet bathing suit, when she came up from surf-boarding. —Unpopularity of Albert Isham (I had known him at Hill School)—his elaborate beachhouse of a most unappetizing brown—the large outbuilding with mosque-like minarets—exactly like a movie set— that was a sort of gymnasium where he tried to get thin, in order to look more attractive—he had all this money—she thought the parents felt terribly about him.

Her footprints in the sand, as we came back from beyond Sandyland, with their firm little imprint of the ball of the foot. —Exploding kelp bulbs—snapping kelp pods underfoot. The green darts of kelp flat on the sand. —Writhen eucalyptus trunks bleached bone-white, like fantastic animal-skulls. —The mists of myriad swarming black fly mites rising from the brown kelp sponges. —The empty reddish casque of a lobster, the antennae trailing limp, straight and rigid. —Workman reading mystery magazine on the rocks.

The trains—the *Padre*, etc.—the men who shoot birds from the trains— made my windows rumble in a faint firm vibration—the sound as of a double pistol shot behind my house, whenever the train went by—not anyone shooting, however, I think. The single track—the train's cry, always the same.

From the Hoffmann beachhouse to town. The long continuous row of bathhouses of the beach club—then the private houses, mostly in dark faded brownish or greenish wood, like grudging odd high-pitched chalets—or with their projecting upper stories and large rectangular curtained windows like the booths of puppet or Punch and Judy shows—occasionally a white one standing out sharply among them—dark spruces rising above them—La Marea, El Mar, La Honda. —Blue-shirted Mexicans with wide straw hats spending their lunch hour on a wall. —A woman on the sand with a Japanese parasol—an old tire—curious little house with flat shingled roof and octagonal tower, which looked as if it had been made of the brown husks of old cigars, with green moss growing in the cracks. —The Hammonds' house, large low and rather ugly raw yellow tint, with its high swings, embowered in palms. —Tall aloe stalks with their flowers like wrought-ironwork, delicate, exact and stiff against the flat blue sky—stiff tendrils. —An open stretch—the mountains brown and friable, streaked with cracks against the sooty discoloration of forest fires. Coarse banks of ice plant—ice plant crawling down over embankment or cliff. —The Biltmore: imposing palms planted at careful intervals—the American flag—a low white Spanish building roofed with tiles of dry dull rose. —A mother with a child wading in the surf—stringy rangy Californian young woman, California-burnt and dressed in old jersey with wide burnt red stripes. — Eroded cliffs of clay—the formless fallen boulder of yellow puddingstoned soil—dislodged no doubt by the earthquake. —The round and hollow rocks of the beach—the slimy silky margin left by receding waves—its film mirroring blue. The rust-riveted beam of a wreck. Dark trees—above the cliffs—the gray unshaven beard of palms, an oppressive disproportionate weight. —Noonday and the beach and sea, empty, bright and dry. —We came out opposite the children's playground (the building in light bright pink, with slides, swings and benches)—at the bird refuge— the stinking mire where they were draining it (a large enclosed estate on rise of the ground to the right)—birds hold conventions in the open there— birds with a "squeaky cry"—pink villas on the friable clay hills—black coots as motionless as decoys on the dark sheets of the dark mire-bottomed puddles. —Sinister roadhouse, with indistinct picture of dancers under high peaked roof—lit up with colored bulbs like a Christmas tree at night. A slender child in a white hat and pale suit, which made it look almost naked, standing on the beach at the playground and apparently eating a lollypop. —The broad railroad place, where Reggy Fernald, having run his car on the beach one night, tried to send for a locomotive. —The yellow string of the freight cars of the Pacific Fruit Express, with stars-and-stripes shield on each, bending away from the road along an easy curve. —The lamp-studded bright gray walk of the boulevard—a small grove of palms—one sometimes saw people riding. A signboard or two with a bright cigarette advertisement—the memorial tablet to Carrillo—the car tracks—the lightly orange gasoline station: the main street of the town.

Notes made on Morgan Adams's yacht. The steady spaced Pacific crash—the ocean breaking outside, a series of slow soft explosions. —On the way to Los Angeles, the mountains in their soft fresh watercolors of blue and brown—and the gleaming white-silver of the long low waves, cresting not on the shore but on the wide napery sheet of blue water. —The high irregular screens of crooked eucalyptus trees and the trellis of long shadows across the dry yellow road—the dry fawn-colored mountains, the beauty of dust, the smell of the air with no sea rankness—the aromatic smell of the light eucalyptus logs burned in the fireplace. —Looking out on some open street of Los Angeles, full of gay and flimsy houses, a group on a porch with a high solid rail, above which one could see the bare arms of two women, apparently reclining in siesta in comfortable chairs with their arms above their heads. —The women and little girls, with their dullish but fair towheads and their bare legs buff and brown, a brownness altogether different from the Jersey tan. —The vogue of the yo-yo (Jimmy's slang: "Oh, that's keen! The heck you do! Haven't got no," etc.) (Jimmy Canby, Margaret's son).

The bright coldish blue afternoon, into which the yacht set sail—the gunboats stationed at intervals—the sailors in the back of motorboats with prows lifted up from the water—out at sea, a white and concave sail, a patch like the print of a thumb on the blue sky—at last, Los Angeles seemed a mirage or phantom city which encumbered the horizon now as little as fog or foam—the black drawbridge, with its square bulk, from which its wonderful folding up to let us through was operated.

Coming back, we hadn't put out lights in time, almost got into trouble and fined—people shouted at us. The *Enchantress* was brought in through the narrow pass between the high steep dark walls of two tankers.

Morgan Adams—glad to get back not drunk—always called the girls "you fellows"—way of telling stories about hydroplane experience at Panama, aeroplane stunts, mutiny of crew at Cuba. Mistress who worked at modiste's—her long cigarette holder clenched at an angle in her mouth. "I'd vote for Smith [Al Smith] if I had the nerve." Guest who had climbed up to crow's-nest when tight one night—Adams had sent sailor up after her—she had been kittenish and tried to evade him. Our swim to Catalina —the lonely graves on the hillside, which we reached over pebbles, dirt and cactus—the man in the boat, seen from above, waiting on his oars against the peacock blues and greens of the little bay. The no-trespassing sign, which also forbade smoking, building fires, etc. —Looking down into the water from the yacht—dropping a ribbon with a buckle or something on it—its slightly impeded but direct progress to the bottom, where twenty feet down we saw it lie. The schools of little fish flickering silver or turning less distinct sides of purple or blue in the green depths—the large fish leisurely and fattish, moving through different colors of purple, silver or blue—all broken and re-forming as the surface of the water was broken. — Our midnight plunge from the put-put, whiskey within and the dash of slashed spray against the night without. —Going to bed, wandering around in pajamas—people visiting other people's rooms. —Thin plank we walked across to get from one yacht to the next, in the harbor at Los Angeles.

Merle Wilhoyt's attempt to arouse Clarence's jealousy. Prettiest in green dress—lightish green, clear complexion. Her little boy, not saying a word, holding down the keys inside the piano while she was trying to play. Ivy that grew in through the cracks in the fireplace and window frame—Mary Craig (a cousin of Ted's) had asked her how she had made it do that. Merle said that she hadn't deliberately trained it to, but if any little growing thing wanted to come in and see her . . . she was supposed to be a great teaser—when Margaret had taken it for granted that she and Clarence were lovers—"I won't think any worse of you, though, Margaret, for thinking that!" Only really at home and at ease at piano—discrepancy between good entertainer manner at piano and insipid artificial English-comedy manner in ordinary intercourse had a certain beauty—one set off the other—element of artificiality, in one relation happy, in other relation, humorless and irritating. —Her little niece—Miss California—never been East—very tall, wholesome, pretty, Irene Rich type, smart, got into Stanford (limited to five hundred girls)—I said that I thought more girls went to college in the West—"Isn't it prevalent in the East?"—When I said goodbye to her, she said that it had been very interesting to get my points of view on all these things. All for Hoover—had had to study different sides of election at college—they had to know something about Norman Thomas, too—but he was "just a curiosity"—Socialists would "try to do away with all militarism." —Her father and mother had fallen in love at Stanford—their initials were still there on the trunk of a tree and somewhere else, too. They lived at Santa Monica—bad undertow—boy almost drowned, while they were all out on the raft. —Merle telling me how carefully this little niece had been brought up—used to come in and sit on Merle's bed and want to talk—didn't drink and boys seemed to like it better, Merle said. —Clarence trying to keep Merle's drinking within bounds.

Mr. Ed [see p. 127]. Ted used to give the Swedish servant girls Havelock Ellis and Dr. Robie to read, demoralizing the household. He gave his father Havelock Ellis, and Mr. Ed sat up in bed reading it, with his eyes popping out. He made a few passes at Miss Mary, but there was nothing doing.

Margaret used to go up there and find him tippling all alone.

She would go down to the beach, where the Paramores had a little beach-house, and see him at the other end in a bright blue bathing suit, walking on the beach with his little mincing steps. He would do like this (arm exercise) about once—"and then go back and have another drink, I suppose."

They used to let him drive his car out to the ranch alone. When he felt a heart attack coming, he would take a pill and be all right. When he died, he had only time to stop the car beside the road. They found the pill on the floor.

Mr. Ed's birthday dinner, when his toupee came off and he put it back wrong, with the part running sideways. He had got up to make a speech, full of high humor, politeness and gallantry toward the ladies. (Ted remembered this scene as heartbreaking.)

When Miss Mary gave a formal party and Mr. Ed went out for the evening, he would always come home roaring drunk before the guests had gone—when they were playing bridge, no doubt.

His difficulty in crossing legs. He liked to sing Heine's *Morgenrot*.

Jim Paramore's singing—his mouth working in French songs—*Je suis un petit oiseau*—his fingers would be held rigid in claws—Mrs. Paramore playing the piano—Mr. Ed sitting by and thinking what a wonderful voice his son had. —Ted told me that his father was always convinced that whatever they had was the best that could be had.

My call on Mrs. Paramore. The sitting room was dark—I couldn't see the face of the enormous round portrait of her above the couch—as she had been when she was first married. Now she seemed shrunken—she had aged: she was dressed in black and wore high tennis shoes—when we left the house, she walked with a stick. But in the darkness of the room, when she lifted her chin, I could almost see the pretty girl that she had once been—her face was pale through the gloom, and the wrinkles and erosions of life disappeared. She was very sober and nice. —The sitting room had always had a little air of a smoking room in a men's club: the rather shapeless comfortable upholstered men's chairs; the well-worn and random collection of books in the bookcase. —She said that she couldn't tell how Ted had been affected by his father's "going"—he wouldn't hear about him, and she had wanted to give him some of his father's things, but he wouldn't have them. Frances, Jim's wife, had been wonderful, but Jim couldn't do anything either—I walked around the room, depressed, while she went out to give orders to someone: I looked out the long high horizontal window from which you see the lawn, the trees, a bush with some yellow flower. —She wanted to sell the house rather than let it: you hated to have tenants misuse your things: but she had let it that summer. She had come in to have a few little things done, because people wouldn't buy it, if it hadn't looked attractive: it made such a difference just putting a few flowers around, you know. She made no plans. —On the way out, she and Mrs. Drummond discussed the improvement that cutting down a tree which had stood in front of one of the windows had made—perhaps it was that long horizontal window. Mr. Paramore had loved every one of the trees so, Mrs. Drummond told me, that it had been just like pulling teeth for him to have any of them cut down. I thought what an interesting shape the house was—Mr. Ed's idea, I suppose—a certain quality of surprise, rather a rambling effect.

looked out into the upstairs sun porch, where I had read to Ted and his father my scenario, and it made me sad to think how, the last time I had been in that house, it had been full of gaiety, highballs and sunlight. I saw nothing of the other rooms, and it still seemed to me that they were rooms in the house of a dream.

Migs's story about having been with the Paramore boys and Mrs. Paramore's having said something about their father—and their having gotten in an awful state over it—they seemed to think she ought to apologize.

Mr. Ed used to sing *The Ship That Never Returned* and *I Learned about Women from Her*—the latter with "much arching of the eyebrows—oh, yes: very coy."

Jim's story about going with his father to Colonel Norton's, who didn't offer them a drink—finally Mr. Ed nudged Jim, and said, "Let's go back to our house, where we've got more active control of the liquor!"

Mr. Ed's dude accent, a relic of the Old West—Jim used to drop into it to be facetious.

Shoeto Johnson. Famous last words: Let's cut out this sissy drinking! — Margaret had come down from San Francisco with him once and they'd gone zipping along, just missing the cars all the way.

Ye Olde Pearre Ranche (Jim had inherited it from his father). Irony of anybody having to manage a pear ranch "who hates pears as much as I do."

Mrs. Paramore landing with smuggled liquor. When custom inspector asked her if she had any liquor, she said, "Why, I thought that was against the law—I thought it was against the law to bring in anything to drink!" —Ready to go out for the evening, black dress, black velvet band around neck—powdered white—effect of soft skin, though partly softness of age. —Her looking toward the portrait at her house, as soon as she had turned the light on. —Mr. Ed had always taken care of her so completely—a pretty, spoiled girl all her life.

One of the things that made Margaret furious was a certain occasion when she went out in the car with Ted and his father and they had a puncture, and she and Mr. Ed changed the tire while Ted sat in the car and read the funny paper, laughing loudly and obscenely. The situation was strained all the rest of the way, without Ted's knowing quite what it was all about.

Tommy Lincroft had been a friend of Mr. Ed, but much younger. Had run into a woman and killed her, had also tried to rape somebody: Elliot had had to go and take in all his checks. The family all said thumbs down on Tommy: he lived at home, and one of the women of the family did most of the work, and he spent far too much money, always sportily dressed, always a sporty car. His chagrin over not having become a judge, like his father. His mistress, a married woman: he behaved when she was around, but on the loose, depressed, looking for company, when she was away. Would come in or call up drunk at any hour of the night. Brought people to the Neustadts' house and when they didn't answer the bell, stood under their window saying in a low appealing voice, "It's me—it's Tommy!" Had once been the gay blade of the community—Margaret brought up to think he was a wicked rake. In later years, he used constantly to come to her house—kept wine there for himself, because he couldn't drink anything else, according to doctor's orders—she was the only person who understood how he felt on his days of hangover and despondency. Told me that he'd thought he was all right, that he wouldn't make a fool of himself again, and had then gone out and gotten stewed and done the same thing again. On another occasion, he showed up at the *Daily Press* office (he was the editor) in what he thought was pretty good order, and then a few minutes afterwards, somebody had brought his hat in. The man from Scribner's who had sold him a complete set of Roosevelt and given him a big cigar— he had been in a state of mind that morning where he would have bought anything from anybody who treated him in a friendly fashion. His admiration for his nephew in the diplomatic service—had more above the chin than any young fellow he knew. Campaigning for Hoover: Republican principles only thing for the state of California: halfhearted management of the *Press:* drunk several days after election. His almost hysterical readiness to laugh loudly whenever anyone told him about having been drunk: laughter of a man who is glad to find an excuse for his vice.

Merle Wilhoyt and Sally Neustadt—the former in her light green dress and with her smooth soft skin and her yellow eardrops—and the latter with her sport shoes, white stockings, white embroidered dress, and with her hard firm features and Mexican beak and green eyes.

Long kisses and naked embraces—the curtains, in the afternoon, transparent in the afternoon sun, their pattern of brown flowers growing liquid and shadowy-amber, and finally fading in the dusk. —The cold Adirondack-camp interior.

"Gee, those bears were cunning, weren't they?—We are, too!" (Two bears we had seen necking in the private zoo: they were lying on the floor in an amorous embrace and making low cuddly sounds.)

The gallop of the windowpanes when the train is remotely approaching.

Philip Owen's driving (typical New England boy)—cutting like wind, in the cold night air, across the curves of the road—swinging the car straight, dashing it to its destination.

He never loved her more than when he'd called on her at night, flashing a searchlight through her window, and saw her in that imperfect light, piling out of bed with her thick, brown and naked legs. [I have transferred this to some character in a story.]

A pelican flying, with its head long, dark and thick on the neck like a Scotch terrier—flapping slowly, absurdly, but with an absurdity which one found sympathetic.

Mountains stained by blue shade—and later, the pale brown rungs of the eucalyptus screens all pink in the setting sun and the mountains colored warm chalk-pink in that strange California light at once dry and warm, their shapes at once flimsy and monumental.

The child playing in the room with the yo-yo, flinging it toward some-one he doesn't like. The child, hearing that someone has to go back to work, says, "Goodbye—I hope you get a promotion."

The man who owned the zoo; he had a demoralized animal look—the man who bought real estate had the grounds laid out and the cellar of the house dug—landscaped-gardened with a triple cascade, avenues lined with California foliage, an artificial stagnant lake, dark and smooth, all in the swift Pacific sunset, obscured before one knows it—the aloes with their cones of deep-pink flowers so dashing and so bright for nobody in the dusk, above the stars of their stiff leaf clusters, and that strange flower—like some baked sea bird fattened on sand crabs and gaping on the beach—gaping with thin sharp bill and vibrating a helpless blue stiff tongue—the distant song of a Sunday evening hymn—the encampment which we saw through the foliage of the drive and which Margaret so soon forgot. —Finally he shot his wife one night but didn't kill her—she left him.

The mountains dark blue-purple in the folds and elephantine wrinkles of the bald volcanic surfaces and, above them, streaming northward, the blue-gray clouds smoking northward.
When the very soft foam seems violet and the smooth sand blue.
Orange-green of late afternoon sun on the coarse-leaved glass-plant banks.
The sea-bright blue of those butterfly wings.
The tire ensanded near the surf.

The stink, stagnant and sanded.

The gray boards, going up to the house, faintly purpled by the hour.

"A Japanese child fell in, and the other child jumped in after it—and then all the Japanese families came out—and sat in circles on the sand—waiting for the bodies to be washed up. —And it made such an impression on me as a child—because I always think Japanese are such funny little people, anyway—and it seemed sad somehow!"

The bright flecks of the gulls, and, beyond, the brighter pinker piles of the Miramar pier—and the warmer and pinker legs of the little girl and her nurse coming toward us across the sands.

Now (5:30, December 14) the sky was violet, the hills darker violet, and, below, the lamps twinkling at Sandyland, the water violet like the sky.

Orange in the west, a little wintry and cheap, behind the black rails of the pier and above the steel blue of the sea.

December 14. First, the tanned clouds against the whitened sky—then the purple of the mountains dark and dulled, cutting clearly on the white bank of cloud above it, the white bank of cloud white and dulled, but clear against the dulled blue sky. The villas bright as the edges of new coins on the hillside against the dark of the trees. On the way back from Santa Barbara to Montecito, the white fences against the green, darkened and blued, of the eucalyptus trees.

The sea with its long steel-blue streaks and, above them, the flat gray clouds all streaming, crested, northward, notching the sky, and, above them, the diluted orange against the blue sky, faded, and with the clear crescent moon above the clouds.

The waves empty and loud, resounding upon the shore.

The light hollow look of the round stones, pale brown in the beds of dry streams, behind the light dry green of the foliage, which even in December masks nature, like a scene painter's landscape (the beauty of a bad backdrop also imposes upon us), even at broadest noon and even entering the drive where anybody lives.

The Paramores' place—and the bridge above the dried-up stream—in its bower of dry leaves.

The pale dull green dresses of the film actors—the very amusing smart well-formed flapper who turned out to be a Baroness von Romberg—she was supposed to be watching the race with a field glass and then suddenly, when the man falls off his horse, dashes forward; the mushy-faced blonde in movie green—Laura LaPlante—she walks through the stand and takes her place—pasty and without distinction; the director: white and dark sport shoes, white golf stockings and plus-fours, a Jew, dark and well formed—he sat on a spiked stick, whose ends gave an effect of silver—while his dark close-curled hair had a certain dignity of iron-gray—his folded camel-nose. —The mother sitting frozen and stiff in her ermine wrap. —The second man, much more presentable and decent—he said, "I *don't* think that, at polo games, people stand between the chairs and the stand. Please sit down," etc.—thanks the spectators—sorry that the trick horse didn't arrive—Langdon Mitchell (the author of *The New York Idea* and the play based on *Vanity Fair*): "You ought to be modeled in bronze."—The polo player in green, Laura LaPlante in green, the Romberg girl in green, which would show white in the movies. —The great tin reflectors—the equivalents, in that sun, of klieg lights. —The combination, in the stand, of movie actors—one wearing a false mustache and a green and black V on a white vest—sweater under his brown coat—*pour le sport*—and with a pulled-down soft hat—dreary local people, with a sprinkling of smart local people, who, at the same time that they were fascinated by the movies, kidded all the rest.

Tighe Wheeler. The room with its colored and focused view of the Pacific—the palm tree outside the window repeating the palm tree on the wallpaper—and there was a vague white stagecoach, too—blue sea, green coarse foliage, the steady Pacific sun.

She was Mrs. R. L. Stevenson's daughter—always spoke of RLS as "Mr. Stevenson." A masculine creature with, as I remember, rather a feminine husband.

Trip home by way of New Orleans, December

An abrupt and barren gorge, after the glaring signs; the lichenous look of the hills; factitious hill of movie villas; Texaco; that trumpery skyline against the diamond California sky—dry diamond faintly blue, as the sun goes west.

The dry snow-veined Nevadas—silver against pale blue.

The salver-form of the silver-blue surf on the smooth sand.

The stiff twigs and frost-gray stems of the walnut groves.

The yellow-green cottonwood in Wyoming.

Down in de Canebrake.

Horses on the dark hill like Noah's ark animals.

The crumpled cars from accidents.

The red cactus-stung desert—the colorless brown lemon hills.

Pleasure of passing from West to East—just beyond Beaumont, a few tall modern buildings in the wilderness—people, women in bright dresses, at the lunch hour, passing fast across the tracks—the white bayou boats in the

---

muddy water, a big Gulf boat—the cold air and moister vaguer atmosphere even on the clear winter day—life more unstable, uncertain, a different kind of movement, evading the weather, washed in it as by a sea, and not the Pacific—pace less even, quickened and relieved.

The swamps and the muddy water—the sticks hung with Florida moss, like the tatters of sordid garments caught in thickets—the niggers—unpainted houses—pines—pigs crossing tracks—fallen tree sprawling in water—the dead gray swamp of sticks as colorless as a photograph—the moss itself, which had killed the trees, withered and fading away, and, below, a vivid undergrowth of palms.

Chicory in the coffee—rich shrimp soup, with okra—Louisiana food.

New Orleans. "Who in hell is Hoover?"; Rex in bone glasses (the last Mardi Gras); safety week; Tim Healy, chief of police; gambling and cotton exchange; Père Antoine; girls at Berkeley; Mayor who ran on Dreyfus; Mississippi demands that Virginia give up bodies of Jackson and Lee; candles burnt for Al Smith in the *Picayune* office—to Bishop Canon, "May God rest your bigoted soul this Christmas morning"; Mayor holding hat over abdomen, with cigar sticking out of his mouth.

New York, Clifton Springs

[I came back to New York from the Coast in order to spend Christmas with Rosalind in Red Bank. After that, sometime in January [1929], I took a cheap furnished room at 224 West Thirteenth Street, a block or two north of *The New Republic*, a narrow stale-smelling little hole, with no bathroom attached—I had to go down a flight to use a bathroom with the other lodgers. I thought that I could live there alone and begin writing *Axel's Castle*; but I had only just got *I Thought of Daisy* off to a publisher and was suffering from the letdown that sometimes follows finishing a book. I no longer had Margaret and missed her. Rosalind was at Red Bank with my mother. Anna now and then came to see me, though, as I remember, it was difficult for her then, and my room was anything but a delightful, or even convenient, place in which to entertain a girl. I was planning to marry Margaret, but felt some sort of obstruction against it—compounded, I suppose, of a loyalty to Mary [Blair] and unwillingness to divorce her, though we had not lived together for so long, a feeling of disloyalty to Ted [Paramore], who was still to have hopes of Margaret, and a feeling that, fond though I was of Margaret and well though we got along, we did not have enough in common. I was getting into the same neurotic state of mind as in the spring of 1917, when the United States had just gone into the war and I couldn't decide what to do—indecision is the only thing that has demoralized me completely; and with even worse results. One day I got a letter from Winifred in Europe, about whom I felt very guilty, especially since I had been tight at the time I took her to bed and thought that, if I had been sober, I should have had sense enough not to. I think that it was just at that time Winifred wrote me she had had a miscarriage (which I afterwards understood was imaginary). At any rate, I had written her by then of my intention of marrying Margaret. I found that I couldn't sit down in the evening and work at my book in that ghastly little room, and I took to drinking and going alone to Noël Coward's current revue, which would appear to me at the time amusing but, when I was sober, come to seem disgusting, as the silly little tunes ran through my head. *Teach me to dance as Grandma did* has always been associated in my mind with the nauseating smell of my room. At last, when I set out, at the end of one week, to go down, as usual, to Red Bank, I found myself seized with panic as soon as I got into the taxi. The symptoms were a good deal more serious than they had been on my visit to Princeton, at the time of my anxiety about the war: I began to tremble violently, and I realized that I could not go down to my mother's. I called up Aunt Caroline and asked her to recommend a doctor. She sent me to a young G.P., who simply thought I had been drinking too much and had me spend a couple of days in a hospital, putting me to sleep with a shot of morphine. When I got out, the symptoms returned. I was afraid I was going insane and got Aunt Caroline to look up a psychiatrist. I had always, I suppose, had a fear of this kind, on account of Father and Sandy. She sent me to John M. McKinney, who received me late at night in his bathrobe and convinced me I was not going insane. I told him about my father, and he pointed out—what I had not thought of—that Father had had his first serious breakdown at the same age that I was then. I went to McKinney two or three times a week, and this just made life possible for me, but the panics and depressions continued. The weeks when this was at its worst were the most horrible experience of my life. I told McKinney one day that I felt I could not live through my crises of depression, when it seemed to me I was condemned, by some power I could not control, to destroy myself in some violent way; and he gave me a purchase on the rock down which I seemed to be slipping by assuring me, "Yes, you can. You can get through it just as you can a headache. You know that it will pass away just as a headache does." He finally sent me to Clifton Springs sanatorium. It was the dreariest point of the winter, and the bleakest part of northern New York. The spell I spent waiting in a reception room that has a plain wooden clock on the wall was something I cannot describe, but I suppose I was trying to escape from the various women with whom I had got myself so badly entangled. I forced myself to get through the page proofs of *Daisy*, to finish my Provincetown poem ("We never from the barren down" . . .) and to work on an earlier draft of the first chapter of *Axel's Castle*. My satisfaction in rewriting the passage in which I tried to explain symbolism was a sign of the beginning of recovery; I made the acquaintance of Robert Reid, an old mural artist, suffering from arthritis, who died in the sanatorium. The sanatorium was boring beyond description. I could not do any drinking there, but soon became addicted to a drug called paraldehyde (belonging to the same series as ether), which has a very offensive odor but produces an exhilarating relaxing effect. I charmed my elderly nurse—to whom I read poetry in the evening—so that she gave me more than I was supposed to have, and I went on with it after I left the hospital, continually getting my prescription refilled, till, suddenly realizing one day at the suggestion of McKinney that I was in danger of becoming a real addict, I abruptly broke off the habit. Such places as Clifton Springs are rackets: they never want to let you out. They give you baths, electric treatments and massages, which partly filled up the day but annoyed me. I kept telling the doctors I had always thought that I was a strong personality and that I couldn't understand my going to pieces. The man at Clifton Springs said, "Personality can play us some very strange tricks," or something of the sort. McKinney had said, when I complained to him of finding myself weak: "Neurotics are strong people. It's like polarization in physics. The neurosis is the negative end of a positive assertion of will." He would say, "You haven't gone to pieces: you're still holding down your job." I tried partly to make amends by writing my girls letters.

I don't know whether I stayed at Clifton Springs two or three weeks, but I finally insisted on leaving, in spite of their reluctance to release me. I was grateful to Mary for calling up one day and saying, "Remember the doctors have to live, too!" I continued for a time to go to McKinney, but I hate the sense of dependence and—in spite of his reluctance—detached myself; overcame the neurotic indecision and the sense of floating in a void outside the world of other human beings, where one's ties are not felt as binding, the dreadful feeling of not being real, of not being a part of society through either purpose or relationship, the strain of associating with people combined with the fear of being alone. I got off to Dennis on Cape Cod with Rosalind and Stella, worked in the mornings in the hotel room (at the last group of poems in *Poets, Farewell!*) and read Valéry on the beach for my chapter on him in *Axel's Castle*. In the meantime, I had to face Winifred, who had quickly come back from Europe and with whom I had harrowing interviews. I corresponded all the time with Margaret. [I destroyed all my letters to her in Santa Barbara after her death, though I still have hers to me.] It was years before I recovered from what I suppose were manic-depressive "mood swings": moments of liveliness or heartiness would be followed by a despondency and silence that people did not understand and that made me, I am afraid, at this time, a rather uncomfortable companion. In the days before Margaret came back, Anna continued to visit me, and it was one of the signs of her sensitiveness that, though I tried to conceal my collapses, she always knew at once what was happening, and this made me feel a little better, for it meant that my solitary experience, my frightening isolation, was being understood, and hence shared, by another human being.

A telegram had been sent me in Santa Barbara telling me that Herbert Croly had had a stroke. When I got back, he asked me to stay on at *The New Republic*, which I had been on the point of leaving. Although partially paralyzed, he was hoping to get back to work; but he had another stroke and died. The group of editors still continued, with their theoretically equal powers. My salary was raised to put me on a level with the others. This arrangement worked for a while.]

New York

Central Park. Sun going down red over Jersey, and yellow and white buildings at the south end of the Park taking on a grayness of shadow that gave them a comparative insubstantiality and mitigated the oppressiveness of their bulk—the light greenery of May in the Park gave it, for New York, a pleasant vagueness—the double-towered apartment houses instead of cathedrals.

—old black fur rug in the hack.

Anna. After I've been with you—I'm so sleepy the next day—I'm not exactly sleepy—I'm kinda dreamy—and you know why (with renewed animation)—because I'm thinking about it!

She was lying at the foot of the bed—I at the head—I saw her eyes over her hips—soft-hard and round—like cunning burs—burs like agate marbles—with their unexpected depth, especially when the rest of her face was hidden.

Her blue short chiffony dress, with more or less flesh-colored stockings and bluntish-toed white shoes, that always made me want to go down on her: "Oh, don't do that—it makes me so weak the next day!"

I said, "You were never so happy with me as with Sam, were you?"—"I was never happy with Sam: I used to cry when he made love to me."—"Oh, you didn't always do that, did you?"—"Not at first."

Sister deaf because her mother used to hit her on the head so hard when she was a child ("We did'un have such a good time in the home, you know")—so she did'un hear bell ring—it was a wonder she heard it—she thought it was a bill collector—it's so faint you can hardly hear it—there's bill collectors there every day (example of Anna's humor—her real sense of the comic)—her little short feet—fucking her when she had the monthlies—m'm—cheeks so flushed—"Oh, don't" when I began to tongue her—"Can I love you?"—"But how?"—that rank herring smell, which I had gotten on my hands—pillow and bath towel—rust stains on pillowcase—"That was you did that, not me!"—So cute in her light and yellow uniform at Child's.

He scratched her foot on the sole with his nail—the friendly, the loyal communication, without clothes and half sunken in stupor, between human and human—her short feet on her long straight ankles—on her pretty, slender girl's thighs.

Child's, Fifty-seventh Street. Can't wear bloomers on balcony—the uniforms were hot—she got in wrong for wearing rolled stockings—they picked on her—couldn't afford a girdle—so put her at back tables, where she only made $2 and some cents—(time I saw her before, the hostess had been nice to her—a lady-lover?—used to pinch her arm and say, "Why, you dear little thing!")—she was soon transferred, however—and she thought she was going to be made a hostess—she had had to stand up all the time, on a rainy April day, when no customers came (she was sore at night when she came to my house)—the manager saw her talking to girls and spoke to her—when she paid no attention, he said, "Do you understand English?"—she answered, "Yes! can you speak it?"—he said, "Hey, Katherine!"—she said, "My name's Anna!"—"Maybe they'll fire me—I hope they do!"—"You can't get a place any place else if you quit"—"You have to get fired—the girls do all kinds of things to get fired, y'know."

She'd learned a lot since she'd been up there from hearing the girls talk—"One of them's been pregnant a month"—she says, "'Well, I'll have to get somebody to marry me!'"—Anna was rather innocent about this—apparently took what the girl said at its face value.

Tips anywhere from 5¢ to half a dollar—women tip nickels—man who came in with his girl and said, "Don't be in a hurry: the lady wants to get dry!"—"They stayed there three hours—the darned fool—he didn't know that I only had so many tables to wait on."—When the men tried to flirt with her, it put her in better humor.

Party in Brooklyn. Had all kinds of different colored things to drink—you know: what you call 'em (liqueurs)—everybody was crazy. —She went down in the morning to fix the furnace, with just a blanket wrapped around her—and all the fellows were lying around asleep and one of them grabbed and put his hand way up (she laughs embarrassedly)—it was a christening party.

Her mother used to say that she was glad that the children who had died were dead. Anna: "That's a terrible thing to say!" —Tonight (April 21, 1929) she said that her mother "was cryin' all the time, because she could'un pay the mortgage—two of the tenants have moved out upstairs—and I can' stan' that, y'know."

Worried for fear her daughter would turn out like Sam—"She's mean, y'know.—I want to bring her up right—but I don't know what's the right way to bring up a child." —tells her not to wet herself, not to lie, etc.—punishes her, reasons with her, tries to persuade her—threatens her. —"Such a little lady, when she came back from Oswego—and now she's just like any city kid, y'know." —Had ringworm on face, infected toe. —Sister's children were starving.

55 Charles Street (Ann Cummings's apartment, which I rented for the summer, while they were at Silver Lake). The bulking gray and yellow downtown buildings—but wider-spaced—of Seventh Avenue—after a drink, in the late May afternoon—velveted with the drink—mysteriously softened and colored, against the pale blue sky.

Driving in the Park on an afternoon of mid-May [1929]. The day before, after a first morning and afternoon of New York summer stuffiness and stagnancy, the late afternoon had cleared like cool water—and this afternoon it was neither too cool nor too hot—the driver, a North Irishman, asked us a riddle, after we had given him a drink of straight gin, and he had drunk our health—the light green, a little dim, of spring foliage, and, above it, the sheer gray banks of buildings—coming back to the Plaza, at Fifty-ninth Street, was like approaching a mountain range—we lay and looked up at the buildings, came back along Fifth Avenue at five—New York seemed more interesting—one had a feeling of voyage and adventure as one looked up at the varying skyline—the brownish yellow French buildings—then a rather pretty domino wall of pure blank chalk-white against the pale blue sky of early spring. —The rare bluish lakes of the Park, with their baldish shores—the reservoir. —A deserted apartment house or hotel on the west side of the Park, brown, with semi-Romanesque windows, obsolete already—it displayed great auction signs (the Waldorf was going, too). —We remarked a smart car at the Plaza, robin's-egg blue, with a set of brass bars or rods behind, and canary-yellow hubs and other trimmings—the woman who drove it wore a red hat (fashionable that year—cloches)—the cops in the Park, who never paid any attention to our Lily cups.

Tulips: May 12 (Mother's garden at Red Bank). Low canary-yellow ones in front row, varied, toward one end, by tulips of a deeper yellow and a different shape, with vermilion-lipped thorny-pointed petals, and behind these, a few all vermilion within and outside, a deep peach-blush; in the second row, among the iris clumps, taller pink tulips, and at the end, straight slender-stemmed goblets of a pale dry champagne yellow; beyond these, pink again and a temperate red—along one side of the bed, brightest vermilion within and without, and in the corner, a few of pure white— there should have been more of these—Mother indignantly said—but most of the bulbs, to her surprise, turned out small spiny-petaled flame-like flowers with red stripes along the middle of yellow petals; the tallest flowers of the last rows were deep purple, deep-stained or washed out, and finally, rose red. —The flowers of the second year were stunted and meager; there was one great pink bastard cabbage. Among the white ones was one little tulip with pink-brushed pointed petals.

The border along the drive was full of great tall-stemmed bright-red tulips with big black centers like poppies, and behind them, short shrub-like flowers, almost brown, in whose dusky mouths the triple pistil showed distinct but dryish yellow. There were two exquisite groups of ovular shell-like flowers, one coral, the other roseate. The big bed was like a basket of brightly dyed Easter eggs. The lilacs in their early stages, purple and white.

The fairly abundant parsley row; the first tender foamings of lettuce rosettes; the first growth of sweet peas, just beginning to climb their nets.

Among the tulips, a few sprays of some lily-of-the-valley-like, snow-drop-like flower, of which she did not know the name, but which she had taken over from Grandmother.

Early dandelions in the grass.

Early lettuce rosettes of lightest green foaming in their lightly drawn rows; the young tender tentacles of onions.

An early white iris—the first.

A soft pale sky of pale blue, with small, lightly floating cottony clouds, infinitely slowly floating.

She was trying to grow a young elm, a cherry tree, and a silver birch; to train a trumpet vine on one of the locusts; and she had had trellises for ivy put along the front of the house.

The cucumber frame contained a rectangular box, where little clusters of round leaves, like the paddles of water beetles, pricked regularly the gray earth, and a section of little tin flowerpots, from which there rose sprays of very fine leaves, like the antennae of moths.

On a neighbor's place, the rich bronze brown of the feather-fan fronds of some shrub and that flat pink coral canopy of something else, pink dog-wood perhaps.

Lying down in my bedroom at Red Bank in late afternoon—falling sound asleep and half waking, as afternoon sun fades to darkness, amid the waving of thick dark green leaves all around the house, abundant but vague, and the vague locomotives and cars humming past along the road—all the abundant, vague, content world of summer and the countryside, the seaside—the coolest happiest last day of June, the eve of July and deep summer.

Bruce Bliven's folk dancing, etc. He did "exhibition dancing"—and was rather exhibitionistic about it—Gathering Peasecods, Hit or Miss, Christ Church Chimes—he had just learned a new one, Old Noel's Jig.—"They're very difficult to remember." —Taught by specially imported disciple of Cecil Sharp.

Anna: June 27, 1929 (after not having seen her for about three weeks). She was annoyed with me but she forgot about what—Oh, about my saying I was only going to be away a week ("Oh, I'm so tired and sick of you!")—I still loved her so I kissed her till her mouth was bruised—and she said, "My mouth is sore from you kissing me!"—she'd just begun her monthlies—they started in Child's, and she couldn't think at first what it was (just like all the dreadful things in life)—"I'd been thinking about you all day, and what a break!" —She sat on the couch in her red hat (fashionable, like pansy dresses, that spring) with her legs apart and her feet in slightly futuristic straw shoes, and her darling dark Ukrainian eyes. —Her hair was done a little differently—longer and tacked behind her ears—she looked a little depleted by the hot weather, but said she had gained a pound—by the scale in the bathroom—her breasts, so pretty, plump and fashionable, as her legs were fashionable and slim—during menstruation her breasts were firm, pretty and pert under her "bruzzeeers." —Her darling dark deep eyes.

June 29, 1929. She worried all the time about her daughter—asked me if I worried about my little girl falling and cutting her lip, getting run over by a truck, and things like that—she'd seen this little girl in the subway who'd cut her lip—"Well, she really had no lip, y'see—I worry about her all the time—because she's wild, y'know—she sits on the windowsill." —"You oughtn't to allow her to." —"She's not allowed to, but she does it—I'm so afraid she's going to fall!—Sam was just like that—he'd get up on the roof and jump off—he'd try to jump off the roof and catch the branch of this tree." —"Well, would he make it or did he fall?"—"He fell—and then he'd jump off again and fall again—and the little girl will stand at the top of the stairs, y'know, and she wants to jump down."

Sam would write and ask her to come and see him in jail and ask her to send him money—"He really don't deserve it—just only things for himself." —One of the kids in Brooklyn had said, when they asked the daughter why her father wasn't there, "Because he's in jail!—That's a fine thing for her to hear!"

Her mouth, soft, wet and red—kissing her, after not having seen her for so long—asking if she liked to be kissed—"I like it, being made love to—I could be made love to forever!"

July 5, 1929. Used to say prayers—Hail Marys and Our Fathers—every night—didn't want to say them, y'know, after she'd been with me—but she couldn't get to sleep until she had—so finally she would say them. —She was afraid she was going to burn in hell—you had to believe in hell if you believed in God and Jesus Christ.

She had been to see Sam on Friday, her day off—he wanted her to give him $6 a month, but he'd been so mean to her—"and when he gets out, he'll just ill-treat me.—He was all dolled up in his prison clothes—he thought he looked fine, but he just looked funny."

Her little feminine sighs when I made love to her, held her against me.

Debating sending little girl to her aunt's—would rather send her to some home, where she could go to see her once a week.

Her new clothes: little pink and dappled new dress—light and summery, with scarf in bow around the neck, with flesh-colored stockings and squarish-toed big-bowed shoes, which gave her a lot of sex appeal—mouth and eyes small, strongly colored, sensual in their small cute bright way—her nose was all swollen from my whiskers kissing her—her hair, which was almost smooth, only slightly waved, smelled clean of tar soap.

New Republic. (1) Insurance man who was so much inconvenienced in subway by necessity of opening paper to find continuations of first-page stories inside that he made prolonged and insistent efforts to induce newspapers to continue them to back page. Had appealed to Walter Lippmann: "He's supposed to be a liberal," he said in a brokenhearted way.

(2) **Man** who had only pure ergot in U.S. and was prevented from selling it by Squibb's and other big drug companies, who were importing impure Polish ergot. —My attempt to have cocktails served at this lunch.

Pauline Emmett's April-fool chocolate éclair with cotton inside. —S. K. Ratcliff was there: "Is this supposed to be eaten?" he asked. Bruce, who didn't know about it, answered him it was a chocolate éclair, and Ratcliff is supposed to have gone through with it. —Bruce thought the butler had done it.

Hillsdale (New York), early July (visiting Raymond Holden and Louise Bogan, then married). The old ore pit, forty-seven feet deep, a dark oval pond with a white float in the middle of the blue-green water—dull opaque blue, with green ripple flecks, or smooth shining green with blue ripples—the deep dark water, with warm gusts and icy veins of springs—the smell of grass and water. Swimming past the float, I saw, against the white light of the setting sun, the bodies of the bathers, like spirits drawn by Blake, outlined in the light, as if half transparent and radiant themselves—seen through the air and water—then, as I watched them from the shore, leaving the raft one by one and smearing the green with blue, they swam to the landing place and clambered up, as Louise said, like dogs. She said, too, that the water looked as if it were braided—and that the ripples were like willow leaves.

When Louise whipped the water with a twig, there was a sudden stripe as of green paint, on the transparent, the crystal depths near the shore.

Catching salamanders— "salami from fresh salamanders—it's the way I

make a living—diddling for salamanders."—Dace and little spotted fish—
a school of tiny gnat-like fish, just hatched, transparent and almost invisible,
save for dark squarish heads.

—The clear green tree nearby against the dim darkening bluing mountains. —At night, the fireflies against the background of the dark foggy
opaque dull-blued mountains.

—On the ridge—the Taconic—behind the Holdens', just below the
screen of slim-stemmed, pale-stemmed poplars or aspens that make the edge
of the wood. —Lying in the long summer grass, I saw—beyond the lovely
valley—the sun dropping over the lower opposite ridge and leaving a dullish discolored orange—the moon the thinnest, hardly shining crescent—to
the east, an irregular sheet of water shone above the valley, part way up the
hill, like a lake painted on an old-fashioned map. Two lights came out along
the road that ran through the valley—they seemed a deep lemon almost
greenish, like the rank green summer grass and trees they showed against—
trains sounded through the valley, long, dull, honest, daily country trains, I
thought. —As I came down, the hills to my right were misting into night,
their folds and shoulders softened by the mist seemed at once more wild
with nature's unconscious grandeur and somehow more comforting, more
peaceful—the sky above the nearer hills glowed to intenser orange, and the
moon, though only a wisp, was bright and clear—then, as I descended
below a grassy bank, all palely furred with meadow hay, the sky above its
line was purest white. —Now the orange was dimmer and smokier again,
as I descended toward the house—and found the lamp-lit interior—the
tired people buried in their chairs.

Dennis, Cape Cod (where I spent part of the summer of 1929 with Rosalind
and Stella, her nurse). The gray sparse houses—the gray sea and sky, the
gray mist of the first afternoon we came, blowing up rainy and cold—the
green already rather meager—the sandy banks, the wave-wet solid
beach—a tangled mass of net encrusted and stuffed with crabs—the old-
fashioned dreary dry clean rather cheerful hotel—empty room with stiff
cushionless chairs in which I read a rabbit story to Rosalind—a little Gluck
by the hotel three-piece orchestra Sunday evening—old ladies—no running water in the rooms—the last gray clouds and pale gold of the Cape—
afterwards rose, and night.—Sweet pith of sweet-grass stalks, chewed
while walking on beach—rainy day—sandy shore and gray sea—that
misty damp gray and light green weather of bad Cape Cod days—the
houses white with gray roofs—the misty dunes or hills—telegraph poles.
—In the hotel—Nobscusset—the yellow faded wardrobes and bureaus.
—The moaning and murmuring of the wind in the halls on windy days—
the green young sea crabs on the beach, washed up and killed by surf, dark

green, with gilding, as it were—like the features of some mysterious
mask—the greenish sea urchins' shells, horseshoe crabs—the pools left by
low tide, clear water with stones covered with barnacles—little rivulets
through which tiny fish stream back to the sea again.

—Deep bright blue of the sea, gashed with white, on a windy day—
then, in the afternoon, as the wind abated, the shallow water near the shore
had the mirror-like blue and shine of blue butterflies' wings.

As the sun was going down, the sea was pale bright blue, perfectly flat,
and the horizon a long unbroken line—the sands were a tender gray, and
the big pools left by the tide were almost lavender—great collapsed Jell-O
molds of jellyfish, with their internal rust patterns intact, among the rocks
beside the waves—later, as we walked, the moon, waning, rose, a luminous
yellow globe—to which its irregularity gave a fluid insubstantial look—
and the sea now just brimmed on the shore, almost as if it were the lapping
of an inland pond—where the faint rhythmic wave was deadened by the
ooze of a border of seaweed, one saw merely a back and forth movement, as
if it were quivering in the respiration of sleep—the loud quack of a gull—
the low sand cliffs with grass at the top—the sand rippled like a pond where
the low tide had left it—the winking of Highland light. —Then a night,
with the moon up, all gray—followed by a gray cloudy day.

Belle Gilman (they came to see me in Dennis). She had grown stouter, but
was just as attractive—looked smart in her new clothes (bought with
Clem's $127,000 made on the stock market in a year), driving the new
car—breasts under her blue-gray jersey, shoes with blue and rose flowered
chintz patterns across instep on white—or lounging against a pillow on the
back seat—her dark bright eyes and her mouth made for love. —When
X had "tried to seduce" her, taking her in a taxi to his apartment for a
drink of water, "almost begging" her, when she balked— "I told him I
didn't do that with men, unless I was in love with them." —Z had never
forgiven her for her failure to respond to his advances in Paris—"because
I wouldn't kick him back under the table." —She said that Y "had a
mean streak, too." —I said that, Oh, everybody had. —"No: some
people are nice and some people are mean."

Dennis. The pool behind the wooden breakwater, where the little row-
boats were moored, had the deep purple and green of paint. —The
water, when I went in swimming, a little blown, was like a mint jelly.

In the green transparent water, schools of little snake-like fish, green,
with sea-horse heads and eyes, and as if gilded with spots—they had the
look of something precious—some article of luxury, fancifully imitated
from the animal world, with no attempt to catch the look of life. —
Walking down the beach in the afternoon, the little dog chasing the

sandpipers, which flew off with sharp-cut white wings—the steady succession of small waves, frilling white, one just behind the other—they
seemed laying a soft fluid transparent purplish-blue on the edge of the sea—
the tide was going out—and they left the brown sands blued. —The
families of straight tanned young people—one girl in blue, with frizzed
hair—Diana—one in green—would let down their shoulder straps to tan
themselves more completely—younger girl, with perfect slim long-legged
boy's build, but with sharp firm little female breasts emphasizing themselves
above—she wore a man's yachting hat rakishly askew—a little boy who
wore no bathing-suit top, with an extremely broad and well-developed
chest and strong young arms. —At evening, the sun a bright cherry-gold
checker partly screened by white-gray clouds, whose edges it tinged with
gold-red—and the sea gray-white above tenderest gray of the sand emerging in round smooth islets from the water left by low tide and where a dark
violated turf or mold darkening almost purplish, a darkening as of rich
earth, went exquisitely with the delicate pale-gray tints. —The girl with
the yachting cap had also white sailor's breeches, from which the long dark
straps of her bathing suit went up over her brown boy's shoulders—her
crooked slender arms slapping the sea in a crawl. —"Mary, you're a
bum!"—"No, I aren't."—"Yes, you are."—"I still aren't."

Swimming away from the hotel float—the gray waves, among which I
was myself tossed, sometimes exposed, sometimes concealed the float, on
which one girl was sitting and another, with her long hair down, was standing up.

A dull mist-impregnated day, with the sky opaque gray, not as if it were
shadowed with cloud, but as if the daylight had been thickened with mist.
—White lungy-looking sprays of Irish moss, which "makes a fine puddin'
for sick people." —Gulls, worried about their eggs, who squeak about my
head, swoop toward me with their sharp beaks, then suddenly, afraid, veer
up and off, miaowing. —A walk in bathing suit in the rain—below
Dennis, I came finally to sight of other shores—an island, low dim dark
blues and greens, with a tower or chimney of some building, beyond the
misty waters. —The old man who had followed the sea for fifteen years—
his son had been lost out there, a fine tall fellow, forty-four, right in the
prime of life—had been caught by the anchor rope or something—the old
man had caught an enormous hundred-pound sea turtle, tangled in net
rope—afraid to tie a rope to it for fear it would drag us down—fifty-five-
foot whale—full-grown blackfish weigh a ton. —Small crabs on beach
either green on underside or turning green—ocean gray-green and choppy,
sands emerging from low-tide lagoons like giant clam shells, a dull deep
brown or brown with a tinge of ginger—shells of bigger sea crabs, like big

petrified spiders—a dripping evening. —Small crab shells, all the hues of bronze from brown to green.

Cummings, in the course of one of our conversations at Silver Lake: "I know you'd—well, you'd take one step and cross the river, instead of building a bridge and going across—like me!"

Attitude—half timid, half aggressive, about killing the snake.

I had told him about my qualms in connection with certain things I had done. He replied very soundly that at the time in his life when he had certainly behaved worst, he made a point of taking earthworms off the pavements for fear they would get stepped on.

Of somebody: "He's one of those composite boys!"

When all our ideas of honor and loyalty, derived from our social class, from our Renaissance education, from our foolish early fantasies of ourselves, have been broken up and carried off by the currents in which we find ourselves drowning, we are at a loss as to what to fall back on, but we are bound to fall back on something; and this is perhaps where the real conscious solidarity of the human race begins—though we still communicate most easily, though we still seek most eagerly the companionship—or, failing that, the correspondence or the reading (I had just been reading Edna Millay's *The Buck in the Snow*), of those educated and "conditioned" most nearly as we have been—brought up in some romantic, or classical, myth of egoism—thinking them great or good or important, because, though possessing a good deal of energy, they are in the same situation as ourselves.

Walking about midnight in August in the neighborhood of Katze's old address—against the blank solid-looking walls of the warehouses and dark apartments and shops, which even by day seemed not quite living—the figures of the two girls—there was one man, who stood to one side—one in blue, the other in white, graceful in the slender straight-legged way, and live and fresh—the natural smartness of the city—human life so alive in that apparently blankest deadest wall of the city at night.

New York, mid-August. Seabright boat—dullish colorlessish blue of late afternoon (sea and sky)—city looks as if covered in faded brownish leather—big old perforated cubic masses—uniform color in dulling light—the red setting sun from Hoboken struck out a few red isinglass windows, like the tin back of an electric heater which has been turned on in the winter.

This was a list for an ideal party!
Ted and Edith Paramore
John and Marion Amen
Gilbert and Alice Seldes

Paul Rosenfeld
Tom and Julie Matthews
Sew Collins and Dorothy Parker
Benchley
Ted and Florence Leisen
Katze
Raymond and Louise Holden
Don Stewart and his wife
Scott and Zelda Fitzgerald
Thornton Wilder
Cleon and Julia Throckmorton
Allen Tate and his wife
Jean and Herbert Gorman
Cummings and Ann Barton
Dos Passos, Léonie Adams, John Bishop and wife, Edna Millay and Gene,
    Hemingway and wife, Margaret Canby
Henrietta and Louise Fort—Percy Wendell?
Howard Cox.

   Slang and songs:
O.K. (K.O.)—All right?
to get a break
to crack wise
doesn't make sense
doesn't know what it's all about
It's a howl.
Get a load of this!
I left my Sugar standing in the rain.
The Varsity Drag
My Heart Stood Still from *Connecticut Yankee*: I used to play it on Margaret's
    phonograph at Santa Barbara
My Blue Heaven
Ole Man River—Can't Help Lovin' that man!
Oh, my one and only,
What'm I gonto do if yuh turn me down, when I'm so crazy over you?

   Walter Winchell:
The Main Stem; a phrail; Garbo-Gilberting; So-and-so is that way about
    So-and-so.
ready to cry at card tricks
to give'm th' bird
to go haywire

Helen Kane:

Button Up Your Overcoat; I Want to Be Bad; Get Out and Get Under the Moon; Is There Anything Wrong in That?

August 31: Coming into New York on the Sandy Hook boat. The bridges and the buildings painted light—in silhouette, with a few grayish-yellow buildings—against the gray sky—and from that dimness, a tug swimming to distinctness and to the vulgarity of day, dark, practical and hard, as it approached the boat. —The harsh honk of the boat blew behind me, scratching raucously my eardrums—there was honking and howling on the harbor, and the prolonged diapason of a small steamer with one smokestack, just off the brown cliffs above the Battery—our boat answered with another honk. —The shipping all quiet and deserted, just before the dinner hour—only early points of light on the quiet tugs. —When I got started in the taxi, the sun was farther down, and suddenly everything was a gray blot: docks, sky and street.

Anna: August 31, 1929. Along with her dark-blue clothes, she had a make-up which seemed in unusual relief—sharp red lips—sharp dark eyebrows—and her sea-dark eyes which took that deepness.

Always keep picking on her little girl: "They'd say, for instance, she's homelier than Anna—she's clumsier than Anna." —I had just said how pretty her hands were—the hands of some fine European petit-bourgeois shopkeeper's daughter—one ring on one finger. —"You praise me all the time—nobody ever praised me before."—I had wanted to go down on her but she wouldn't let me—I don't like you to do that—I never did like you to do that, did I? —Later, when she became a little gayer and I was playing the phonograph—Irving Berlin's *Coquette*, her favorite record—and she had admitted that she always felt better after she'd been here awhile, she said, "You know, I'm awful dirty—I haven't had a bath for three days" (she had been drinking—first with the waitresses at Rockaway, then the next night but one, with Jane)—I said, Oh, that's why you didn't want me to go down on you. —No, but—! —Her pretty long slender body under the dark blue velvety cloak (she was wearing a bright dark autumn blue cloche hat, too, and looked, for the first time, quite smart)—her long waist, her round solid buttocks, when I embraced her, as we kept playing the phonograph, though she was just on the point of going.

(JA character in my story must develop toward her—just after the Follies girl?—sadistic ideas of throttling her, *au fur et à mesure,* as he becomes more and more determined to marry the girl. His interest, too, was all thrown off fucking—all the more because she was worried about having drunk too much just before and about Adele and was a little cold when she first came—and his excess sexual energy more than usually applied to studying her character and situation.)

Upset, after Rockaway party, because Jane didn't want to take care of the little girl—girls were going to Atlantic City and Florida—she couldn't go, because of her daughter, see—couldn't bear to send her to a home or anything—"She comes in and gets in bed with me every morning"—announced on the phone, apropos of Jane's refusal to keep the little girl any longer, that she was going out and get drunk every night. —Her pretty feet, in their still smart, though worn, light-brown strapped shoes, protruding from under the blanket which I had thrown over her when she was naked, save for her brassière and stockings, on the couch in the front room. —When I saw her darling dark soft eyes, "Oh, my darling!"

September 4, 1929. She came at eight, getting out early from Child's, but had gotten up at five and had to get back to put the little girl to bed. —She called up and found out that Jane had just gone out to the movies and that her mother hadn't come home yet—the child was playing in the front yard with a little girlfriend, and she had to get back to put her to bed. —Her practical grasp of things in her telephone conversation with her cousin. — She didn't even know who her father was.

One of those rapid energetic solid fucks which are snatched when one is pressed for time—she had all her clothes on but her little bloomers, which she rapidly took off while I was hastening to the bathroom to put a condom on—I made it last a long time—the first pillow didn't lift her high enough and I put another one under her—when it was over, she said, "My shoul'er—you're hurting my shoul'er." —Her eyes had that darling dark velvety organic-animal-human look—and my fingers where I had put them in her vulva smelled rich and animal-human under the nails. —I was to see her the next night.

September 5 or 6, 1929. Contrast between her and X on the baby question: she would go to doctor who always did it for her and Jane ("He always does it for us")—Only charged $35—but her mother had had a hemorrhage and they almost lef' her for dead once.

Her pretty hands—her left hand, with the dead mother-in-law's ring, which had been stolen, then pawned, then got out of hock at considerable expense, was always cleaner and prettier than the right—the hand with its smooth well-rounded longish white fingers and the slenderer wrist rounding slowly into the thicker round arm.

"Funny to have a little Edmund running around the house, huh?—I think I'm swelling up down there—I don't know whether it's because I eat a lot and have been drinking a lot . . . [laughing] I'm worried!—I'm gonta be sick and I don't think I'll see you any more all week. —Everybody would know if I took a mustard bath—it makes me faint, I'm afraid I'm gonta faint—I have to have somebody to stay in with me." —Even at that, she wanted me to come in her again after we got started.

How cute she was, sitting on the couch, hitching up her rolled stockings, her bare thighs exposed with no attempt to cover them—I spoke to her about her pretty velvety darkish eyes, and she said, "They're green—my eyes are green—if I wear a green hat, they're green."

A thoroughly satisfactory fuck, exhausted with previous exertions though I had thought I was.

September 23, 1929. Her little mouth under the moist kisses of my mouth and my finger on her little moist cunt rubbing its most sensitive spot—I felt that I was in contact with her two tenderest places—tiny, infinitely delicious, those two little spots on her slight small body where flesh, where personality melted into magic and delight.

The first time, I was so anxious not to come in her that I withdrew and came on the pillow—she had said, when I whispered I didn't want to come in her: I w-a-nt . . . !, holding me to her, not wanting to let me go. —Then, to make up for that first miscarriage, I did it a second time and came in her.

The night she arrived at an inopportune time and I parked her at Julius Ranganeschi's. She turned out (it was at a time when I was least prepared to face it, least willing to have it so) to be bursting with eagerness—after the time she had come to me so tired, after having told me, for the benefit of her family, over the phone, that she never wanted to see me again as far as she was concerned—with sex appeal, her hair all the stronger brass for the new dark green dress she was wearing, and her color high—she was so pretty at Julius's, staring around, shy, but assuming for the occasion a woman's dignity—she said of the lumpish chunky patrons of Julius's, "They all look so nice!"—When we got back to the apartment, I began to kiss her. "I'm way ahead of you," when I apologized.

She had been quarreling with the family—they thought she let every man she knew lay her—she had stayed out late at night to help take care of the five children of a man she knew— "I don' know what he does, well, he's a gennulman, anyway" —he was the husband of a "good friend" of theirs who had died. —But the real reason, she said later, was that she'd taken the little girl out for a walk and the child had said that Aunt Jane didn't care whether she got anything to eat or not—she just gave her cornflakes any time of the day—so Anna took her away and left her to board with some people whom she'd never seen before but who she was sure were all right—she hadn't spoken to Jane since.

Her mother and Aunt Lilly had been going to have a conference about her—about having her divorce Sam—they were afraid she was going to the bad—her mother had said she would split my head if she ever saw me (I had threatened to go in at Anna's when I took her home)—but Anna, calling up and finding her mother wasn't there, went back to Brooklyn with some sly-naïve triumph. —They'd said nothing, she told me, when I asked her about it later—her mother had called her darling that morning—you ought to have heard all the names she's called me—and she wanted to get back early, as she'd promised. —She had to go see Sam Friday, her day off—and she might be late coming down to see me, because the child hated so to have her leave her—"I don' want to go back to Brooklyn," she'd say, "but I don' want you to go!"

September 27, 1929. All worried, nervous and restless—"Oh, I wish I hann'un smoked so many cigarettes!" —Long talk about Sam and family situation—had been afraid to go see him at Sing Sing on her day off (Friday) for fear she'd tell'um everything—the last time she'd been there, after not having written or visited him for two months, he came in and looked terrible—"What do you mean?"—"He just stared at me and didn't say anything like he was sore—then I talked to'um and told'um I still loved'um and everything and after a while he calmed down.—He thinks that everybody is through with'um.—He's a bad egg—he's just about as bad as they come—I'm afraid of him—I'm afraid he might cut me up—he would'un kill me—he says he wouldn't kill me because he doesn't want to burn in the chair."

She looked so cute in my white pajamas when she cold-creamed her face for the night. —It was so sweet to have her little gentle young body in bed with me—her soft dear shadowed eye hollows with the cunning sincere greenish eyes—and her little pink amorous mouth—her new light stockings and new dark brown shoes which made her legs look pretty. —She was very cunning, saying, "Well, you said you'd leave me alone.—Well, let's go to sleep!" at the same time that she would respond with a little soft tender pressure, when I turned her to me and put my arms around her. I had persuaded her to spend the night by embracing her, as she half reclined across the foot of the day bed, and rubbing her cunt—her green dress was up from her lap—gently and persuasively with my finger—she had wanted to go at first without doing anything.—We slept uneasily, I continually turning from one side to the other and switching over the pillow, and the mosquitoes harrying us.

In the morning, a capable young woman, in her green dress, ironing her apron on the card table.

The whole evening and night left me, through the following day, a memory of sweetness and dearness—affection, satisfaction.

"Hannun assident" (had an accident).

Mid-October 1929. "Have you come yet" —Her cunning little dark-fringed eye opening and looking up at me when she had turned away toward the wall and I leaned over and stared at her three-quarters hidden face.

When she was having her monthlies and spent the night with me and wouldn't do anything with me, she got me into such a state that I went to the restaurant the next day to arrange to meet her when she left in the afternoon and tried to induce her to live with me—my mind was full of the picture of her in bed in my pajamas and lying between me and the wall—I was continually getting tumescent even walking in the street until, the night before I was to see her again, I went off in my sleep.

The night she came and took a bath while I went out and got some dinner—when I came back, she looked very clean, in my pajamas, which were white and the upper half of which, except for the top button, didn't button—and Russian, with a broad face, flattish-looking nose and blond-looking hair parted in the middle—eyes seemed clear foreign light green, as if they had been washed, too—she smelled sweet from powder and soap—it was nice to have her without that slightly sour tarnish of the smell of poverty.

When she was a little girl, she had always thought she was homely, had been told so—used to sit in back of schoolroom, so people wouldn't see her. Sister used to go with sailors and chauffeurs and everybody and get all kinds of presents and give them away, but never gave her any. She thought when she saw other girls' mothers make a fuss over them that they were just putting on. She never had anyone fuss over her the way I did—had never had a father. I asked her whether the husbands in the family didn't fuss over the wives—she said no, they expected them to do things for them—then added, after a little thought, that she supposed they did take care of them.

His letter from Sing Sing (So-and-so Street, Ossining)—*done* for *did, of* for *have*—taxed her with infidelity, apparently hoping to make her confess it—she had told him she had been drunk—"and what Christ-like creature am I not to forgive you?—I know that I am a phony crook and a liar and that I haven't been fair and just to you, but I still love you, etc.—pay no attention to what other people say—use your own judgment—sixteen more months—I am only in here two years, and I expect to live with you fifty years if you will have me—I am going to sing a song for you in the show—bring up Lizzie." —The other letters she had had from him had made her cry.

November 1929. She had thought that men's cocks were stiff all the time because whenever they got close enough to her for her to notice, they always were—when men danced with her and when she was a little girl and when they'd held her on their legs—(with sudden bitterness) "The dirty things!"

Period when I got jealous of her (following the week when I'd seen her almost every other day, but she wouldn't do anything with me the night she stayed when she was having her monthlies and when I got all hot about her and went around to Child's to ask her to live with me)—I found her at 220 West Forty-ninth, which had a door like a garage: you pushed and went right in—with a girlfriend named Ethel Mildred, whom I suspected of having Lesbian designs on her—my scene with her in the cab—she wanted me to go to Child's, so that they could see Marty, Ethel's "big moment"—I kept ragging Anna when I got her home, piling up barriers between her and me—she said, "You don't care about me, anyway!"—that I must be getting tired of her because I was beginning to pick on her—I kept asking her in bed whether she still loved me—"I don't like the way you ask—all right, if you don't think so—I could say I did, anyway, couldn't I?"—The cheap drinks at the speakeasy and the Limburger cheese we had, made her sick to her stomach and had given her bad breath—our love-making was perfunctory—we scarcely kissed, she turned her head away.

The time before this (we had left off using condoms during her safe period), I had screwed her on the couch with her green dress on—peculiar satisfaction of fucking without condoms—the comfortable magic feeling of the fusion of moistures afterwards when you lie together a few moments still coupled—human sub-superhuman.

The time I took her to Peter's and afterwards to the National Winter Garden—brought her home at the end of the first half—she was having her monthlies and passionate, begged me not to take her to my apartment but evidently wanted to be taken—as I was opening the front door, I asked her if she didn't want me to get her a drink—"Don't you want one?"—she: "I want you!"—passionate embrace, once inside the apartment—she started to go down on me but stopped and wouldn't finish (perhaps on account of directions I had given her as to how to do it)—steadfastly refusing to be screwed, she threw herself on top of me and kissed me—I finally took off her Kotex, etc., unpinning safety pins—"Do you want it that bad?"—and went through her on the edge of the bed. She had bought a new cheap ($3) black dress, with orange trimmings on the skirt and over the right breast, for the occasion; and at the restaurant had said, "I should think you'd be ashamed to come here with me—so many nice people come here—I could watch these people all night!" She thought that the loudmouthed cut-up, who was impersonating a radio announcer, looked like Sam—Sam had used to be a cut-up, too—"I never thought he was funny, but everybody used to laugh at him."

Her brother-in-law over in Brooklyn always used to be asking, "Well, did Mr. Wilson get it in tonight?—Why don't you let poor Mr. Wilson get it in?"—or, "I can see that you had it tonight!"—"He says that every night I come back."

The night she brought the child around, because, after having taken her back to Brooklyn for a visit, she couldn't get her to stay with the Ukraines who had been taking care of her—they were more strict with her, see—and the little girl would cry and wouldn't let Anna leave her—Lizzie was extremely pretty and attractive on this occasion, neatly dressed and her dark hair cut straight in a bang—her big dark eyes, peculiarly intense, but with a winning intelligent smile of the eyes for Anna—my rubber peanuts, mechanical mouse and rubber pretzel—I broke the mouse winding it too tight and tried hard to fix it—Anna finally said, "Never mind: Mac will fix it—he's a mechanic." I asked Lizzie how she'd like to spend the night here, and sarcastically: "Like fun!" —Anna disapproved of her talking like this, said she learned it from tough children. —Anna would give her orders and correct her very roughly and sternly. —Little flat nose contrasted with conspicuous intense eyes—Lizzie's eyes made Anna's green ones look pale—legs crossed, mature shoes of a young married matron. She embraced me behind Lizzie's back, till Lizzie heard my kiss and turned around. Her aunt's family used to tell her that Lizzie was ugly, but on another occasion, Anna when I told her that Lizzie was unusually cute, said, "That's what everybody says." Lizzie had rather a hoarse little voice—spoke laconically but, as it were, firmly and fully.

When I was moving out of Ann Cummings's apartment, she wanted the Helen Morgan record, *Mean to Me*, that I had bought, and also Irving Berlin's *Coquette*, which had always been her favorite—I told her at first that she couldn't have *Coquette* because it belonged to Ann—when I finally said, "All right, take it," she was suddenly transported with excitement and delight. —She told me later that Jane had been crazy about it—"They were all crazy about it"—but that Jane had sat on it, and now she cried about it—she used to be playing it all the time and she'd put her head right in to listen to it—now there was only part of it she could play.

> "You treat me coldly
> Each day in the year!
> You always scold me
> When anyone else is near!
> Mean to me—you're mean to me!! . . .
> Can't you see what you mean to me?"

Cold gray Sunday afternoon when she came to see me—funny effect of having her in broad gray daylight between the cold white sheets in her prosaic mid-afternoon brassière, etc. (she had taken off her pink stiffer winter slip), reminded me of afternoon when she had come to see me at Twelfth

Street—perhaps for this reason, in spite of the cold gray afternoon, it had a certain flavor and romance—the warm body and rank mossy underparts, the mystery, the organic animal, the human furnace of heat and juice, between the cold afternoon sheets and in the tomb of the gray Sunday room.

Her brother-in-law was a wop from Palermo—his name was Buzzant and they called him Buzzard—he was stupid—he didn't have much to say—he just asks questions—he's so stupid, he just asks the same questions over and over again. —When she'd come back from seeing me, he'd ask, "Didn't he get it in tonight!"—You think I wouldn't razz'um [Al?]—boy, I'd razz'um, and how! —I told her that, if she failed to come the night she promised, I'd knock her block off—she said, All right, fine!—I like to fight! I can't hit, but I can scratch and kick.

Effect of moving into Ninth Street from Charles Street: our love-making was informal and sloppy on the old familiar day bed, more a matter of course, without ceremony. —She was wonderful when I screwed her the second time lying on her face—her pretty bare behind and thighs between her black dress and her gray stockings—just as I was about to get on her, she kicked up a foot, with its black neat waitress's shoe, in a last gesture of wantonness, of playful pretended resistance—her round pink buttocks and thighs in the midst of her black clothes in the darkish room of shaded light extremely provocative and satisfactory. —She said, "Aren't you terrible!"—a kind of thing she almost never said. —Time on Thirteenth Street, when she said, Pig! humorously, when she wanted to go, in an evening gown, and I wanted to put it under her arm—We've been bad enough already!

Her little low-slung behind, which gave her a long straight back—so that her dresses were made to hang rather smartly through catching under the scooped-in curve of her buttocks—caught up by the fashion in front—her green dress.

Her attempts to convince her sister that she should come over to her mother's house in Brooklyn to have her baby—the sister didn't like the mother on account of her paramour Alex. But her mother would be gone then, which would make it possible for Anna to rent the house from her mother. Had talked all afternoon—was tired talking—the sister was so dumb she couldn't see it—"She don't like my mother, that's why." —I asked about the child with the running ear, was he all right?—"Yes"— very scornfully—"He's a big pain in the neck!" —She couldn't get over her sister's dumbness—"Jesus, can you imagine it? Jesus!"

November 26. In bad state of mind—first time I think I ever saw her cry—I think I'll commit suicide—"What's the best way to commit suicide?" — After we had made love, I asked her if she felt better, and she said, "Yes—I always do." She had persuaded her sister to bring her family to Brooklyn, but Johnny had drawn up a paper which he wanted her to sign in the presence of a notary public, agreeing to pay the rent and pay for the food in Brooklyn, and if they didn't like the arrangement, to pay two months' rent in advance on some other apartment. The sister was expecting a baby, and there was no one but Anna to be with her—she knew that, if they came to Brooklyn, Johnny would stop work—the sister, it seems, thought that it would be a fine idea to leave Johnny, then she could qualify to put the children in a home—"Imagine! having children to put them in a home!" —If she went to live with them, she'd have to support them all—"I can't live with those people!" —Besides, the boy was terrible— "I'm afraid he'd do something to Lizzie"—he'd cut her lip—"Honestly, he's *terrible*—you can't do a thing with him—he breaks the windows!—and he don't pay attention to anything you say—he just sits and looks at you—I think he's crazy." —"Also, in Brooklyn, Lizzie just opens the door and she's out—but over there, she's out running in the streets and I'd be afraid she'd get hurt." The sister's family tried to live on $24 a week.

She put her arms around me and kissed me as if I meant something to her—as if to embrace me and be embraced brought her some relief.

Anna and Lizzie had just a couch to sleep on in Brooklyn—Lizzie wouldn't stay with the Ukraines, she used to make herself sick—the mother couldn't afford the house any more, she was moving to New York; but Jane couldn't move in with Anna, because she had to stay with her mother—couldn't take all the furniture away—wouldn't live with mother's furniture, which her mother would simply store in the basement—six-room apartment. —Jane didn't have as much money as Anna had always thought, either—she had hard time paying rent on the six-room house.

After Sam and Alex had been in jail the first time, they used to go out to Coney Island, where there wouldn't be nobody else, and they'd take great quantities of wine and they'd all get cockeyed—her mother and all. —She wished they could have one of those parties like they used to have in Brooklyn—I offered to pay for the liquor, but she replied with some scorn that it would cost $50— "Why, it would cost $100! you have to have sandwiches and everything—when we give a party, we give a party, I'm tellin' you!—The husbands never see their wives at these parties—but there isn't anything mushy, you know—I hate petting parties, don't you?—I sleep without any clothes on, and I went downstairs to fix the furnace and I wrapped a blanket around me and boys were laying asleep on the floor and every old thing, and they tried to pull off the blanket—there was one layin' in his underclothes with his thing out."

She was so darling—little white thighs—breasts so much fuller than when I first knew her—Shall I tongue you a little?—I don't know that I ever enjoyed loving her more—I told her so, and she asked, "Why tonight?" —Cunning black waitress's shoes, which she had taken off—nice to have her with rolled stockings again—at Child's she had had to wear long garters like harness attached to a thing around her waist.

One night at Charles's she had said, "You're no good any more—you used to be able to do it twice!"

Later on, she felt for my cock and took it out—it was as small and limp as possible—a mere little tassel of flesh. —"This is terrible!" —I laughed. —"I should think you'd be ashamed to take it out!" —I said later, after she had been coaxing it along for some time, "Is it any bigger now?"—"Yes, but not enough." —I did it behind the second time; straight smooth young little back, legs and unobtrusive bottom. —She slept about an hour and a half—then got herself up and went back to Brooklyn—"I wish I didn't have to go back: my eyes sting so!"—gray-eyed, pale-eyed, tarnished with fatigue, in the staleness of clothes put on in the evening, taken off and put on again to go in the middle of the night, with her mouth pressing in goodbye against mine, she left.

New York from New Jersey ferry, etc.

December 7, 1929. Coming out of Pennsylvania Terminal into a world of white thawing mist—all lost, dissolved in mist—only, above, the brightening-through white clouds of a buried noonday sun and, below, in the foreground, the distant coat of snow with the stiff brown marsh grass growing out of it. —The dark square shacks in the marsh—and later, the square blind dark factories.

December 8. From the ferry at Jersey City, the city against the pale flat bluish air, its planes to the south brought out distinctly by the dim noonday sun, like the peaks of mountain ranges, and all below, the steep enormous bulk like the bulks of mountains left in shadow, darker, bluer, but the same color as the sky, was like the painting of something solid rather than the solid thing itself—the painting in light forms and colors—till, nearing the Liberty Street slip, the grooves and windows of the great sides of the buildings became prosaic and lost the hues of distance—became colorless and lost the composition of high and low, light and shade.

(The weather was still unnaturally mild—too warm—the change had given me a sore throat.)

December 9, 1929. She began laughing, as I was talking to her on phone—"These kids are certainly well trained!" —She told me in the evening that Jane had trained her little daughter to say, "Mamma's not home," when bill collectors called, but this time she had been looking out the upstairs window, so the bill collector came right in.

December 11. The buildings gray, varnished and arid as the winter walls and pavements of the town, among which one would soon be making one's colorless way.

10 Bank Street. Ainsworth (the man who lived there) had been in it seven years—dirty—dreary, shabby: horse-racing picture; silhouette; *American Mercury*; couch which turned into folding bed, if you propped it upright; couch admirably adapted for petting, cigarette holes burnt in it; *jour blafard* of bedroom and bathroom; phonograph so antiquated that it ran down on twelve-inch records, and records so old that they only had music on one side; pieces of rare furniture, china and glass which he'd picked up, under china closet (which had shades like window shades, one with idealized peasant boy kissing little lass, one other with the lad going away and leaving the little lassie in tears); bottles of Gordon's gin, carefully evenly stacked, and gallon containers; window in front room, which, when you'd pulled down shade and tried to close it all the way, went slowly but inexorably shooting up behind the shade; handsomely bound telephone book on nice old desk; telephone, with European receiver-mouthpiece, long since disconnected, photographs of Ainsworth in navy costume on dresser in bedroom with girlfriend, presumably also seven years ago, looking rather cute.—Ainsworth seemed mildly cocky and in an inoffensive way self-satisfied in the photograph—he looked now both too stringy and too loose—colorless phase with two heavy lines in it—ice pack with records under china closet; small hot-water bag in bathroom—Remington Indian, large intolerable poster picture in bright colors; complete Scribner set of F. Hopkinson Smith, *The Rubáiyát*—the rugs very dirty and worn, the grime of city streets of countless winters tramped and stamped into them till the original patterns and tints were almost indistinguishable.

Anna. She was all hopped up over her sister's baby—I could hear it when she first announced its birth to me over the telephone—in spite of her previous misgivings and objections. —On the old dark shabby couch, she looked so pretty, desirable, that reddish-orange touch of color in the muffled electric light—her legs crossed and stuck out straight before her, with her little black waitress's shoes. —She wanted it right away—lost no time. —Afterwards, she said, "I want some more."—"Wine?"—"No"—she laughed. —"I'm going to get somebody who can do it eight or nine times." —When I told her that I was going to get married, she clung to me without saying anything. "So you were thinking about marrying somebody else all the time!" —I told her about everything and asked her if she understood and she said, "Yes."—Then she began to tell me the true story of her affairs since I had known her—told me about Jimmy, whom she had met at the Tango Gardens—he used to go out with her and never tried to start anything—he didn't know how to make love to a woman or anything—she finally became annoyed with this and made him kiss her, after which he wouldn't let her alone and got to be a pest, so that she wouldn't see him—"I kinda liked you."—She'd gone to Baltimore to get away from Sam.—She said something about her life—I had never heard her talk so about it—"I'm never really happy or anything." (When I talked to her about marrying her once, she had said that she couldn't bear to marry anybody and have him unfaithful, after her experience with Sam.) She was sorry she hadn't invited me to the family dinner party.—Second time: "Take that thing off! . . . Maybe I want a little baby, too" . . . (I had already taken it off but went to the bathroom and put on another one.) . . . I didn't mean what I said. My hot whiskey, sugar and lemon for my cold—I drank it in the dark on the little narrow cot, with her on another cot on the other side of the room— comfort of having her there, contentment—but it turned out in the morning that she'd been cold all night—she set the alarm for five, then, when it went off, roused up and shut it off and went back to sleep. —In the morning I got into bed with her and, feeling from behind, ran forefinger along little wet soft slimy slit—strangely juicy compared to her dry averted apparently somnolent morning back—hair seems dry and tintless in the morning.

Next time. She liked to order her sister's family around—it gave her authority and importance—Johnny didn't like her but he did what she told him.—She thought Jane knew that she hadn't stayed at her sister's—she gave her dirty looks.

Last days, December 1929. She used to say, when I took her to a restaurant or, at first, when I went out with her on the street and I was silent, "Well, why don't you say something?"

She didn't think of writing as work—didn't think of me as working because I didn't work with my hands.

She looked chic and glowing, under the hall electric light, in her green dress coming downstairs to open the door for me—I loved to watch her movements as, sitting on a bed, she pulled on her sister's small gray galoshes—one knee lifted, back bent, arms pulling, head with reddish hair lowered.

Last day. Narrow escapes from callers—pulled down shades (afternoon) and, after one prompt bout, lay quiet in each other's arms on the couch till our tender silence was broken by somebody, whom I didn't let in, ringing the doorbell—she seemed sad, but didn't say so—gray eyes brooding and desolate—she said, "Well, I'll have to look for another lover."—She told me not to cheat on Margaret—then when I dropped her with the taxi over on Second Avenue, she said, "Goodbye, be good to Margaret." —She had told her family that I was going to get married—"Well, so he gave you the air!"

My visit to her sister's—the grouchy-looking baby, brutalized-looking—"She looks mad"—"steam-heated apartment," apropos of coal stove. —The gray dreary drizzling day, going over to the East Side.

Discovery on Christmas Eve of crabs—shaved myself and spent evening removing them—pathetic horrid little blind beings—didn't know what had happened to them when detached—waved little claws around gropingly, at a loss—a whole community in various stages of development.

When I suspected her of having stolen the keys—I interpreted her constrained anxious manner a "consciousness of guilt"—I was so much relieved and pleased when I discovered that she hadn't, and when I got in by climbing down the fire escape from the window of the apartment above—knocked out old screen and got into bedroom.

After we had parted and I had discovered the crabs, she began to fade into the dinginess of some of my first impressions of her, to blend with and disappear in the grayness of the winter pavements. —And when I went to see her at the Broadway and Seventy-second Street Child's, she seemed to me flat-complexioned, pale-eyed and rather plain under the too relentlessly bright light, among the almost Babylonian black onyx marble walls and in front of the cascading gilded fountain lit with electric light (the even thin tinselly waters themselves a kind of gilt)—she had just started in work, she said, and was tired and felt sick—wanted money for dress to wear to New Year's party, the hostess taking her and providing a boyfriend—I asked her why she didn't wear her green dress and she said that she had had it washed and it had shrunk—she hadn't been sleeping lately—then, as I was talking to her, I saw her little firm round red mouth.

I went up again New Year's Eve, when I had just been to the Neugasses' cocktail party for Genevieve Taggard, and, ordering corned-beef hash with a poached egg, slipped her $10 in a package of cigarettes.

—and mistresses who cannot stay
Leave loneliness behind and drunken nights.

Cummings's marvelous mimicking of the New Playwrights Theatre plays: two men sitting around: "When does the strike begin?" Then the other says in a high falsetto voice, "Mother's over at the house sewing her eyes out!"

The New York streets from a taxi. That misty gap at the end of the Avenue. Beyond the bright windows, loaded with color and light—

beyond the green and yellow lights—the misty rift in the stone—those buildings beyond the Arch—gray on the gray-pale sky—beyond Madison Square—the sun on the biscuit-box buildings and the clock tower—beyond the cigar stores of the Avenue and the red lights of the Flatiron corner drugstore, the trolleys and the trucks on Twenty-third Street—that stop my taxi—girls in nude summer stockings—those personalityless international eating places—we're nearer the Arch—Fourteenth Street—a slab of sun—turns down Twelfth Street toward the El—Jefferson Market Court.

Moment of evanescent—brief, dissolving—clarity in the darkness—shining darkly from the muffling and obscurity of intercourse under the covers—seeing in a clear and tranquil flash the imperfection of the present sexual relationship, the satisfactoriness of some other woman.

Anna. Early in January 1930. When I said or intimated that she might have caught the crabs from living in filth at home, she stiffened up and said so indignantly that they had everything clean at home—the only time I had ever seen her defend the dignity of her family in this way—so that I told her—as if apologetically—how clean her sister's apartment had seemed to me. —Her green dress was torn through the elbow—I thought she looked a little *abruti*—I asked her why she was living at her sister's: "Because Johnny hasn't got a job, that's why!"

In the taxi, as I was taking her home, she said, "You're suppose' t' care so much for me an' then yuh live with another woman—and I could'un even kiss a man unless I liked him: —Well, you threw me over for her."

When I had accused her of being unfaithful: "G' Lord, I'm the best girl living! I'm so good—so decent!—only you, that's all!"

"Gosh, I only wish Johnny works now—my mother's holding the apartment for us out there now—oh, it'll be lovely!"

Like Pauline, had heavy cadences weighting the ends of what she said—a note of dull accustomed sadness at the constant hard condition of things.

I kept saying, Why did you give me those wild animals?—Wild animals?—You'll make me laugh calling them wild animals.

[In spite of the vermin, it never occurred to me to accuse her of having been unfaithful; and though she had given me gonorrhea, I assumed she had caught it from her husband and didn't know she had it.]

Riverton, Connecticut, mid-January 1930. Black and white nights—dark walls of the foothills of the Berkshires and round and oval spots of snow in the dark river bed. —Then thaw, everything blurred with the mist of melting snow. —Then snow turning to hail, which scratched the landscape across, already etched by brush and birch. —Then the cold: a night rung clear, the snow crisply crashing underfoot, the stars contracted to pinpoints but jeweling the sky, the moon, gibbous, coming up over the eastern wall of hills, a globule of rarefied yellow, weighted but too firm to burst—the translucent lemon luminance of a window laying a longer, dimmer but clear-marked panel along the snow. —The next day, clearness, snow, sun—the dark hill flat as a tapestry (as at Austerlitz early in the spring) where the white of the birch stems showed like a fine pale stitch. —The next night, darker, going out for a short walk, I saw the tiny stars glistening, as I moved, through the branches of the high fine black broom skeletons of the elms. Muffled night, hills, houses and river all buried, dumbly present in the dark, hardly a dog barking, shut in the house—warmer, the eve of a thaw?

The inn—applejack and Canadian beer ($1.50 a bottle) and very bad alcohol sold as gin, rye and Scotch at the bar, with its plaster bas-reliefs of Paul Revere, its coyote head, with, on each side, old top hats of the stage-coach days (it was on the old Albany stagecoach route) and various guns, large imitation dice, etc. —English waiter (former second huntsman in England) and wife (hours in private service too long in New York, so came up here and started to raise chickens)—substantial big white house next door, regular New England squarish windows and open green blinds, squa-rish red chimneys, but with large Japanese vase filling middle pane of decor-ous, restrained and, as it were, flattened bow window, of which each of the reddish-brown shades was pulled down to the bar which cut the pane in half (the vase filled the section below). The windows next to the door, we noticed, had only one blind, and we assumed that it was double and opened all the way across.—The bow window with the (blue and red) vase had the look of being a concession—there was nothing generous about the ampli-tude of its bulge—the bow-window idea had been moderated so as to seem a little stiff and chaste (starched, cold). —Old factory where Hitchcock chairs had been made, now rubber-nipple factory—pinkish, not painted for a long time, looked abandoned—wood-pulp mill which had gone bank-rupt. —House mysteriously darkened toward street, but where heavy heady rhythm of mechanical contraption was always heard throbbing—an occasional building of brick.

Attractive appropriate ribbed-iron bridge just in front of inn—the river always falling at the door—

—Here am I among elms again that ribbed with iron pillars the clear night, strong as the heavenly vault—

Silver pane above frozen puddles in the road, the rondures of the edge followed with cloisonné veins—wintergreen in the woodpath—wood roads that follow the river on either side—climbing the road that goes straight up behind the inn—starting a partridge at the top, which whirred up like an airplane.

—Vast double beds that sag in the middle and that tilt on uneven floors, through the cracks in the boards of which one sees the gleam of the light from the bar.

Twilight on a snowy day. An unsteady pale light, as if not of night, with faint dull pink above the western hills and all the white houses secure and comfortable at the end of a snowy day, one with the windows at the side, orange with the light of the evening lamp, down almost to the snow, as if on close and unterrified terms with the winter world of the north but still clearly marked off and delimited, in its firm and fastidious civilization, by the clear and almost elegant outline of its white sides, from the essentially rude and wild uncouth world of the snow—even the falls were crusted.

—At night, it was cold, evidently freezing—and the snow, above the hard basic ice, was fine underfoot just as it had fallen in the morning.

Deer tracks—deer flashing across road as we came down hill in the twilight—[hemlocks slim trees, *birches* for poplars]—old men in the hills, with the soil pounded into their faces, yet, though blackened, not dirty-looking. —A fine fast energetic voluble walk in the snow, on a couple of stiff drinks of applejack, while it got colder all the time and froze our shoes as we were coming home to the inn, and, in our room, we confronted one another with faces as red as peonies or beets.

The next day (January 23), looking out the inn window, after a couple of applejack highballs at the bar—the massed buildings of the small town—to the right, the faded brick of the chair factory, with its high square-notched roof of snow, the white houses beyond the bridge, under the fine sea-fan black spreading lines of their elms, and in the foreground the black arc of the iron bridge, with its rim of ice and its trimming of icicles, bright in the declining light and answering the bright edge of the brick factory's roof. — When we went out and walked along the river road, the pale lovely orange light lay in strips from between the buildings on the farther bank across the soft absolutely untouched counterpane of the snow on the frozen river— the softest most inviolate surface ever seen. —Beyond, the river was marbled by the current running, with a low urgent murmur, among the oval islands of snow, and, on the other side of the road, the brush was burnished bronze-pink by the sun and veined by the white of poplars. —Farther along the river road, where the road had begun climbing and falling, taking turns as the river commenced to wind among the hills outside the town, the brush and saplings, in that still gentle and steady light of day that took away the sharpness of winter sunsets in New York, had a green at once soft and dark, and against it the dry leaves were soft and brown, matching the diluted winter pink of the last light—even the white of the snow underfoot soft and not glaring or blank, at that hour in that home of snow. —When we returned, we saw the square windows of the inn, hung with curtains of illuminated orange peel, extending back along the unexpectedly capacious building to the out-buildings and black trees behind.

(Before this, the slightly unhealthy-hued yellowish-green ice in the icy running current of the river.)

I found a little field mouse in the snow today—brown and with a blunt nose—I picked it up, it thought it had concealed itself by running under the snow.

—At night, as we lay in bed—under the patchwork quilt in little octagons, of which the white ones were inscribed in a clear and fine, though rather faded, hand with Bible texts—the ebb and flow of the radio bringing incongruously the wavering fluid gold of Debussy, the music of old Victor Herbert operas and the *St. Louis Blues*—after which our reading would be punctuated by the regular rhythmic activity of the electric refrigerator, which, when it started, would cause the lights we were reading by to blink a moment and grow dim till, with the end of the refrigerator's buzzing, they came on somewhat brighter again.

—Brindled with birch, the brindled hills—Margaret's brindled hair.

—In the morning, on those white bright cold days of snow, we would see out the window, as we lay in bed, the teams hauling wood on low sledges.

January 24. Walked out in the afternoon on the farther side of the river, and on the opposite side, saw the hills, where a dried-ink black of blotting paper was brushed with brown and silvered with birches. —We found the snow-carpeted ice firm on the river and we walked across, exploring a little island on the way—the friendly dog followed us—he always deserted other people for us, no doubt because we were always setting out on walks as they were coming back. —That night the stars were dim. —While, on our right, we would see above the dark hills, the radiance, as it were, both candid and gray—better, sober—and yet, even in that winter air, with its luminance of glory.

—Red bricks of old chair factory worn to a pink without warmth, but with its own delicacy, and in places even whitened.

—The next days, cold as blazes—went out for a walk at four and came back with hands and faces freezing.

—Saturday night drinking and talking in bed—while sounds of sociability and conviviality in the other parts of the inn made us feel we were participating in the general cheer—consumed whole pint of apple—political conversation, after we had turned the lights out, coming up through the cracks of the floor, on Woodrow Wilson, etc. —I kept saying to Margaret, "I bet you never heard a discussion like that in California!"

—the clogged encrusted cauliflower falls.

—Monday. Warmer, after a night of 14 below 0, a few feeble attempts to snow, resulting in the emission of a flaccid sprinkling of snowflakes—our walk up the hill back of the hotel to first a deserted farm, then a live one, lighted and rather mysterious and intriguing on the dim and muted warmed winter night, when, on our way up, the view below us, the town and the opposite hills, had seemed to be dissolving, as they blurred, in the mist that emanated from or absorbed the snow, and on our way back the lights of the town were only a soft growing to luminosity in the blurred soft deep cunt-depression of the valley.

—That night (27 January), when I went out for a walk, there was a fine steady snow falling, and everything was completely blotted—you could hardly even see the whiteness of the snow on the ground or the relative clarity of the sky above the trees, and you couldn't raise your eyes, because the fine sharp snow fell in them—as I got nearer to the wood road, I heard the low dull murmur of the river. —George, the waiter, had been down to New York and caught a chill in his back—in his low confidential eager way: "I wouldn't have a dog the way I was—my bahck all doubled up—my word!" This was the first day he'd been back at work.

—The next day was warm, bright and soft, a relief, as if one were restored to some summer "normalcy"—life seemed easier, requiring less effort—walked out without my coat.

—But we heard it blowing up cold in the night (change in sleeping relations in the same bed caused by drop in the temperature—seek and cherish each other less, no idea of sticking together, by warming each other, against the elements)—and the next day a day of cold wind unlike any we had yet had, with—at one, when I went out for a walk—a cold oblique light from a slightly clouded sky.

The next day (January 31) all gray and dreary wintry weather—the bad blank chill side of winter even in these Connecticut hills—we walked in to Winsted, fortifying ourselves with cider brandy—sky gray as the hard asphalt motor road—I took a turn at night and heard the limbs of the trees breaking or the ice cracking or whatever it was, as I walked along the river.

—Boys coasting at night down the hill beside the hotel and along past my windows as I worked.

Notes for Riverton poem. Here am I among elms again—sledge, edge—low urgent murmur—The river always falling at the door—The clogged encrusted cauliflowered falls—translucent lemon luminance—The bridge's black iron is ribbed with ice—Night edge of brick factory's roof—The brown brush stitched with birch—Etched with brush and birch and scratched across with hail—The hills hatched across with hemlock—the day scratched with hail—silvered with birch—fast, and firm.

Mary [Blair], January 1930. When I came in after she had been in court that morning (when we were getting our divorce), I found her crying and tight on the day bed—she said it was on account of Throck's (Cleon Throckmorton) behavior and did a good deal of raving, sobering up, however, somewhat, during dinner at the Lafayette. When I finally left her in her apartment, after dinner, she gave me a human intelligent look, as she said good night, which made me feel her friendliness and her strength—a look of understanding between us on a level away above our wrangling—I could count on her, she counted on me.

Index